ENVIRONMENTALISM IN HEALTHCARE

ENVIRONMENTALISM IN HEALTHCARE

Caring for Tomorrow Ecologically

edited by

Jacqueline A. Stagner

David S.-K. Ting

JENNY STANFORD

PUBLISHING

Published by

Jenny Stanford Publishing Pte. Ltd.
101 Thomson Road
#06-01, United Square
Singapore 307591

Email: editorial@jennystanford.com
Web: www.jennystanford.com

British Library Cataloguing-in-Publication Data
A catalogue record for this book is available from the British Library.

Environmentalism in Healthcare: Caring for Tomorrow Ecologically

ISBN 978-981-5129-95-3 (Hardcover)
ISBN 978-1-003-74869-4 (eBook)
DOI 10.1201/9781003748694

Dedication

To everyone who cares for other souls.

Contents

Preface

Environmentalism in Healthcare: Caring for Tomorrow Ecologically draws together international experts from the fields of healthcare, engineering, architecture, sociology, policy, and others to disclose the latest insights into forging viable means to care for an aging society ecologically. It focuses on the challenges and areas where remedies can be most feasibly implemented to mitigate the current shortfalls. Some adjustments in the way we currently operate can substantially furnish a healthier tomorrow.

Ayoub, **Ceesay**, **Daglilar,** and **Tahan** confront the challenges of an aging society and sustainable healthcare head-on in the opening chapter, "Sustainability in Healthcare and Its Future Impact on the Aging Generation." Their comprehensive chapter addresses an aging population and within this backdrop, the coupled human–environment interactions. Green initiatives mean well, but they must also be cost- and implementation-effective. For example, to fully realize the potential of green chemistry, environmentally friendly materials must also be easily recyclable for reuse. Circular systems that extend from cradle to grave to cradle to cradle pave the path forward.

Beauty is much more than skin deep. In Chapter 2, "Environment- and Microbiome-Friendly Skincare Products," **Kaur**, **Noorbakhsh**, **Arzani Birgani**, and **Sidhu** enlighten us with the dynamic ecosystem of microorganisms of the skin microbiome. With increasing environmental stressors, healthy skin is an indispensable shield that also safeguards a viable immune system. They propose bettering tomorrow's health via a holistic approach of integrating cutting-edge science with environmental consciousness. Shifting towards eco-friendly natural alternatives can further skin and related health while simultaneously lowering environmental damage.

Our tendency to fall and injure ourselves tends to increase as we age. It follows that fall-related health is a growing issue with an aging population. **Ebrahimi**, **Ting**, and **Carriveau** propose strategies to mitigate this in Chapter 3, "Mitigating Falls among the Aging Population." Our healthcare system is confronted with one in three adults over 65 years old falling at least once a year. Studies have shown that this can be drastically reduced with the help of technologies such as wearable sensors, real-time monitoring, and artificial intelligence. To further the multi-pronged remedy, the built environment also needs to be revamped into an age-friendly one. Above all, exercise programs and community involvement are essential. It is thus clear that collaborative efforts between healthcare providers, policymakers, and technology developers are pivotal for healthier aging.

On the topic of digital healthcare, Chapter 4 is "Healthcare Digital Twin: Transformative Perspectives in Socio-Technical Systems." **Mohanty**, **Vaishali**, and **Alla** delve into the transformative potential of digital twin (DT) technology in healthcare. DT aims at bridging physical systems and virtual models to enable real-time monitoring, simulation, and predictive analytics. Fragmented health records, dynamic governance structures, cultural and linguistic diversity, and the emotional sensitivity inherent to medical data are added challenges in the successful application of DT as compared to its application in an industrial setting. Interdisciplinary collaboration that is built on an inclusive, adaptive, and ethically sound platform is the healthy way forward.

At the intersection of healthcare, environmental sustainability, and non-communicable diseases, an appropriate balance is sought. **Aylı** presents "Towards Sustainable Care: Green Solutions for Managing Chronic Conditions" as Chapter 5. Details, including how healthcare practices affect the environment and how pollution and climate change contribute to the increase in non-communicable diseases, are elucidated. The trajectory is characterized by high resource consumption and serious waste production, which fuel the very diseases we aim to treat. The author calls for a paradigm shift toward a multi-disciplinary remedy that invokes green hospital programs, sustainable pharmaceutical solutions, and ecologically friendly therapeutic approaches.

In terms of its carbon footprint, healthcare is a serious culprit, and hence, "Eco-friendly Practices: Reducing Healthcare's Carbon Footprint" is the topic of Chapter 6. In this chapter, **Qadrie**,

Ashraf, **Maqbool**, and **Dar** advocate the integration of renewable energy sources such as solar and wind within healthcare facilities. They further recommend replacing conventional systems such as lighting and heating, ventilation and air conditioning (HVAC) with the latest green options such as LED and smart HVAC systems. It would be remiss not to attend to healthcare waste. It's time to practice "do no harm."

With HVAC consuming a substantial portion of the total energy usage, Chapter 7 is devoted to hospital HVAC, "Recent Advances in Energy-Saving Technologies for Hospital Heating, Ventilation, and Air Conditioning Systems." **Wang**, **Carriveau**, and **Ting** remind us that ensuring optimal indoor air quality, temperature, and humidity is essential for patient comfort, health, and safety; it is worth pointing out that Florence Nightingale was the statistician, nurse, and pioneer on this front. Integrating renewable energy sources such as solar power, geothermal energy, wind, and biomass into HVAC systems is a given. To fully capitalize on efficiency, minimize waste, and improve system adaptability to meet varying operational demands, advanced energy management strategies involving machine learning and artificial intelligence are necessary.

Human behavior plays a critical role in the implementation and operation of promising solutions. In Chapter 8, "The Effect of Social Capital on Eco-Friendly Behavior," **Abbasi**, **Sheykhi**, **Shokati Amghani**, and **Savari** make known social capital as a valuable resource to mitigate environmentally harmful actions. Social capital accounts for the role of social factors in environmental psychology. The benign idea is to enhance residents' sense of belonging and trust within their communities so that good stewardship comes naturally. They expound on the key dimensions of social capital that affect pro-environmental behaviors. Imagine widespread embracement of social capital, healthier psychology, healthier environments, and healthier health, drastically reducing the tax on the healthcare system.

This volume ends with a chapter on urban water quality by **Sharma**, **Dehalwar**, and **Pandey**, "Measures to Manage the Urban Water Quality for Public Health." The recent surge in urbanization stresses the importance of life-sustaining potable water. To protect public health, measures must be taken to ensure a safe and high-quality water supply, including that for healthcare facilities. Community engagement and public awareness campaigns are needed to foster responsible water use, pollution prevention, and adoption of sustainable practices. Much can be learned from the presented case studies from urban areas in Delhi.

This volume reveals our healthcare status. There are as many promising solutions as the number of challenges. Together, we can realize Caring for Tomorrow Ecologically. Environmentalism in Healthcare is the very essence of a healthy tomorrow.

David S.-K. Ting and Jacqueline A. Stagner
Turbulence & Energy Laboratory
University of Windsor

Acknowledgments

This book would not have been realized without the assiduous experts who compiled the chapters and the anonymous reviewers who uplifted the quality. The editors truly enjoy working with the amazing publishing team, who invoke simplicity to ease our striving and boost our efficiency. Providence alone transformed this dream into a reality.

and available options, and avenues for future initiatives with their modes of application and cost.

1.1.1 Sustainability in Healthcare and Its Future Impact on the Aging Generation

This chapter explores the relationship between aging, environmental factors, and healthcare sustainability (Fig. 1.1). It highlights the complexities of aging, distinguishing between normal aging and changes driven by disease. Research from the Baltimore Longitudinal Study of Aging (BLSA) reveals common age-related changes, stressing that aging is influenced by both programmed genetic alterations and random cellular damage. These processes affect different age groups in varying ways, with older populations being particularly vulnerable to environmental toxins and stressors. The challenges of separating the effects of aging from environmental influences complicate efforts to understand how these factors impact life expectancy and disease.

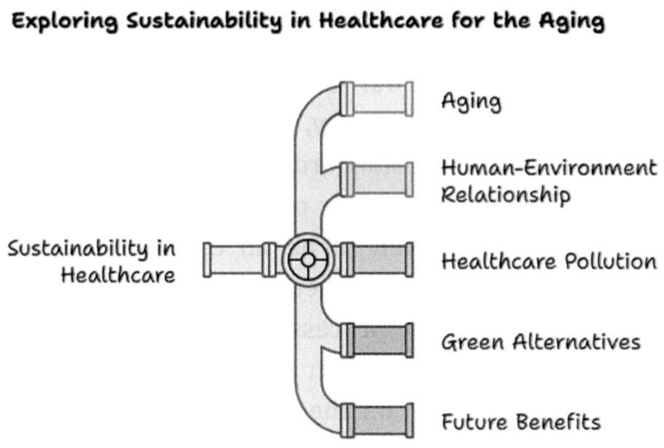

Figure 1.1 Chapter outline.

The chapter also addresses the environmental burden of healthcare, especially highlighted during the COVID-19 pandemic, due to the surge in single-use medical supplies such as personal protective equipment (PPE). As the healthcare sector contributes significantly to global pollution, the text advocates for adopting sustainable alternatives, such as biodegradable materials and energy-efficient processes. By moving toward greener practices, healthcare institutions can reduce their environmental impact while maintaining high standards of patient care, ultimately contributing to a more sustainable future.

1.2 Aging

What is aging? The BLSA aims to understand "normal aging" by separating age-related changes from those caused by disease or other factors. This research has revealed common changes that nearly everyone experiences as they age. By studying aging and disease together, scientists have identified links between various health conditions and the aging process. Overall, discoveries from the BLSA have reshaped our understanding of aging and laid the groundwork for future research on disease prevention and healthy aging. With continued participation from study participants, the BLSA aims to address questions about disease resistance and healthy aging, potentially leading to innovative approaches for extending health span and lifespan [1].

Within the older population, heterogeneity is notable, with characteristics varying notably across different age groups. Thus, analyses often segment the older population into specific age brackets, such as 55–64 years, 65–74 years, 75–84 years, and 85 years and older. The effects of aging on health, social dynamics, and economic aspects are typically more pronounced in these older age groups, warranting closer scrutiny in demographic studies. Moreover, shifts in life expectancy, reductions in mortality rates, and changes in the proportion surviving to various ages provide tangible indicators of the evolving demographic landscape, reflecting advancements in public health and healthcare interventions [2].

Theories of aging can be broadly categorized into deterministic and stochastic mechanisms. Deterministic theories propose programmed alterations in gene expression or structure, while stochastic theories suggest random alterations in macromolecules, cells, and organ systems [3]. However, the line between these categories can blur, as stochastic alterations in individual cells may lead to predictable outcomes in larger cell populations. For instance, terminal differentiation, where populations of cells cease dividing after differentiation, can be seen as both stochastic and deterministic [3].

Programmed aging is observed in species with single massive episodes of reproduction, while placental mammals experience various stochastic processes due to their extended reproductive phases. The relative contributions of these mechanisms may vary based on the organism's reproductive strategy. Several theories of aging have been proposed, including deterministic theories such as developmental switches in gene expression and neuroendocrine-cascade theories, and stochastic theories like intrinsic mutagenesis and protein-synthesis error catastrophe. These theories have implications for understanding the impact of environmental agents on aging processes [4].

Deterministic theories like the neuroendocrine-cascade hypothesis of aging suggest that age-related changes in hormone regulation may contribute to various age-associated problems. Stochastic theories propose mechanisms such as intrinsic mutagenesis, protein-synthesis error catastrophe, and free radical damage, which can lead to the accumulation of cellular damage over time. Thymic involution, a hallmark of immunosenescence, is an early and significant precursor of aging in humans and other mammals, suggesting potential targets for environmental modulation. Understanding these theories provides insights into how environmental agents may influence aging processes and age-related diseases (Fig. 1.2) [5].

1. **Deterministic:** Developmental Switches in Gene Expression, Neuroendocrine-Cascade Theories.
2. **Stochastic:** Intrinsic Mutagenesis Theory, Protein-Synthesis Error Catastrophe, Free Radicals, Posttranslational Glycation of Proteins and DNA, Thymic Involution as a Pacemaker of Immunosenescence.

Being one of the most populous countries in the world, with approximately 320 million inhabitants, the United States of America has experienced steady population growth over the past decade, indicating improvements in living conditions and

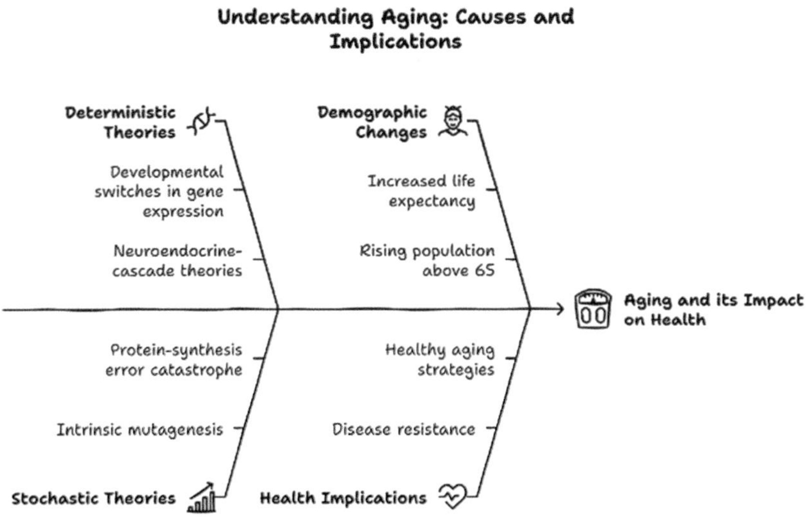

Figure 1.2 Schematic review of the aging process using the Deterministic and Stochastic theories with consideration of population demographic changes and the overall health implications.

healthcare. Such advancement has led to a steady increase in life expectancy at birth in the United States. This is evident in the age distribution of the United States. In 2012, 13.58% of the population was above 65 years of age, and in 2022, 17.13% of the population was above 65 years of age [6]. Figure 1.3 shows a comparison between the population of the U.S. in the years 2000, 2010, and 2020, and the increase in the number of people above 65 years of age over time using the U.S. Census Bureau [7].

The inquiry into whether environmental factors are shortening both lifespan and life expectancy, or if we are nearing natural limits in both realms, precipitates a profound exploration of aging processes and environmental influences. A discourse ensues, contemplating the potential redirection of research away from the intricate mechanisms of aging towards attenuating the impact of environmental toxins on longevity. The argument is that by targeting age-associated diseases caused by environmental factors not inherently linked to aging, we could potentially improve the quality of life in old age.

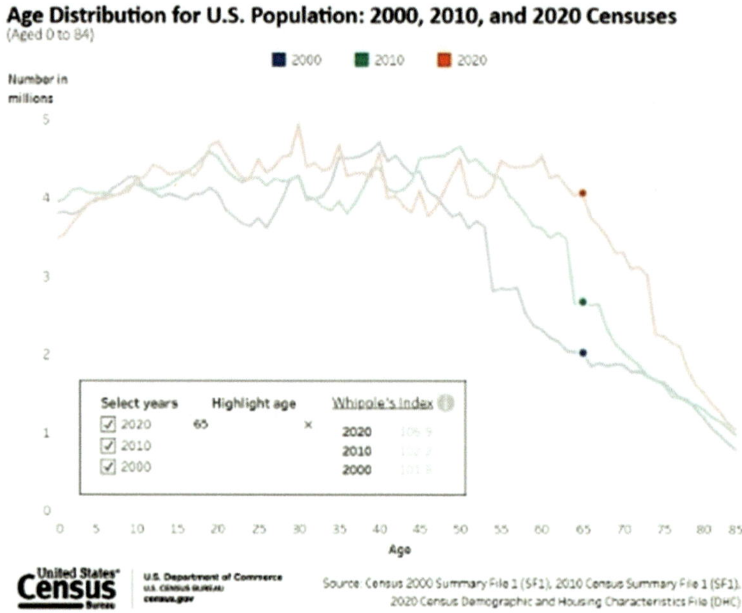

Figure 1.3 Graph comparing trend of U.S. population with age 65+ in years 2000, 2010, and 2020.

Yet, the understanding of precisely how environmental agents modulate aging processes remains enigmatic, primarily due to the scarcity of comprehensive research in this domain. It is conjectured that exposures to environmental factors during pivotal developmental stages could imprint upon age-related phenomena later in life. For instance, the exposure to certain agents during fetal development or early childhood may predispose individuals to age-related neurodegenerative conditions, such as Parkinson's disease. Moreover, elderly individuals may exhibit heightened susceptibility to environmental toxins owing to age-related alterations in cellular function and diminished physiological resilience [8].

Classic studies indicate a gradual decline in the functional capacity of physiological systems with age, affecting responses to environmental stresses. Whereas young adults are shielded by their homeostatic reserves, older individuals may exhibit attenuated adaptive responses, rendering them more vulnerable to environmental challenges. This heightened vulnerability is reflected in elevated mortality rates among the elderly in response to environmental stressors that may not prove fatal in younger cohorts [9].

Distinguishing between age-related changes and those induced by environmental exposures presents a scientific challenge, exacerbated by the intertwining of aging and chronic environmental exposure. Laboratory inquiries into aging within controlled settings possess limited generalizability to real-world contexts, where aging unfolds amidst multifaceted environmental dynamics. Moreover, the pursuit of biomarkers that are exclusively indicative of aging or toxicity has yielded only partial success, reflecting the incomplete understanding of the underlying mechanisms [10].

These challenges extend to epidemiological and demographic studies of human aging, where disentangling the contributions of intrinsic aging and environmental factors remains a difficult task. Consequently, it is challenging to predict the impact of environmental exposures on life expectancy and disease prevalence in old age. Addressing these complexities requires interdisciplinary collaboration and a comprehensive approach to studying aging and environmental influences [11].

As individuals age, they exhibit greater variation in biological responses compared to younger individuals. This variation can impact their vulnerability to the effects of toxic substances, with physiological aging playing a role but not fully explaining the susceptibility. Elderly populations are more vulnerable to environmental insults due to increased incidence of disease and age-related changes in physiological functions. Figure 1.4 illustrates how changes in skin anatomy, immune function, and drug metabolism affect the elderly negatively.

Studies have shown that older individuals respond differently to drugs and environmental agents compared to younger individuals, often experiencing more adverse reactions. Diseases and chronic conditions are common among the elderly, further complicating their susceptibility to environmental factors. Physiological changes associated with aging, such as alterations in drug metabolism and immune function, can influence their response to toxic agents [12].

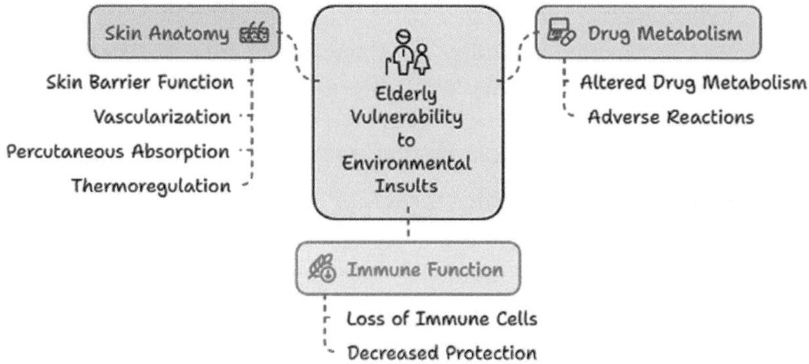

Figure 1.4 Physiological changes associated with negative outcomes in the elderly.

Changes in the immune system, nervous system, and skin anatomy and function occur with age, affecting susceptibility to environmental insults. For example, age-related changes in skin barrier function and vascularization can increase percutaneous absorption of chemicals and impair thermoregulation. Loss of immune cells and melanocytes in the skin may decrease protection against radiation and foreign antigens. Additionally, age-related decreases in sensory perception, including pain perception, make the elderly more vulnerable to environmental injuries [5].

1.3 Human-Environment Relationship

Toxicology involves the examination of how harmful effects are exerted by environmental agents, along with empirically determining their toxicity and risk to human populations. This field heavily depends on comparing experimental findings with extensive databases gathered from standardized testing protocols applied to various chemicals and types of radiation [13].

To comprehend how environmental agents might worsen aging processes, it is necessary to consider the mechanisms of aging in relation to known toxic substances. Identifying screening tests that assess interactions between environmental agents and aging processes or increased risks to elderly individuals is crucial. Additionally, assessing these agents in whole-animal systems that reflect human responses and utilizing existing databases are essential steps [14].

Aging exhibits similarities to toxic processes, as age-related changes often resemble those induced by toxic substances. Studying aging as a toxic process is justified by its link to age-related diseases and its consistent presence during experiments. Although many environmental agents can induce aging-like changes at high doses, such mimicry tends to be partial and specific to certain tissues [14].

The significance of neurotoxicology and immunotoxicology cannot be overstated, as many environmental agents have yet to be tested for their effects on the nervous and immune systems, which are particularly vulnerable in the elderly. Challenges in understanding the relationship between the environment and aging include the unknown mechanisms of aging and the absence of comparative data for validating tests [14]. To understand the roots of the challenges of studying toxicology in the aging population, we depicted the following graph (Fig. 1.5).

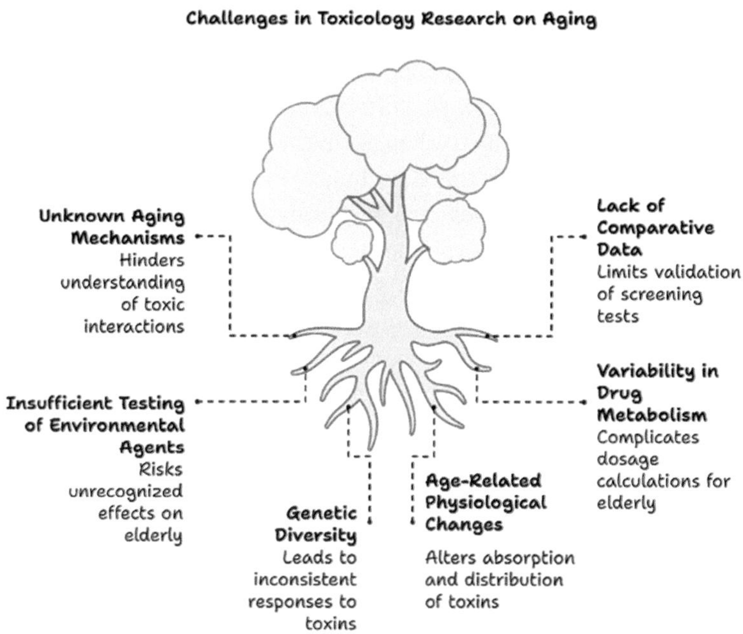

Figure 1.5 An overview of the major challenges facing toxicology research in the aging population.

To overcome these challenges, it is crucial to identify agents that interact with aging processes, sensitize individuals to other agents, or pose increased risks to the elderly. Furthermore, assessing the effects of acute or subacute exposures at various life stages and predicting how old animals respond to environmental agents are important considerations in toxicological research related to aging [15].

Chemicals can enter the body via inhalation, ingestion, or skin contact, potentially exerting local or systemic effects. While the liver primarily metabolizes toxic substances, other organs like the kidneys, lungs, and gastrointestinal tract also contribute. Most toxicants are eliminated through urine or bile, with some volatile ones expelled through exhaled air [16].

Research on how aging affects the body's handling of chemicals has mainly focused on drugs rather than environmental toxins. However, insights from drug studies are relevant to toxicology, as many toxic substances undergo similar metabolic pathways. Age-related changes in carcinogen metabolism are complex and not fully understood, with limited and conflicting data available [17].

Alterations in pharmacokinetics, such as absorption, distribution, metabolism, and elimination, can influence drug responses, particularly in the elderly, who often exhibit increased sensitivity to certain medications due to changes in these processes. Absorption mainly occurs through the skin, lungs, and gastrointestinal tract, with age-related changes like reduced gastrointestinal motility potentially affecting absorption rates [15, 18, 19].

The distribution of toxicants throughout the body depends on factors like body composition and binding to plasma proteins. Age-related changes, such as decreased lean body mass and alterations in protein binding, can affect the volume of distribution. Metabolism and elimination processes can also be impacted by age, with some evidence indicating reduced hepatic enzyme activity in older individuals [20].

Renal function commonly declines with age, affecting the elimination of drugs excreted through the kidneys. While there is variability in the extent of renal decline among individuals, adjustments in drug doses are often necessary in elderly patients to prevent toxicity [20].

Variations in drug elimination rates are also observed among fetuses, neonates, children, and adults, underscoring the importance of considering age-related pharmacokinetic differences in drug dosage calculations and treatment strategies. Additionally, the genetic diversity within the human population leads to varying responses to environmental chemicals, even among individuals with similar exposures [21–25].

The process of absorption plays a crucial role in transporting toxic substances across body membranes, primarily occurring through the skin, lungs, and gastrointestinal tract. Skin, being a significant absorption site, can be affected by injuries or other factors, altering its permeability. Similarly, toxicants can enter the bloodstream through the lungs, especially when inhaled as gases or aerosols. The gastrointestinal tract also serves as a route for absorption, influenced by factors like gastrointestinal motility and the properties of the toxicant [26–30].

Physiological changes associated with aging, such as increased gastric pH and reduced gastrointestinal motility, can affect absorption from the gastrointestinal tract in older individuals. However, while some studies suggest a delay in the time to peak plasma concentration after oral drug administration in the elderly, the extent of absorption generally remains unchanged compared to younger subjects [31, 32].

Once absorbed into the bloodstream, toxicants are distributed throughout the body. The distribution depends on factors like cell membrane permeability and affinity for body components. Age-related changes, such as alterations in body composition and plasma protein binding, can affect the volume of distribution and thus the concentration of toxicants in the blood [20].

Metabolism and elimination processes transform and remove toxicants from the body. Metabolism can alter the chemical nature of toxicants, facilitating their elimination. Aging can affect hepatic drug metabolism, but the evidence is indirect and varies depending on the drug and individual factors. Renal function declines with age, impacting the elimination of drugs excreted by the kidneys [28, 33, 34]. Differences in drug metabolism and elimination exist across various age groups, emphasizing the need for tailored dosages and further research into pharmacokinetic processes in different populations [35–37]. The interplay of environmental chemicals and aging underscores the complexity of human responses to toxic exposures, which are influenced by genetic variability and individual characteristics (Fig. 1.6) [20].

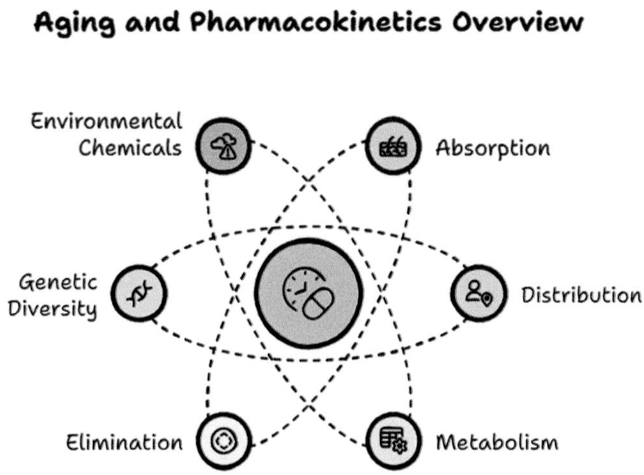

Figure 1.6 Interplay of different factors influencing pharmacokinetics in the aging population.

The mechanisms through which toxic substances exert their effects are highly varied and can differ between specific agents and even at different doses of the same agent. These mechanisms are often characterized by the dose required to induce the toxic effect and the specificity of that effect. This characterization is particularly relevant when considering aging, as the decline in physiological functions associated with age affects various tissues without specificity to particular cells or tissues, although the precise mechanism of aging remains unknown [38].

At the molecular level, toxic agents can cause damage by creating harmful chemical species that target specific components of biological molecules. The search for toxic mechanisms common to both aging and specific agents should include those with broad actions, given that aging affects all tissues broadly. Additionally, identifying agents that affect specific aspects of the aging phenotype would allow for a more detailed understanding of the underlying mechanisms.

Damage can occur in specific molecules, leading to a wide range of toxic effects. For instance, damage to DNA can have pleiotropic effects (Fig. 1.7). Some agents induce general toxic effects by producing damaging species, such as free radicals, which can interact with various biomolecules. Different tissues can be susceptible to toxicity at different exposure levels. For example, ionizing radiation can induce different toxic effects at varying doses, illustrating the importance of dose-dependent responses [39].

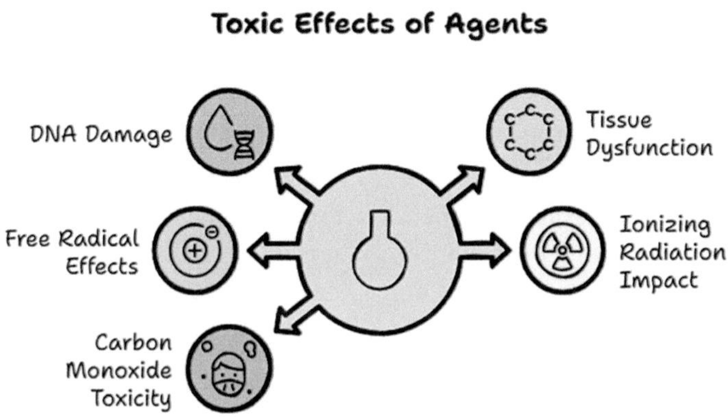

Figure 1.7 Overview of how various agents exert their toxic effects.

Toxic agents may exhibit both specific and nonspecific actions. For instance, carbon monoxide binds to hemoglobin, reducing its oxygen-carrying capacity and causing toxicity. Some agents produce nonspecific toxic effects that can affect multiple tissues, although the specific response may vary depending on exposure dose [40].

Cellular mechanisms of toxicity can lead to tissue-level effects. Toxic agents may cause tissue dysfunction by altering the function of enough cells in a specific tissue. Alternatively, toxic stress on individual cells can result in various toxic effects, including cancer, heritable mutation, and teratogenesis. Aging is characterized by alterations in most cells across various tissues, suggesting a similarity to the cellular effects of toxic agents [41].

While aging research has aimed to identify the molecular changes underlying cellular aging, establishing a definitive molecular etiology has proven challenging. Therefore, comparisons at the cellular and tissue levels between toxic agents and aging may provide valuable insights [42].

Toxic effects at the tissue level are commonly observed in intact animals, often due to toxic stress at the site of exposure or metabolic action, or in susceptible target cells. Understanding the toxic mechanisms at the tissue level requires consideration of their cellular and molecular etiology [42].

The study of individual differences in response to drugs, influenced by environmental, age-related, and genetic factors, is termed pharmacogenetics [43]. This field is particularly significant in toxicology as it elucidates how genetic variations can predispose individuals to toxic effects from xenobiotics [30]. Genetic differences in drug metabolism pathways and enzyme activities can affect susceptibility to tissue damage caused by reactive metabolites [44].

The expression of genetic factors and their impact on drug toxicity may manifest differently depending on age, with certain conditions being expressed only later in life [24]. With drugs being more commonly prescribed to older individuals, the incidence of pharmacogenetically related toxicity may increase with age [45]. Age-related effects on gene frequencies in pharmacogenetic conditions have been observed, such as with the acetylation polymorphism [46].

Pharmacogenetic conditions, characterized by aberrant enzymatic conversion of drugs, often result in toxic responses due to drug accumulation [43]. For example, slow acetylators, resulting from gene mutations, may exhibit increased susceptibility to adverse drug reactions [47]. Geographic variations in gene frequencies of pharmacogenetic conditions further complicate the understanding of their effects [48].

Environmental factors, such as smoking and diet, can interact with genetic factors to influence drug disposition [49]. The total interindividual variation in drug elimination among heterogeneous populations is attributed to both genetic and environmental factors [50]. This complexity underscores the challenge of identifying specific factors contributing to variations in drug response [45].

Understanding the dynamic interactions between genetic, environmental, and developmental factors is crucial for comprehensively studying drug response [45]. This interdisciplinary approach helps elucidate the mechanisms underlying inter-individual variations in drug metabolism and toxicity, ultimately informing personalized medicine strategies.

1.4 Healthcare Pollution

It is well established in our scientific community that global warming is an imminent threat to our society. The United Nations recently surveyed 50 Nobel laureates, and more than one-third cited "population rise/environmental degradation" as the biggest threat to mankind, followed by nuclear war [51]. Climate-related hazards include extreme weather events, sea level rise, an increase in air pollution, an increase in water- and vector-borne illnesses, just to name a few. According to World Health Organization (WHO) research, 37% of heat-related deaths are attributed to human-induced climate change, and heat-related deaths in those over 65 years of age have risen by 70% in the last two decades. Additionally, WHO projects an increase in yearly deaths due to climate change impacts on diseases like malaria and coastal flooding by 250,000 [51]. Climate change has a direct implication for our healthcare system.

The COVID-19 pandemic has shed light on many aspects of our healthcare system, specifically, it has brought attention to the healthcare waste sector. The increased use of PPE (i.e., gloves, masks, surgical gowns, face shields) during the pandemic was astronomical. During the early stages of the COVID-19 pandemic, the WHO estimated a global demand of 89 million medical masks, 76 million examination gloves, and 1.6 million goggles per month, which were used by healthcare professionals [52]. This raises a question: How is medical waste disposed of and managed?

Healthcare waste is generated by hospitals, laboratories, nursing homes, and research centers and can be broken down into non-hazardous (80–85%) and hazardous waste (15–20%) [53]. Hazardous materials include needles and syringes, body parts, blood, soiled dressings, pharmaceuticals, toxic chemicals, and PPE. Infectious waste must be disposed of and managed carefully to prevent harm and further spread of disease. The concern about how healthcare waste is managed arose in the 1980s after medical waste was found washing up on coastal beaches. This prompted Congress to enact the Medical Waste Tracking Act (MWTA) of 1988. The regulations of this short two-year program expired after the EPA concluded that the disease-causing potential of medical waste is the greatest at the point of generation and naturally tapers off after that point [54]. After the MWTA expired in 1991, states took on the role of regulating medical waste based on the data collected during that program. Many states have since further developed their programs regulating waste disposal [54].

Healthcare waste contains highly toxic metals, chemicals, pathogenic viruses, and bacteria that have the potential to cause disease and contaminate the environment (Fig. 1.8). Therefore, healthcare waste must be treated before disposal to ensure public safety. Current treatment methods of healthcare waste treatment and disposal include thermal processes (i.e., incineration, autoclaving), chemical processes, irradiation processes, and others, which include recycling, reusing, and sanitary landfilling [55]. The incineration process appears to be the most preferred method of treating waste, given its success in reducing waste quantities and in eliminating microorganisms [56, 57]. Incinerators have been shown to create organic pollutants such as dioxins [58]. Dioxins are also called persistent organic pollutants because they take a very long time to break down once they are in the environment. These are highly toxic and carcinogenic pollutants, and the EPA estimates 90% of human exposure comes from animal fats [59]. One study showed that cows grazing near incinerators had a higher concentration of dioxins than those grazing further away from incinerators [60]. This supports the idea that incinerators can lead to bioaccumulation from the pollutants they produce.

In the U.S., the annual growth in health services spending is now higher than before the COVID-19 pandemic, as shown in Fig. 1.9 [61].

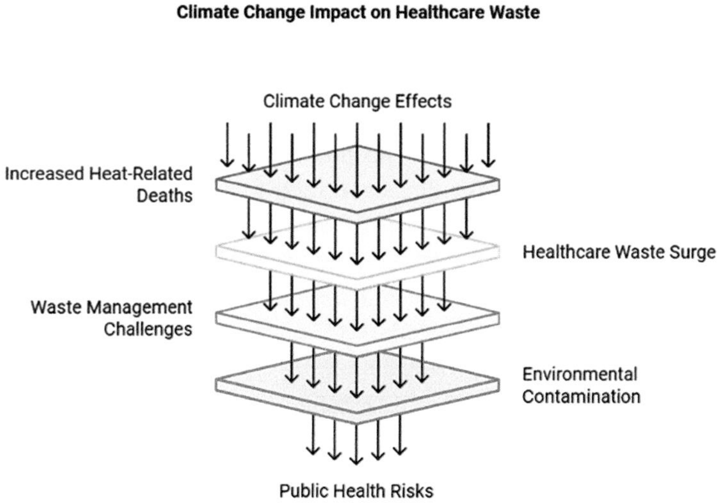

Figure 1.8 Cumulative impact of modern healthcare waste and climate change on public health.

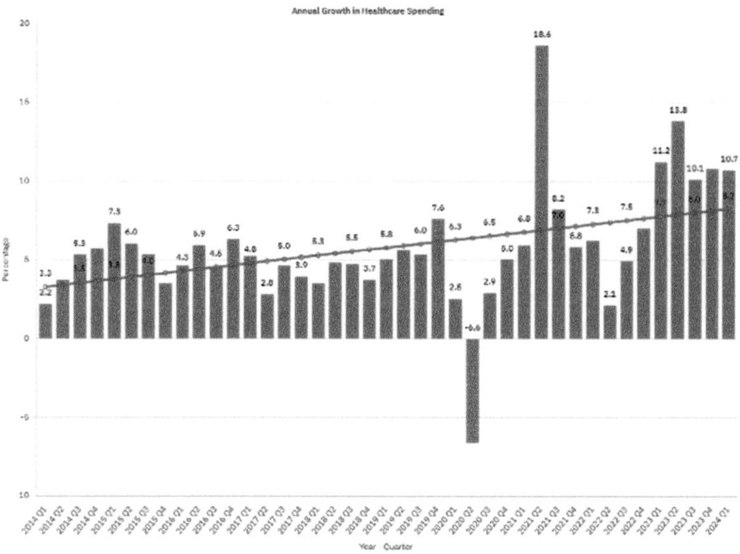

Figure 1.9 Trend of annual spending in healthcare services from 2014 to 2024 using data from the U.S. Census Bureau.

The economic impact of healthcare delivery extends far beyond medical expenses, touching every aspect of patients' and caregivers' lives. Understanding this economic burden is essential to raising awareness of the public health crisis posed by expenditure, informing policy proposals, and ultimately improving the lives of affected individuals and their families. This knowledge encompasses not only out-of-pocket costs but also the ripple effects on labor market participation and productivity, which influence how policymakers and the public allocate resources. It also equips healthcare providers to uncover and address hidden costs and barriers to care [62].

Medical waste encompasses any waste generated through healthcare activities, such as treatment, diagnosis, immunization, and research. If not handled and disposed of properly, it can pose significant risks to public health and the environment. Proper management of medical waste ensures the safety of patients, healthcare workers, and the surrounding community, maintaining hygienic conditions within healthcare facilities. The disposal of medical waste is not merely about adhering to regulatory requirements—it carries substantial financial implications. Inefficient or improper waste management can result in increased operational costs, legal penalties, and reputational damage. By gaining insights into the costs associated with medical waste disposal, healthcare facilities can implement cost-effective and compliant strategies to manage this crucial aspect of their operations.

Medical waste is classified into several categories based on its characteristics and risks (Fig. 1.10):

1. **Infectious Waste:** It includes materials that can transmit infectious diseases, such as contaminated blood or laboratory cultures.
2. **Sharps Waste:** This includes items like needles, syringes, and scalpels that can cause injuries and spread infections.
3. **Hazardous Waste:** It covers materials with toxic properties, including certain chemicals, pharmaceuticals, and devices.

4. **Pharmaceutical Waste:** This includes expired or unused medications that require careful disposal to prevent misuse or environmental harm.

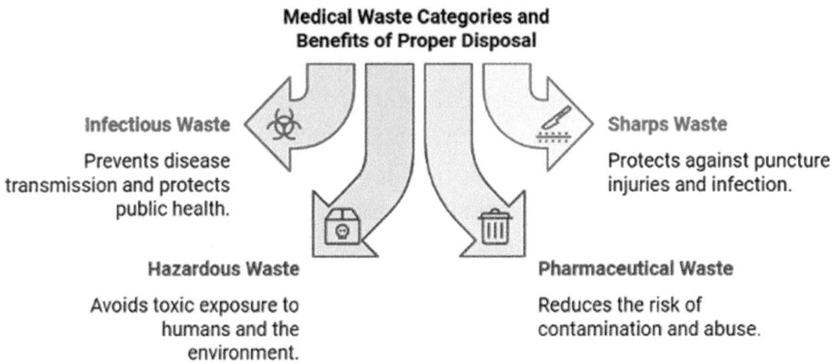

Figure 1.10 Different categories of medical waste as described by the WHO and the outcomes of their proper disposal.

Each category of medical waste demands compliance with specific regulatory requirements to minimize risks:

1. **Infectious Waste:** Prevents disease transmission.
2. **Sharps Waste:** Protects against puncture injuries and infection.
3. **Hazardous Waste:** Avoids toxic exposure to humans and the environment.
4. **Pharmaceutical Waste:** Reduces the risk of contamination and abuse.

According to the WHO, about 85% of waste generated by healthcare activities is general, non-hazardous waste comparable to domestic waste [63]. The remaining 15% is considered hazardous material that may be infectious, chemical, or radioactive [63]. In contrast, in 2023, only 25% of health facilities had basic healthcare waste management services [64]. Such contrast between production and proper disposal underscores the importance of adhering to the previously mentioned guidelines, which ensure safe disposal practices while preventing financial repercussions to ensure a greener environment.

1.5 Green Alternatives

As environmental degradation intensifies, the healthcare sector is increasingly recognized for its significant role in contributing to global pollution. Human health is intricately connected to the health of our planet, and it is becoming clearer that our efforts to improve health can inadvertently exacerbate environmental issues. The healthcare sector, which includes hospitals, public health systems, and pharmaceutical companies, is responsible for approximately 4.4% of global greenhouse gas (GHG) emissions, with hospitals alone being among the most energy-intensive facilities [65, 66]. In countries like the U.S., healthcare contributes up to 8.5% of total emissions, highlighting the urgent need for a shift toward greener practices [67].

The production and disposal of single-use medical equipment, coupled with energy consumption in healthcare facilities, significantly impact the environment. The COVID-19 pandemic further underscored this issue, generating vast quantities of waste from PPE and other disposable medical supplies. The disposal of these items, often through incineration, adds to the pollution burden, releasing harmful chemicals into the atmosphere if not managed properly [68, 69].

Moreover, the healthcare sector's reliance on fossil fuels for energy use in cooling, heating, and powering facilities compounds its contribution to environmental degradation (Fig. 1.11) [70]. Given the healthcare industry's mission to improve and safeguard human health, it must take a more active role in addressing climate change. From reducing emissions through energy-efficient systems to adopting biodegradable materials and promoting sustainable practices across supply chains, the sector has a unique opportunity—and responsibility—to lead in the fight against climate change. Embracing these green alternatives is not only essential for the environment but also vital for ensuring long-term health and well-being [71, 72]. According to the U.S. Energy Information Administration (EIA), the Commercial Buildings Energy Consumption Survey (CBECS) revealed that inpatient healthcare buildings were the third most energy-intensive buildings in 2018, despite a downward trend from 2012 (Fig. 1.12) [73].

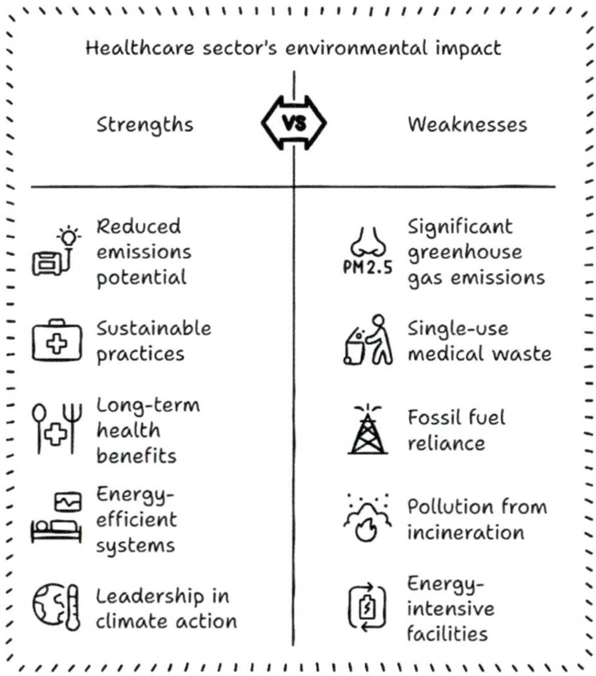

Figure 1.11 Strengths and weakness of modern healthcare impact on the environment.

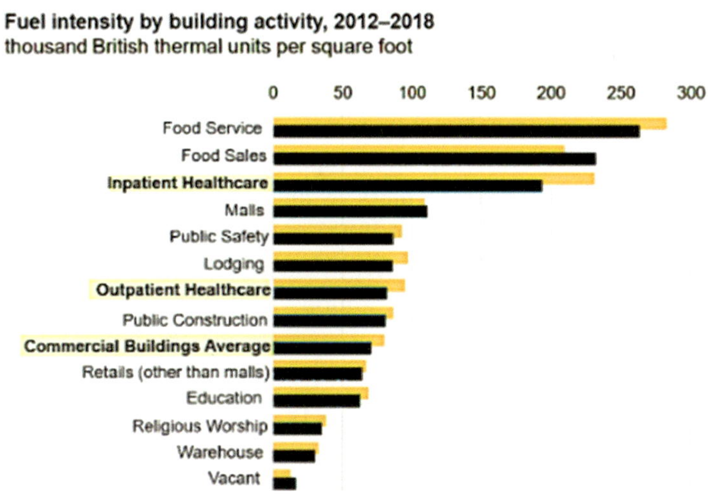

Figure 1.12 Fuel intensity level by building activity showing the consumption of healthcare in comparison to average buildings in 2012 (Yellow) and 2018 (Black) using data from the CBECS by the U.S. EIA.

1.5.1 Importance of Green Alternatives in Healthcare

Pollution is a major contributor to morbidity and mortality, accounting for an estimated 9 million premature deaths globally in 2015, or 16% of all deaths. Most of these environmentally mediated deaths are linked to air pollution, with many experts identifying climate change as the most pressing public health issue of the 21st century [74]. Disruptions in food production, water supplies, and coastal areas are expected unless substantial action is taken to reduce GHG emissions [75]. Ironically, healthcare systems significantly contribute to pollution that negatively impacts human health. In fact, healthcare in the U.S. [76], Australia [77], England [78, 79], and Canada [80] emits around 748 million metric tons of carbon dioxide equivalents annually. If these healthcare systems were considered a nation, they would rank seventh globally in terms of GHG emissions [81].

Ensuring quality in healthcare includes preventing harm to patients, improving efficiency, and eliminating unnecessary care. To reduce healthcare-related pollution, addressing overuse of resources and optimizing the sector's environmental footprint could lead to better population health. Environmental sustainability, although often overlooked, is an essential component of healthcare quality.

The healthcare industry's reliance on traditional instruments, particularly disposable plastics and energy-intensive devices, has a significant environmental footprint. The use of single-use items like syringes, gloves, and PPE, especially during the COVID-19 pandemic, contributed to massive amounts of waste, including an estimated 87,000 tons of PPE waste in 20 months [69, 76]. Additionally, the sector's energy use for sterilization, heating, cooling, and equipment operation further exacerbates GHG emissions. For example, hospitals account for around 60% of the healthcare sector's total energy consumption [67]. These practices increase emissions and contribute to resource depletion, ultimately harming public health.

The shift toward green alternatives in healthcare is crucial to reduce the sector's environmental damage. By adopting biodegradable medical tools, energy-efficient sterilization methods, and sustainable packaging, the industry can reduce its overall carbon footprint while maintaining high standards of care. Green alternatives, such as those developed by emerging companies like EcoMed Innovations, offer biodegradable polymers for gloves and other supplies, significantly reducing landfill waste [72]. Moreover, companies like Sterilis Solutions are introducing energy-efficient sterilization devices that consume less power, helping to address the healthcare sector's heavy reliance on fossil fuels for energy [76]. These sustainable practices can lessen healthcare's environmental impact and improve public health outcomes by reducing pollution. In 2003, the California Sustainable Building Task Force provided evidence for the claim that applying green building practices to government buildings is a strong financial investment, as shown in Table 1.1, which shows 20-year net savings for different categories [82].

Table 1.1 Financial benefits of green buildings as reported by Kats in 2003

Category	20-Year Net Present Value
Energy savings	$5.80
Emissions savings	$1.20
Water savings	$0.50
Operations and maintenance savings	$8.50
Productivity and health benefits	$36.90 to $55.30
Subtotal	$52.90 to $71.30
Total 20-year net benefit	$50 to $65

1.5.2 Biodegradable and Recycled Medical Instruments

Biodegradable and recycled medical instruments are becoming crucial components in reducing healthcare's environmental footprint. Traditional medical tools, such as single-use plastic syringes, gloves, and packaging, generate significant waste, much of which ends up in landfills or is incinerated, contributing to pollution. In contrast, biodegradable alternatives offer a more sustainable solution by decomposing naturally or through industrial composting processes, reducing their environmental impact.

One key player in this space is EcoMed Innovations, a company dedicated to producing biodegradable medical tools. They offer products made from plant-based polymers that break down over time, unlike traditional plastics that persist for hundreds of years. Their biodegradable gloves, for instance, provide the same protection as traditional latex gloves while significantly reducing waste. These innovations are designed to maintain quality and sterility while being environmentally friendly, addressing a major concern in the medical industry [72].

Several studies have shown that biodegradable materials, such as polylactic acid (PLA) and other plant-based biopolymers, can replace traditional plastic items used in healthcare. Mechanism of bio-degradation, and example of natural and synthetic biodegradable polymers are shown in Figures 1.13, 1.14, and 1.15. These materials degrade naturally under the right conditions, turning into non-toxic byproducts. According to research, these alternatives can reduce the carbon footprint of medical institutions by up to 30%, as they require less energy to produce and degrade naturally rather than undergoing incineration [67]. Companies like GreenMed Supplies have also developed biodegradable syringes, bandages, and wound dressings that perform as well as their conventional counterparts but decompose in landfills or compost facilities within months [83].

A notable example of such a product is biodegradable syringes, which are made from bioplastics derived from corn starch or sugarcane. These syringes maintain the sterility required in medical settings but can be safely composted, reducing plastic waste. Biodegradable sutures are another example, which not only break down in the body after healing but also prevent the need for removal, minimizing hospital visits and further reducing environmental strain.

Additionally, Sterilis Solutions has contributed to this green movement by introducing sterilization machines that work in tandem with biodegradable instruments. Their system ensures that biodegradable products are sterilized using energy-efficient methods, enhancing the eco-friendliness of the entire process [75, 76, 83–85].

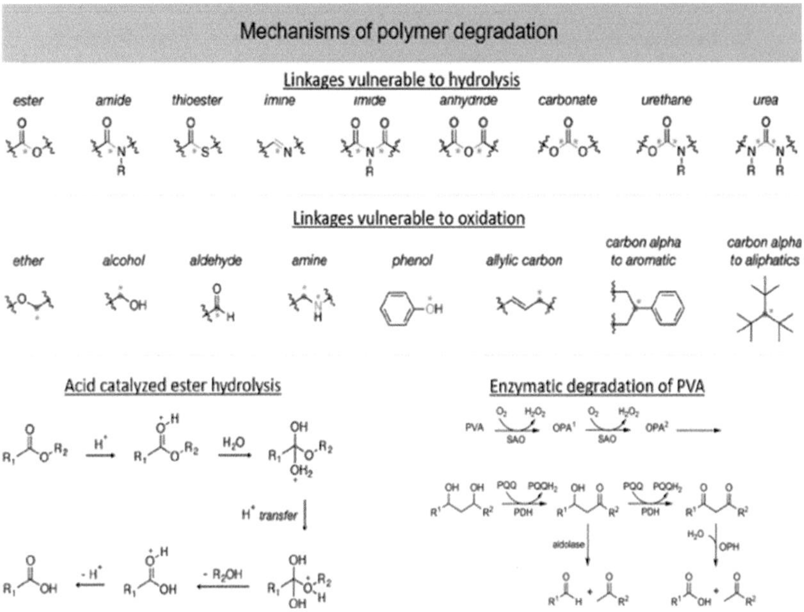

Figure 1.13 Different mechanisms of polymer degradation.

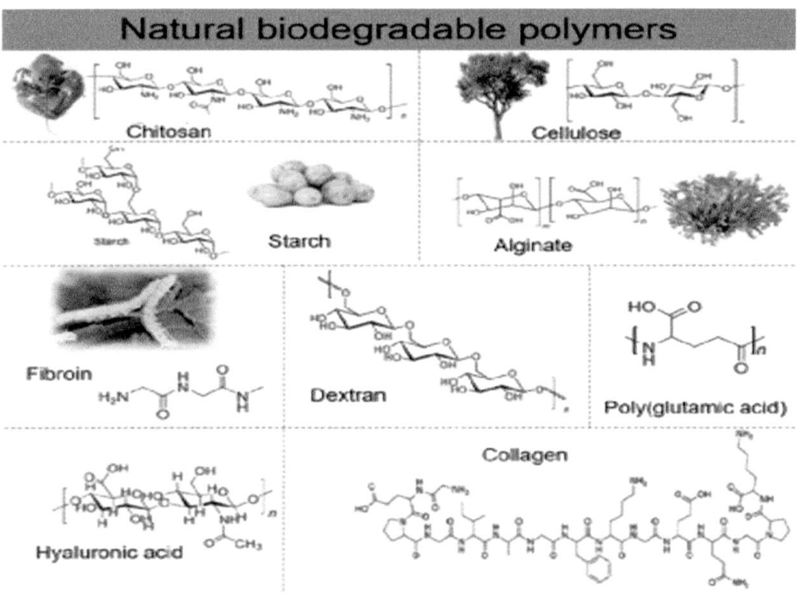

Figure 1.14 Natural biodegradable polymers.

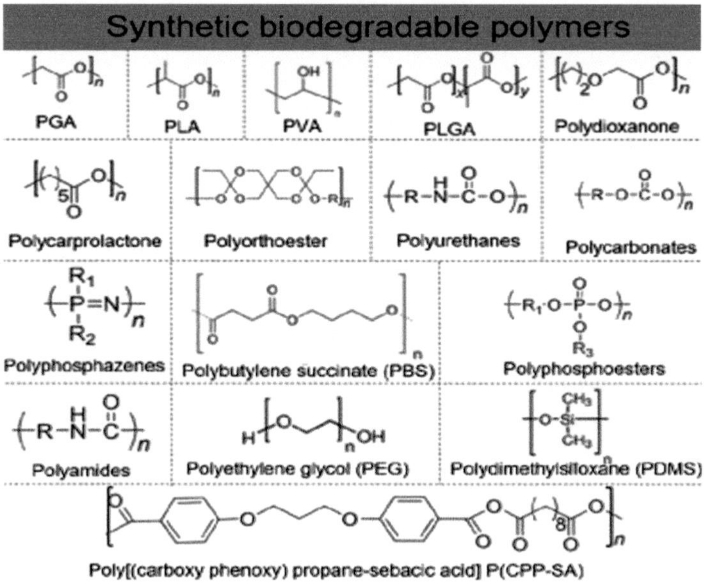

Figure 1.15 Synthetic biodegradable polymers.

The healthcare industry's shift towards biodegradable and recycled medical instruments is essential for reducing environmental impact. With companies like EcoMed Innovations and GreenMed Supplies leading the way, biodegradable syringes, gloves, and other tools offer a viable and sustainable alternative to traditional plastic products. As more institutions adopt these eco-friendly innovations, the potential for healthcare to reduce its carbon footprint becomes increasingly tangible.

1.5.3 Energy-Efficient Sterilization and Medical Equipment

The introduction of single-use plastics in the mid-20th century transformed healthcare by offering improved sanitation due to their disposability and flexibility. While plastics have long been the go-to material for medical tools worldwide, the focus has now shifted toward reducing the amount of non-recyclable waste generated by hospitals and other healthcare facilities (Fig. 1.16) [86].

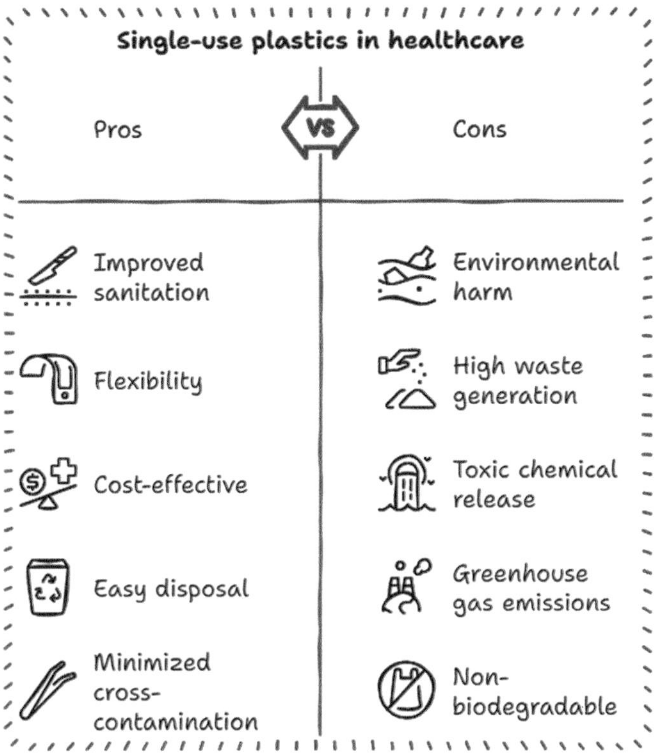

Figure 1.16 Pros and cons of using single-use plastics in healthcare.

Healthcare professionals favor single-use plastics for their sterility, which minimizes the risk of cross-contamination. Additionally, plastics are cheap and easy to dispose of, reducing the potential risks posed to waste handlers. Despite these benefits, hospitals generate enormous waste, estimated at 25 pounds per patient per day, amounting to over 5 million tons annually. Around 80% of this is general waste, of which 55% is plastic, but only about 20% of it is recycled [87].

Hospitals use materials like polyvinyl chloride (PVC), polyurethane, and polyethylene, which are environmentally harmful due to the release of toxic chemicals. PVC is problematic as it emits chlorine-based pollutants that disrupt ecosystems. PVC is used in both construction and disposable medical devices, contributing to both human and environmental health hazards [88].

The massive production of non-biodegradable plastics has led to environmental crises, particularly with microplastic pollution. It can take centuries for plastics to break down in landfills, where much of it eventually ends up in oceans. These microplastic particles are toxic to marine organisms and are absorbed at the base of the food chain, including by algae and other microorganisms [89].

Plastics made from fossil fuels also contribute to GHG emissions. In 2019, the Center for International Environmental Law estimated that plastic production and incineration produced over 850 million metric tons of GHGs, which is equivalent to the emissions of 189 coal power plants. While plastic production emits less than paper, its environmental toll is still significant [90].

There is a pressing need for materials that meet the demands of healthcare while minimizing environmental damage. However, the challenge lies in finding cost-effective alternatives that still ensure the sterility required for patient safety. The growing global population adds further pressure to produce these materials at a large scale [91].

Companies have been making efforts to meet these demands. For example, in 2019, the FDA approved the Enviropouch, a reusable steam sterilization pouch, to reduce single-use plastic waste. Similarly, ecoMedSupply introduced biodegradable materials for hospitals, including patient gowns and gloves, while NewGen Surgical developed a plant-based skin stapler that prevents 500 pounds of plastic waste for every 10,000 used [92].

While these technologies are not yet widespread, they represent significant steps toward sustainable healthcare. Organizations like Practice Greenhealth are helping hospitals reduce their waste and carbon emissions by offering strategies to cut back on waste. Their efforts have led to hospitals avoiding the generation of over 140,000 tons of waste and cutting 180,000 metric tons of carbon emissions [72].

Through the guidance of Practice Greenhealth, Kaiser Permanente in California recently became the first major healthcare system to achieve carbon neutrality. This shift is estimated to offset an 800,000-ton carbon footprint. Programs like Practice Greenhealth's Environmental Excellence Awards encourage other hospitals to follow suit, with centers like Boston Medical Center and Seattle Children's Hospital leading the way [93].

1.5.4 Future Trends in Green Healthcare Products

In future trends for green healthcare, efforts are being made to assess emissions at the state level, linking them to healthcare spending, energy intensity, and access to care. States with higher healthcare expenditures tend to have higher per capita GHG emissions. Moving forward, strategies that reduce unnecessary care and prioritize disease prevention and public health will lower healthcare-related pollution and costs [94, 95].

To incorporate environmental accountability, healthcare facilities will need valid metrics and data-sharing technologies. The Centers for Medicare and Medicaid Services (CMS) framework will require reforms to incentivize sustainability. Linking financial incentives to emissions reduction could promote greener practices, with measures such as integrating emissions metrics into existing health quality assessments. For example, the Hospital Value-Based Purchasing Program could include sustainability metrics, encouraging Medicare-participating organizations to reduce their carbon footprints while improving population health [96, 97].

Additionally, state-level interventions could involve adjusting federal aid based on healthcare sector emissions or the energy intensity of electricity grids, pushing states to adopt more sustainable operations. Payment reductions in states with higher emissions or more energy-intensive grids could drive systemic change. Accountability for resource conservation and waste reduction can be further incentivized through programs like the Quality Payment Program, encouraging providers to minimize emissions associated with clinical care [96, 97]. These evolving frameworks indicate a strong push toward integrating sustainability into healthcare's financial and operational structures, shaping future trends in green healthcare products and practices (Fig. 1.17).

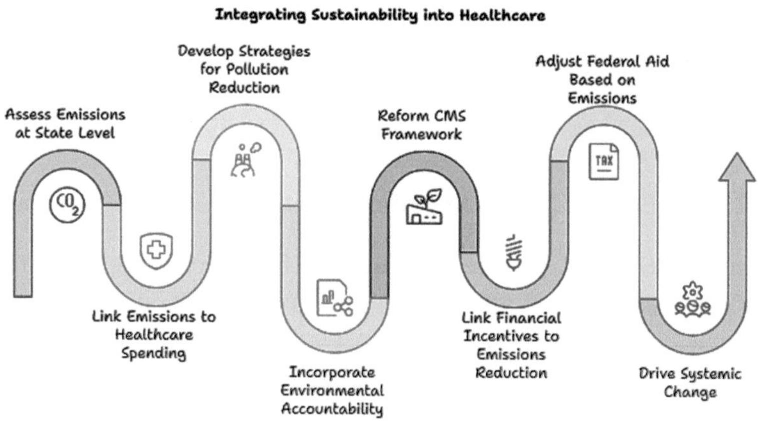

Figure 1.17 Pathway to achieving a worldwide systemic change to integrate sustainability in healthcare.

1.5.5 Conclusion

The shift to green alternatives in healthcare is no longer an option but a necessity. As hospitals continue to generate vast amounts of plastic waste and contribute significantly to GHG emissions, it is imperative to adopt sustainable practices. The introduction of biodegradable medical tools by companies represents a significant leap toward reducing the environmental burden. These companies exemplify the role of innovation in rethinking healthcare systems. Additionally, they are helping healthcare facilities reduce waste and emissions by providing guidance and support for sustainability initiatives (Fig. 1.18).

The growing awareness of healthcare's environmental impact highlights the urgent need for sustainable materials that maintain sterility and safety while minimizing harm to the planet. Solutions like reusable sterilization equipment and biodegradable plastics provide practical alternatives to traditional tools, helping healthcare institutions to reduce their ecological footprint without compromising care quality. Moving forward, healthcare systems must integrate these innovations on a larger scale, setting a precedent for other industries to follow.

As we face increasing global challenges related to climate change, the healthcare industry has a crucial role to play. By embracing green alternatives and implementing forward-thinking strategies, the industry can not only reduce its environmental impact but also contribute to the global effort toward sustainability. The future of healthcare is inextricably linked to the health of the planet, and the adoption of eco-friendly practices is a critical step toward a healthier world for all.

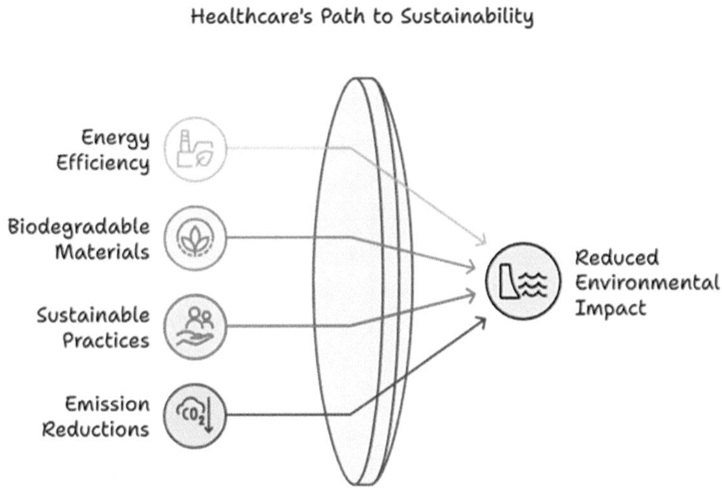

Figure 1.18 Reducing harmful environmental impact can be achieved by using energy efficient modalities, biodegradable materials, sustainable and practical practices, and reducing emission.

1.6 Future Green Benefit

1.6.1 Introduction

Exposure to air pollutants has a range of harmful effects on human health, contributing to increased mortality and morbidity [98]. Air pollution, arising from both human activities such as vehicle emissions, industrial processes, and agricultural practices, as well as natural sources like fires, is the largest environmental risk factor today [99]. Pollutants sometimes form indirectly through complex atmospheric reactions, making air pollution a complex issue. The Clean Air Act (CAA), enforced by the U.S. Environmental Protection Agency (EPA) in collaboration with state and local governments, aims to improve air quality through regulatory standards. Since its passage in 1963, the CAA has undergone significant expansions in 1970, 1990, and 1997 [100]. These amendments have set national standards for major pollutants (ozone, particulate matter (PM), carbon monoxide, sulfur dioxide, lead, and nitrogen dioxide) while reducing emissions of other toxic substances (e.g., benzene, asbestos) and metals like mercury and cadmium. A timeline of the CAA and its amendments is shown in Fig. 1.19 [101].

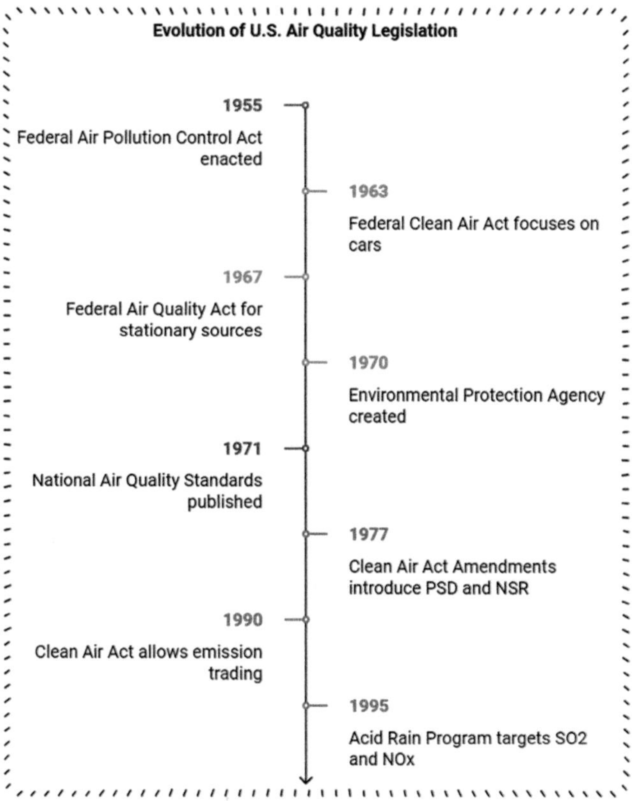

Figure 1.19 Federal CAA chronological evolution over time.

Among these pollutants, PM2.5, fine particulate matter with a diameter of 2.5 μm or less, has been most closely studied for its health impacts. Exposure to PM2.5 is a significant concern, especially since these particles can penetrate deep into the lungs and enter the bloodstream, potentially reaching vital organs like the brain [102]. This has been linked to structural and functional brain damage, accelerating cognitive decline, especially in older adults (Fig. 1.20). Studies have shown that higher levels of air pollution correlate with increased risks of cardiovascular and respiratory diseases, as well as elevated hospitalization and mortality rates, particularly among older individuals [103]. This population is more vulnerable due to physiological aging, chronic diseases, and prolonged exposure to pollutants over a lifetime [104, 105].

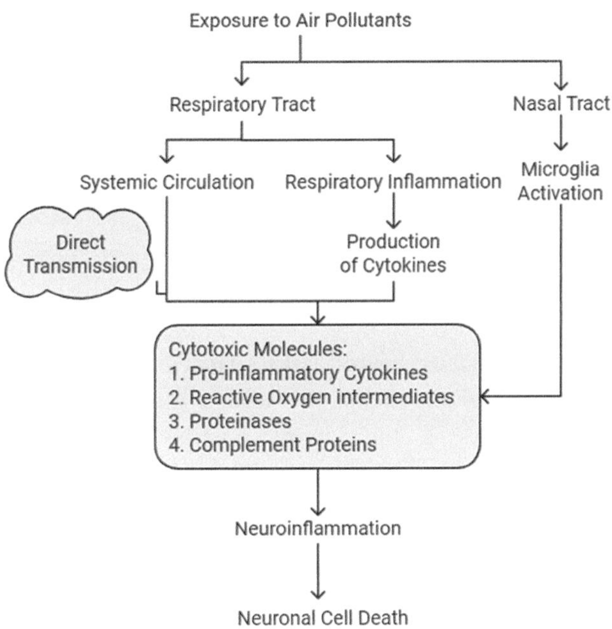

Figure 1.20 Impact of air pollutants on the brain.

According to the WHO's report on the global assessment of exposure (Fig. 1.21), living in areas with high concentrations of $PM_{2.5}$ is associated with cognitive decline in older adults [103, 105–111]. Fine particulate matter has been implicated in brain inflammation, white matter loss, and beta-amyloid buildup-factors associated with Alzheimer's disease [112–115]. Despite the clear short- and long-term health impacts of air pollution, research is still limited in assessing the effects of lifetime exposure, particularly since air quality monitoring began only in the 1970s. This gap highlights the need for more comprehensive studies to better understand the full extent of pollution's impact on human health across the lifespan.

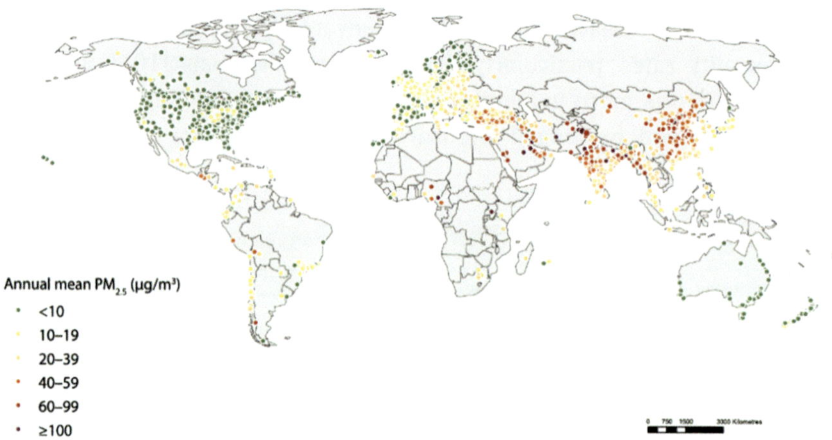

Figure 1.21 Location of fine particulate matter of 2.5 microns of less ($PM_{2.5}$) in nearly 3,000 human settlements between 2008 and 2015.

Given the serious health risks, particularly for vulnerable populations like older adults, the WHO's Air Quality Guidelines recommend achieving the lowest possible concentrations of particulate matter to minimize health damage [98]. Deaths due to air pollution were depicted by the WHO in 2012 worldwide in Fig. 1.22 [111].

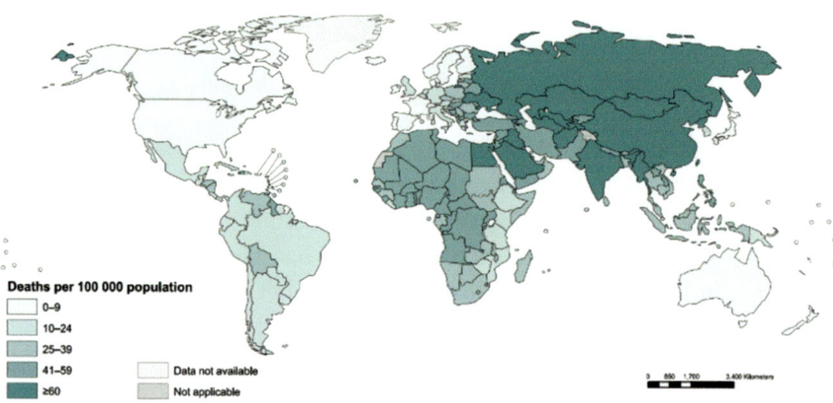

Figure 1.22 Deaths attributable to ambient air pollution in 2012, worldwide.

1.6.2 Transition to Environmentally Neutral Products

In an era where environmental concerns are paramount, green chemistry has emerged as a critical framework for fostering sustainability across various industries. For over three decades, green chemistry has provided chemists and engineers with principles and tools that contribute to global efforts toward sustainability. By minimizing waste, reducing hazardous substances, and supporting innovations in chemical processes, green chemistry plays a crucial role in addressing the challenges of pollution and resource depletion [116, 117]. As the world moves toward a circular economy, green chemistry offers solutions that not only protect the environment but also enhance public health and economic stability [118].

At the heart of green chemistry is a set of guiding principles that emphasize the reduction of environmental impact throughout the entire lifecycle of chemical products. These principles encourage the design of processes that minimize waste, use less hazardous substances, and rely on renewable materials [117]. By focusing on efficiency and sustainability, green chemistry aims to create safer and more eco-friendly products for both industrial and consumer use. The importance of this approach cannot be overstated, as the traditional chemical industry has historically contributed to significant pollution and resource depletion [118, 119]. By adopting green chemistry principles, industries can not only reduce their environmental footprint but also improve their economic resilience [120].

1.6.3 Green Chemistry and the Circular Economy

A key theme in the advancement of green chemistry is its role in promoting the circular economy. This concept focuses on the continual reuse and recycling of materials, aiming to reduce waste and ensure that resources are used as efficiently as possible. The 2021 Green Chemistry & Engineering Conference, with its theme "Sustainable Production to Advance the Circular Economy," underscored the need for industries to embrace lifecycle thinking [116]. This approach ensures that every stage of a product's lifecycle, i.e., from raw material extraction to disposal, considers its environmental impact [120].

In the context of green chemistry, the circular economy is supported by designing products and processes that allow materials to be reused, recycled, or upcycled [117]. By reducing the dependency on finite resources like fossil fuels and emphasizing renewable materials, green chemistry enables the creation of products that are not only sustainable but also economically viable in the long term. This shift is especially critical as industries face increasing pressure to reduce their carbon emissions and waste production [116].

One of the most exciting aspects of green chemistry is the technological innovations that have emerged in recent years. These innovations are making it possible for industries to adopt more sustainable practices without sacrificing efficiency or performance. For instance, catalysis has become a cornerstone of green chemistry, enabling the efficient transformation of raw materials into valuable products with minimal waste [118, 119]. Innovations in biobased chemicals are also gaining traction, as renewable feedstocks replace traditional fossil fuels in chemical manufacturing [120].

CO_2 capture technologies represent another area of significant advancement. These technologies are designed to remove carbon dioxide from industrial emissions and repurpose it for use in the production of chemicals and fuels [121]. This not only reduces the environmental impact of industries but also helps mitigate climate change by preventing the release of CO_2 into the atmosphere. Additionally, alternative solvents, such as deep eutectic solvents and ionic liquids, are being developed to replace hazardous solvents traditionally used in chemical processes [122]. These innovations are revolutionizing the way industries approach sustainability, offering practical solutions that align with the principles of green chemistry [120].

Green chemistry is not only about reducing the environmental impact of chemical production but also about protecting human health. The chemicals used in industrial processes have long been associated with various health risks, from respiratory issues to cancer. As such, a critical aspect of green chemistry is the development of chemicals with minimal toxicity. This involves creating new materials that are safe for both the environment and human health. The challenge lies in assessing the toxicological risks of thousands of chemicals already in use, as well as those being developed. To address this, green chemistry promotes interdisciplinary research to better understand the interaction of chemicals with biological systems and to design safer alternatives.

Moreover, the design of biodegradable plastics and sustainably produced materials is becoming increasingly important. Conventional plastics, for example, are notorious for their long degradation periods, which lead to pollution in oceans and landfills. Green chemistry offers alternatives, such as bioplastics, that decompose more rapidly and have a lower environmental impact [123, 124]. By focusing on safer, more sustainable materials, green chemistry is helping industries minimize their ecological footprint while protecting human health.

1.6.4 Future Directions and Research Needs

Despite the progress made, there are still challenges that need to be addressed for green chemistry to fully realize its potential in supporting a sustainable future. One of the key areas for future research is the depolymerization and defunctionalization of existing materials, particularly plastics [125]. These processes are essential for creating circular systems that can reuse and recycle materials without generating harmful byproducts. Another critical area is the need for improved lifecycle assessment (LCA) methodologies that accurately evaluate the environmental impact of products and processes [126].

Additionally, the integration of machine learning and big data analytics into green chemistry research holds promise for driving innovation. These tools can help researchers identify new materials and processes that align with sustainability goals, accelerating the transition to a circular economy [118, 120]. By addressing these challenges, green chemistry can continue to play a pivotal role in reducing pollution, conserving resources, and protecting both the environment and public health [120].

Green chemistry has proven to be an essential framework for achieving sustainability in the chemical industry and beyond. Its principles of waste reduction, renewable resource use, and the development of safer chemicals offer a path toward a more sustainable future. As industries continue to adopt green chemistry practices, the transition to a circular economy will become more achievable, benefiting both the environment and society [116]. The technological innovations driving green chemistry today (e.g., catalysis, CO_2 capture, and alternative solvents) are laying the foundation for a future where environmental sustainability and economic growth go hand in hand [120]. Through continued research and collaboration, green chemistry will remain at the forefront of efforts to create a cleaner, healthier planet for generations to come [118, 119].

1.6.5 Costs and Benefits of Environmental Sustainability

The transition to a low-carbon and resource-efficient global economy is not only an environmental imperative but also an economic necessity. The traditional "grow now, clean up later" approach to development, while successful in lifting millions out of poverty, has led to severe environmental degradation, increased health risks, and significant future economic costs [127]. This strategy has strained ecosystems, accelerated climate change, and placed human well-being in jeopardy. A new path forward is essential, one that balances economic growth with environmental sustainability.

A sustainable future requires the adoption of three key strategies: decarbonization, detoxification, and dematerialization. Decarbonization focuses on reducing GHG emissions to mitigate climate change, while detoxification targets the reduction of harmful pollutants. Dematerialization involves minimizing the environmental impact of resource extraction and consumption. Together, these strategies provide a framework for addressing the environmental crises we face while fostering economic resilience [128].

The economic costs of transitioning to a sustainable economy are often overstated. Many conventional models fail to account for the role of innovation in reducing long-term costs. Clean technologies, such as renewable energy, have already demonstrated their potential to lower costs while driving economic growth. Innovation, once triggered, becomes self-reinforcing. As clean technologies become more widespread, economies of scale and continuous improvement reduce costs even further, making the transition more affordable than initially anticipated.

The transition to a low-carbon economy is not only about managing environmental risks but also about seizing opportunities. Early action can stimulate innovation, create new industries, and generate economic benefits. Delaying this transition, on the other hand, will lock societies into unsustainable carbon-intensive infrastructure, increasing future costs. The longer the delay, the higher the financial and environmental price.

Embracing environmental sustainability is not just about protecting the planet; it is about securing long-term economic prosperity. The sooner societies invest in clean technologies and sustainable practices, the more they stand to gain. A future that integrates sustainability into economic decision-making is one that offers growth, innovation, and a healthier environment for all. The cost of inaction is too great to bear, and the time to act is now [128].

1.6.6 Conclusion

The transition to environmentally neutral products presents a clear pathway toward reducing pollution and protecting vulnerable populations, particularly the aging demographic. By adopting green chemistry principles and embracing innovations like CO_2 capture technologies, biobased chemicals, and biodegradable materials, industries can significantly reduce their environmental impact. This shift not only offers ecological benefits but also enhances economic resilience through sustainable practices. As the global economy moves toward a circular model, green chemistry and other environmentally neutral approaches will be essential for fostering long-term sustainability. Continued research and development in these areas will ensure that both the environment and human health are safeguarded, making the future brighter and cleaner for generations to come.

1.7 Summary

As the aging population continues to grow globally, the demand for healthcare services and resources is expanding rapidly. Older adults typically experience a higher incidence of chronic diseases, mobility issues, cognitive impairments, and other age-related health conditions that require long-term care, specialized treatments, and frequent medical interventions. This increased demand on healthcare systems can lead to significant strain on resources, making sustainability not only an environmental consideration but also a critical factor in ensuring the long-term viability of healthcare services for older adults.

Sustainability in healthcare for the aging population addresses several key concerns. First, it helps reduce the environmental impact of healthcare systems, which are major contributors to pollution and waste. By adopting sustainable practices, such as energy-efficient buildings, waste minimization strategies, and reducing the carbon footprint of healthcare facilities, healthcare systems can better manage their environmental resources without compromising the quality of care for the elderly. For instance, older adults often spend more time in healthcare settings such as hospitals, nursing homes, and long-term care facilities. Creating sustainable, healthier environments within these facilities can improve the overall experience for aging patients, fostering better recovery and well-being.

Moreover, sustainability is essential for financial stability. As the aging population increases, healthcare costs are expected to rise dramatically. Sustainable practices, like reducing waste, improving energy efficiency, and optimizing resource usage, can help lower operational costs in the long run. This allows healthcare providers to focus more on patient care while managing the financial burden of an aging population. In turn, these savings can be reinvested into improving care standards, increasing access to services, or supporting innovation in geriatric care models.

Finally, sustainability in healthcare also promotes a more equitable system. By prioritizing long-term, cost-effective, and resource-efficient strategies, healthcare providers can ensure that care remains accessible to all, including underserved elderly populations. This is particularly crucial for communities that may face economic challenges in supporting their aging citizens. Implementing sustainable healthcare practices helps ensure that all older adults, regardless of their background or socioeconomic status, have access to high-quality care, which is essential for maintaining their dignity and health as they age.

In essence, sustainability in healthcare for the aging population is not just about environmental responsibility; it is about creating a system that can meet the growing and evolving needs of older adults in a financially sustainable, equitable, and environmentally conscious manner. As we continue to confront the challenges of an aging society, sustainable healthcare will be key to maintaining a high standard of care for older generations without compromising the ability of future generations to thrive.

References

1. What is Normal Aging? Lessons from the BLSA | National Institute on Aging. https://www.nia.nih.gov/research/labs/blsa/what-normal-aging. Accessed 2 Mar 2024.
2. Aging NRC (US) C on CT (1987) *The Aging Population and the Psychosocial Implications of Aging*.
3. Arking R (2006) The biology of aging: Observations and principles. *The Biology of Aging Observations Principles,* 604.
4. Rothstein Morton (2014) *Biochemical Approaches to Aging,* 329.
5. Aging NRC (US) C on CT (1987) *Principles of Gerontology*.
6. United States - Age distribution 2022 | Statista. https://www.statista.com/statistics/270000/age-distribution-in-the-united-states/. Accessed 2 Mar 2024.
7. Age Distribution for U.S. Population: 2000, 2010, and 2020 Censuses | Tableau Public. https://public.tableau.com/app/profile/us.census.bureau/viz/AgeDistributionforU_S_Population20002010and2020Censuses/AgeDistribution. Accessed 1 Dec 2024.
8. Navarro C, Salazar J, Díaz MP, et al. (2023) Intrinsic and environmental basis of aging: A narrative review. *Heliyon,* 9:e18239.
9. Goldspink DF. Ageing and activity: their effects on the functional reserve capacities of the heart and vascular smooth and skeletal muscles. *Ergonomics*. 2005 Sep 15-Nov 15;48(11–14):1334-51. doi: 10.1080/00140130500101247. PMID: 16338704.

10. Poole R, Sharples F, Sawyer K (eds) (2020) *Integrating the Science of Aging and Environmental Health Research.* https://doi.org/10.17226/25908.
11. Aging NRC (US) C on CT (1987) *Aging and Environmental Exposure.*
12. Varghese D, Ishida C, Patel P, Haseer Koya H (2024) *Polypharmacy.*
13. Krewski D, Acosta D, Andersen M, et al. (2010) Toxicity testing in the 21st century: A vision and a strategy. *J Toxicol Environ Health B Crit Rev,* 13:51–138.
14. Aging NRC (US) C on CT (1987) *Environmental Effects on Age-Associated Diseases and Changes in Organ Function.*
15. Aging NRC (US) C on CT (1987) *Principles of Toxicology in the Context of Aging.*
16. Clements BW, Casani JAP (2016) Chemical hazards and disasters. *Disasters and Public Health,* 181–218.
17. Birnbaum LS (1987) Age-related changes in carcinogen metabolism. *J Am Geriatr Soc.,* 35:51–60.
18. Schmucker DL (1985) Aging and drug disposition: An update. *Pharmacol. Rev.,* 37.
19. Lee EJ (1987) Disposition of drugs in the elderly. *Ann Acad Med Singap.,* 16:128–32.
20. Mangoni AA, Jackson SHD (2004) Age-related changes in pharmacokinetics and pharmacodynamics: Basic principles and practical applications. *Br J Clin Pharmacol.,* 57:6–14.
21. Reidenberg MM, Levy M, Warner H, Coutinho CB, Schwartz MA, Yu G, Cheripko J (1978) Relationship between diazepam dose, plasma level, age, and central nervous system depression. *Clin Pharmacol Ther,* 23:371–374.
22. Van Brummelen P, Buhler FR, Kiowski W, Amann FW (1981) Age-related decrease in cardiac and peripheral vascular responsiveness to isoprenaline: Studies in normal subjects. *Clin Sci.,* 60:571–577.
23. Vestal RE, Wood AJJ, Shand DG (1979) Reduced β-adrenoceptor sensitivity in the elderly. *Clin Pharmacol Ther,* 26:181–186.
24. Bellville JW, Forrest WH, Miller E, Brown BW (1971) Influence of age on pain relief from analgesics: A study of postoperative patients. *JAMA,* 217:1835–1841.
25. Kaiko RF (1980) Age and morphine analgesia in cancer patients with postoperative pain. *Clin Pharmacol Ther,* 28:823–826.

26. Divoll M, Ameer B, Abernethy DR, Greenblatt DJ (1982) Age does not alter acetaminophen absorption. *J Am Geriatr Soc*, 30:240–244.

27. Divoll M, Greenblatt DJ, Ameer B, Abernethy DR (1982) Effect of food on acetaminophen absorption in young and elderly subjects. *J Clin Pharmacol*, 22:571–576.

28. Vestal RE, McGuire EA, Tobin JD, Andres R, Norris AH, Mezey E (1977) Aging and ethanol metabolism. *Clin Pharmacol Ther*, 21:343–354.

29. Salem SAM, Rajjayabun P, Shepherd AMM, Stevenson IH (1978) Reduced induction of drug metabolism in the elderly. *Age Ageing*, 7:68–73.

30. Brooks PM, Kean WF, Kassam Y, Buchanan WW (1984) Problems of antiarthritic therapy in the elderly. *J Am Geriatr Soc*, 32:229–234.

31. Schmucker DL, Wang RK (1987) Effects of aging on the properties of rhesus monkey liver microsomal NADPH-cytochrome c (P-450) reductase. *Drug Metabolism and Disposition*, 15.

32. Woodhouse JH, Dziewonski AM (1989) Seismic modelling of the Earth's large-scale three-dimensional structure. *Philosophical Transactions of the Royal Society of London. Series A, Mathematical and Physical Sciences*, 328291–308. http://doi.org/10.1098/rsta.1989.0037.

33. Smithard D, Langman M (1978) The effect of vitamin supplementation upon antipyrine metabolism in the elderly. *Br J Clin Pharmacol*, 5:181–185.

34. Wattenberg LW (19714) Studies of polycyclic hydrocarbon hydroxylases of the intestine possibly related to cancer. Effect of diet on benzpyrene hydroxylase activity. *Cancer*, 28(1):99–102. doi: 10.1002/1097-0142(197107)28:1<99::aid-cncr2820280118> 3.0.co;2-m. PMID: 5110649.

35. Alvares AP, Kappas A, Eiseman JL, Anderson KE, Pantuck CB, Pantuck EJ, Hsiao KC, Garland WA, Conney AH (1979) Intraindividual variation in drug disposition. *Clin Pharmacol Ther*, 26:407–419.

36. Campbell TC, Hayes JR (1974) Role of nutrition in the drug-metabolizing enzyme system. *Pharmacol Rev*, 26.

37. Alvares AP, Pantuck EJ, Anderson KE, Kappas A, Conney AH (1979) Regulation of drug metabolism in man by environmental factors. *Drug Metab Rev*, 9:185–205.

38. Markers NRC (US) C on B (1989) *Markers of Exposure*.

39. Kay J, Thadhani E, Samson L, Engelward B (2019) Inflammation-induced DNA damage, mutations and cancer. *DNA Repair (Amst)*, 83:102673.

40. Parry GJ (2008) Neurological complications of toxin exposure in the workplace. *Neurology and General Medicine: Expert Consult,* 749–768.

41. Zhang Y (2018) Cell toxicity mechanism and biomarker. *Clin Transl Med,* 7:34.

42. Guo J, Huang X, Dou L, Yan M, Shen T, Tang W, Li J (2022) Aging and aging-related diseases: From molecular mechanisms to interventions and treatments. *Signal Transduction and Targeted Therapy,* 7:1–40.

43. La Du BN (2003) *Pharmacogenetics: Defective Enzymes in Relation to Reactions to Drugs,* 23:453–468. https://doi.org/101146/annurev.me23020172002321.

44. Sipes IG, Gandolfi J (1991) Biotransformation of toxicants. 88–126.

45. Vesell ES (1982) Complex, dynamically interacting host factors that affect the disposition of drugs and carcinogens. *IARC Sci Publ,* 427–37.

46. Price Evans DA, Manley KA, McKusick VA (1960) Genetic control of isoniazid metabolism in man. *Br Med J,* 2:485–491.

47. Vesell ES (1970) Recent progress in pharmacogenetics. *Adv Pharmacol,* 7:1–52.

48. Patel CJ, Cullen MR (2012) Genetic variability in molecular responses to chemical exposure. *Exp Suppl,* 101:437–457. doi: 10.1007/978-3-7643-8340-4_15. PMID: 22945578.

49. Vesell ES (1980) The influence of host factors on drug response. IV. Occupation. *Ration Drug Ther,* 14:1–5.

50. Vesell ES (1973) Advances in pharmacogenetics. *Prog Med Genet,* 9:291–367.

51. United Nations Population growth, environmental degradation and climate change | United Nations. https://www.who.int/news-room/fact-sheets/detail/climate-change-and-health. Accessed 20 Sep 2024.

52. Shortage of personal protective equipment endangering health workers worldwide. https://www.who.int/news/item/03-03-2020-shortage-of-personal-protective-equipment-endangering-health-workers-worldwide. Accessed 20 Sep 2024.

53. Zikhathile T, Atagana H, Bwapwa J, Sawtell D (2022) A review of the impact that healthcare risk waste treatment technologies have on the environment. *Int J Environ Res Public Health.* https://doi.org/10.3390/IJERPH191911967.

54. Medical Waste | US EPA. https://www.epa.gov/rcra/medical-waste. Accessed 1 Dec 2024.

55. Kenny C, Priyadarshini A (2021) Review of current healthcare waste. Management methods and their effect on global health. *Healthcare*, 9:284.

56. Ranjbari M, Shams Esfandabadi Z, Shevchenko T, Chassagnon-Haned N, Peng W, Tabatabaei M, Aghbashlo M (2022) Mapping healthcare waste management research: Past evolution, current challenges, and future perspectives towards a circular economy transition. *J Hazard Mater*. https://doi.org/10.1016/J.JHAZMAT.2021.126724.

57. Nadiah Syafei, A, Warno Utomo, S (2022). Comparison of COVID-19 Medical Waste Management Strategies for Hospitals in Developed and Developing Country. *KESANS : Int J Health Sci*, 1(9):853–862. https://doi.org/10.54543/kesans.v1i9.89.

58. Ramesh Kumar A, Vaidya AN, Singh I, Ambekar K, Gurjar S, Prajapati A, Kanade GS, Hippargi G, Kale G, Bodkhe S (2021) Leaching characteristics and hazard evaluation of bottom ash generated from common biomedical waste incinerators. *Journal of Environmental Science and Health, Part A*, 56:1069–1079.

59. US Environmental Protection Agency. Learn about Dioxin https://www.epa.gov/dioxin/learn-about-dioxin. Accessed 20 Sep 2024.

60. Mayilsamy M, Sangeetha S, Nakamura M, Ko S, Govarthanan M, Vimalkumar K (2022) Screening of PCDDs/Fs and DL-PCBs by AhR-CALUX bioassay in bovine milk and environment ash from India. *Toxicol Environ Health Sci*, 14:223–234.

61. Business and Industry: Time Series / Trend Charts. https://www.census.gov/econ/currentdata/?programCode=QSS&startYear=2003&endYear=2024&categories[]=000000A&dataType=QREV&geoLevel=US&adjusted=1&notAdjusted=1&errorData=0;https://www.census.gov/econ_timeseries/. Accessed 1 Dec 2024.

62. The Cost of Medical Waste Disposal - Medical Waste Disposal. https://www.getbiomed.com/medical-waste-disposal/the-cost-of-medical-waste-disposal-2/. Accessed 1 Dec 2024.

63. Healthcare waste. https://www.who.int/news-room/fact-sheets/detail/health-care-waste. Accessed 1 Dec 2024.

64. WASH in health care facilities 2023 data update: Special focus on primary health care. *JMP*. https://washdata.org/reports/jmp-2024-wash-hcf. Accessed 1 Dec 2024.

65. Institute of Medicine (US) Roundtable on Environmental Health Sciences R and M (2007) Introduction.

66. Lenzen M, Malik A, Li M, Fry J, Weisz H, Pichler PP, Chaves LSM, Capon A, Pencheon D (2020) The environmental footprint of health care: A global assessment. *Lancet Planet Health*, 4:e271–e279.

67. The environmental impact of healthcare | Pursuit by the University of Melbourne. https://pursuit.unimelb.edu.au/articles/the-environmental-impact-of-healthcare. Accessed 20 Sep 2024.

68. Khan MT, Shah IA, Hossain MF, Akther N, Zhou Y, Khan MS, Al-shaeli M, Bacha MS, Ihsanullah I (2023) Personal protective equipment (PPE) disposal during COVID-19: An emerging source of microplastic and microfiber pollution in the environment. *Sci Total Environ*, 860:160322.

69. Rume T, Islam SMDU (2020) Environmental effects of COVID-19 pandemic and potential strategies of sustainability. *Heliyon*. https://doi.org/10.1016/J.HELIYON.2020.E04965.

70. US Environmental Protection Agency. Climate Change and the Health of Older Adults. https://www.epa.gov/climateimpacts/climate-change-and-health-older-adults. Accessed 20 Sep 2024.

71. Ebi KL, Hess JJ (2020) Health risks due to climate change: Inequity in causes and consequences. *Health Aff*, 39:2056–2062.

72. Home Page ecoMedsupply. https://www.ecomedsupply.com/. Accessed 20 Sep 2024.

73. Energy Information Administration (EIA)-Commercial Buildings Energy Consumption Survey (CBECS) Data. https://www.eia.gov/consumption/commercial/data/2018/index.php?view=characteristics. Accessed 1 Dec 2024.

74. Landrigan PJ, Fuller R, Acosta NJR, et al. (2018) The Lancet Commission on pollution and health. *The Lancet*, 391:462–512.

75. Steffen W, Richardson K, Rockström J, et al. (2015) Sustainability. Planetary boundaries: Guiding human development on a changing planet. *Science*. https://doi.org/10.1126/SCIENCE.1259855.

76. Eckelman MJ, Sherman J (2016) Environmental impacts of the U.S. health care system and effects on public health. *PLoS One*. https://doi.org/10.1371/JOURNAL.PONE.0157014.

77. Malik A, Lenzen M, McAlister S, McGain F (2018) The carbon footprint of Australian health care. *Lancet Planet Health*, 2:e2–e3.

78. SDU NHS (2016) Carbon update for the health and care sector in England 2015.

79. THE NHS: CARBON FOOTPRINT Sources of NHS carbon emissions.

80. Eckelman MJ, Sherman JD, MacNeill AJ (2018) Life cycle environmental emissions and health damages from the Canadian healthcare system: An economic-environmental-epidemiological analysis. *PLoS Med.* https://doi.org/10.1371/JOURNAL.PMED.1002623.

81. Muntean M, Guizzardi D, Schaaf E, Crippa M, Solazzo E, Olivier J (2019) Emissions Database for Global Atmospheric Research, version v5.0_FT_2017 (fossil CO_2 time-series).

82. The Costs and Financial Benefits of Green Buildings | icma.org. https://icma.org/documents/costs-and-financial-benefits-green-buildings. Accessed 1 Dec 2024.

83. Single-Use Plastics and Their Alternatives in Modern Healthcare | The Emerald Review. https://emeraldreview.com/2023/08/single-use-plastics-and-their-alternatives-in-modern-healthcare/. Accessed 20 Sep 2024.

84. About Us | Sterilis Solutions. https://sterilissolutions.com/about/. Accessed 20 Sep 2024.

85. Tsou AY, Pavlides S, Koepfler L, Drummond C (2020) No-touch modalities for disinfecting patient rooms in acute care settings.

86. When plastics revolutionised healthcare | PVCMed Alliance. https://pvcmed.org/healthcare/when-plastics-revolutionised-healthcare/. Accessed 20 Sep 2024.

87. Single use plastics in healthcare and hospitals. https://www.trvst.world/waste-recycling/plastic-pollution/single-use-plastic-in-healthcare-and-hospitals/. Accessed 20 Sep 2024.

88. How plastics contribute to climate change? Yale Climate Connections. https://yaleclimateconnections.org/2019/08/how-plastics-contribute-to-climate-change/. Accessed 20 Sep 2024.

89. Go PVC-Free - Greenpeace USA. https://www.greenpeace.org/usa/toxics/pvc-free/. Accessed 20 Sep 2024

90. Plastic Proliferation Threatens the Climate on a Global Scale Plastic & Climate. https://www.pacificenvironment.org/what-we-do/ending-plastic-pollution/?gad_source=1&gad_campaignid=21301767023&gclid=EAIaIQobChMIycTSjaCLjwMVrjcIBR1p0ABWEAAYASAAEgKG-vD_BwE.

91. How dangerous is microplastic? https://phys.org/news/2019-01-dangerous-microplastic.html. Accessed 20 Sep 2024.

92. About EnviroPouch®, Medical Device Manufacturer of Steam Sterilization Equipment. https://www.enviropouch.com/about-us. Accessed 20 Sep 2024.

93. NewGen Surgical - Leading the Way for Sustainability in Healthcare. https://newgensurgical.com/. Accessed 20 Sep 2024.

94. Berwick DM, Hackbarth AD (2012) Eliminating waste in US health care. *JAMA*, 307:1513–1516.

95. Maciosek M V., Coffield AB, Flottemesch TJ, Edwards NM, Solberg LI (2017) Greater use of preventive services in U.S. health care could save lives at little or no cost. https://doi.org/101377/hlthaff2008070129:1656–1660.

96. Sherman JD, Thiel C, MacNeill A, et al. (2020) The green print: Advancement of environmental sustainability in healthcare. *Resour Conserv Recycl*, 161:104882.

97. Sherman JD, MacNeill A, Thiel C (2019) Reducing pollution from the health care industry. *JAMA*, 322:1043–1044.

98. Regional Committee for Europe, 56th session. (2006). Fifty-sixth Regional Committee for Europe: Copenhagen, 11-14 September 2006: the future of the WHO Regional Office for Europe. World Health Organization. Regional Office for Europe. https://iris.who.int/handle/10665/342270

99. WHO (2018) Burden of disease from ambient air pollution for 2016 description of method.

100. Epa U, of Policy Analysis O (2011) The benefits and costs of the Clean Air Act from 1990 to 2020, Final Report, Revision A, April 2011.

101. The Definitive Guide to Air Emissions Regulations - ESC Spectrum. https://escspectrum.com/home/learn-and-support/source-blog/the-definitive-guide-to-air-emissions-regulations/. Accessed 1 Dec 2024.

102. Peters R, Peters J, Booth A, Mudway I (2015) Is air pollution associated with increased risk of cognitive decline? A systematic review. *Age Ageing*, 44:755–760.

103. Schikowski T, Vossoughi M, Vierkötter A, et al. (2015) Association of air pollution with cognitive functions and its modification by APOE gene variants in elderly women. *Environ Res*, 142:10–16.

104. U.S. EPA. Integrated Science Assessment (ISA) for Particulate Matter (Final Report, Dec 2019). U.S. Environmental Protection Agency, Washington, DC, EPA/600/R-19/188, 2019. https://www.epa.gov/isa/integrated-science-assessment-isa-particulate-matter.

105. Manisalidis I, Stavropoulou E, Stavropoulos A, Bezirtzoglou E (2020) Environmental and health impacts of air pollution: A review. *Front Public Health*. https://doi.org/10.3389/FPUBH.2020.00014.

106. Weuve J, Puett RC, Schwartz J, Yanosky JD, Laden F, Grodstein F (2012) Exposure to particulate air pollution and cognitive decline in older women. *Arch Intern Med*, 172:219.

107. Tonne C, Elbaz A, Beevers S, Singh-Manoux A (2014) Traffic-related air pollution in relation to cognitive function in older adults. *Epidemiology*, 25:674.

108. Gatto NM, Henderson VW, Hodis HN, St. John JA, Lurmann F, Chen JC, Mack WJ (2014) Components of air pollution and cognitive function in middle-aged and older adults in Los Angeles. *Neurotoxicology*, 40:1.

109. Ailshire JA, Clarke P (2015) Fine particulate matter air pollution and cognitive function among U.S. older adults. *The Journals of Gerontology: Series B*, 70:322–328.

110. Ailshire JA, Crimmins EM (2014) Fine particulate matter air pollution and cognitive function among older US adults. *Am J Epidemiol*, 180: 359–366.

111. Ambient air pollution: A global assessment of exposure and burden of disease. https://iris.who.int/handle/10665/250141. Accessed 1 Dec 2024.

112. Wilker EH, Preis SR, Beiser AS, et al. (2015) Long-term exposure to fine particulate matter, residential proximity to major roads and measures of brain structure. *Stroke: A Journal of Cerebral Circulation*, 46:1161.

113. Levesque S, Surace MJ, McDonald J, Block ML (2011) Air pollution & the brain: Subchronic diesel exhaust exposure causes neuroinflammation and elevates early markers of neurodegenerative disease. *J Neuro-inflammation*, 8:105.

114. Chen JC, Wang X, Wellenius GA, Serre ML, Driscoll I, Casanova R, McArdle JJ, Manson JE, Chui HC, Espeland MA (2015) Ambient air pollution and neurotoxicity on brain structure: Evidence from women's health initiative memory study. *Ann Neurol*, 78:466.

115. Calderón-Garcidueñas L, Reed W, Maronpot RR, et al. (2004) Brain inflammation and Alzheimer's-like pathology in individuals exposed to severe air pollution. *Toxicol Pathol*, 32:650–658.

116. Anastas PT (2020) Circularity. What's the Problem? *ACS Sustain Chem Eng*, 8:13111.

117. Erythropel HC, Zimmerman JB, De Winter TM, et al. (2018) The Green ChemisTREE: 20 years after taking root with the 12 principles. *Green Chemistry*, 20:1929–1961.

118. Meier MAR, Tam MKC (2021) Shaping effective practices for incorporating sustainability assessment in manuscripts submitted to ACS

sustainable chemistry & engineering: Biomaterials. *ACS Sustain Chem Eng*, 9:7400–7402.

119. Debecker DP, Kuok (mimi) Hii K, Moores A, Rossi LM, Sels B, Allen DT, Subramaniam B (2021) Shaping effective practices for incorporating sustainability assessment in manuscripts submitted to ACS sustainable chemistry & engineering: Catalysis and catalytic processes. *ACS Sustain Chem Eng*, 9:4936–4940.
120. Subramaniam B, Licence P, Moores A, Allen DT (2021) Shaping effective practices for incorporating sustainability assessment in manuscripts submitted to ACS sustainable chemistry & engineering: An initiative by the editors. *ACS Sustain Chem Eng*, 9:3977–3978.
121. Halliday C, Hatton TA (2020) Net-negative emissions through molten sorbents and bioenergy with carbon capture and storage. *Ind Eng Chem Res*, 59:22582–22596.
122. Jiang Y, Shi XC, Tan P, Qi SC, Gu C, Yang T, Peng SS, Liu XQ, Sun LB (2020) Controllable CO_2 capture in metal-organic frameworks: Making targeted active sites respond to light. *Ind Eng Chem Res*, 59:21894–21900.
123. Napper IE, Thompson RC (2024) Annual review of environment and resources plastics and the environment. *Guest*, 53:49. Downloaded from www.annualreviews.org.
124. Napper IE, Thompson RC (2019) Environmental deterioration of biodegradable, oxo-biodegradable, compostable, and conventional plastic carrier bags in the sea, soil, and open-air over a 3-year period. *Environ Sci Technol.*, 53:4775–4783.
125. Chamas A, Moon H, Zheng J, Qiu Y, Tabassum T, Jang JH, Abu-Omar M, Scott SL, Suh S (2020) Degradation rates of plastics in the environment. *ACS Sustain Chem Eng*, 8:3494–3511.
126. Luo Y, Ierapetritou M (2020) Comparison between different hybrid life cycle assessment methodologies: A review and case study of biomass-based p-xylene production. *Ind Eng Chem Res*, 59:22313–22329.
127. O'Connor, D. (1996), "Grow Now/Clean Later, or the Pursuit of Sustainable Development?", OECD Development Centre Working Papers, No. 111, OECD Publishing, Paris, https://doi.org/10.1787/043786612388.
128. Ekins P, Zenghelis D (2021) The costs and benefits of environmental sustainability. *Sustain Sci*, 16:949–965.

Chapter 2

Environment- and Microbiome-Friendly Skincare Products

Tranum Kaur,[a] Negin Noorbakhsh,[a] Tarokh Arzani Birgani,[a] and Sohila Kaur Sidhu[b]

[a]*Department of Chemistry and Biochemistry, University of Windsor, Windsor, Ontario, Canada*
[b]*Department of Integrative Biology, University of Windsor, Windsor, Ontario, Canada*

tranum@uwindsor.ca

In 2023, the global skincare industry experienced a substantial 8% growth, solidifying its position as one of the fastest-growing markets worldwide. This surge in demand has been driven by an increasing public awareness of skin health and advances in the field of the skin microbiome. The skin microbiome is a dynamic ecosystem of microorganisms, such as bacteria, viruses, and fungi, which plays a vital role in regulating skin health, immune responses, and protection against environmental stressors. A comprehensive understanding of the microbiome, along with the interplay of genetic, environmental, and lifestyle factors, is essential for designing advanced skincare solutions that promote both skin health and microbial diversity. This chapter explores

Environmentalism in Healthcare: Caring for Tomorrow Ecologically
Edited by Jacqueline A. Stagner and David S.-K. Ting

ISBN 978-981-5129-95-3 (Hardcover), 978-1-003-74869-4 (eBook)
www.jennystanford.com

DOI: 10.1201/9781003748694-2

the latest research on factors that influence skin microbiome diversity, dysbiosis, and skin disorders. Further, it delves into the development of microbiome-friendly and sustainable skincare formulations that reduce the ecological footprint of the skincare industry. Emerging biotechnological techniques for analyzing the skin microbiome, such as metagenomic sequencing and gene expression profiling, are examined to provide a foundation for innovative product development. By integrating cutting-edge science with environmental consciousness, this holistic approach offers a pathway toward healthier skin and a more sustainable future for the skincare industry.

2.1 Introduction

The skin, as the largest organ of the human body, is crucial for maintaining balance and protecting against external threats [1]. Its functionality is intricately connected with its diverse microbial communities, collectively known as the human skin microbiome [2]. Colonized by beneficial microorganisms, the skin microbiota varies across different physiological sites and changes over time [3]. Understanding the complexities of the skin microbiome is essential for exploring its interactions with various factors, including skincare products, age, genetics, hormonal differences, environmental pollutants, and lifestyle choices. Each of these factors can influence the composition and functionality of the skin microbiome, with implications for both local skin conditions and systemic health. These considerations are critical for developing skincare solutions that are not only effective but also environmentally sustainable. A comprehensive understanding of these interactions is vital for developing targeted skincare strategies that can adapt to individual needs while minimizing ecological footprints.

2.2 Factors Impacting Skin Microbiome

Microbiota colonization begins at birth and continues to impact the composition and stability of the skin microbiome.

This process is influenced by a multitude of factors, including genetics, age, sex, environment, lifestyle, and hygiene. Genetics is one of the factors that determines skin properties such as pH and sebum production, which, in turn, affect microbial diversity and immune interactions [4].

Age is another critical factor that influences microbiome diversity. Newborns acquire their initial microbial communities from their mothers during birth and through breastfeeding. As children grow, their microbiome diversity increases, adapting to new environments and exposures. Puberty brings significant changes, with increased sebum production and hormonal shifts altering microbial communities. For example, sebum production during puberty supports the growth of lipophilic bacteria. In elderly individuals, microbial diversity often decreases due to changes in sebum production and skin barrier function, which can affect overall skin health [5].

Hormonal influences result in distinct microbial communities between males and females [6]. Higher levels of testosterone in males contribute to increased sebum production, which influences the types of microbes that thrive on the skin [7]. In women, hormonal changes, particularly fluctuations in estrogen, significantly affect the composition of the skin microbiome. Estrogen plays a key role in regulating the skin's pH and sebum production, both of which are essential for maintaining a balanced microbial environment [8]. A reduction in estrogen levels, such as during menopause or certain phases of the menstrual cycle, leads to decreased sebum production, resulting in a drier skin environment. This dryness, combined with a shift toward a more alkaline skin pH, can favor the growth of harmful bacteria such as *Cutibacterium acnes* (formerly known as *Propionibacterium acnes)* and *Staphylococcus aureus*, while beneficial bacteria like *Staphylococcus epidermidis* may decrease in abundance. These notable changes in the microbiome can contribute to skin issues like acne, eczema, and increased sensitivity [9, 10].

Environmental factors such as climate, temperature, humidity, and sunlight exposure significantly impact microbial diversity. The World Health Organization (WHO) considers ambient (outdoor) and household (indoor) air pollution as the most significant environmental health risk factors, causing 7 million premature deaths annually.

Air pollutants like ozone (O_3) and particulate matter (PM2.5) [11], and other toxic substances induce oxidative stress, lipid peroxidation, and DNA damage, depleting hair follicle stem cells and disrupting the skin microbiome. This leads to skin disorders such as acne vulgaris and hair loss through increased squalene oxidation and keratinocyte apoptosis-based mechanisms (Fig. 2.1) [12, 13].

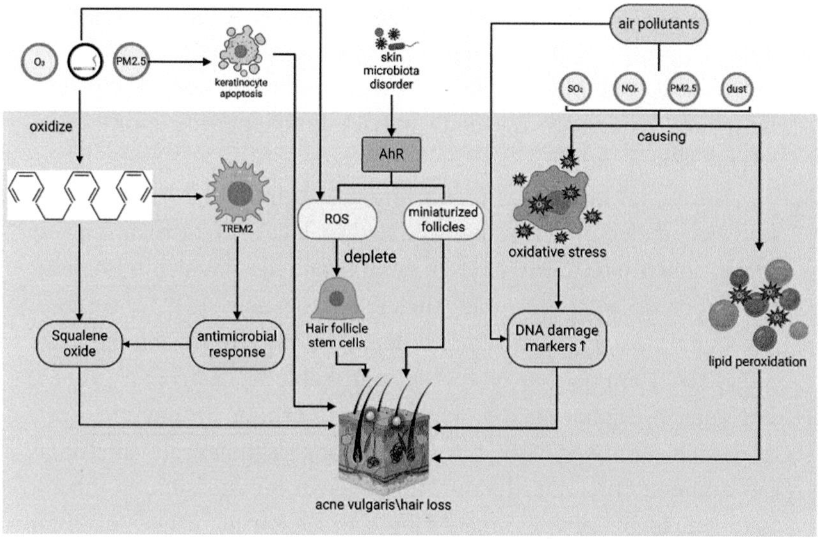

Figure 2.1 Impact of air pollutants on skin health and the microbiome. The figure is reproduced with permission from [12].

Humid and warm climates tend to increase microbial diversity, while urban pollution can alter the composition of microbial populations on the skin. These environmental factors highlight the importance of considering local conditions when developing skincare routines [13]. Hygiene practices, including the frequency of bathing and the use of antimicrobial soaps, have a profound effect on the skin microbiome. Over-washing can disrupt the skin barrier and remove beneficial microbes, leading to an imbalance, while insufficient hygiene can result in the overgrowth of harmful microbes. The use of skincare products also plays a role in altering the skin's pH and influencing microbial growth [2]. Lifestyle choices, such as diet, stress levels, sleep quality, and physical activity, indirectly affect the skin microbiome by impacting immune function, hormone levels, and skin physiology. A healthy gut microbiome, supported by a balanced diet, contributes to overall skin health, while stress and sleep deprivation can weaken the skin barrier, making it more susceptible to microbial imbalances and skin conditions [13]. These factors underscore the need for sustainable practices in skin healthcare. Understanding how genetic, environmental, and lifestyle factors influence the skin microbiome allows for the creation of eco-friendly skincare routines.

2.3 General Composition of the Skin Microbiome

As shown in Fig. 2.2, skin structures include hair follicles, sebaceous glands, and sweat glands. On a skin cross-section, various microorganisms, including viruses, bacteria, fungi, and mites, are located on the skin surface and found deep within hair follicles and glands [14].

The skin's appendages, including hair follicles, sebaceous glands, and sweat glands, support the microbiome's balance and function. On the surface, rod-shaped and spherical bacteria, such as *Proteobacteria and Staphylococcus* species, form interconnected communities with other microorganisms. Commensal fungi, such as *Malassezia* species, exist both as branching filaments (hyphae) and as individual cells [15]. Viruses are present both freely on the skin and inside bacterial cells. Tiny skin mites, such as *Demodex folliculorum* and *Demodex brevis*, live in or near hair follicles [14].

The skin microbiome is a complex ecosystem composed of a diverse array of microorganisms, including bacteria, fungi, viruses, and mites, which vary significantly across different body sites due to the unique environments created by oily, dry, and moist areas [16].

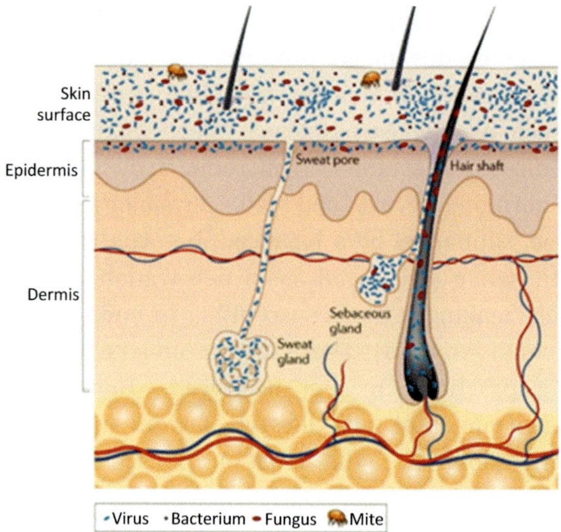

Figure 2.2 A cross-section of skin showing microorganisms and structures. The figure is reproduced with permission from [14].

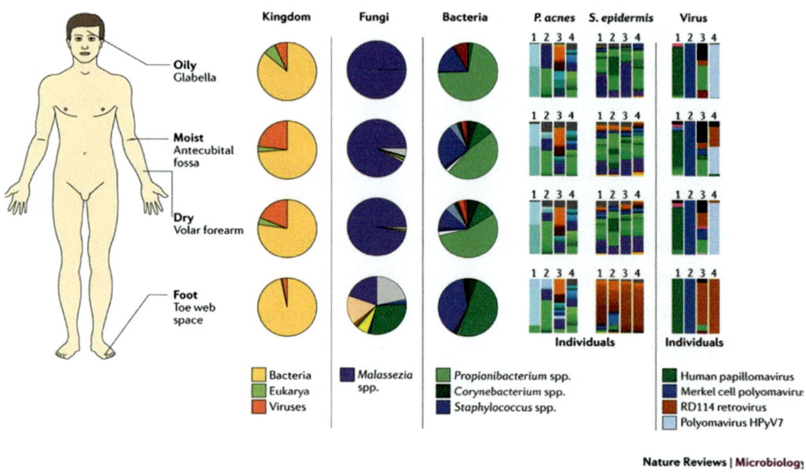

Figure 2.3 Four major skin microenvironments: sebaceous (oily), antecubital fossa (moist), volar forearm (dry), and toe web space (foot). Bacteria are the most abundant kingdom across sites, and fungi are the least abundant among these four microenvironments. Pie charts represent consensus relative abundances of the kingdom, fungi, and bacteria across healthy adults. For the kingdom, fungi, bacteria, and virus relative abundance plots, the major taxa colors are identified in the legend. Unlabeled colors may be grouped as 'Other'. The figure is reproduced with permission from [17].

As seen in Fig. 2.3, sebaceous (oily) areas, such as the forehead and back, are rich in lipophilic bacteria, including *Cutibacterium* species, which thrive on the sebum produced by the sebaceous glands. Humid areas, such as the armpits and groin, are predominantly inhabited by *Staphylococcus* and *Corynebacterium* species, which favor the higher humidity and lower pH of these regions. In contrast, fungal communities tend to be more consistent across different body sites, with the notable exception of the feet, which exhibit a higher diversity of fungi [17]. Bacteria are the most abundant members of the skin microbiome, with genera such as *Cutibacterium, Staphylococcus,* and *Corynebacterium* species being particularly prevalent. These bacteria play crucial roles in maintaining skin health by competing with pathogenic microorganisms for resources and space, producing antimicrobial substances, and modulating the immune response. Fungi, primarily *Malassezia* species, are significant components of the skin microbiome, although they are less abundant than bacteria. Further, fungi are involved in the breakdown of lipids on the skin surface and can influence skin conditions such as dandruff and seborrheic dermatitis [18].

Viruses and mites, including a species of *Demodex*, form a smaller yet essential part of the skin ecosystem. *Demodex* mites live in hair follicles and sebaceous glands, where they feed on oils and dead skin cells. Although they are usually harmless, an overgrowth of these mites can lead to skin problems like rosacea with recurrent episodes of redness on the face in different forms, as shown in Fig. 2.4 [19]. Viruses, including bacteriophages that infect skin bacteria, also help shape the skin's microbial balance by affecting bacterial populations. This diverse community of microbes is essential to protect the skin from harmful pathogens, help train the immune system, and maintain the skin's protective barrier [14].

Preserving the delicate balance of the skin microbiome and understanding the competition among diverse skin microbes can guide the development of sustainable skincare practices. This approach supports long-term skin health and reduces reliance on environmentally harmful skin formulations. This can include the use of prebiotics, which nourish beneficial microbes, and probiotics, introducing beneficial bacteria to the skin. Postbiotics, byproducts of microbial fermentation, can also be used to enhance the skin's barrier function and overall health [20]. These practices help maintain a healthy microbiome, which is crucial for protecting against environmental stressors and pathogens while also supporting the development of environmentally friendly skincare products. Overall, sustainable skincare practices, which prioritize both microbiome health and environmental responsibility, represent the future of dermatology.

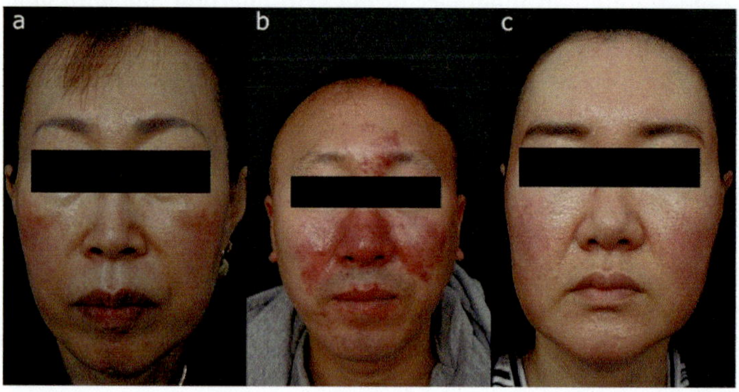

Figure 2.4 Different forms of rosacea: (a) Redness in the center of the face with a few small bumps. (b) Redness in the center of the face, changes in the shape of the nose, and bumps. (c) Redness in the center of the face, mild nose changes, bumps, and swelling (shared with the patients' consent). The figure is reproduced with permission from [19].

2.3.1 Competition Among Skin Microbes

Competition among skin microbes shapes the dynamics of the skin microbiome by significantly influencing its composition and function. Limited resources on the skin surface, such as space and nutrients, drive this competitive interaction, impacting both the microbial community and host health [21, 22]. Many skin microbes produce substances that inhibit or kill competitors. For example, *Staphylococcus epidermidis* secretes antimicrobial peptides (AMPs), such as bacteriocins, which target pathogenic bacteria, such as *Staphylococcus aureus,* to maintain beneficial microbes [23]. Microbes compete for scarce resources, such as amino acids, fatty acids, and sugars, which are critical for their survival. *Staphylococcus epidermidis* bacterial species excel in this competitive environment by breaking down sweat components into usable nutrients, thus surpassing rival bacteria and enhancing skin health by preventing pathogen growth [24]. This ability to utilize available resources efficiently allows beneficial microbes to outcompete harmful ones, maintaining a healthy balance within the skin microbiome.

Certain microorganisms, like *Cutibacterium acnes*, modify the skin environment to enhance their growth. Through the production of acidic byproducts from skin oils, they decrease the skin's pH, creating a favorable condition for their proliferation while hindering competitors that thrive in neutral or alkaline environments [23, 25]. This adaptive strategy not only promotes their survival but also shapes the diversity of the skin microbiome, as various microorganisms flourish under specific pH levels.

Understanding these competitive dynamics is pivotal for advancing sustainable skincare strategies. This allows for the creation of products that support beneficial microbes while inhibiting harmful ones. Traditional skincare products often employ harsh chemicals and preservatives to achieve desired outcomes, often at the expense of environmental health. By harnessing the inherent competitive dynamics among skin microbes, skincare formulations can be developed for the treatment of skin disorders while remaining environmentally sustainable. Fostering a balanced skin microbiome through these innovative strategies fortifies natural defenses, reducing the risk of infections and skin disorders by preventing pathogens from overgrowing and disrupting the skin's barrier function [14]. Such approaches support broader environmental objectives, ensuring that skincare practices do not contribute to ecological harm. Integrating principles of microbial competition into product design will allow the skincare industry to embrace sustainable practices that benefit both consumers and the planet [26].

2.3.2 Dysbiosis and Skin Disorders

Dysbiosis refers to an imbalance in the microbiome, which can affect the skin similarly to the gut, often leading to skin disorders like acne, eczema, psoriasis, and rosacea. Addressing dysbiosis is crucial for developing treatments that restore microbial balance and improve skin health [27].

Acne involves an overgrowth of bacteria such as *Cutibacterium acnes,* which causes inflammation and pimples. Treatments, including antibiotics and probiotics, aim to balance the skin microbiome [28]. Eczema, a skin disorder, is characterized by dry, itchy, and inflamed skin, often showing decreased microbial diversity and colonization of bacteria, such as *Staphylococcus aureus,* which can alleviate skin disorder-related symptoms as covered in Table 2.1 [29].

Table 2.1 Skin disorders linked to microbiome dysbiosis and treatment approaches

Skin Disorder	Type of Dysbiosis	Key Microorganisms Involved	Symptoms	Treatment Approaches	Source
Acne Vulgaris	Bacterial overgrowth	*Cutibacteri-umacnes*	Inflammation, pustules, comedones	Antibiotics (topical/oral), probiotics, prebiotics to restore balance	[28]
Eczema	Decreased microbial diversity, colonization of *Staphyl-ococcus aureus*	*Staphylococcus aureus*, reduced beneficial microbes	Dry, itchy, inflamed skin	Topical steroids, moisturizers, probiotics, reducing *S. aureusco-lonization*	[29]
Psoriasis	Dysbiosis of both skin and gut microbiota	Various bacteria and fungi, including *Streptococcus* and *Candida* species	Red, scaly patches, skin inflammation	Immune-modulating treatments, probiotics, anti-inflammatory agents	[30]
Rosacea	Overgrowth of skin mites and associated bacteria	*Demodex folliculorum* and *Demodex brevis*, associated bacteria (e.g., *Bacillusoleronius*)	Facial redness, swelling, pustules	Anti-microbials, managing mite population, probiotics	[32, 33]

Psoriasis, an autoimmune disorder causing rapid skin cell buildup, is linked to dysbiosis in both skin and gut microbiomes, contributing to inflammation and autoimmunity [30]. Rosacea, marked by facial redness and swelling, may be exacerbated by an increased density of mites like *Demodex folliculorum* and *Demodex brevis*. Managing these populations could alleviate skin disorder symptoms and help in treatment approaches [31, 32].

Research on dysbiosis and skin disorders focuses on genetics, immune responses, and environmental factors that contribute to microbial imbalances. Treatments include topical and oral antibiotics, probiotics, prebiotics, and postbiotics to promote beneficial microbes while inhibiting the growth of harmful ones [31]. Using natural and eco-friendly treatments, such as probiotics and prebiotics, reduces the reliance on synthetic chemicals and antibiotics.

2.3.3 Prebiotics, Probiotics, and Postbiotics Integration

Skincare science has recently made significant strides by incorporating popular ingredients, namely, prebiotics, probiotics, and postbiotics, in skincare products. This not only enhances their effectiveness but also promotes environmental sustainability.

Prebiotics, such as konjac glucomannan hydrolysate, a natural fiber from the konjac plant, provide nourishment to beneficial microbes, fostering a robust skin microbiome that naturally resists pathogens and reduces the need for chemical interventions [33, 34].

Probiotics introduce live beneficial bacteria through ingestion or topical application that maintain microbial balance and enhance skin health by reducing acne, inflammation, and improving hydration [34]. These microbes colonize the skin and produce bioactive compounds that protect against harmful pathogens. This further reduces the reliance on synthetic preservatives and antibiotics in skincare formulations [35].

Postbiotics, the metabolic byproducts of these beneficial bacteria, contribute additional protective properties to skincare products, enhancing skin resilience while being completely biodegradable and environmentally friendly [36]. The term postbiotic was recently defined by the International Scientific Association of Probiotics and Prebiotics as "a preparation of inanimate microorganisms and/or their components that confers a health benefit on the host" [34].

The synergy of prebiotics, probiotics, and postbiotics not only nurtures a beneficial relationship between the skin and its microbial community but also promotes a holistic approach to skincare. By integrating these bio-based ingredients, skincare products not only promote healthier, more resilient skin but also align with sustainable practices by significantly reducing their ecological footprint through the minimal use of synthetic additives [37, 38]. Using natural, biodegradable ingredients with less reliance on synthetic chemicals, microbiome-friendly skincare products benefit the skin while minimizing environmental impact.

Table 2.2 summarizes the different types of microbiome-friendly prebiotic, probiotic, and postbiotic skincare products, their key ingredients and benefits, synthetic chemicals, and antibiotics. This not only restores the microbial balance of the skin but also minimizes the environmental impact of skincare products.

2.3.4 Bioactive Compounds: Polyphenols and Peptides

The inclusion of bioactive compounds, such as polyphenols and peptides, in skincare products offers significant environmental and health benefits [56]. As shown in Fig. 2.5, known for their powerful antioxidant effects, polyphenols help reduce oxidative stress, which, in turn, maintains a balanced skin microbiome and decreases the need for harsh chemical additives in skincare products [57]. This reduction in harsh chemicals improves skin health and minimizes environmental pollution by limiting the release of synthetic compounds into ecosystems.

Peptides, such as collagen, are another type of bioactive compound that support skin regeneration and repair processes, leading to stronger and healthier skin barriers that are more resilient to environmental stressors. According to the literature, peptides play a crucial role in supporting cellular signaling and repair in cellular models and tissue culture studies, highlighting their role in promoting skin health at the molecular level [57].

Table 2.2 Microbiome-friendly skincare products

Product Type	Description	Key Ingredients	Benefits	Impact on environment	Source
Prebiotic Skincare Products	Promote a healthy skin microbiome by stimulating beneficial bacteria growth, reducing the risk of infections, maintaining skin's acidity, and enhancing barrier function.	Inulin, Fructooligosaccharides (FOS), Galacto-oligosaccharides (GOS), Beta-glucan, Xylitol, Glycerol	Strengthen skin barrier, prevent moisture loss, reduce inflammation, improve skin hydration and texture, and boost collagen production.	Supports sustainable agriculture, minimal environmental footprint.	[39–43]
Probiotic Skincare Products	Application of beneficial bacteria to maintain a healthy skin microbiome, improve barrier function, reduce skin sensitivity, and diminish signs of aging.	*Lactobacillus, Bifidobacterium, Streptococcus* species	Reduce skin sensitivity, improve hydration, diminish signs of aging, enhance skin barrier function, and regulate the immune system.	Reduces the need for synthetic preservatives, and biodegradables.	[44–48]
Postbiotic Skincare Products	Utilize non-viable bacterial products to support skin microbiome, enhance barrier function, modulate the immune system, and provide antioxidant and anti-inflammatory benefits.	Short-chain fatty acids (SCFAs), Peptides, Enzymes, Polysaccharides, Cell surface proteins, Secondary metabolites	Enhance skin barrier function, modulate immune response, provide antimicrobial and antioxidant effects, and improve skin hydration.	Utilizes natural fermentation processes, with a low ecological impact.	[49–52]
pH-Balancing Skincare Products	Maintain optimal pH balance to support microbial composition, enhance skin resilience, and reduce inflammation.	Organic acids (e.g., Lactic Acid, Citric Acid, Malic Acid, and Glycolic Acid)	Enhance skin resilience, reduce inflammation, maintain microbial flora balance, and improve moisture retention.	Reduces the need for harsh chemicals, supports natural skin functions.	[53, 54]
Fermented Skincare Products	Leverage fermentation to enhance ingredient efficacy, improve bioavailability, create beneficial compounds, and support the skin's natural defenses.	Fermented microorganisms (bacteria and yeast)	Improve bioavailability of active ingredients, introduce beneficial compounds, support skin's natural defenses, and enhance barrier function.	Biodegradable product promotes the sustainable use of natural resources.	[55]

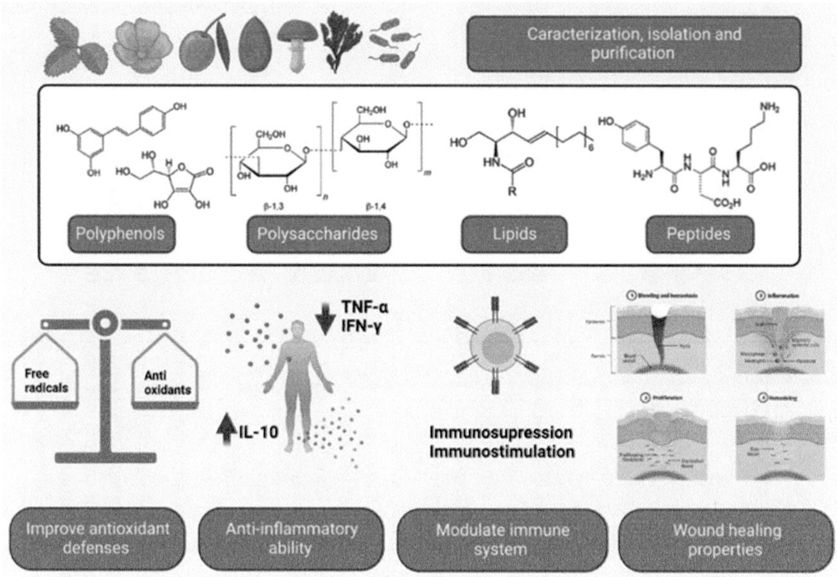

Figure 2.5 Bioactive compounds such as polyphenols and peptides targeting inflammation, wound healing, and photo-aging. The figure is reproduced with permission [57].

These bioactive compounds enhance the skin's appearance, making it more vibrant and youthful, while supporting microbial balance for overall better skin health. By preserving a healthy skin microbiome, these compounds prevent various skin disorders [57–59]. Advanced research methods, such as mass spectrometry and gene expression analysis, have highlighted the positive impacts of these bioactive compounds in precise and measurable ways. It has been demonstrated that these bioactive compounds mitigate oxidative stress using in vitro assays that measure reactive oxygen species (ROS) levels, showing their effectiveness in protecting skin cells from oxidative damage [60]. This body of research underscores the substantial environmental benefits of integrating polyphenols and peptides into skincare products. Around the world, skincare products are emerging as key players in supporting skin health and addressing various skin conditions [61]. The industry's shift from synthetic chemicals to natural bioactive ingredients presents a significant opportunity to reduce its environmental impact.

2.4 Skincare Products and Skin Health

Skincare products worldwide play a vital role in maintaining and enhancing skin health through a diverse array of formulations targeting specific needs [61]. Cleansers, ranging from foaming types to micellar water, effectively remove impurities and prepare the skin for subsequent treatments. These products are essential for maintaining the skin's hygiene and ensuring that other skincare products can penetrate and perform effectively. Moisturizers available in various forms, such as lotions, creams, and serums, ensure optimal hydration by replenishing the skin's moisture barrier and preventing dryness. They are crucial in maintaining the skin's softness, elasticity, and overall appearance. Regular use of sunscreens helps preserve the skin's health and youthful appearance by blocking harmful ultraviolet rays [62]. Sunscreens are essential for shielding the skin from UV damage, which can cause premature aging, hyperpigmentation, and a heightened risk of skin cancer [63]. Anti-aging products, often formulated with ingredients such as retinoids, peptides, and antioxidants, specifically address wrinkles, fine lines, and loss of elasticity. These products work by stimulating collagen production and promoting skin cell turnover, helping to maintain a youthful and radiant appearance [64]. Acne treatments, which include ingredients such as benzoyl peroxide, salicylic acid, and retinoids, are designed to combat breakouts by reducing inflammation, unclogging pores, and preventing future blemishes [65]. These treatments are essential for maintaining clear skin and preventing acne-related scarring. Exfoliants, which can be physical (scrubs) or chemical (alpha hydroxy acids (AHAs) and beta hydroxy acids (BHAs)), help remove dead skin cells and promote skin renewal [66]. This process results in a smoother, brighter complexion and enhances the efficacy of other skincare products by allowing better penetration.

Formulations, such as serums, deliver concentrated active ingredients like vitamin C, hyaluronic acid, and niacinamide, targeting specific concerns such as hyperpigmentation, dehydration, and fine lines. In addition, facial masks provide intensive care with ingredients that hydrate, detoxify, or soothe the skin, making them perfect for periodic treatments to boost skin health. They provide a concentrated dose of active ingredients, such as hyaluronic acid for hydration, charcoal for detoxification, and aloe vera or chamomile for soothing irritated skin, thereby enhancing the skin's appearance and health [67]. Moreover, eye creams, designed to address concerns around the delicate eye area, such as puffiness, dark circles, and fine lines, rely on gentle yet effective ingredients. For example, caffeine is often used to reduce puffiness, while peptides and retinol help smooth fine lines. Ingredients like vitamin C and licorice extract work to brighten dark circles, improving the appearance of this sensitive area [68].

Modern skincare formulations incorporate eco-friendly ingredients and sustainable packaging to reduce environmental impact. These eco-conscious choices include the use of biodegradable materials, recyclable packaging, and natural, organic ingredients that are sustainably sourced. By choosing products that support both skin health and environmental sustainability, consumers can contribute to a healthier planet. This dual benefit aligns with the rising awareness and demand for products that are not only effective but also environmentally responsible. Consumers are increasingly looking for brands that prioritize sustainability and ethical practices in their product development. This shift in consumer behavior encourages the skincare industry to innovate and adopt greener practices, leading to a broader availability of eco-friendly skincare options [69].

2.4.1 Active Ingredients in Skincare Products

The study of skincare ingredients and their impact on the skin microbiome is advancing rapidly [70]. Skincare products influence the skin's pH, which is crucial for supporting beneficial microorganisms. The skin's pH, ranging from 4.7 to 5.75, forms the acid mantle, which protects against pathogens [71]. Cleansers with high surfactant levels or alkaline properties can disrupt this balance, while pH-balanced formulations help preserve it [62]. Ingredients such as lactic acid and citric acid play a crucial role in regulating pH levels, fostering an environment that supports the growth of healthy microorganisms [54, 72]. Maintaining the skin's natural pH is essential for skincare products aimed at supporting a balanced microbiome [73]. Notably, excessive use of harsh surfactants like sodium lauryl sulfate (SLS) in cleansers can disrupt the skin's microbiome, leading to imbalances that may contribute to skin conditions such as dryness, irritation, and acne. To counter these effects, moisturizers containing prebiotics and probiotics are gaining attention for their ability to restore the skin's moisture, promote the growth of beneficial bacteria, and strengthen the skin barrier, thereby helping to repair the damage caused by surfactants [5].

Preservatives, while necessary for product safety, can disrupt the skin's microbiome by affecting beneficial microorganisms. To address this, research is focusing on developing preservatives that have minimal impact on the microbiome, as well as preservative-free formulations that maintain product safety while preserving microbial balance. Examples of microbiome-safe preservatives include phenethyl alcohol, ethylhexylglycerin, sodium benzoate, potassium sorbate, and caprylyl glycol, which are used for their antimicrobial properties without significantly disrupting the skin's microbial community [74].

Botanical extracts and antioxidants can act as prebiotics or antimicrobials, influencing microbiome balance [57, 72]. By focusing on ingredients that preserve the skin's natural environment, sustainable skincare products can enhance microbial health and promote overall skin wellness. Utilizing milder, microbiome-supportive ingredients such as mild surfactants, prebiotics, and probiotics benefits individual skin health and contributes to broader environmental sustainability. This is achieved by reducing the need for harsh chemicals and synthetic additives, which minimizes environmental pollution from synthetic chemicals entering water systems. Therefore, this approach fosters the development of products that are both skin-friendly and eco-conscious [73].

While microbiome-friendly skincare products offer promising benefits for both skin health and environmental sustainability, it is important to recognize that not all skincare products have such positive effects. In contrast, some formulations can disrupt the skin's delicate microbial balance, leading to unintended consequences for both the skin and the environment.

2.4.2 Adverse Impacts of Skincare Products

Table 2.3 Recent research on the adverse impacts of skincare products

Author	Focus	Techniques Used	Adverse Impact
Schwingen et al. [74]	Clinical and ecological implications of microbiome disruption	Skin biopsies, eco-toxicological analyses	**Compromised skin barrier function and negative impacts on local wildlife due to chemical runoff.**
Lemoine et al. [79]	Effects of skincare products on molecular pathways and natural habitats	Transcriptomic analyses, habitat disruption studies	**Skincare ingredients alter essential molecular pathways in skin cells and damage the surrounding ecosystems.**
Luger et al. [80]	Protein alterations due to skincare products and their ecological effects	Metaproteomic techniques, sustainability assessments	**Alterations in skin protein profiles that lead to skin irritation and secondary ecological consequences.**
Gueniche et al. [70]	How skincare products disrupt microbial balance and environmental health	Metagenomics sequencing, environmental impact studies	**Loss of microbial diversity on the skin leads to dermatological issues and further environmental stress.**
Khalid & Abdolla [81]	Chemical runoff from skincare products and its environmental pollution	Ecotoxicology assessments	**Introduction of toxic chemicals into waterways affects aquatic life and water quality.**
Patel et al. [82]	Impacts of non-biodegradable skincare elements on aquatic systems	Environmental impact assessments, water quality studies	**Persistent environmental pollutants from skincare products are accumulating in aquatic ecosystems.**
Van den Bogaard et al. [83]	Link between skincare-induced inflammation and environmental stress	Clinical investigations, environmental stress tests	**Inflammation is triggered by skincare products that also exacerbate environmental degradation.**
Bashir et al. [84]	Skincare products as sources of microplastic pollution in aquatic environments	Water sample analysis, environmental modeling	**Microplastics from skincare products are polluting oceans and affecting marine ecosystems and biodiversity.**

Despite beneficial effects, recent research has highlighted the detrimental effects of skincare products on the skin microbiome, leading to imbalances or dysbiosis that may cause various skin disorders. Advanced methodologies, such as metagenomic sequencing, gene expression profiling, and clinical investigations, have been instrumental in revealing how these products disrupt the natural microbial balance [49, 75]. This disturbance not only impacts skin health but also raises concerns about the environmental sustainability of these products [76]. Table 2.3 outlines pivotal recent studies, focusing on the methods used to uncover these adverse effects and emphasizing the need for developing skincare products that are both effective and environmentally responsible [77].

As scientific advancements continue to shed light on the unintended consequences of some skincare products, it becomes clear that more sophisticated tools are needed to better understand and mitigate these adverse effects [76, 78]. Biotechnological techniques offer a more precise analysis of the skin microbiome, providing valuable insights that can guide the formulation of safer and more sustainable skincare products and play a crucial role in shaping the future of dermatology in healthcare [78].

2.5 Biotechnological Techniques for Microbiome Analysis and Therapies

Advanced methodologies not only enable the creation of products that promote long-term skin health but also advocate for sustainable and environmentally friendly skincare solutions [76]. By integrating traditional culture-based methods with cutting-edge DNA sequencing technologies such as 16S rRNA gene sequencing and shotgun metagenomics, this research minimizes the ecological impact of skincare products. While culture-based methods have been foundational, they often miss many uncultivable microorganisms. In contrast, DNA sequencing provides a broader and more detailed analysis of the skin's microbial diversity without the constraints of cultivation [17].

Furthermore, meta-transcriptomics, meta-proteomics, and metabolomics have become essential tools for a precise understanding of microbial communities, their active functions, and biochemical interactions, which are pivotal for developing non-invasive and natural skincare products. By combining these methods with bioinformatics and machine learning, researchers can perform comprehensive analyses of large datasets, identifying patterns and predicting microbial behavior in ways that support the natural microbial community while reducing reliance on synthetic chemicals [85]. Additionally, technological analysis allows for an enhanced understanding of the skin microbiome, enabling the effective management of skin conditions such as acne, eczema, and psoriasis, while promoting healthier skin through a balanced microbial environment [86]. Consequently, it paves the way for a range of dermatological treatments and skincare products that are more environmentally sustainable.

A pivotal study by Gueniche et al. (2022) examined how probiotics, such as *Lactobacillus, Bifidobacterium, Streptococcus thermophilus,* and *Lactococcus lactis,* can strengthen the skin's barrier, improve hydration, and alleviate inflammation, ultimately promoting overall skin health and resilience. This microbiome analysis study identifies specific probiotic strains that support a balanced skin microbiome and strengthen the skin's barrier, minimizing the reliance on synthetic additives. Another study by Thakur et al. (2024) explores botanical extracts, including green tea, aloe vera, and chamomile, in healthy skincare. Using high-performance liquid chromatography (HPLC) and antioxidant assays, the study demonstrates that polyphenol-rich plant extracts neutralize free radicals and reduce oxidative stress on the skin [87]. By sourcing active ingredients from plants, this approach reduces reliance on synthetic chemicals, minimizes environmental impact, and supports sustainable agriculture practices. Another study by Khatri et al. (2021) examines bioactive peptides from marine organisms, showing their potential in promoting collagen synthesis and improving skin elasticity. This research employs mass spectrometry and cellular assays to confirm the effectiveness of marine-derived peptides in skincare products, highlighting the sustainable use of marine resources. By utilizing byproducts from the fishing industry or sustainably harvested marine organisms, this approach helps minimize waste and promotes the conservation of the marine ecosystem [88].

2.5.1 Bacteriophage Therapy in Skincare

Bacteriophage therapy represents a promising approach to address inflammatory skin disorders, particularly in conditions like acne vulgaris. Bacteriophages are viruses that infect and lyse bacterial cells, such as *Cutibacterium acnes*, a major contributor to acne. Bacteriophages provide superior clinical efficacy in addressing *Cutibacterium acnes* without affecting beneficial skin microbiota. Importantly, this differentiates bacteriophages from traditional antibiotics, which often disrupt the broader skin microbiome and contribute to the development of antibiotic resistance [89]. A study by Brown et al. found that cream formulation containing *Cutibacterium acnes* phages at a concentration of 2.5×10^8 PFU/g successfully lysed bacterial colonies in agar lawn culture plates and remained effective up to 90 days at 4°C in light-protected bottles [90].

This suggests a bacteriophage-based simple therapeutic option for acne treatment. In addition, *Cutibacterium acnes* phages can penetrate biofilms, which are dense bacterial layers usually resistant to antibiotics, with the help of endolysins, which are enzymes that break down bacterial cell walls. This ability helps them target bacteria within biofilms more effectively [91, 92]. A recent study by Rimon et al. (2023) has shown promising results with topical phage therapy applied in a mouse model of *Cutibacterium acnes*-induced acne-like lesions, supporting superior clinical and histological outcomes. Phage therapy led to a notable reduction in inflammatory markers, such as CXCL2 and IL-8, and neutrophil infiltration, highlighting phages' potential to modulate inflammatory responses specific to acne pathology [93]. Clearly, bacteriophages have the potential to enhance therapeutic effectiveness for chronic acne management and reduce the risk of antibiotic resistance [94]. As microbiome research progresses, bacteriophage therapy exemplifies how biotechnological approaches can enable sustainable interventions while reducing reliance on traditional chemical treatments [95].

2.5.2 Revolutionary CRISPR-Cas9 Technology in Dermatology

Recent advancements in Clustered Regularly Interspaced Short Palindromic Repeats (CRISPR) systems have transformed gene editing research in dermatology. Programmable RNA-guided CRISPR-associated (Cas) nucleases and CRISPR-based genome-editing systems allow for the precise modification of specific sites in the human genome. Studies utilizing this gene-editing tool explore personalized skincare based on genetic factors, allowing for precise modifications of genes related to skin health. Specifically, CRISPR-Cas9 offers unprecedented accuracy in skincare interventions, reducing the environmental footprint by tailoring treatments to individual needs and minimizing waste [96].

In a study conducted by Jacków et al. (2019), the authors explored the use of CRISPR/Cas9 gene editing technology to correct mutations responsible for recessive dystrophic epidermolysis bullosa (RDEB), a severe genetic skin disorder resulting in fragile skin, blistering, and wound formation. The study utilized induced pluripotent stem cells (iPSCs) derived from patients with RDEB to correct specific mutations in the COL7A1 gene, which is responsible for encoding type VII collagen and plays a vital role in maintaining skin integrity by anchoring the epidermis to the dermis, ensuring skin stability and structure. By applying CRISPR/Cas9 and homology-directed repair, the authors successfully restored the expression of type VII collagen (C7), a crucial protein for skin stability, in gene-edited iPSCs [97].

These corrected iPSCs were then used to create human skin equivalents (HSEs), which were grafted onto immunodeficient mice, showing normal expression of type VII collagen and functional anchoring fibrils two months post-grafting. The study's results highlighted the high efficacy of the CRISPR/Cas9 system in correcting both homozygous[1] and heterozygous[2] mutations within the COL7A1 gene. Moreover, the research demonstrated

[1]Refers to having two identical alleles for a specific gene, one inherited from each parent.

[2]Refers to having two different alleles for a specific gene, one inherited from each parent.

that gene-corrected iPSCs were able to differentiate into functional keratinocytes and fibroblasts. These differentiated cells, when incorporated into 3D skin models, exhibited restored skin integrity and collagen VII expression. The findings provide strong evidence that CRISPR/Cas9-mediated gene editing, in combination with iPSC technology, represents a promising therapeutic strategy for the treatment of RDEB and potentially other genetic skin disorders [97].

Advancements in skincare, such as probiotics, botanical extracts, and marine peptides, together with CRISPR-Cas9 technology (Fig. 2.6), promote a multifaceted approach to healthier skincare while reducing the need for synthetic chemicals and minimizing waste [96–99]. Future advancements in microbiome research will pave the way for targeted skin therapies that align with environmental goals.

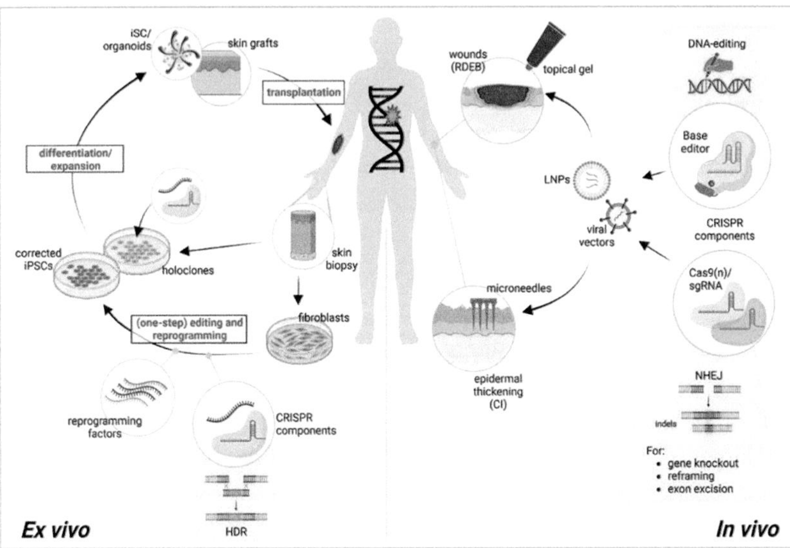

Figure 2.6 CRISPR-Cas9 technology in dermatological gene editing. The figure illustrates ex vivo and in vivo applications. In ex vivo, iPSCs are edited via CRISPR, expanded, and used for skin grafts. In vivo, CRISPR is delivered via lipid nanoparticles (LNPs) or viral vectors to edit DNA in skin wounds, promoting regeneration and personalized skincare. The figure is reproduced with permission [98].

2.6 Future Directions in Microbiome Research

Innovations in microbiome-friendly skincare products are becoming increasingly apparent as research advances. This section briefly explores the emerging machine learning (ML) and artificial intelligence (AI) tools for the personalized design of skin therapeutics, the development and challenges of smart skincare devices, the expansion of probiotic skincare ranges, the exploration of the gut-skin axis, and probiotic interventions in clinical settings.

2.6.1 Integration of AI and ML

The application of AI and ML in analyzing the skin microbiome's intricate data promises to uncover complex patterns and interactions among microbial species and skincare ingredients [100]. These emerging technologies are poised to develop predictive models capable of anticipating the effects of specific skincare formulations on the microbiome's equilibrium. By leveraging vast datasets, AI can identify subtle interactions that might be missed by traditional analysis methods. ML algorithms can identify correlations between microbial composition and skin health, uncovering critical biomarkers for conditions such as acne, eczema, and psoriasis. These emerging predictive models are also capable of revealing the effects of specific skincare formulations on the microbial signatures [101]. AI analysis of changes in microbial composition upon application of skin product(s) could equip consumers to make informed lifestyle modifications. For example, SkinBug is an ML-based tool that predicts the metabolic reactions of skin biomolecules, enzymes, and bacterial species. Its highly accurate prediction is based on its curated database of 1,094,153 metabolic enzymes and substrates from approximately 900 bacterial species. Leveraging a database comprising over 1 million metabolic enzymes from 897 bacterial species across 19 distinct skin sites, SkinBug achieves a multilabel accuracy of 82.4% and binary accuracy of 90.0%. This tool uniquely identifies metabolic reactions, enzymes, bacterial species, and the specific skin sites involved, enabling precise predictions of how skincare products, pollutants, or pharmaceuticals interact with the microbiome. By addressing the complexity and diversity of skin metabolic pathways, SkinBug not only enhances the design of microbiome-friendly cosmetic and therapeutic products but also significantly contributes to exposome studies and dermatological research, offering insights into metabolism-related toxicity and efficacy challenges [102]. Predicted metabolism of cosmetics and other therapeutics by the skin microbiome could facilitate the design of more efficient skincare products. Readers are directed to Jaiswal et al.'s paper on SkinBug for more details [102]. Such advancements aim to introduce highly personalized and eco-friendly skincare solutions, reducing waste and enhancing product effectiveness. Personalized skincare products tailored to an individual's unique microbiome composition will not only improve skin health outcomes but also minimize the environmental impact by reducing the need for a broad range of generic products.

2.6.2 Development of Smart Skincare Devices

As advancements in technology continue to revolutionize the beauty industry, smart skincare devices have emerged, offering consumers more personalized and effective skincare solutions [103]. One example of a smart skincare device is the **Foreo LUNA 3** by Foreo Sweden, which combines sonic pulsations with a soft silicone brush to deeply cleanse the skin while providing real-time feedback via a mobile app [104, 105]. Another example is the **Neutrogena Skin360** by Johnson & Johnson. This device scans the skin using a smartphone camera and provides personalized skincare advice based on moisture levels, pores, and fine lines [106, 107]. These devices represent the next generation of personalized skincare solutions. The emergence of smart technologies capable of analyzing the skin's microbiome composition in real-time presents new possibilities. At present, real-time skin microbiome analysis via smartphone applications remains unavailable in the commercial market. Technologies like HelloBiome, which utilize next-generation sequencing combined with AI-powered insights, rely on physical skin swab samples that need to be sent to a laboratory for detailed analysis. The results, delivered within 48 hours, provide personalized insights into an individual's skin microbiome reference. Advancements in nanotechnology and biosensors are showing promise for real-time microbiome scanning through smartphones [108, 109]. The development of non-invasive, user-friendly devices that offer immediate insights into skin health could revolutionize the skincare industry. These devices can help consumers choose the most suitable microbiome-friendly products based on their unique skin conditions. Additionally, smart skincare devices can monitor changes in the skin microbiome over time, providing valuable data that can be used to refine and optimize skincare routines [103]. By reducing unnecessary product use and waste, these technologies contribute significantly to environmental sustainability. The integration of smart skincare devices into daily routines can also empower consumers to take a more active role in managing their skin health, fostering a greater sense of control and awareness regarding the products they use and their environmental impact.

2.6.3 Challenges in Smart Skincare Devices

Despite significant advances in smart skincare technologies, multiple challenges must be addressed for commercial viability and success in the market. This includes further development in functionality, accessibility, and user engagement with smart skincare devices. One major hurdle is sensor accuracy and sensitivity, as devices designed to monitor skin characteristics such as moisture, pH, and microbial diversity must incorporate highly accurate sensors to produce reliable data [110]. However, achieving this level of precision in compact, non-invasive devices remains complex, and current technology often falls short of the standards necessary for dependable, at-home use [111]. Data privacy, ethics, and security represent serious concerns, as these devices gather sensitive personal health data. This requires robust security protocols ensuring consumer trust and protecting user information [112]. Another significant challenge is the cost and affordability associated with advanced sensors and complex algorithms, which contribute to their high production costs. Rising inflation and the high cost of skincare devices would restrict device accessibility to a broader market. Furthermore, battery life and device longevity are technical challenges that need attention without compromising the compact design and functionality of these home-based devices [111]. Addressing these challenges will be vital to the commercial viability of smart skincare technologies in the evolving and rapidly expanding skincare market.

2.6.4 Expansion of Probiotic Skincare Range

According to Yahoo Finance (2024), probiotic skincare products are projected to reach $981.3 million by 2034 and are driven by consumer perception of their skin appearance, significant reduction in skin wrinkling, acne, and other skin conditions [113] (Fig. 2.7).

Figure 2.7 Probiotic skincare cosmetic product market growth projections (2024–2034). This chart illustrates the projected growth of the probiotic skincare cosmetic product market, valued at $320.3 million in 2023, with an expected compound annual growth rate (CAGR) of 11.0% from 2024 to 2034. The market is anticipated to reach $981.3 million by 2034, reflecting the increasing demand for probiotic-infused skincare products driven by consumer awareness of natural, health-focused beauty solutions. The figure is compiled with data from [113].

Advancements in the next-generation probiotics are evolving, yet many probiotic strains with potential benefits for skin health remain unexplored [113]. Further research into these novel probiotic species for their efficacy and safety in skincare products could lead to innovative and sustainable skincare solutions. These probiotics can help restore and maintain the natural balance of the skin microbiome, providing benefits such as reducing inflammation, enhancing hydration, and protecting against environmental stressors. The expansion of the probiotic skincare range has the potential to offer a more diverse selection of products that cater to various skin types and conditions, ultimately leading to more effective and targeted eco-friendly skincare solutions.

Recent advances in dermatological research emphasize the therapeutic potential of novel probiotic species in skincare products. Probiotics, such as *Vitreoscilla filiformis, Streptococcus thermophilus,* and *Lactobacillus johnsonii,* have been shown to enhance the skin barrier, particularly in conditions like atopic dermatitis and psoriasis, by reducing inflammation and restoring microbial balance [114, 115].

Probiotic microorganisms have shown promise in managing various skin disorders through their ability to balance the skin microbiome, as illustrated in Fig. 2.8.

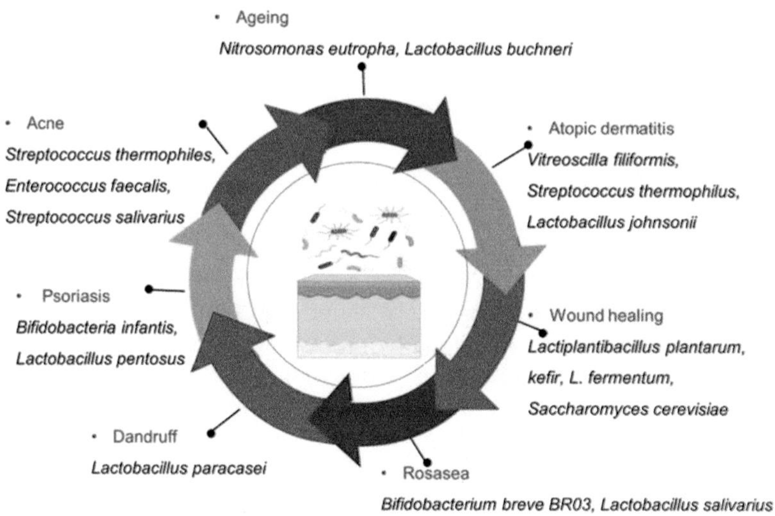

Figure 2.8 Different probiotic microorganisms useful in the management of various skin disorders. The figure is reproduced from [116] and under the Creative Commons Attribution (CC BY) License (https://creativecommons.org/licenses/by/4.0/).

These probiotics, including species like *Lactobacillus, Streptococcus thermophilus,* and *Bifidobacterium,* work by modulating immune responses and reducing inflammation, which is crucial for treating skin conditions such as acne and rosacea.

By maintaining a healthy microbial balance, these beneficial bacteria enhance skin resilience and repair. The mechanism of action of probiotics in improving skin health is depicted in Fig. 2.9, where probiotics block inflammatory pathways that otherwise contribute to skin irritation and damage. Through the production of AMPs and other bioactive compounds, probiotics prevent the colonization of harmful pathogens, promote hydration, and support the skin's barrier function, ultimately leading to a healthier and more robust skin environment. This anti-inflammatory action is key to reducing the symptoms of common skin disorders, thereby promoting overall skin health [116].

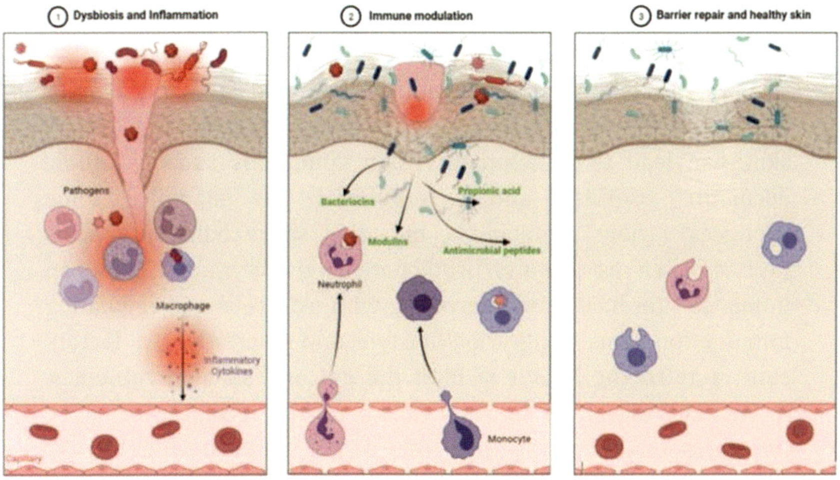

Figure 2.9 Mechanism of action of probiotics via blocking the inflammatory pathways in improving skin health. The figure is reproduced from [116] and is under the Creative Commons Attribution (CC BY) License (https://creativecommons.org/licenses/by/4.0/).

2.6.5 Hospital and Probiotic Interventions

Hospital settings pose a significant risk for the spread of infections, often facilitated by the contamination of staff clothing, linens, and other textiles. Traditional methods of addressing this issue involve the use of antimicrobial agents in laundry processes. A sustainable and emerging novel approach incorporates probiotics into hospital garments to combat harmful microorganisms and reduce the risk of infection [117]. Recent advancements in topical probiotics have led to the development of probiotic-coated hospital apparel, and current literature supports their ability to maintain effectiveness even after several washes. Studies have shown that probiotic-infused clothing helps to maintain skin balance, reduce harmful bacterial colonization, and prevent nosocomial infections, which are a major concern in healthcare environments [116, 118, 119].

2.6.6 Exploration of the Gut-Skin Axis

The link between gut health and skin conditions, known as the gut-skin axis, has garnered significant attention. Both the gut and skin are heavily populated with microbial communities that regulate immune responses, nutrient metabolism, and barrier integrity. Dysbiosis, or microbial imbalance in either the gut or skin, can lead to inflammatory skin conditions such as atopic dermatitis, psoriasis, and acne vulgaris. The gut microbiome produces various metabolites, including short-chain fatty acids (SCFAs) such as acetate, propionate, and butyrate, which can influence skin health by interacting with skin cells and regulating immune functions [120]. Diet, lifestyle, and environmental factors contribute to the health of both the gut and skin microbiomes. A Western diet high in saturated fats, for example, has been linked to acne vulgaris and other skin disorders due to its effect on gut microbiome composition and immune responses [121, 122]. Similarly, gut dysbiosis is associated with diseases like atopic dermatitis, where specific bacterial species may trigger inflammatory pathways that lead to skin barrier dysfunction [123]. This suggests that interventions targeting gut health, such as probiotics, dietary changes, and lifestyle modifications, could be potential therapeutic strategies for managing skin disorders [27]. Future studies are needed to explore the mechanisms behind this connection, investigating how changes in the gut microbiome affect skin health and how skincare products support this interplay [20].

2.6.7 Sustainability in the Skincare Industry

Growing environmental concerns promote the creation of sustainable, eco-friendly skincare products. Future research is needed to identify and employ biodegradable ingredients that support microbial health while minimizing environmental impact [124]. This includes the development of formulations that use natural, renewable resources such as aloe vera, shea butter, or coconut oil, and avoid harmful chemicals that can disrupt both the skin microbiome and the environment. Furthermore, sustainable skincare formulations should consider the entire lifecycle of the product, from sourcing raw materials to manufacturing processes and packaging. Developing recyclable packaging can further reduce the ecological footprint of skincare products, aligning with broader environmental conservation goals. By prioritizing sustainability in skincare formulations, the industry can lead by example, demonstrating the feasibility and importance of environmentally responsible practices that benefit both consumers and the planet.

2.6.8 Clinical Trials in the Skincare Industry

To ensure the development of effective and sustainable microbiome-friendly skincare products, it is essential that clinical trials recruit participants of diverse ages and ethnicities to address the needs of various skin types. Existing literature indicates that Caucasian skin exhibits a higher resistance to water barrier damage, while African skin demonstrates greater resilience to transcutaneous penetration. Transepidermal water loss (TEWL), a critical indicator of skin surface moisture, is defined as the loss of water from the body that diffuses and evaporates through the epidermis [126]. Research indicates that TEWL is typically higher in African skin compared to Caucasian skin. Furthermore, TEWL and skin surface moisture levels tend to decrease with age across all populations, with a more pronounced decline observed in Caucasian skin, likely due to a thinner stratum corneum [125].

In addition to the differences in moisture loss, aging also brings about changes in epidermal structure, particularly in the rate of desquamation and the variability of corneocytes. These factors contribute to xerosis or dryness, a condition that is more frequently observed in African skin. To manage these conditions, a range of moisturizing products is currently available, designed to restore the integrity of the stratum corneum by replenishing the skin's natural moisturizing components. Active ingredients in these products, categorized as emollients, occlusives, and humectants, work by softening the skin, retaining water in the stratum corneum, and preventing excessive TEWL [125]. A comprehensive approach is essential to understanding how various skin microbiomes respond to different formulations, leading to inclusive products that address a wide array of skin types while minimizing environmental impact.

In a study conducted by Hong et al. (2020), titled *"Changes in the Diversity of Human Skin Microbiota to Cosmetic Serum Containing Prebiotics,"* a double-blind, placebo-controlled clinical trial with 60 participants evaluated the impact of a galacto-oligosaccharides (GOS)-based serum on skin health. Authors assessed crucial parameters such as skin hydration, TEWL, and microbial diversity. Participants were divided into two groups: one that used the GOS-containing serum and the other that received a placebo. The results indicated that the GOS serum led to significant improvements in skin hydration, reduced harmful bacteria like *Staphylococcus aureus*, and promoted beneficial bacteria like *Pediococcus*, which are key to enhancing the skin's barrier function. This improvement in skin barrier function was evidenced by a decrease in TEWL and an increase in the skin's water retention capacity. The study suggests that prebiotics, such as those found in GOS, can play a pivotal role in rebalancing the skin microbiome and promoting overall skin health [43].

Together, the future of skincare and microbiome research holds immense potential for innovation and sustainability. By integrating advanced technologies, expanding the range of probiotic skincare, exploring the gut-skin axis, developing smart skincare devices, and focusing on sustainability, the skincare industry can make significant strides toward creating personalized, effective, and environmentally responsible products. The continued collaboration between researchers, industry professionals, and consumers will be crucial in driving these advancements forward, ultimately transforming the landscape of skincare and promoting a holistic approach to health and wellness.

2.7 Conclusion

This chapter underscores the pivotal role of the skin microbiome in dermatological health and the potential of microbiome-friendly skincare products, ranging from promoting skin health (e.g., reduction in wrinkles) to addressing dysbiosis, treatment of various skin disorders, and environmental sustainability. The interplay between microbial communities, skincare formulations, and lifestyle choices emphasizes the importance of developing effective and sustainable skincare solutions. Several microbial strains exhibit beneficial effects in various skin disorders and in restoring microbial balance. Notably, a significant shift toward natural alternatives is emerging, including the integration of prebiotics, probiotics, and postbiotics, and is in line with the growing public awareness of beneficial applications in skin health. These new directions in the skin industry not only bolster skin health but also aim to minimize environmental harm, promoting eco-friendly practices. Implementing biodegradable materials, reducing the use of harmful synthetic chemicals, and adopting sustainable packaging are essential steps toward decreasing the ecological footprint of skincare products. Furthermore, these practices align with broader environmental goals, reinforcing the skincare industry's commitment to ecological conservation. As the landscape of skincare evolves, the convergence of microbiome research and sustainable practices offers a promising future where products are not only effective and personalized but also environmentally responsible. To sum it up, innovations in microbiome-friendly skincare products coupled with eco-friendly goals would foster a healthier future for both individuals and the planet.

References

1. Hsu, Y. C., & Fuchs, E. (2022). Building and maintaining the skin. *Cold Spring Harbor Perspectives in Biology, 14*(7), a040840.
2. Loomis, K. H., Wu, S. K., Ernlund, A., Zudock, K., Reno, A., Blount, K., & Karig, D. K. (2021). A mixed community of skin microbiome representatives influences cutaneous processes more than individual members. *Microbiome, 9*, 1–17.
3. Egert, M., & Simmering, R. (2016). The microbiota of the human skin. *Microbiota of the Human Body: Implications in Health and Disease*, 61–81.
4. Skowron, K., Bauza-Kaszewska, J., Kraszewska, Z., Wiktorczyk-Kapischke, N., Grudlewska-Buda, K., Kwiecińska-Piróg, J., ... & Gospodarek-Komkowska, E. (2021). Human skin microbiome: Impact of intrinsic and extrinsic factors on skin microbiota. *Microorganisms, 9*(3), 543.
5. Khmaladze, I., Leonardi, M., Fabre, S., Messaraa, C., & Mavon, A. (2020). The skin interactome: A holistic "genome-microbiome-exposome" approach to understand and modulate skin health and aging. *Clinical, Cosmetic and Investigational Dermatology*, 1021–1040.
6. Woo, Y. R., & Kim, H. S. (2024). Interaction between the microbiota and the skin barrier in aging skin: A comprehensive review. *Frontiers in Physiology, 15*, 1322205.
7. Townsend, E. C., & Kalan, L. R. (2023). The dynamic balance of the skin microbiome across the lifespan. *Biochemical Society Transactions, 51*(1), 71–86.
8. Ottman, N., Smidt, H., De Vos, W. M., & Belzer, C. (2012). The function of our microbiota: Who is out there and what do they do? *Frontiers in Cellular and Infection Microbiology, 2*, 31601.
9. Park, M. G., Cho, S., & Oh, M. M. (2023). Menopausal changes in the Microbiome—A review focused on the genitourinary Microbiome. *Diagnostics, 13*(6), 1193.
10. Pawlica, P. J. (2019). Corresponding address: The influence of cosmetics on the bacterial flora of the skin. *European Journal of Medical Technologies, 3*(24), 44–52.
11. Kan, H. (2022). World Health Organization air quality guidelines 2021: Implication for air pollution control and climate goal in China. *Chinese Medical Journal, 135*(5), 513–515.

12. Gu, X., Li, Z., & Su, J. (2024). Air pollution and skin diseases: A comprehensive evaluation of the associated mechanism. *Ecotoxicology and Environmental Safety, 278,* 116429.

13. Boxberger, M., Cenizo, V., Cassir, N., & La Scola, B. (2021). Challenges in exploring and manipulating the human skin microbiome. *Microbiome, 9,* 1–14.

14. Grice, E. A., & Segre, J. A. (2011). The skin microbiome. *Nature Reviews Microbiology, 9*(4), 244–253.

15. Saunte, D. M., Gaitanis, G., & Hay, R. J. (2020). Malassezia-associated skin diseases, the use of diagnostics and treatment. *Frontiers in Cellular and Infection Microbiology, 10,* 112.

16. Pistone, D., Meroni, G., Panelli, S., D'Auria, E., Acunzo, M., Pasala, A. R., .. & Drago, L. (2021). A journey on the skin microbiome: Pitfalls and opportunities. *International Journal of Molecular Sciences, 22*(18), 9846.

17. Byrd, A. L., Belkaid, Y., & Segre, J. A. (2018). The human skin microbiome. *Nature Reviews Microbiology, 16*(3), 143–155.

18. Limon, J. J., Skalski, J. H., & Underhill, D. M. (2017). Commensal fungi in health and disease. *Cell Host & Microbe, 22*(2), 156–165.

19. Kim, H. S. (2020). Microbiota in rosacea. *American Journal of Clinical Dermatology, 21*(Suppl 1), 25–35.

20. Salem, I., Ramser, A., Isham, N., & Ghannoum, M. A. (2018). The gut microbiome as a major regulator of the gut-skin axis. *Frontiers in Microbiology, 9,* 1459.

21. Booth, S. C., Smith, W. P., & Foster, K. R. (2023). The evolution of short-and long-range weapons for bacterial competition. *Nature Ecology & Evolution, 7*(12), 2080–2091.

22. Hibbing, M. E., Fuqua, C., Parsek, M. R., & Peterson, S. B. (2010). Bacterial competition: Surviving and thriving in the microbial jungle. *Nature Reviews Microbiology, 8*(1), 15–25.

23. Cros, M. P., Mir-Pedrol, J., Toloza, L., Knšdlseder, N., Maruotti, J., Zouboulis, C. C., .. & Fábrega, M. J. (2023). New insights into the role of *Cutibacterium acnes*-derived extracellular vesicles in inflammatory skin disorders. *Scientific Reports, 13*(1), 16058.

24. Swaney, M. H., Nelsen, A., Sandstrom, S., & Kalan, L. R. (2023). Sweat and sebum preferences of the human skin microbiota. *Microbiology Spectrum, 11*(1), e04180–22.

25. Nakamura, K., O'Neill, A. M., Williams, M. R., Cau, L., Nakatsuji, T., Horswill, A. R., & Gallo, R. L. (2020). Short chain fatty acids produced by *Cutibacterium acnes* inhibit biofilm formation by *Staphylococcus epidermidis*. *Scientific Reports, 10*(1), 21237.

26. SanMiguel, A., & Grice, E. A. (2015). Interactions between host factors and the skin microbiome. *Cellular and Molecular Life Sciences, 72*, 1499–1515.

27. De Pessemier, B., Grine, L., Debaere, M., Maes, A., Paetzold, B., & Callewaert, C. (2021). Gut–skin axis: Current knowledge of the interrelationship between microbial dysbiosis and skin conditions. *Microorganisms, 9*(2), 353.

28. Dessinioti, C., & Katsambas, A. (2024). The microbiome and acne: Perspectives for treatment. *Dermatology and Therapy, 14*(1), 31–44.

29. Zeng, J., Dou, J., Gao, L., Xiang, Y., Huang, J., Ding, S., .. & Lu, J. (2020). Topical ozone therapy restores microbiome diversity in atopic dermatitis. *International Immunopharmacology, 80*, 106191.

30. Chen, L., Li, J., Zhu, W., Kuang, Y., Liu, T., Zhang, W., .. & Peng, C. (2020). Skin and gut microbiome in psoriasis: Gaining insight into the pathophysiology of it and finding novel therapeutic strategies. *Frontiers in Microbiology, 11*, 589726.

31. Jarmuda, S., O'Reilly, N., Żaba, R., Jakubowicz, O., Szkaradkiewicz, A., & Kavanagh, K. (2012). Potential role of Demodex mites and bacteria in the induction of rosacea. *Journal of Medical Microbiology, 61*(11), 1504–1510.

32. Daou, H., Paradiso, M., Hennessy, K., & Seminario-Vidal, L. (2021). Rosacea and the microbiome: A systematic review. *Dermatology and Therapy, 11*, 1–12.

33. De Almeida, C. V., Antiga, E., & Lulli, M. (2023). Oral and topical probiotics and postbiotics in skincare and dermatological therapy: A concise review. *Microorganisms, 11*(6), 1420.

34. Salminen, S., Collado, M. C., Endo, A., Hill, C., Lebeer, S., Quigley, E. M., .. & Vinderola, G. (2021). The International Scientific Association of Probiotics and Prebiotics (ISAPP) consensus statement on the definition and scope of postbiotics. *Nature Reviews Gastroenterology & Hepatology, 18*(9), 649–667.

35. McLoughlin, I. J., Wright, E. M., Tagg, J. R., Jain, R., & Hale, J. D. (2022). Skin microbiome—The next frontier for probiotic intervention. *Probiotics and Antimicrobial Proteins, 14*(4), 630–647.

36. Thorakkattu, P., Khanashyam, A. C., Shah, K., Babu, K. S., Mundanat, A. S., Deliephan, A., .. & Nirmal, N. P. (2022). Postbiotics: Current trends in food and pharmaceutical industry. *Foods, 11*(19), 3094.

37. Endale, H., Mathewos, M., & Abdeta, D. (2023). Potential causes of spread of antimicrobial resistance and preventive measures in one health perspective: A review. *Infection and Drug Resistance,* 7515–7545.

38. Lombardi, F., Augello, F. R., Artone, S., Bahiti, B., Sheldon, J. M., Giuliani, M., .. & Cinque, B. (2022). Efficacy of probiotic *Streptococcus thermophilus* in counteracting TGF-β1-induced fibrotic response in normal human dermal fibroblasts. *Journal of Inflammation, 19*(1), 27.

39. Al-Ghazzewi, F. H., & Tester, R. F. (2014). Impact of prebiotics and probiotics on skin health. *Beneficial Microbes, 5*(2), 99–107.

40. Lam, K. L., & Cheung, P. C. K. (2013). Non-digestible long chain beta-glucans as novel prebiotics. *Bioactive Carbohydrates and Dietary Fibre, 2*(1), 45–64.

41. de la Rosa, O., Flores-Gallegos, A. C., Ascacio-Valdés, J. A., Sepúlveda, L., Montáñez, J. C., & Aguilar, C. N. (2022). Fructooligosaccharides as prebiotics, their metabolism, and health benefits. *Probiotics, Prebiotics and Synbiotics: Technological Advancements Towards Safety and Industrial Applications,* 307–337.

42. Di Lodovico, S., Gasparri, F., Di Campli, E., Di Fermo, P., D'Ercole, S., Cellini, L., & Di Giulio, M. (2020). Prebiotic combinations effects on the colonization of Staphylococcal skin strains. *Microorganisms, 9*(1), 37.

43. Hong, K. B., Hong, Y. H., Jung, E. Y., Jo, K., & Suh, H. J. (2020). Changes in the diversity of human skin microbiota to cosmetic serum containing prebiotics: Results from a randomized controlled trial. *Journal of Personalized Medicine, 10*(3), 91.

44. Paetzold, B., Willis, J. R., Pereira de Lima, J., Knödlseder, N., Brüggemann, H., Quist, S. R., .. & Güell, M. (2019). Skin microbiome modulation induced by probiotic solutions. *Microbiome, 7,* 1–9.

45. Liang, L., Qi, X., Jiang, X., Chen, T., & Dong, L. (2024). *Lactobacillus* plantarum MH-301 as an effective adjuvant to isotretinoin in the treatment of acne vulgaris: A randomized and open-label trail. *Frontiers in Medicine, 10,* 1340068.

46. Woo, J., & Ahn, J. (2013). Probiotic-mediated competition, exclusion and displacement in biofilm formation by food-borne pathogens. *Letters in Applied Microbiology, 56*(4), 307–313.

47. Kim, M. S., Lee, M., Oh, H., Seo, W., Kim, G. S., Ban, O. H., .. & Yang, J. (2021). Enhanced ceramides production by *Lactobacillus* rhamnosus IDCC 3201 and its proposed mechanism. *Applied Biological Chemistry, 64*, 1–9.

48. Klaenhammer, T. R., Kleerebezem, M., Kopp, M. V., & Rescigno, M. (2012). The impact of probiotics and prebiotics on the immune system. *Nature Reviews Immunology, 12*(10), 728–734.

49. Bouslimani, A., da Silva, R., Kosciolek, T., Janssen, S., Callewaert, C., Amir, A., .. & Dorrestein, P. C. (2019). The impact of skin care products on skin chemistry and microbiome dynamics. *BMC Biology, 17*, 1–20.

50. Roudsari, M. R., Karimi, R., Sohrabvandi, S., & Mortazavian, A. M. (2015). Health effects of probiotics on the skin. *Critical Reviews in Food Science and Nutrition, 55*(9), 1219–1240.

51. Rawal, S., & Ali, S. A. (2023). Probiotics and postbiotics play a role in maintaining dermal health. *Food & Function, 14*(9), 3966–3981.

52. da Silva Vale, A., de Melo Pereira, G. V., de Oliveira, A. C., de Carvalho Neto, D. P., Herrmann, L. W., Karp, S. G., .. & Soccol, C. R. (2023). Production, formulation, and application of postbiotics in the treatment of skin conditions. *Fermentation, 9*(3), 264.

53. Prescott, S. L., Larcombe, D. L., Logan, A. C., West, C., Burks, W., Caraballo, L., .. & Campbell, D. E. (2017). The skin microbiome: Impact of modern environments on skin ecology, barrier integrity, and systemic immune programming. *World Allergy Organization Journal, 10*, 1–16.

54. Lukić, M., Pantelić, I., & Savić, S. D. (2021). Towards optimal pH of the skin and topical formulations: From the current state of the art to tailored products. *Cosmetics, 8*(3), 69.

55. Verardo, V., Gómez-Caravaca, A. M., & Tabanelli, G. (2020). Bioactive components in fermented foods and food byproducts. *Foods, 9*(2), 153.

56. Zappelli, C., Barbulova, A., Apone, F., & Colucci, G. (2016). Effective active ingredients obtained through biotechnology. *Cosmetics, 3*(4), 39.

57. Fernandes, A., Rodrigues, P. M., Pintado, M., & Tavaria, F. K. (2023). A systematic review of natural products for skin applications: Targeting inflammation, wound healing, and photo-aging. *Phytomedicine, 115*, 154824.

58. Rajha, H. N., Paule, A., Aragon s, G., Barbosa, M., Caddeo, C., Debs, E., .. & Edeas, M. (2022). Recent advances in research on polyphenols:

Effects on microbiota, metabolism, and health. *Molecular Nutrition & Food Research, 66*(1), 2100670.

59. Suleria, H. A. R., Butt, M. S., Anjum, F. M., Saeed, F., & Khalid, N. (2015). Onion: Nature protection against physiological threats. *Critical Reviews in Food Science and Nutrition, 55*(1), 50–66.

60. Michalak, M., Pierzak, M., Kręcisz, B., & Suliga, E. (2021). Bioactive compounds for skin health: A review. *Nutrients, 13*(1), 203.

61. Surber, C., & Kottner, J. (2017). Skin care products: What do they promise, what do they deliver. *Journal of Tissue Viability, 26*(1), 29–36.

62. Skotnicki, S. (2020). Skin pH, epidermal barrier function, cleansers, and skin health. *Local Wound Care for Dermatologists*, 5–12.

63. Dondos, V. (2022). *The Glowing Skin Plan: Proven Ways to Optimise Your Skin Health and Radiance, Whatever Your Age*. Random House.

64. Domagała, A., Wojtowicz-Prus, E., Dubis, J., Witkiewicz, W., & Czarnecka, A. (2019). Evaluation of plasma levels of tissue factor and tissue factor pathway inhibitor in patients with psoriasis. *Advances in Dermatology and Allergology/Postępy Dermatologii i Alergologii, 36*(4), 442–448.

65. Agountaf, I. (2023). Optimizing the use of topical retinoids in Moroccan patients with acne. dspace.nuph.edu.ua

66. Liu, J. K. (2022). Natural products in cosmetics. *Natural Products and Bioprospecting, 12*(1), 40.

67. Zhang, X., Zhang, Z., Tao, H., He, X., Hsu, K., Wang, W., .. & Steel, A. (2023). Comprehensive assessment of the efficacy and safety of a clay mask in oily and acne skin. *Skin Research and Technology, 29*(11), e13513.

68. Hamie, H., Yassine, R., Shoukfeh, R., Turk, D., Huq, F., & Moossavi, M. (2024). A review of the efficacy of popular eye cream ingredients. *International Journal of Women's Dermatology, 10*(2), e156.

69. Sasounian, R., Martinez, R. M., Lopes, A. M., Giarolla, J., Rosado, C., Magalhães, W. V., .. & Baby, A. R. (2024). Innovative approaches to an eco-friendly cosmetic industry: A review of sustainable ingredients. *Clean Technologies, 6*(1), 176–198.

70. Gueniche, A., Perin, O., Bouslimani, A., Landemaine, L., Misra, N., Cupferman, S., .. & Khodr, A. (2022). Advances in microbiome-derived solutions and methodologies are founding a new era in skin health and care. *Pathogens, 11*(2), 121.

71. Sehgal, A., & Singh, A. (2022). The influence of pH on skin's surface. *Journal of Pharmaceutical Negative Results*, 2012–2023.

72. Büyükköroğlu, G., Şenel, B., & Sevim, G. (2022). Biotechnology in cosmetics. In *Biotechnology in Healthcare*, 273–287. Academic Press.

73. Pan, Y., Ma, X., Song, Y., Zhao, J., & Yan, S. (2021). Questionnaire and lactic acid sting test play different role on the assessment of sensitive skin: A cross-sectional study. *Clinical, Cosmetic and Investigational Dermatology*, 1215–1225.

74. Schwingen, J., Kaplan, M., & Kurschus, F. C. (2020). Current concepts in inflammatory skin diseases evolved by transcriptome analysis: In depth analysis of atopic dermatitis and psoriasis. *International Journal of Molecular Sciences, 21(3),* 699.

75. Li, M., Mao, J., Diaz, I., Kopylova, E., Melnik, A. V., Aksenov, A. A., .. & Boyd, T. (2023). Multi-omic approach to decipher the impact of skincare products with pre/postbiotics on skin microbiome and metabolome. *Frontiers in Medicine, 10,* 1165980.

76. Han, J. H., & Kim, H. S. (2024). Skin deep: The potential of microbiome cosmetics. *Journal of Microbiology*, 1–19.

77. Nagar, P., & Hasija, Y. (2018). Metagenomic approach in study and treatment of various skin diseases: A brief review. *Biomedical Dermatology, 2,* 1–8.

78. Godlewska, U., Brzoza, P., Kwiecień, K., Kwitniewski, M., & Cichy, J. (2020). Metagenomic studies in inflammatory skin diseases. *Current Microbiology, 77,* 3201–3212.

79. Lemoine, L., Dieckmann, R., Al Dahouk, S., Vincze, S., Luch, A., & Tralau, T. (2020). Microbially competent 3D Skin: A test system that reveals insight into host–microbe interactions and their potential toxicological impact. *Archives of Toxicology, 94,* 3487–3502.

80. Luger, T., Amagai, M., Dreno, B., Dagnelie, M. A., Liao, W., Kabashima, K., .. & Schmuth, M. (2021). Atopic dermatitis: Role of the skin barrier, environment, microbiome, and therapeutic agents. *Journal of Dermatological Science, 102*(3), 142–157.

81. Khalid, M., & Abdollahi, M. (2021). Environmental distribution of personal care products and their effects on human health. *Iranian Journal of Pharmaceutical Research: IJPR, 20*(1), 216.

82. Patel, A. K., & Sharma, A. K. (Eds.). (2023). *Sustainable Production Innovations: Bioremediation and Other Biotechnologies.* John Wiley & Sons.

83. van den Bogaard, E. H., Elias, P. M., Goleva, E., Berdyshev, E., Smits, J. P., Danby, S. G., .. & Leung, D. Y. (2023). Targeting skin barrier function in atopic dermatitis. *The Journal of Allergy and Clinical Immunology: In Practice, 11*(5), 1335–1346.

84. Bashir, S. M., Kimiko, S., Mak, C. W., Fang, J. K. H., & Gon alves, D. (2021). Personal care and cosmetic products as a potential source of environmental contamination by microplastics in a densely populated Asian city. *Frontiers in Marine Science, 8*, 683482.

85. Ding, J., Wei, D., An, Z., Zhang, C., Jin, L., Wang, L., .. & Li, Q. (2020). Succession of the bacterial community structure and functional prediction in two composting systems viewed through meta transcriptomics. *Bioresource Technology, 313*, 123688.

86. Dréno, B., Dagnelie, M. A., Khammari, A., & Corvec, S. (2020). The skin microbiome: A new actor in inflammatory acne. *American Journal of Clinical Dermatology, 21*(Suppl 1), 18–24.

87. Thakur, A., & Kumar, A. (2024). Polyphenols for dyes application. *Science and Engineering of Polyphenols: Fundamentals and Industrial Scale Applications*, 157–210.

88. Khatri, M., Naughton, R. J., Clifford, T., Harper, L. D., & Corr, L. (2021). The effects of collagen peptide supplementation on body composition, collagen synthesis, and recovery from joint injury and exercise: A systematic review. *Amino Acids, 53*(10), 1493–1506.

89. Castillo, D. E., Nanda, S., & Keri, J. E. (2019). *Propionibacterium (Cutibacterium) acnes* bacteriophage therapy in acne: Current evidence and future perspectives. *Dermatology and Therapy, 9*, 19–31.

90. Brown, T. L., Petrovski, S., Dyson, Z. A., Seviour, R., & Tucci, J. (2016). The formulation of bacteriophage in a semi solid preparation for control of *Propionibacterium acnes* growth. *PLoS One, 11*(3), e0151184.

91. Rimon, A., Rakov, C., Lerer, V., Sheffer-Levi, S., Alkalky-Oren, S., Shlomov, T., .. & Hazan, R. (2022). Towards phage therapy for acne vulgaris: Topical application in a mouse model. *BioRxiv*, 2022–02.

92. Li, X., Ding, W., Li, Z., Yan, Y., Tong, Y., Xu, J., & Li, M. (2024). vB_CacS-HV1 as a novel pahexavirus bacteriophage with lytic and anti-biofilm potential against *Cutibacterium acnes. Microorganisms, 12*(8), 1566.

93. Rimon, A., Rakov, C., Lerer, V., Sheffer-Levi, S., Alkalky-Oren, S., Shlomov, T., .. & Hazan, R. (2022). Towards phage therapy for acne vulgaris: Topical application in a mouse model. *BioRxiv*, 2022–02.

94. Ambawade, M. S., Gugale, G. S., Bankhele, K. R., Nirgude, R. S., Bhusare, B. P., Pathade, G. R., & Abhang, P. D. In vitro study on improving antiseptic efficiency of cosmetics using bacteriophage-cosmetic formulation. (2021). *Int J Pharm Sci, 12*(3), 75–85.

95. Natarelli, N., Gahoonia, N., & Sivamani, R. K. (2023). Bacteriophages and the microbiome in dermatology: The role of the phageome and

a potential therapeutic strategy. *International Journal of Molecular Sciences, 24*(3), 2695.

96. Khetpal, S., Ghosh, D., & Roostaeian, J. (2023). Innovations in skin and soft tissue aging—A systematic literature review and market analysis of therapeutics and associated outcomes. *Aesthetic Plastic Surgery, 47*(4), 1609–1622.
97. Jacków, J., Guo, Z., Hansen, C., Abaci, H. E., Doucet, Y. S., Shin, J. U., .. & Christiano, A. M. (2019). CRISPR/Cas9-based targeted genome editing for correction of recessive dystrophic epidermolysis bullosa using iPS cells. *Proceedings of the National Academy of Sciences, 116*(52), 26846–26852.
98. Piñón-Hofbauer, J., Guttmann-Gruber, C., Wally, V., Sharma, A., Gratz, I. K., & Koller, U. (2024). Challenges and progress related to gene editing in rare skin diseases. *Advanced Drug Delivery Reviews*, 115294.
99. He, J., & Jia, Y. (2022). Application of omics technologies in dermatological research and skin management. *Journal of Cosmetic Dermatology, 21*(2), 451–460.
100. Ogawa, K., & Okada, Y. (2020). The current landscape of psoriasis genetics in 2020. *Journal of Dermatological Science, 99*(1), 2–8.
101. Patil, M. S. V., Patil, M. R., & Gaikwad, M. P. *Cosmetic Science.* JEC Publication.
102. Jaiswal, S. K., Agarwal, S. M., Thodum, P., & Sharma, V. K. (2021). SkinBug: An artificial intelligence approach to predict human skin microbiome-mediated metabolism of biotics and xenobiotics. *Iscience, 24*(1), 101925.
103. Majidian, M., Kolli, H., & Moy, R. L. (2021). Management of skin thinning and aging: Review of therapies for neocollagenesis; hormones and energy devices. *International Journal of Dermatology, 60*(12), 1481–1487.
104. Mangtani, N., Bajpai, N., Sahasrabudhe, S., & Wasule, D. (2020). Importance of artificial intelligence and augmented reality in cosmetic and beauty industry post Covid 19. *World Journal of Pharmaceutical Research, 9*(8), 2296–308.
105. Yang, L., & Ting, L. (2024). Researching the modular design of beauty products for home use. *Methods, 8*(2), 58–68.
106. Eriksson, G., & Kenalemang, L. M. (2023). How cosmetic apps fragmentise and metricise the female face: A multimodal critical discourse analysis. *Discourse & Communication, 17*(3), 278–297.

107. Masterson, D. (2023). NutraCast: Neutrogena and nourished use biometrics to deliver 3D-printed, personalized beauty supplements. *Global Cosmetics.*

108. Kanaska, S. D. (2022). Is the future of beauty personalized case study for microbiome skincare brand skinome. weblink.

109. HelloBiome. AI-powered microbiome platform. (n.d.). Retrieved September 29, 2024, from https://hellobio.me/.

110. Prakashan, D., Kaushik, A., & Gandhi, S. (2024). Smart sensors and wound dressings: Artificial intelligence-supported chronic skin monitoring: A review. *Chemical Engineering Journal*, 497, 154371.

111. Ha, M., Lim, S., & Ko, H. (2018). Wearable and flexible sensors for user-interactive health-monitoring devices. *Journal of Materials Chemistry B*, *6*(24), 4043–4064.

112. Sun, C., Hu, G., Yi, L., Ge, W., Yang, Q., Yang, X., .. & Chen, W. H. (2024). Integrated analysis of facial microbiome and skin physio-optical properties unveils cytotype-dependent aging effects. *Microbiome*, *12*(1), 163.

113. Probiotic skin care cosmetic product market size, forecast 2034. (n.d.). Retrieved September 29, 2024, from https://www.alliedmarketresearch.com/probiotic-skin-care-cosmetic-product-market-A06317.

114. Mahmud, M. R., Akter, S., Tamanna, S. K., Mazumder, L., Esti, I. Z., Banerjee, S., .. & Pirttilä, A. M. (2022). Impact of gut microbiome on skin health: Gut-skin axis observed through the lenses of therapeutics and skin diseases. *Gut Microbes*, *14*(1), 2096995.

115. Hrestak, D., Matijašić, M., Čipčić Paljetak, H., Ledić Drvar, D., Ljubojević Hadžavdić, S., & Perić, M. (2022). Skin microbiota in atopic dermatitis. *International Journal of Molecular Sciences*, *23*(7), 3503.

116. Habeebuddin, M., Karnati, R. K., Shiroorkar, P. N., Nagaraja, S., Asdaq, S. M. B., Khalid Anwer, M., & Fattepur, S. (2022). Topical probiotics: More than a skin deep. *Pharmaceutics*, *14*(3), 557.

117. Sydnor, E. R., & Perl, T. M. (2011). Hospital epidemiology and infection control in acute-care settings. *Clinical Microbiology Reviews*, *24*(1), 141–173.

118. Erem, A. D., Nıehaus, K. L., & Nıerstrasz, V. (2018). Development of probiotic printings for polyester fabrics. *Tekstil ve Mühendis*, *25*(111), 208–213.

119. Niehaus, K. L., Dural-Erem, A., & Nierstrasz, V. (2018). Probiotic printed PET fabrics for biocontrol in hospital textiles. *Textile and Apparel, 28*(3), 195–198.

120. Bowe, W. P., & Logan, A. C. (2011). Acne vulgaris, probiotics and the gut-brain-skin axis-back to the future? *Gut Pathogens, 3*, 1–11.

121. Kober, M. M., & Bowe, W. P. (2015). The effect of probiotics on immune regulation, acne, and photoaging. *International Journal of Women's Dermatology, 1*(2), 85–89.

122. Vaughn, A. R., Notay, M., Clark, A. K., & Sivamani, R. K. (2017). Skin-gut axis: The relationship between intestinal bacteria and skin health. *World J Dermatol, 6*(4), 52–58.

123. Zhu, T. H., Zhu, T. R., Tran, K. A., Sivamani, R. K., & Shi, V. Y. (2018). Epithelial barrier dysfunctions in atopic dermatitis: A skin–gut–lung model linking microbiome alteration and immune dysregulation. *British Journal of Dermatology, 179*(3), 570–581.

124. Subhadarshani, S., & Mishra, H. S. (2020). Letter to editor in response to the article 'Position statement: LEPROSY: diagnosis, treatment and follow-up.' *Journal of the European Academy of Dermatology and Venereology, 34*(2), e72–e73.

125. Markiewicz, E., & Idowu, O. C. (2018). Personalized skincare: From molecular basis to clinical and commercial applications. *Clinical, Cosmetic and Investigational Dermatology, 11*, 161–171.

126. Dolečková, I., Cápová, A., Machková, L., Moravčíková, S., Marešová, M., & Velebný, V. (2021). Seasonal variations in the skin parameters of Caucasian women from Central Europe. *Skin Research and Technology, 27*(3), 358–369.

Chapter 3

Mitigating Falls among the Aging Population

Mehdi Ebrahimi, David S.-K. Ting, and Rupp Carriveau

Turbulence and Energy Laboratory, Ed Lumley Centre for Engineering Innovation, University of Windsor, Windsor, Ontario, Canada

mehdi.ebrahimi@uwindsor.ca

Falls among the aging population are a significant public health concern. Each year, approximately 33% of adults aged 65 and older experience at least one fall. Muscle weakness, balance problems, and medication use are among the top contributors. Through comprehensive risk assessments and the utilization of wearable sensors, real-time monitoring of movement patterns can aid in identifying high-risk individuals. Integrating fall prevention strategies can reduce fall rates by up to 35%. This approach encompasses exercise programs, home modifications, medication reviews, and community-based interventions. Moreover, research has shown that combining physical therapy with environmental adjustments can decrease fall incidents by 25%. In addition, artificial intelligence (AI) technologies provide innovative solutions for fall prevention. Predictive analytics and machine learning (ML)

Environmentalism in Healthcare: Caring for Tomorrow Ecologically
Edited by Jacqueline A. Stagner and David S.-K. Ting

ISBN 978-981-5129-95-3 (Hardcover), 978-1-003-74869-4 (eBook)
www.jennystanford.com

DOI: 10.1201/9781003748694-3

models can identify high-risk individuals with an accuracy of up to 95%. Additionally, AI-driven wearable devices provide real-time alerts and personalized intervention strategies, demonstrating a potential 16% reduction in fall-related hospitalizations. The integration of risk factor assessment, multifactorial interventions, and AI applications holds promise for significantly reducing the incidence and impact of falls among older adults. By addressing these key areas, this paper aims to provide a comprehensive overview of current strategies and technological advancements in fall prevention for the aging population.

3.1 Introduction

Falls among the elderly represent a critical and growing public health emergency that extends far beyond individual injuries. Each fall not only risks immediate harm and long-term disability but also imposes substantial emotional and financial burdens on patients, families, and healthcare systems. The consequences of falling, which include fractures, head injuries, loss of independence, and, in severe cases, fatalities, intensify the challenges faced by an aging society. According to the World Health Organization (WHO), approximately 33% of adults aged 65 and older experience at least one fall annually, with this figure rising to nearly 42% among those aged 70 and older [1]. Such alarming statistics underscore the cascading impact on public health infrastructures, demanding coordinated efforts in community planning, medical care, and innovative prevention programs. These data underscore the cascading impact of falls on both personal well-being and broader socioeconomic stability, highlighting the urgent need for effective and scalable prevention strategies [2].

The etiology of falls is complex, transcending the widely recognized physical impairments. Emerging research indicates that subtle declines in neurocognitive and sensory functions can significantly hinder the rapid processing of environmental cues. Diminished executive functioning and slower reaction times may impede the ability to adjust during unexpected perturbations. At the same time, reductions in visual clarity, especially in-depth perception and contrast sensitivity, can compromise spatial awareness, while even minor auditory deficits might disrupt the perception of critical ambient signals. Psychological factors, including the fear of falling following a previous incident, further exacerbate this vulnerability by altering natural movement patterns. Together, these cognitive, sensory, and psychological elements form an intricate web of risk factors, many of which remain only partially understood [3].

In addition to the interplay of neurocognitive and sensory factors, systemic health deterioration plays a critical role in elevating fall risk among older adults. Chronic low-grade inflammation and the resulting oxidative stress, inherent in the aging process, subtly erode neuromuscular coordination over time. Furthermore, episodes of orthostatic hypotension, often stemming from impaired cardiovascular regulation, limit the body's ability to fluidly adapt to postural changes. Nutritional deficits, particularly regarding vitamin D and essential micronutrients, further weaken bone integrity and muscle performance [4]. These systemic and biochemical factors highlight that fall risk extends beyond immediate physical or environmental challenges, reflecting an overall decline in physiological resilience that warrants deeper investigation.

Numerous mitigation strategies have been advanced to curb fall incidents, yet many interventions address only isolated facets of this multifactorial challenge. Traditional measures such as targeted exercise programs designed to enhance balance and strength, strategic home modifications to minimize environmental hazards, and regular medication reviews have each demonstrated benefits in controlled settings [5]. More recent technological innovations, including AI-driven wearable devices and predictive analytics, offer promising avenues by enabling real-time monitoring and personalized intervention strategies. However, these approaches often operate from a single-dimensional perspective, highlighting the absence of a cohesive, all-encompassing preventative framework. The development of integrated models that synergize conventional interventions with emerging technologies may hold the key to significantly reducing both the incidence and severity of falls among older adults.

Consequently, several studies in the literature have focused on identifying various parameters that can impact fall risk in the aging population. Bergen et al. evaluated geographic, demographic, functional, and health characteristics associated with fall injuries among adults aged 65 years and older [6]. Their analyses included multivariable logistic regression and descriptive statistics to produce crude and adjusted percentages by characteristic. Their work showed the importance of screening and assessing elderly patients to identify their specific risk factors. Ting and Ting studied various reasons that falls can occur and how they can be prevented or mitigated. Given that more than 80% of fall-related deaths among the elderly occur in this demographic, they concluded that it is crucial to design communities with age-friendly amenities to support older adults [7]. Kim et al. [8] analyzed data from 391,902 patients across 580 hospitals, uncovering that influential factors for falls included advanced age, the use of multiple medications and treatments, and impaired mobility. The role of assistive devices in fall prevention has also been a focus of several studies [9]. Can et al. performed a pilot study on the effectiveness of a fall detection device, studying a total of 26 participants with a mean age of 82 ± 10 years, whereas 89% of the residents were female [10]. They reported the significance of a fall detection device in fall prevention. Aldailami et al. studied predictors of fall-related injuries among elderly people at the emergency department in the United States between 2007 and 2017 [11]. In their work, 538 thousand injuries with ED visits were analyzed. Two-thirds of these visits were fall-related, of which 33% were among those 85 years and older, 29% needed hospitalization, about 63% occurred at home, and 38% had head trauma.

Interventions targeting specific populations and settings have also been explored. Nickerson et al. examined the circumstances of falls among older adults using walkers in long-term care facilities [12]. They identified design deficits in walkers that can cause falls. Their findings highlighted the importance of individual interventions to address the unique needs of different elderly populations in different communities. Snyder et al. explored the characteristics of falls among wheelchair users in long-term care facilities [13]. Their study highlighted the need for specialized interventions to address the unique challenges faced by this population. Nowakowski and Gronostajska discussed the design of movement spaces for the elderly in construction law [14]. They concluded that accessible and safe environments are crucial for fall prevention. Schmucker et al., in a similar work, concluded that user-friendly designs can enhance safety and mobility and reduce fall risks [15]. Shi et al. studied unintentional fall-related deaths and their circumstances in Utah to evaluate the underlying and contributing causes associated with these deaths [16]. Their findings showed the importance of targeted interventions to prevent fatal falls.

Environmental modifications are another component of fall prevention. Drahota et al. conducted a systematic review of shock-absorbing flooring [17]. They reported a significant reduction in fall-related injuries. Montero-Odasso et al. developed a guideline for falls prevention and management recommendations applicable to older adults [18]. Camara et al. studied the impact of the length of walking canes on postural stability in older women [19]. They reported that the role of assistive technologies in enhancing balance and reducing fall risks was significant. A wide range of fall prevention methods has been addressed in this guideline. Gharghan et al. reviewed some elderly fall detection systems (FDSs), examining different aspects such as fall detection methods, system architecture, wireless communications, sensor types, performance metrics, system challenges, and limitations [1]. By categorizing FDSs into traditional and AI-based methods and critically reviewing and comparing AI techniques like ML and deep learning, they studied the accuracy of deep learning-based systems in fall detection. They also investigated methods to optimize energy consumption by employing wireless power transfer to recharge the device's battery and implementing power-saving techniques to extend the battery life of FDSs [20]. Jindal et al. [21] showed that falls among the elderly in North India have a prevalence of 28.7%, with key risk factors including slippery floors, hearing loss, vertigo, hypertension, use of multiple medications, and functional disability. The study highlights the importance of addressing preventable factors through environmental modifications and exercise programs to reduce the incidence of falls and related injuries.

Applying tech equipment is another way to prevent falls among the elderly. Cerqueira et al. developed a robot to help prevent falls for older adults [22]. They reported that the robot achieved an accuracy rate of about 97% in detecting user movement intention and 90% in recognising the user's gait phase. Wearable sensor technologies have emerged as a valuable tool for assessing fall risk. Nouredanesh et al. examined the use of wearable sensors in free living conditions [23]. This research introduced techniques to apply advanced technologies to prevent routine falls among the aging population. Kou et al. studied the fall risk of aged workers using wearable inertial measurement units [24]. They developed an ML model using inertial motion data. Their findings showed that the method had excellent performance in assessing fall risk, allowing aged workers to assess their fall risk before a clinical diagnosis. Patel et al. [25] showed that vision-based technologies utilizing deep neural networks and transfer learning significantly enhance the accuracy of fall detection in elderly individuals, achieving a test accuracy of 98.15%. Their methodology incorporates explainable AI, ensuring transparency and trustworthy decision-making, particularly in critical healthcare contexts for vulnerable elderly populations.

Mitigating falls among the aging population requires a comprehensive approach that involves identifying and assessing risk factors, implementing multifaceted interventions, and utilizing AI technologies. Identifying specific risk factors and addressing both modifiable and non-modifiable factors are important keys for effective fall prevention among the aging population. Assistive devices, including FDSs, mobility aids, and properly designed walking canes, have proven to enhance the safety of elderly people. Multifactorial interventions that combine physical therapy, home modifications, and community-based programs have also shown significant reductions in fall rates. Moreover, innovative AI applications, such as predictive analytics, wearable sensors, and robotic technologies, have emerged as invaluable tools for real-time risk assessment. This paper aims to provide a comprehensive overview of current strategies and technological advancements in fall prevention, addressing these key areas to significantly reduce the incidence and impact of falls among older adults.

3.2 Identification and Assessment of Fall Risk Factors

Identifying and assessing various risk factors is crucial to addressing falls among the elderly. Intrinsic factors, such as muscle weakness, gait deficits, balance impairments, visual deficits, impaired activities of daily living, and cognitive impairments, are some of the major risk contributors to falls in the aging population. These factors can result from natural aging processes, chronic health conditions, or a sedentary lifestyle, leading to a decline in strength and stability. Various studies have examined these parameters to better understand their impact on falls among the elderly; however, the reported impact in different studies varies. In Fig. 3.1, the average percentage, minimum, and maximum from 16 different datasets are presented to illustrate the impact of various intrinsic risk factors on falls among the elderly [26]. Each percentage represents the increased likelihood of falls associated with a specific risk factor. For instance, a value of 100% signifies that the chance of falling is doubled. The minimum and maximum ranges indicate the lowest and highest reported increases in fall risk, respectively, across the datasets. These ranges help capture the variability observed in different studies, which can be attributed to differences in study populations, methodologies, and settings.

Extrinsic factors, such as poor lighting, slippery floors, and inappropriate footwear, also play crucial roles in fall risk. The environment in which an elderly person lives or frequents can substantially influence their risk of falling. Poor lighting, for example, can make it difficult for older adults to see potential hazards, such as loose rugs or obstacles in their path, increasing the likelihood of tripping and falling. Slippery floors, often found in bathrooms and kitchens, pose a significant risk, especially if they are not equipped with non-slip mats or if spills are not promptly

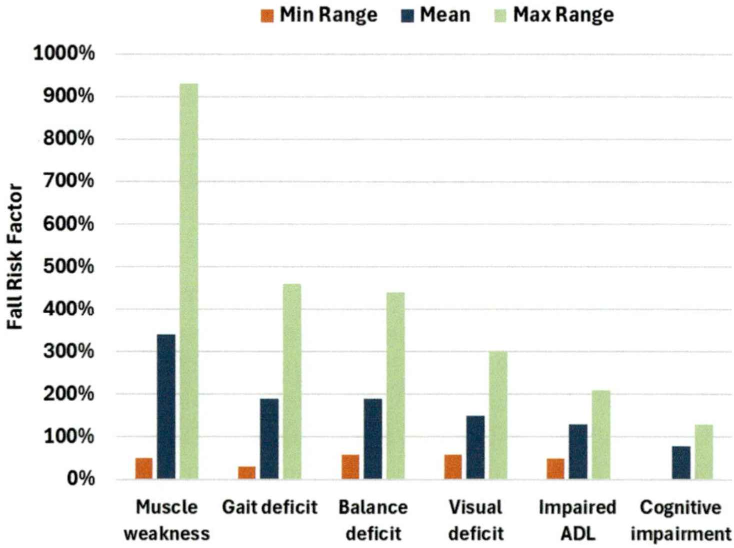

Figure 3.1 The impact of primary risk factors on falls in the elderly population across 16 studies; based on [26].

cleaned. Inappropriate footwear, such as shoes with high heels, slippery soles, or poor support, can also contribute to instability and falls. Therefore, conducting thorough home safety assessments and making necessary modifications, such as installing grab bars and improving lighting, can significantly reduce the risk of falls among the elderly. In Table 3.1, various intervention strategies from several studies are compared. This table repeatedly highlights interventions involving home evaluations by occupational therapists, showcasing their consistent role in advising on modifications and supervising the implementation of safety measures. This repeated emphasis underscores the importance and effectiveness of such assessments in reducing extrinsic fall risk factors among the elderly.

It should be noted that an individual's risk of falling is often impacted by a combination of multiple factors. This means that these factors can overlap and contribute to the same fall incident. For example, muscle weakness might make an older adult more prone to losing balance, and if they are also dealing with a vision impairment, their risk of falling is further heightened.

Table 3.1 Summary of studies evaluating home assessments and modifications for extrinsic factors in fall prevention

Study	Methodology	Participants	Effectiveness
[27]	Home evaluation by a trained assessor; advice and provision of materials and labor for modifications (e.g., rails, grab bars, etc.).	1090 participants with a mean age of 76	8%
[28]	Home assessment by an Occupational Therapist; advice on modifications and strategies for living safely with fixed hazards	60 participants with a mean age of 65	13%
[29]	Occupational therapist conducted home evaluations and supervised home modifications	530 participants with a mean age of 65	36%
[30]	Home evaluation by an occupational therapist and physiotherapist; guidance on modifications and training in the use of assistive devices	360 participants with a mean age of 81	37%

This overlapping nature is critical in understanding fall risk, as it better explains the complexity and multifactorial nature of fall incidents among the elderly. In practice, it is not about each factor standing alone; it is about how they interact and compound one another to elevate fall risk. Therefore, the combined percentages in this context are more informative as they reflect the compounded vulnerabilities and underline the importance of a comprehensive risk assessment that considers the interplay of various intrinsic and extrinsic factors. Tinetti et al. [31] conducted a survey among elderly individuals living in the community and discovered that the percentage of those who experienced falls rose from 27% among individuals with no or one risk factor to 78% among those with four or more risk factors. A similar study showed that the percentage of community-dwelling individuals with recurrent falls increased from 10% to 69% as the number of risk factors grew from one to four or greater [32].

Comprehensive risk assessments are pivotal in crafting personalized prevention strategies that address both intrinsic and extrinsic factors. Tools like the Timed Up and Go (TUG) test and the Berg Balance Scale are widely employed to evaluate an individual's fall risk [18, 33]. The TUG test measures the time it takes for an individual to stand up from a chair, walk a short distance, turn around, walk back, and sit down. Longer completion times suggest a higher risk of falling. Meanwhile, the Berg Balance Scale assesses a person's ability to perform specific tasks such as standing up, sitting down, reaching, and turning, with lower scores indicating poorer balance and a heightened risk of falls. Utilizing these tools enables healthcare providers to gain a comprehensive understanding of an individual's fall risk and develop targeted interventions to mitigate this risk. Table 3.2 showcases the TUG test results for 58 elderly participants, including 30 healthy older adults and 28 elderly individuals with health conditions [33]. This table summarizes their average performance times across three different obstacle heights (0 cm, 5 cm, and 17 cm). The time taken to complete the TUG test increased with the obstacle height for both groups. Healthy older adults consistently outperformed their counterparts with health conditions in all test conditions, demonstrating significantly shorter completion times. The average TUG completion times for the 0, 5, and 17 cm obstacles were 27.6 seconds, 28.9 seconds, and 30.3 seconds, respectively, for elderly individuals with health conditions, compared to 12.3 seconds, 12.2 seconds, and 12.6 seconds for healthy older adults.

In general, as reported in [33], both groups required more time to complete the task as the obstacle height increased. Also, the elderly with health conditions took approximately twice as long as their healthy counterparts to finish the test. The differences in TUG completion times were significant across the 0 cm, 5 cm, and 17 cm obstacle heights for the elderly with health conditions. However, for healthy older adults, the TUG completion time remained relatively stable across different obstacle heights, with a slight increase at 17 cm. By evaluating the information from this table, healthcare providers can develop personalized interventions to reduce the likelihood of falls and enhance the overall safety and well-being of older adults.

Table 3.2 TUG test results for healthy older adults and the elderly with health conditions at varying obstacle heights [33]

Obstacle Height (cm)	Healthy Older Adults		People with Health Conditions	
	Mean (sec)	Standard deviation	Mean (sec)	Standard deviation
0 cm	12.3	1.3	27.6	10.6
5 cm	12.2	1.4	28.9	11.7
17 cm	12.64	1.55	30.32	12.29

Figure 3.2 illustrates the TUG test times, for instance, at a 0 cm obstacle height. This figure shows the TUG test times for elderly participants with health conditions at a 0 cm obstacle height. The recorded times, presented in seconds, reflect the participants' mobility and agility. Lower TUG times generally indicate better mobility and agility, while higher times suggest challenges in these areas. By analyzing these times, we can assess the impact of health conditions on participants' functional mobility. Figure 3.3 displays the corresponding Fugl-Meyer Assessment (FMA) scores for the same group of elderly participants with health conditions. The FMA is a quantitative measure used to assess motor functioning, balance, sensation, and joint functioning in individuals who have experienced a stroke or other neurological conditions. Higher FMA scores indicate better motor functioning, whereas lower scores suggest greater impairment. By examining these scores, we can evaluate the extent of motor deficits among the participants. By combining these data points, we can gain a more comprehensive and nuanced understanding of an individual's fall risk, contributing to the creation of a robust and thorough risk profile. This comprehensive approach enables the development of personalized interventions to enhance safety and well-being.

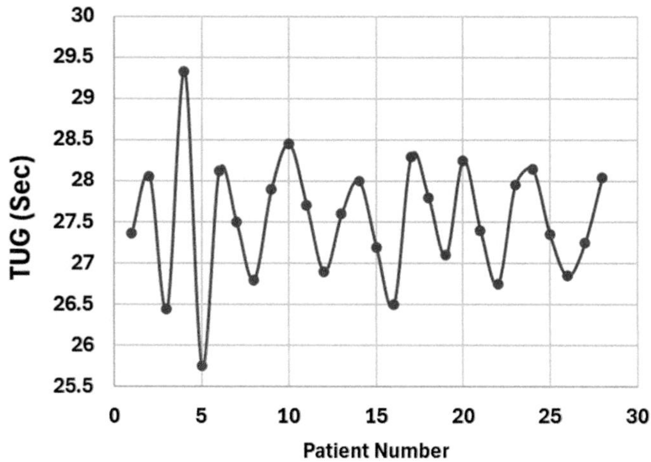

Figure 3.2 TUG test times at 0 cm obstacle height for elderly participants with health conditions.

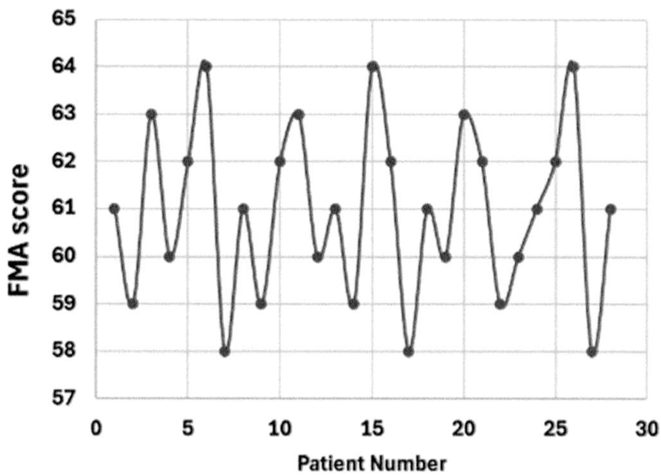

Figure 3.3 FMA scores for elderly participants with health conditions.

3.3 Multifactorial Interventions

Multifactorial interventions are comprehensive strategies designed to address the multiple risk factors contributing to falls among older adults. These interventions typically involve a combination of exercise programs, medication reviews, environmental modifications, and education on fall prevention. For instance, exercise programs aimed at improving strength, balance, and mobility are a core component of these interventions. Medication reviews help identify and adjust medications that may increase the risk of falls, such as those causing dizziness or drowsiness. Environmental modifications, such as improving lighting, installing grab bars, and removing tripping hazards, also play a crucial role in reducing the risk of falls.

Multifactorial interventions need to be effective and relevant to the specific circumstances of the older adult. For example, a comprehensive fall risk assessment can identify specific intrinsic and extrinsic factors that need to be addressed. Based on this assessment, a personalized intervention plan can be developed. This may include targeted exercises, home safety modifications, and education on safe practices. Engaging older adults and their caregivers in the intervention process is essential for ensuring adherence and effectiveness.

Research has shown that multifactorial interventions can significantly reduce the incidence of falls among older adults. A systematic review and meta-analysis of 41 trials involving almost 20,000 participants found that these interventions can reduce the rate of falls by approximately 21% compared to usual care [34]. The effectiveness of these interventions highlights the importance of addressing multiple risk factors simultaneously to achieve a significant reduction in fall risk. By combining various strategies, multifactorial interventions provide a holistic approach to fall prevention, ultimately improving the safety and well-being of older adults.

Sherrington et al. [35] reviewed 116 studies involving 25,160 participants and found that exercise reduces the rate of falls by 23%. Their subgroup analysis revealed variations in the effects of different types of exercise: balance and functional exercises reduced falls by 24%, while programs incorporating multiple types of exercise achieved a 28% reduction in falls. Ming et al. [36] examined the effectiveness of medication review in preventing fall-related injuries among older adults. Fourteen randomized, controlled studies were analyzed, indicating that medication review as a stand-alone intervention reduced fall-related injuries by 6%. Environmental modifications have also proven to be highly effective in fall prevention. Cost-effectiveness modeling suggests that investing AUD$244 per person (as of 2010) in a home modification program can reduce the risk of falls by 25%, specifically by addressing safety hazards such as poor lighting and tripping hazards [3]. Additionally, a systematic review included 43 studies, with 23 in the meta-analyses, examining the impact of education and training on fall risk reduction among the elderly. This intervention demonstrated a significant reduction in fall rates and the odds of falling, as reported by [37]. A summary of these studies is illustrated in Fig. 3.4.

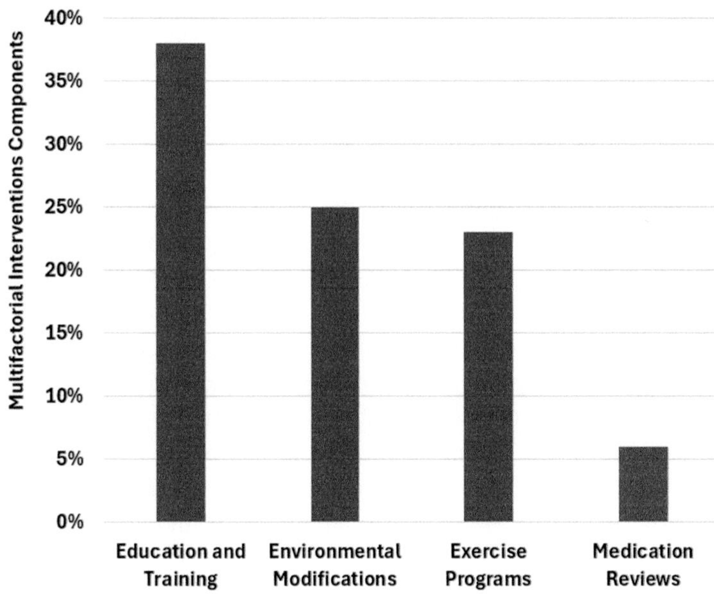

Figure 3.4 Distribution of multifactorial interventions components for fall prevention; based on [3, 35–37]

Figure 3.5 illustrates the effectiveness of key multifactorial interventions in reducing fall rates among older adults, comparing data from before and after the intervention. The graph demonstrates significant reductions in fall incidents, with fall-related injuries decreasing by 10% [38], hospital admissions due to falls by 15% [39], and medical attention required due to falls by 16%

[40]. Additionally, there is a notable improvement of 20% in the health-related quality of life of older adults following these interventions [38]. In conclusion, the graph shows that multifactorial interventions are highly effective in mitigating fall risks and improving overall health outcomes for older adults.

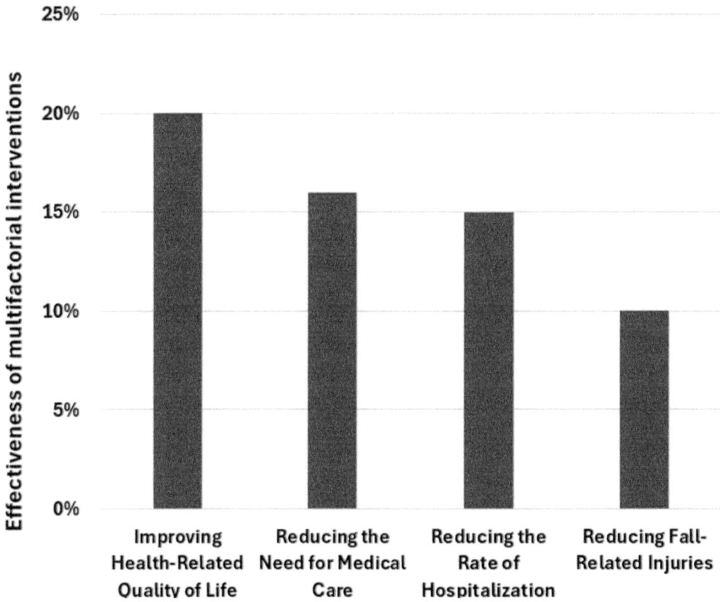

Figure 3.5 Effectiveness of multifactorial interventions among older adults by comparing various parameters; based on [38–40].

3.4 AI Applications in Fall Prevention

AI applications in fall prevention are revolutionizing the way the safety and well-being of older adults can be achieved. By leveraging advanced algorithms and ML, AI can analyze vast amounts of data from wearable sensors to detect patterns and anomalies in movement that may indicate a fall risk [41]. Chauhan et al. [42] investigated multiple AI algorithms for fall prediction, discovering that XG-Boost achieved the highest accuracy at 94.5%, successfully identifying almost all fall instances. Conversely, the random forest algorithm had the lowest accuracy, at 86.9%. Data from studies like this can be provided to AI applications through accelerometers and gyroscopes in wearable devices. These applications can then continuously monitor an individual's balance and gait, providing real-time alerts to caregivers when a potential fall is detected. This proactive approach allows for timely interventions, significantly reducing the likelihood of falls.

One notable application of AI in fall prevention is the use of predictive analytics. By analyzing historical data, AI models can identify individuals at high risk of falling and suggest personalized fall prevention plans. For example, a study conducted at El Camino Hospital in California showed a 39% reduction in hospital fall rates over six months by using predictive analytics to monitor high-risk patients [43]. This demonstrates the potential of AI to not only prevent falls but also to improve overall health outcomes for older adults.

Virtual reality (VR) technology is another innovative AI application in fall prevention. VR can simulate real-world environments and situations, allowing seniors to practice their balance and mobility in a safe and controlled setting. This helps build confidence and reduce the risk of falls in everyday life. Inspir Carnegie Hill, a senior living community, implemented a pilot program using VR technology and saw promising results in reducing fall incidents among residents [44].

AI-driven solutions also extend to smart home technologies, which can create safer living environments for older adults. For example, Microsoft Kinect sensors placed around retirement residences can log residents' baseline gait speed and stride length, alerting staff if these variables decrease, indicating a higher risk of falling. This integration of AI into home environments enhances the ability to monitor and respond to fall risks effectively [45].

Image-based detection frameworks have shown immense potential in managing fall-related risks among the elderly, enabling timely medical interventions to mitigate injury severity. Umer et al. [46] proposed an optimized NASNet model integrated with Local Binary Patterns to enhance adaptability under varying lighting conditions. This innovative approach achieved a remarkable accuracy of 99.69%, surpassing benchmarks such as 99.20% from earlier methodologies, 98.80% by YOLOv7, and 98.50%

by DenseNet [46]. Polynomial classification models performed significantly lower, with an accuracy of 92.30%. The integration of LBP not only simplified computational requirements during training but also significantly improved model performance across various deep learning paradigms [46]. However, the reliance on image-based data is limited by environmental factors such as lighting variations and obstacles, which may hinder classification accuracy. To address these limitations, the authors advocate incorporating sensor-based data such as accelerometers, gyroscopes, and inertial measurement units, alongside vision-based approaches to enhance reliability and fidelity in FDSs. This advancement underscores the crucial role of combining AI-driven technologies to ensure effective fall prevention for the elderly.

In conclusion, AI applications in fall prevention offer a multifaceted approach to enhancing the safety and quality of life for older adults. By combining wearable sensors, predictive analytics, VR technology, and smart home solutions, AI provides a comprehensive strategy to mitigate fall risks and improve overall well-being. As the global population ages, the importance of these innovative technologies in fall prevention cannot be overstated.

3.5 Conclusion

Falls among older adults are a significant public health concern, necessitating comprehensive strategies to effectively mitigate this risk. Through the identification and assessment of fall risk factors, it was discussed that both intrinsic and extrinsic factors contribute to the likelihood of falls. Addressing these factors requires a multifaceted approach that includes detailed assessments, personalized intervention plans, and ongoing monitoring to ensure efficacy. It has been discussed that the likelihood of recurrent falls increases from 10% with a single risk factor to 69% with four or more, highlighting the importance of comprehensive risk assessments. Also, data from home assessments and modifications show significant reductions in fall risks, with effectiveness ranging from 8% to 37%, depending on methodologies and participant demographics. Furthermore, TUG tests revealed that elderly individuals with health conditions took, on average, 27.6 seconds at 0 cm obstacle height compared to 12.3 seconds for healthy counterparts, underscoring mobility challenges. The discrepancy in TUG completion times became even more pronounced as the obstacle height increased, with elderly individuals with health conditions requiring approximately 30.3 seconds at a 17 cm obstacle height compared to only 12.6 seconds for their healthier peers. These results highlight the compounded impact of health conditions on mobility and agility, particularly when faced with environmental obstacles, to enhance functional mobility and reduce fall risks in vulnerable populations.

It has been shown that multifactorial interventions are highly effective in reducing the incidence of falls among the elderly. By combining various components such as exercise programs, medication reviews, environmental modifications, and education, these interventions address the multifactorial nature of fall risk. The impact of these interventions is substantial, yet it varies across the reviewed studies, with notable outcomes such as a 10% reduction in fall-related injuries, a 15% decrease in hospital admissions due to falls, and a 20% enhancement in health-related quality of life. This variability highlights the importance of customizing approaches to maximize their effectiveness across diverse settings and demographics.

The integration of AI applications in fall prevention represents a promising advancement in this field. It has been demonstrated that AI-powered predictive analytics, wearable sensors, VR technology, and smart home solutions can provide methods for identifying high-risk individuals and implementing timely interventions. The substantial improvements in fall rates, health-related quality of life, and overall satisfaction among older adults showed the potential of AI to revolutionize fall prevention strategies.

In summary, a combination of thorough risk factor assessment, multifactorial interventions, and cutting-edge AI applications can provide a comprehensive and effective approach to preventing falls among older adults. By addressing the diverse and complex factors contributing to falls, these strategies not only reduce fall incidents but also enhance the overall quality of life for older adults, ensuring their safety, independence, and well-being. Despite these advancements, there remains a need for greater accessibility and equity in the implementation of these strategies. Further research is essential to refine AI technologies to ensure that they are user-friendly, cost-effective, and adaptable to diverse populations. Collaborative efforts between healthcare providers, policymakers, and technology developers will be pivotal in scaling these solutions and addressing existing gaps in fall prevention initiatives.

References

1. S. K. Gharghan and H. A. Hashim, "A comprehensive review of elderly fall detection using wireless communication and artificial intelligence techniques," *Measurement,* vol. 226, no. 114186, pp. 1–29, 2024.
2. C. Court-Brown, N. Clement, A. Duckworth, L. Biant and M. McQueen, "The changing epidemiology of fall-related fractures in adults," *Injury,* vol. 48, no. 4, pp. 819–824, 2017.
3. S. R. Lord, C. Sherrington, H. B. Menz and J. C. T. Close, "Chapter 14: Modifying the environment to prevent falls," in *Falls in Older People,* Cambridge, Cambridge University Press, pp. 300–310, 2010.
4. B. F. Olij, V. Erasmus, J. I. Kuiper, F. V. Zoest, E. F. V. Beeck and S. Polinder, "Falls prevention activities among community-dwelling elderly in the Netherlands: A Delphi study," *Injury,* vol. 48, no. 9, pp. 2017–2021, 2017.
5. M. Dong, X. Liu, Y. Choi and N. Li, "Effects of Otago Exercise Program and aquatic exercise on fall risk in older adults: A systematic review," *Archives of Gerontology and Geriatrics,* vol. 132, no. 105799, pp. 1–11, 2025.
6. G. Bergen, M. R. Stevens, R. Kakara and E. R. Burns, "Understanding modifiable and unmodifiable older adult fall risk factors to create effective prevention strategies," *American Journal of Lifestyle Medicine,* vol. 16, no. 5, pp. 580–589, 2021.
7. T. Z.-T. Ting and D. S.-K. Ting, "A balancing act: Falling versus aging," *Discover Medicine,* vol. 1, no. 155, pp. 1–11, 2024.

8. J. Kim, E. Lee and S. Lee, "Multilevel factors influencing falls of older patients in hospital: The risk of hospital-induced delirium and the impact of nurse staffing," *Geriatric Nursing,* vol. 61, pp. 13–19, 2025.
9. S. Kulkarni and A. Nagarkar, "Effect of a video-assisted fall prevention program on fall incidence in community-dwelling older adults during COVID," *Geriatric Nursing,* vol. 50, pp. 31–37, 2023.
10. B. Can, A. Tufan, S. Karadag, N. S. Durmus, M. Topcu, Berrin Aysevinc, Songul Cecen Duzel, S. Dagcıoglu, N. A. Fak, G. Tazegul and A. S. Fak, "The effectiveness of a fall detection device in older nursing home residents: A pilot study," *Psychogeriatrics,* vol. 24, no. 4, pp. 822–829, 2024.
11. D. Aldailami, J. E. Banta, K. J. McCleary, R. Mataya, M. M. Ramadan, R. Chinnock and M. S. Suprono, "Predictors of fall-related injuries due to common consumer products among elderly adult emergency department visits in the United States during 2007–2017," *International Journal of Injury Control and Safety Promotion,* vol. 29, no. 2, pp. 186–192, 2022.
12. K. A. Nickerson, K. Diaz and B. C. Muir, "Circumstances of falls among older adult walker users in long-term care and the associated walker design deficits," *Assistive Technology,* vol. 36, no. 3, pp. 248–253, 2024.
13. M. B. Snyder, T. Zanotto, E. Potts and J. J. Sosnoff, "Characteristics and consequences of falls in people who use wheelchairs in long-term care settings," *Journal of the American Medical Directors Association,* vol. 25, no. 5, pp. 796–801, 2024.
14. P. Nowakowski and B. Gronostajska, "Designing movement space for elderly and disabled people in the construction law in selected countries," *Medycyna Pracy,* vol. 75, no. 3, pp. 189–197.
15. M. Schmucker, A. Küpper, C. Mahler and A. Elsbernd, "The usability of rollators as part of the human-centred quality of mobility devices: A systematic narrative literature review," *Disability and Rehabilitation: Assistive Technology,* vol. 20, no. 2, pp. 268–285, 2025.
16. Y. Shi, E. Bennion, C. Ward and L. D. Nolen, "Circumstances of unintentional fall-related adult deaths: Utah, 2010–2020," *Injury Prevention,* vol. 30, pp. 277–282, 2023.
17. A. Drahota, L. M. Felix, J. Raftery, B. E. Keenan, C. C. Lachance, D. C. Mackey, C. Markham and A. C. Laing, "The SAFEST review: A mixed methods systematic review of shock-absorbing flooring for fall-related injury prevention," *BMC Geriatrics,* vol. 22, no. 1, pp. 32–38, 2022.

18. M. Montero-Odasso, N. van der Velde, F. C. Martin, M. Petrovic and et al., "World guidelines for falls prevention and management for older adults: A global initiative," *Age and ageing,* vol. 51, no. 9, pp. 1–36, 2022.

19. C. T. P. Camara, S. M. S. Ferreira de Freitas, C. A. Lima, C. F. Amorim, J. M. Prado-Rico and M. R. Perracini, "The walking cane length influences the postural sway of community-dwelling older women," *Physiotherapy Research International,* vol. 25, no. 1, pp. e1804, 2020.

20. M. Ebrahimi, R. Carriveau, D. S.-K. Ting and A. McGillis, "Conventional and advanced exergy analysis of a grid connected underwater compressed air energy storage facility," *Applied Energy,* vol. 242, pp. 1198–12089, 201.

21. H. A. Jindal, M. Duggal, L. Jamir, D. Sharma, A. Kankaria, L. Rohilla, A. Avasthi, R. Nehra and S. Grover, "Mental health and environmental factors associated with falls in the elderly in North India: A naturalistic community study," *Asian Journal of Psychiatry,* vol. 39, pp. 17–21, 2019.

22. R. Cerqueira, J. Pereira, N. F. Ribeiro and C. P. Santos, "Engineering a safer future: Electronic design and validation of a cane-type robot for fall prevention," in *IEEE International Conference on Autonomous Robot Systems and Competitions (ICARSC),* Tomar, Portugal, 2023.

23. M. Nouredanesh, A. Godfrey, J. Howcroft, E. D. Lemaire and J. Tung, "Fall risk assessment in the wild: A critical examination of wearable sensor use in free-living conditions," *Gait & Posture,* vol. 85, pp. 178–190, 2021.

24. J. Kou, X. Xu, X. Ni, S. Ma and L. Guo, "Fall-risk assessment of aged workers using wearable inertial measurement units based on machine learning," *Safety Science,* vol. 176, no. 106551, pp. 1–14, 2024.

25. A. N. atel, R. Murugan, P. K. R. Maddikunta, G. Yenduri, R. H. Jhaveri, Y. Zhu and T. R. Gadekallu, "AI-powered trustable and explainable fall detection system using transfer learning," *Image and Vision Computing,* vol. 149, no. 105164, pp. 3–19, 2024.

26. N. Lundebjerg, "Guideline for the prevention of falls in older persons," *American Geriatrics Society,* vol. 49, no. 5, pp. 664–672, 2001.

27. L. Day, B. Fildes, I. Gordon, M. Fitzharris, H. Flamer and S. Lord, "Randomised factorial trial of falls prevention among older people living in their own homes," *The British Medical Journal,* vol. 325, no. 7356, pp. 128–131, 2002.

28. V. Pardessus, F. Puisieux, C. Di Pompeo, C. Gaudefroy, A. Thevenon and P. Dewailly, "Benefits of home visits for falls and autonomy in

the elderly: A randomized trial study," *American Journal of Physical Medicine & Rehabilitation,* vol. 81, no. 4, pp. 247–252, 2002.

29. R. G. Cumming, M. Thomas, G. Szonyi, G. Salkeld, E. O'Neill, C. Westbury and G. Frampton, "Home visits by an occupational therapist for assessment and modification of environmental hazards: A randomized trial of falls prevention," *Journal of the American Geriatrics Society,* vol. 47, no. 12, pp. 1397–1402, 1999.
30. T. Nikolaus and M. Bach, "Preventing falls in community-dwelling frail older people using a home intervention team (HIT): Results from the randomized Falls-HIT trial," *Journal of the American Geriatrics Society,* vol. 51, no. 3, pp. 300–305, 2003.
31. M. E. Tinetti, M. Speechley and S. F. Ginter, "Risk factors for falls among elderly persons living in the community," *The New England Journal of Medicine,* vol. 19, no. 26, pp. 1701–1707, 1988.
32. M. C. Nevitt, S. R. Cummings, S. Kidd and D. Black, "Risk factors for recurrent nonsyncopal falls: A prospective study," *The Journal of the American Medical Association,* vol. 261, no. 18, pp. 2663–2668, 1988.
33. S. S. Ng, M. M. Tse, P. Chen, C. K. Chan, E. H. Cheng, K. K. Iu, T. W. Wong and T.-W. Liu, "Reliability, concurrent validity, and minimal detectable change of timed up and go obstacle test in people with stroke," *Archives of Physical Medicine and Rehabilitation,* vol. 104, no. 9, pp. 1465–1473, 2023.
34. S. Hopewell, B. Copsey, P. Nicolson, B. Adedire, G. Boniface and S. Lamb, "Multifactorial interventions for preventing falls in older people living in the community: A systematic review and meta-analysis of 41 trials and almost 20 000 participants," *British Journal of Sports Medicine,* vol. 54, no. 22, pp. 1340–1349, 2018.
35. C. Sherrington, N. Fairhall, W. Kwok, G. Wallbank, A. Tiedemann, Z. A. Michaleff, C. A. C. M. Ng and A. Bauman, "Evidence on physical activity and falls prevention for people aged 65+ years: Systematic review to inform the WHO guidelines on physical activity and sedentary behaviour," *International Journal of Behavioral Nutrition and Physical Activity,* vol. 17, no. 144, pp. 1–9, 2020.
36. Y. Ming, A. Zecevic, S. Hunter, W. Miao and R. Tirona, "Medication review in preventing fall-related injuries in older adults: A systematic review and meta-analysis," *Innovation in Aging,* vol. 2, no. 1, pp. 982–985, 2018.
37. M. Morris, K. Webster, C. Jones, A.-M. Hill, T. Haines, S. McPhail, D. Kiegaldie, S. Slade, D. Jazayeri, H. Heng, R. Shorr, L. Carey, A. Barker and I. Cameron, "Interventions to reduce falls in hospitals: A systematic

review and meta-analysis," *Age and Ageing,* vol. 51, no. 5, pp. 1–12, 2022.

38. S. Gates, J. D. Fisher, M. W. Cooke, Y. H. Carter and S. E. Lamb, "Multifactorial assessment and targeted intervention for preventing falls and injuries among older people in community and emergency care settings: Systematic review and meta-analysis," *British Medical Journal,* vol. 336, no. 7636, pp. 130–133, 2008.
39. J. Suen, D. Kneale, K. Sutcliffe, W. Kwok, I. D. Cameron, M. Crotty, C. Sherrington and S. Dyer, "Critical features of multifactorial interventions for effective falls reduction in residential aged care: A systematic review, intervention component analysis and qualitative comparative analysis," *Age and Ageing,* vol. 52, no. 11, pp. 1–11, 2023.
40. Y. You, H. Zheng, X. Lei, H. Zhou, L. Huang, Y. Zhang, Z. Xie and Q. He, "Development of a falls risk assessment scale for middle-aged and elderly patients with cardiovascular diseases in Chinese community based on AutoScore: A CHARLS study," *Public Health,* vol. 240, pp. 167–173, 2025.
41. M. Ebrahimi, D. S.-K. Ting, R. Carriveau, A. McGillis and D. Young, "Optimization of a cavern-based compressed air energy storage facility with an efficient adaptive genetic algorithm," *Energy Storage,* vol. 2, no. 6, pp. 1–12, 2020.
42. R. Chauhan, A. Satyam, E. Yafi and M. F. Zuhairi, "Predict the elderly fall using IoT and AI technology," in *AI Applications in Cyber Security and Communication Networks*, Singapore, 2024.
43. El Camino Hospital, "Transforming traditional models of fall prevention through the power of prescriptive analytics," 2015. [Online]. Available: https://www.elcaminohealth.org/newsroom/transforming-traditional-models-fall-prevention-through-power-prescriptive-analytics?form=MG0AV3. [Accessed 03 01 2025].
44. Inspir Senior Living Team, "Artificial intelligence breaks new boundaries in senior fall prevention," 2023. [Online]. Available: https://inspirseniorliving.com/senior-living-resources/Artificial-Intelligence-Breaks-New-Boundaries-in-Senior-Fall-Prevention?form=MG0AV3. [Accessed 03 01 2025].
45. L. J. Phillips, C. B. DeRoche, M. Rantz, G. L. Alexander, M. Skubic, L. Despins, C. Abbott, B. H. Harris, C. Galambos and R. J. Koopman, "Using embedded sensors in independent living to predict gait changes and falls," *Western Journal of Nursing Research,* vol. 39, no. 1, pp. 78–94, 2016.

46. M. Umer, A. A. Alarfaj, E. A. Alabdulqader, S. Alsubai, L. Cascone and F. Narducci, "Enhancing fall prediction in the elderly people using LBP features and transfer learning model," *Image and Vision Computing,* vol. 145, no. 104992, pp. 1–19, 2024.

Chapter 4

Healthcare Digital Twin: Transformative Perspectives in Socio-Technical Systems

Joshit Mohanty,[a] Vaishali,[b] and Sujatha Alla[a]

[a]*Engineering Management and Systems Engineering, Old Dominion University, Norfolk, Virginia, USA*
[b]*Biomedical Sciences, Old Dominion University, Norfolk, Virginia, USA*

jmoha003@odu.edu

This chapter delves into the transformative potential of Digital Twin (DT) technology in healthcare, highlighting how it bridges physical systems and virtual models to enable real-time monitoring, simulation, and predictive analytics. While DTs have garnered success in well-defined industrial domains, their application to broader socio-technical systems—particularly healthcare—introduces added layers of complexity. These issues arise from the fragmented or incomplete digitization of health records, dynamic governance structures, cultural and linguistic diversity, and the emotional sensitivity inherent in medical data. The chapter sets the stage for an exploration of key challenges in healthcare contexts, such as data integration, privacy, security, and equitable resource allocation. Emphasis is placed on the crucial role of

Environmentalism in Healthcare: Caring for Tomorrow Ecologically
Edited by Jacqueline A. Stagner and David S.-K. Ting

ISBN 978-981-5129-95-3 (Hardcover), 978-1-003-74869-4 (eBook)
www.jennystanford.com

DOI: 10.1201/9781003748694-4

trustworthiness and accountability. It demands interdisciplinary collaboration to establish that DTs can be catalysts for inclusive, adaptive, and ethically guided healthcare systems.

4.1 Introduction

We are living in a world where digital integration into our lives has become indispensable. Technologies like smartphones and the internet have altered the basic needs of human existence. This necessitates a tight integration of the physical world with the virtual space. In this process, DT technology has emerged as a cornerstone of modern innovation, offering a transformative approach to act as the unifying bridge. DTs are a dynamic, virtual representation of a physical system, object, or process continuously updated through real-time data exchanges (Mohanty & Vaishali, 2025; Thelen et al., 2022a, 2022b). It enables real-time monitoring, predictive analytics, and simulation, providing better insights and predictive capabilities. As societies and organizations evolve, DTs redefine how we design, operate, and optimize systems. Beyond technical setups, their significance lies in their adaptability across various fields, including healthcare, urban development, governance, and others. In healthcare, DTs of human organs can enable personalized treatments and advanced surgical simulations. In urban planning, DTs of cities simulate traffic flow, optimize energy consumption, and enhance sustainability. These applications illustrate their potential to address complex challenges such as efficiency, accessibility, and equity. DTs are not entirely new; their roots lie in creating replicas to better understand and manage systems (V. Singh & Willcox, 2018; Thelen et al., 2022a). Recent advancements in enabling technologies, such as the Internet of Things (IoT), artificial intelligence (AI), and big data analytics, have transformed this concept into a practical and scalable solution. Today, DTs are at the forefront of digital transformation, fostering innovation, operational efficiency, and resilience in the face of evolving global challenges.

Unlike conventional literature on DT, which often delves into its core technological aspect, this chapter takes the path less explored. Initially, it does provide a foundation for its origins, theoretical underpinnings, and practical applications. However, the primary purpose of this chapter is to discuss different wrappers of DTs and their implications for advancing sustainable societies. The discussion is organized into four key sections: an exploration of the historical and technological background of DTs, the possibility in healthcare, challenges beyond complexity, and a fuzzy bridge.

4.2 History

The foundational idea of a "twin" dates to pre-digital times. Before digital computing, physical replicas were used to simulate and understand systems. The National Aeronautics and Space Administration's (NASA) Apollo program in the 1960s utilized physical replicas of spacecraft to simulate conditions and solve real-world problems (Zhang et al., 2024). These replicas were integral to mission success, especially during critical scenarios such as the Apollo 13 mission, where simulations on Earth-based physical twins helped engineers solve the oxygen tank explosion in space (Mohanty, 2020; Mohanty & Ivanov, 2020). Although these physical replicas were not digital, they introduced the core philosophy of mirroring a system [product/service] to understand and manage its behavior. This approach would later inspire the transition from physical analog twins to digital counterparts as technology advanced.

The formalization of the term "Digital Twin" is attributed to Dr. Michael Grieves, who introduced the concept in 2003 during his lectures at the University of Michigan (Thelen et al., 2022a). Grieves envisioned a digital counterpart of a physical product that could exist throughout its lifecycle, enabling seamless data integration across design, manufacturing, and operational phases. Grieves' original framework outlined three key components:

- *Physical Entity*: The real-world product/service.
- *Virtual Representation*: A computational model that mirrors the physical entity.

- *Connection*: The communication and data exchange between the physical and digital entities.

A system undergoes several transitions during the entire lifecycle, from design to operationalization to retirement. The intent of his proposed DT was to have consistent data flow across the lifecycle adherent to accepted standards (Thelen et al., 2022b). This framework remains the foundation of DT today, though the concept has since evolved and expanded to encompass broader applications across industries. After Dr. Grieves's lecture series, the concept of DTs began to gain traction as technological advancements made integrating physical and digital counterparts more feasible (Boschert & Rosen, 2016). During the dotcom bubble of the 2010s, IoT sensors became integral to capturing the physical state of systems, providing a continuous influx of data. These advancements enabled industries such as manufacturing and aerospace to implement early versions of DTs for monitoring and predictive maintenance (van Dinter et al., 2022). Further, developments in computational modeling and simulations, such as finite element analysis (FEA) and computational fluid dynamics (CFD), have enabled physics-guided modeling. These tools helped engineers to simulate real-world scenarios under controlled environments (Boschert & Rosen, 2016). In 2010, NASA formally adopted the concept of DT in its Model-Based Systems Engineering (MBSE) efforts to simulate spacecraft performance and ensure mission success (Grieves & Vickers, 2017). NASA's "Digital Twin Prototyping Project" became the industry benchmark (Glaessgen & Stargel, 2012). This was adopted into the mainstream industry settings by companies like Siemens and General Electric (GE). During the late 2010s, the industrial focus shifted to automation, interconnectivity, and data-driven decision-making (Ferré-Bigorra et al., 2022). Siemens and GE integrated DT predicates into their manufacturing processes to enhance product quality, reduce downtime, and streamline operations. Siemens utilized DTs in their Digital Enterprise Suite. Similarly, GE's Predix platform incorporated DTs for predictive maintenance (Wang et al., 2021). On a shift from conventional industrial engineering settings, countries like Singapore used the concept of DTs for smart city planning and sustaining the needs of their societies (ABI Research, 2021), marking a first-of-its-kind use case of DT for social engineering. Since then, several milestones have highlighted the rapid acceptance and adoption of DT technology (Oppermann et al., 2023; Rosen et al., 2015):

- *2017*: Gartner listed DTs among the Top 10 Strategic Technology Trends.
- *2018*: The DT Consortium was established to standardize and promote DT technologies.
- *2020s*: The COVID-19 pandemic accelerated the adoption of DTs in industries such as healthcare and supply chains.

4.3 A Possibility in Healthcare

The coin of DT soon faced its dual sides. While academia has focused on expanding the theoretical foundation, industry has been instrumental in operationalizing the concept for practical use. Dr. Grieves's perspective prevailed in academia, emphasizing lifecycle management (Bonney et al., 2023; Kritzinger et al., 2018). VanDerHorn and Mahadevan advanced this perspective by stating DTs as "virtual representations of physical systems updated through the exchange of information," underscoring their real-time synchronization and predictive analytics capacity (Sharma et al., 2022). This expanded the scope of DTs to real-time data synchronization, guiding industries to accommodate bi-directional information flow. Although this was intended for industrial settings, Singapore's case study presents a different avenue. This chapter explores the extension of DT implications through the lens of socio-technical setups like Singapore's case study.

4.3.1 Imagine – All You Do

A society where digital interactions are fundamental and bi-directional, in essence, predictive yet uncertain. Uncertainty is what makes humans and society different from human-designed systems. However, the predictive capability of DT is that bridge that "might" connect these two realms to an extent. This chapter "imagines" a unified socio-digital community renowned for its commitment to diversity, opportunity, and inclusion (J. P. Morgan Asset Management, 2025). Recent studies present that DTs can be used to identify disparities in healthcare access, facilitate participatory urban planning, and model the societal impact of policies (Ferré-Bigorra et al., 2022; Grieves & Vickers, 2017; Negri & Abdel-Aty, 2023). Siemens describes DTs as "precise virtual models," and GE refers to them as "digital doppelgängers" of industrial equipment, focusing on performance metrics such as cost reduction and return on investment (ROI) (Thelen et al., 2022b). In a similar fashion, for a society, the most crucial component or equipment is its population. The attributes of the population are situational, unlike the designed piece of machinery. Thus, the true ROI for a society is understanding the attributes of its population. A society is imagined by what constitutes its population, the diversity of that population, and the relative behavior of its members. This implies that the indicators of their attributes may include ethics, data management, and scalability (Alla et al., 2025). Although there can be others, these attributes are generalizable across all spheres. One such sphere of attention in this chapter is equitable healthcare within society (Dhar et al., 2022). Academic studies on the scalability and adaptability of DTs show that while designed industrial setups can have some control elements, societal aspects are genuinely dynamic and uncertain (Li et al., 2022). This poses a challenge in implementing emerging technologies like DT in unpredictable sectors like healthcare (Alla, 2024). Unlike standalone software, a DT integrates real-time physical data, advanced simulations, and machine learning (ML) algorithms to mimic society's dynamic, interactive, and evolving virtual counterpart. This dynamic interaction enables (Aivaliotis et al., 2019; Lehtola et al., 2022):

- *Instant Feedback Loops*: DTs immediately reflect changes in the physical society.
- *Bidirectional Communication*: DT can influence social policies and governing rules through predictive analytics and prescriptive actions.

- *Futuring design space*: Simulate different design scenarios to optimize social setups before operationalizing policies and regulations.

Twinning in the case of healthcare DT will involve major reformations to technology adoption in healthcare (D'Amico et al., 2022). There are multiple facets of twinning in healthcare, such as drug development, illness research, and others. However, this chapter takes a socio-political-technical approach to address diversity and equitable healthcare using DT. The parameters discussed above highlight a particular challenge: rapid reflection of DT actions over its physical counterpart, i.e., healthcare setups in society. Procuring healthcare data and diversity distribution is more straightforward than the counter information-action flow. This is because data insights can, at best, be applied to decision-making, while practical implementation is subject to the acceptance of those decisions by diverse social settings. Hence, enabling equitable healthcare through DT is easier to virtualize than phenomenalizing (borrowed from "phenomenon").

4.3.2 One-Way Twinning

The "subjective" ease of healthcare data procurement regarding equitable access and resource allocation. This can be analyzed by generating an understanding of patients' electronic healthcare records (EHR), local and federal government policies, private medical provider concentration, geographical-economic distribution, and census data. EHR data may reveal a patient's historical data, operating parameters, environmental conditions, and supplementary information such as insurance details. This layer of DT focuses on a patient's spatial and temporal aspects. The data acquisition-cum-analysis layer acts as a bridge between the society-cum-patient physical being and the virtual counterpart. It gathers real-time data from the patient and EHR through sensors, IoT devices, and data streams (Grieves & Vickers, 2017). Parameters, such as temperature, heart rate, and pulse rate, synchronize the patient's active status. Protocols such as MQTT and OPC-UA enable seamless data transmission to the virtual servers

(Alla et al., 2025). Local edge servers may process raw data locally to reduce latency before transmitting it to the central system. These local servers may exist in a healthcare service provider facility to enable access to EHR or a government center to allow access to the socio-economic distribution of the population in relation to healthcare accessibility. Once such data types are procured, a virtual counterpart can be modeled and varied to analyze different "possibilistic" scenarios. In this aspect, the virtual model mirrors the patient or society as a "whole" created using computational models and simulations (Ferré-Bigorra et al., 2022). It can incorporate a physics-based model to dynamically model population movement and economic shifts in the case of a pandemic such as COVID-19. ML models, including data frameworks, predict patient healthcare status in short waves. Such scenarios may or may not directly relate to a patient's healthcare but rather to society as a "whole." The next step is stitching the procured data. The integration layer ensures seamless communication and data exchange between different components, specifically EHR or government data records (Landini et al., 2023). Such a communication channel is facilitated by two interwoven layers, namely, middleware and APIs. Middleware acts as the communication hub, linking sensors, IoT devices, cloud systems, and analytics platforms, while APIs facilitate the integration of the collected data with third-party software and tools. Once a patient's EHR data is analyzed or geographic-based socio-economic data is patterned, AI can step in to generate a story based on pattern recognition. In doing so, DTs rely heavily on analytics and AI to process data, generate insights, and enable decision-making (Shi et al., 2022). This is framed in three steps, namely,

- *Predictive Analytics*: Identifying potential failures or inefficiencies before they occur.
- *Prescriptive Analytics*: Recommending actions to optimize operations.
- *Simulation Engines*: Testing hypothetical scenarios to evaluate different strategies.

These enable users/stakeholders to visualize the "if-else" conditions related to societal patterns in relation to healthcare distribution, such as the number of pharmacy stores or the average distance from a residential community to a healthcare facility. The user interface thus allows stakeholders to interact with the DT and implement recommendations (Oppermann et al., 2023).

4.4 Challenges Beyond Complexity

DT implementations within industrial and organizational settings have enjoyed considerable success, particularly where system boundaries are well-defined and data collection can be systematized at scale. In contrast, implementing DTs in broader societal contexts like healthcare faces complex situations. Societies are inherently fluid, characterized by rapidly shifting demographics and governance structures that evolve according to political and administrative changes. Sections 4.1 and 4.2 introduced DTs by highlighting their conceptual foundations, historical background, and their growing influence across diverse applications like healthcare. This section shifts the focus to the practical challenges of transposing these established DT principles.

Any discussion of DT adoption for healthcare must first acknowledge that healthcare data is notoriously incomplete, fragmented, and governed by disparate rules across regions. While advanced societies have digitized many aspects of patient records and governmental policymaking, a large portion of the global population still exists outside these digitized networks. The potential for bridging these gaps through technologies like optical character recognition (OCR) often collides with operational, infrastructural, and ethical hurdles (Mullankandy et al., 2025). Further complicating this scenario is the sheer diversity present in countries such as India, or indeed any populous democracy, where different languages, literacy rates, and sociocultural norms amplify the challenges of ensuring equitable healthcare distribution. Moreover, the recurring changes in governance structures and agendas in democracies introduce a layer of fluidity. DT systems that were meticulously configured under one administrative priority might find themselves less relevant or even in conflict with the subsequent administration's policy objectives (Chan & Xiang, 2022; Macy & Willer, 2002). An inclusive, accurate, and continually evolving DT collides here with these social, political, and infrastructural constraints. While these problems appear daunting, acknowledging them is an essential step toward forging pathways to more resilient, socially aware DT solutions.

4.4.1 Healthcare Data – Too Much Yet Too Little

One of the foundational principles of a DT is the continuous data stream from the physical environment to its virtual mirror. Standardized sensors and integrated IoT frameworks often generate this data in industrial settings. However, societal contexts involve collecting data from vast repositories of patient records, governmental databases, policy reports, and other scattered sources (Elmaraghy et al., 2012; Endsley & Jones, 2012). A significant portion of these resources has not been digitized. Paper-based healthcare records remain prevalent, particularly in regions lacking robust digital infrastructures. Policy documents, administrative directives, and statistical reports may also exist in hardcopy formats or in electronic forms that are not machine-readable (Mullankandy et al., 2025). Adopting OCR technology to convert paper documents into digital text might be a straight-forward response to this challenge. While conceptually simple, the practical use of OCR in large-scale digitization of healthcare data encounters multiple obstacles. First, OCR engines must handle handwriting styles that vary immensely across cultures, linguistic regions, and generations. The complexity escalates when dealing with multilingual societies, where official documents may be recorded in multiple scripts (Khallouli et al., 2022). In India, healthcare records are available in multiple languages, including Hindi, English, Tamil, Bengali, and others, often intermixed within a single patient file. An OCR system may excel in one language or script yet perform poorly in another. The accuracy declines further when encountering poor print quality, outdated medical forms, or notes hastily scribbled by healthcare providers in semi-formal contexts (Sadri et al., 2022).

Moreover, the concept of "model hallucinations," which typically references large language models that generate incorrect or fabricated outputs, becomes relevant in the realm of OCR when the algorithm misreads handwriting or conflates partial glyphs (e.g., from smudges) into erroneous text (Mohanty, Nayak, et al., 2025; Mohanty, Vaishali, et al., 2025). Adding additional layers of ML to clean up OCR'd text can help mitigate some of these issues. Still, each step introduces more complexity, computational overhead, and the potential for further error propagation. The cost and logistical complexity of conducting mass OCR digitization efforts are currently far from achievable. Any extensive project to scan and digitize healthcare records or large-scale governmental archives requires significant financial resources, well-trained personnel, and robust project management (Alla et al., 2017). The absence of consistent data standards across different hospitals, clinics, or government departments further complicates these efforts, rendering the concept of a seamless DT far more challenging than in a factory-floor environment where data originates from dictated sensor arrays. When speaking of real-time or near-real-time data integration in a DT, reliance on post-scanned documents is already at a disadvantage. OCR digitization is typically a retrospective process, capturing what has been written rather than continuously streaming data. While the retrospective data is valuable for historical analytics, operational real-time applications such as pandemic monitoring or immediate resource allocation in an emergency require up-to-date streams that are notoriously difficult to obtain through scanning.

4.4.2 Elusive Quest

One of the more ambitious aspirations of employing DTs in society is the notion that a well-designed, data-driven mirror of the population could reveal systemic inequities, allowing stakeholders to address them proactively. Section 4.3 briefly mentioned how a DT could map disparities in healthcare access, highlight resource deficiencies, and propose remedial actions. However, the foundation for such equitable outcomes depends on a society's ability to accurately measure, interpret, and respond to social demographics. Many societies, especially large and diverse ones, lack the stable or uniform population distribution necessary for an "optimal" alignment of resources.

Consider the scenario where a rural region has historically been underinvested, resulting in poor hospital infrastructure and minimal clinical data collection. A DT aiming to represent that community comprehensively finds itself starved of credible data. The absence of robust cell-tower coverage and internet services in these regions might mean "chokepoints" for an equitable model that cannot accurately reflect the actual conditions for these communities, potentially leading to misguided or incomplete policy recommendations. This problem is often exacerbated in countries such as India, where the sheer scale and diversity of its population, spanning rural, semi-urban, and urban domains, means that no single data collection approach can uniformly capture the variability in healthcare needs. A region's medical concerns may be overshadowed by more prominent issues of a different region when the aggregated data is viewed nationally (micro vs macro view). Moreover, the concept of "equitable distribution" itself becomes contentious. Different stakeholders may propose competing definitions of equity: Is it about equal per-capita resource allocation or about need-based distribution skewed towards historically marginalized areas? These philosophical differences in how equity is defined and operationalized can significantly impact the design and implementation of a DT, especially when it comes to modeling and simulation algorithms that underpin resource allocation. In a society where multiple languages coexist, any data-driven system that relies primarily on a single language for interfacing or record-keeping risks marginalizing large swathes of the population. Such data gaps inevitably lead to "blind spots" in the DT. Subtle differences in vernacular usage, cultural norms regarding healthcare disclosure, and local forms of alternative medicine (Ayurveda, Unani, etc.) create complexities that standard data frameworks may not capture (Conklin, 2005). The risk is that the DT inadvertently reflects an incomplete or biased representation of society, thereby recommending solutions that fail to address or even worsen existing inequities. In this scenario, there is a temptation to adopt a top-down approach where a central body. While such a strategy can effectively set overarching guidelines, local contexts matter immensely. Cultural traditions might dictate healthcare choices that deviate from what the aggregated data indicates as "optimal." People may prefer local clinics and healers, or resist specific technological interventions due to historical mistrust of government-led initiatives, or simply adhere to their cultural heritage. A DT that does not integrate these social patterns risks oversimplifying the cultural tapestry and compromising the aim of creating genuinely equitable healthcare systems.

4.4.3 Democratic Governance, Policy Shifts, and Societal Adaptability

Any technology thrives on consistency. The continuous feedback loop between a system's physical state and its virtual representation requires stable infrastructural conditions, robust data pipelines, and uniform governance frameworks for the long term (Elmaraghy et al., 2012; V. Singh & Willcox, 2018). In many democratic societies, however, governance undergoes periodic alterations in response to electoral results. A new administration might have different priorities, resources, or even fundamental ideologies about how and where public funds should be spent. When a new governing body assumes power, there can be substantial changes in healthcare policy. If a DT relies on a particular set of data-sharing regulations or standardized EHR protocols, newly instituted rules may abruptly render these assumptions invalid. A national-level push towards universal electronic medical records might be replaced by local-level governance advocating more privatized systems, or vice versa. The result is a potential fracturing or siloing of previously unified data under a single framework (Bonnema et al., 2017; Jain, 2001). Beyond formal governance, democratic societies are also marked by high levels of activism, public engagement, and socio-political awareness. Policies that appear intrusive or paternalistic can generate public pushback, especially when they involve sensitive personal data like medical histories. In extreme cases, local interest groups might lobby for legislation that restricts data sharing, effectively "cutting off" entire regions or population segments from the digital network. Such societies themselves exhibit self-adaptability in ways that are difficult to capture in a single digital model. This adaptiveness stems from governance changes and citizens' everyday actions responding to policy shifts, economic constraints, and cultural trends. DT that remains locked into the formal structures of a previous policy environment might fail to detect, let alone account for, these informal or emergent responses. As a result, the DT's recommendations for resource allocation or public health guidelines could become misaligned with the reality of the on-the-ground (Cohen et al., 2002).

Technological innovations, such as telemedicine platforms or smartphone-based diagnostic tools, further add to this dynamism. These solutions, rapidly adopted by communities, can shift the balance of how and where healthcare data is generated. From the perspective of a DT, this abrupt inflow of data collected through crowd-sourced health applications may conflict with the older, system-centric EHR data or with government-led data frameworks. Thus, in a democratic context where public sentiment, activism, and elected leadership continuously redefine the boundaries of data governance, a DT must be engineered to handle socio-technical complexities and these evolving socio-political dimensions.

4.5 A Fuzzy Bridge

The interplay between incomplete digitization, demographic complexities, and the fluidity of governance shapes a unique context for DTs. Each challenge magnifies the others, creating a butterfly effect. Overcoming these challenges requires broad-based collaboration among stakeholders: governments, healthcare providers, grassroots organizations, technology vendors, and academic researchers. Within this shifting environment, DTs may possibly remain ethically anchored and trustworthy. While trustworthiness and ethics are crucial in any technological adoption, they become especially pivotal in healthcare, where the stakes are quite literally a matter of life and death.

4.5.1 Trustworthiness in Socio-Technical DTs

Combined with the complexities introduced in Section 4.3 and 4.4, especially incomplete digitization and fluid policy environments, underscores the urgent need for a robust ethical framework that addresses socio-technical systems' moral, emotional, security, and accountability dimensions. Trustworthiness encompasses multiple layers. On one level, it requires robust technology to guard against breaches, malfunctions, and manipulations. On another level, it invites scrutiny of how data is gathered and used, specifically whether individuals and communities understand the implications of participating in a real-time, predictive system that can significantly influence resource distribution. The more profound question addresses what the DT does and how it does it, or does it largely remain a "black box"? (Asgari et al., 2024; Lepore, 2023; Pal et al., 2023) Moreover, trust also hinges on issues of ownership and accountability. In the event of an error, be it a misdiagnosis, a flawed policy recommendation, or an unintended breach, who bears responsibility, and what mechanisms exist for redress?

Healthcare DTs inevitably involve interactions with highly sensitive data like patient histories, genetic profiles, and even real-time physiological metrics. Such data, if mishandled, can lead to consequences ranging from personal embarrassment to overt discrimination in employment, insurance, or access to social services. Ethical stewardship in DT starts with the concept of informed consent. Before a patient's medical data enters a twin, the patient should be fully aware of how that data will be utilized, who will have access to it, and for what explicit purposes. This requirement seems intuitive, but it becomes complicated in real-world contexts. Data can be re-analyzed or re-combined in new ways that were unforeseen at the time of initial consent. The iterative and evolving nature of DT applications means that use cases may broaden or shift over time. An ethics-based approach must ensure continuous, dynamic consent processes that allow individuals to revisit and revise their permissions, matching the fluidities of both technology and society. On this note, the question arises: Should the DT's predictive algorithms identify a surge in potential patients in a particular locality, and how should resources be allocated? Does a purely utilitarian approach neglect marginalized pockets in the community? The principle of distributive justice suggests that the DT should be harnessed to rectify inequities rather than reinforce them (Gergen, 2011; Yezdani et al., 2015). Achieving this goal requires deliberate calibration of the twin's algorithms to pay extra attention to underrepresented or historically disadvantaged groups. With the convergence of private and public healthcare systems, large corporations might gain control over extensive health-related data sets. Without adequate governance, there is a risk that these entities prioritize profit motives over societal well-being. Proactive policies that require anonymization, data partitioning, and the prohibition of secondary data used for non-health-related commercial gains will be more integral to establishing moral accountability than ever before (Alla et al., 2018). Public sentiments are neither stagnant nor discrete stamps. They evolve with discussions around data privacy, consent, and policy integration and are framed rationally or legally. Societal divisions, especially the neglected community, frequently experience vulnerability, fear, hope, and relief, sometimes in quick succession. Introducing advanced technological interfaces like DTs can amplify these emotional experiences in unforeseen ways. A digital representation of one's medical condition or community health status might evoke a sense of reassurance for some. Still, it may also trigger anxiety or apprehension for others, especially when the analytics highlight looming health risks. This sentiment represents not merely social negligence or choice governance, but also distrust in the sentiment analysis of digitized health records (Mohanty et al., 2023; Yalim et al., 2023).

In a typical industrial DT for machinery, emotional resonance is a non-factor. An engine's performance metrics or an assembly line's throughput do not evoke concern on a personal level. However, in healthcare DTs, the emotional implications of telling patients that predictive analytics foresee a significant decline in their health can be profound. Even if the predictions or recommendations are accurate, presenting them insensitively can erode trust in the system and the broader medical community. Designers of healthcare DTs thus have a "moral and ethical" responsibility to consider user experience at an emotional level. The aggregated analytics generated by a DT might portray a grim picture for a certain neighborhood, such as high disease prevalence, limited healthcare facilities, or an economic decline that correlates with worsening public health. Local populations informed of these predictions could experience collective anxiety or, conversely, mobilize in solidarity to improve healthcare access. Researchers have noted instances where dire projections can become self-fulfilling prophecies, fueling a narrative of hopelessness, discouraging local investment or participation in health programs (Hallam & Contreras, 2018; Mohanty, Alla, et al., 2025; Rafiei et al., 2024). The emotional undercurrent underscores a broader shift in contemporary technology design that resonates with the concept of patient-centric or human-centric systems. A patient-centric DT aims to monitor, predict, reassure, empower, and support. Achieving that requires an empathetic understanding of how individuals interpret and respond to health-related data, the cultural lenses they bring, and the social pressures they navigate. Emotionally informed design parameters and communication strategies thus become crucial to healthcare DT.

4.5.2 Security and Safety

A vast part of the digital world is a ghost space, implying that data will stay forever beyond its intended use once digitized. This raises concerns about privacy, safety, and security in sensitive domains like healthcare. A single patient's privacy violation might lead to identity theft or targeted discrimination. At the same time, large-scale intrusions could compromise millions of records. The ramifications extend beyond theft or exposure of personal data; malicious actors could manipulate or corrupt the data streams, leading to erroneous predictive outcomes. A compromised DT that indicates no impending shortage of vital supplies might cause public health authorities to delay stockpiling, with dangerous or even deadly outcomes.

While the DT system ingests data from a myriad of IoT devices, hospital information systems, and community-based inputs, all of them can become potential attack vectors. This calls for end-to-end encryption, rigorous authentication procedures, and multi-factor identity checks for all entities interfacing with the twin. Yet, high security often competes with usability. Overly complex authentication can deter healthcare professionals or community workers from operating in resource-limited settings, prompting them to circumvent procedures (M. Singh et al., 2017). Safety, while closely related to security, involves the system's reliability and resilience. A safe DT is designed to prevent catastrophic failures even in the face of partial malfunctions or partial data corruption. Redundancies should be built into data pipelines to guarantee that a localized outage will not collapse the entire system. A similar scenario exists for physical servers and buildings that host the DT. This multi-layer approach is not novel, but the scale and diversity of data in a nationwide or multinational healthcare DT setting accentuate the stakes considerably. Thus, there is an urgent need to establish dialogue and implement crisis protocols in the case of a breach or system compromise. These protocols should define how and when the public, hospitals, and government agencies are alerted, as well as establish a clear escalation pathway. This transparency is crucial for preserving trust, ensuring that stakeholders do not discover a breach only after it has silently persisted for an extended period. Trust-building in DT contexts typically spans five interrelated dimensions: transparency, accountability, performance reliability, ethical alignment, and stakeholder engagement (Ganguly et al., 2023; Rahman et al., 2022).

First, transparency involves openness about the DT's algorithms, data flows, and decision-making processes. A "black box" approach, where predictive models remain inscrutable, is antithetical to a setting where personal health or communal resource allocation is at stake (Centeio Jorge et al., 2023).

Transparent systems allow external audits, publish model architectures, and adhere to recognized data standards. This openness not only reassures experts who can validate the system's integrity but also signals to citizens that their data is handled fairly and comprehensively. Accountability centers on defining who is responsible for the twin's actions or recommendations. As noted in Section 4.4, shifting governmental bodies can create blurred lines of accountability. A robust governance framework assigns definitive responsibility for data management, privacy lapses, and erroneous predictions. It also clarifies the chain of command regarding decision-making, specifically who authorizes changes to the system, who verifies new data sources, and how errors are rectified (Bhatt et al., 2019; Van Bossuyt et al., 2023). Performance reliability reflects the system's consistent ability to produce accurate and relevant predictions. While common in initial phases, DT miscalculations erode trust if not openly acknowledged and rectified. Documenting the system's successes and failures, as well as the steps taken to correct them, shapes a narrative of continuous improvement rather than unassailable perfection. This, paradoxically, tends to enhance trust by making the system's handlers appear sincere and diligent rather than secretive or defensive (Ferrario et al., 2020). Ethical alignment refers to aligning the DT's guiding principles with the community's values. Local traditions, religious practices, and cultural mores often dictate how healthcare is perceived and accessed. A system that disregards these nuances risks being deemed illegitimate or even exploitative. Finally, stakeholder engagement undergirds every preceding dimension. A continuous dialogue with patients, healthcare workers, regulators, and the broader public fosters a two-way exchange (Gebru et al., 2022; Tenhundfeld et al., 2022). The DT implementers gain insights into community concerns and real-world implementation challenges while the stakeholders learn about the twin's potential capabilities and limitations. Public outreach campaigns, multilingual communication strategies, and easily navigable user interfaces extend an open invitation for community participation. This sense of shared ownership cements trust by demonstrating that the system is not imposed from the outside but co-created with those whose lives it ultimately affects. Suppose a city-level DT incorrectly predicts that a surge in respiratory infections will occur in the eastern suburbs. Still, the actual surge happens in the West, leaving medical facilities unprepared. Who is at fault in this scenario? Is it the software developers who wrote the predictive algorithm, the data providers whose incomplete or inaccurate data misled the model, the municipal healthcare officials who made policy decisions based on the model, or the political leadership who mandated the model's use?

Precise definitions of fault are essential in a technologically networked environment; errors are rarely isolated to a single point of origin. They often result from a cascade of partial failures. To foster accountability, system architects must embed traceability throughout the data pipeline: every transformation, every model inference, and every policy directive reliant on the DT's recommendations should be logged. This audit trail allows post-event investigations to pinpoint precisely where and why errors occurred. An extension of this principle includes implementing "graceful fail" modes, where the DT's outputs are flagged as uncertain or incomplete under conditions of abnormal data quality. This ensures that final decision-makers understand the reliability bounds of the predictions. Suppose the sensor network in the western suburbs fails or transmits sporadic data. In that case, the twin should highlight that region as a high-uncertainty zone, prompting municipal authorities to exercise additional caution and possibly revert to supplementary data collection. From a legal perspective, emerging data protection and digital governance frameworks will also influence how fault is assigned. In certain jurisdictions, laws might hold technology vendors liable for inaccurate or negligent system design, whereas in others, the responsibility may be more distributed. The presence of well-established protocols for accountability not only clarifies post-incident adjudication but also fosters trust in the system's day-to-day operation. Accepting that no digital system is error-free is part of building realistic and resilient DT solutions. Rather than guaranteeing perpetual correctness, well-governed DTs acknowledge the potential for error and put mechanisms for prompt detection, transparent disclosure, and collaborative remediation in place. Far from discrediting the technology, such candor often solidifies stakeholder trust. People are generally more willing to accept mistakes from a system that is explicit about its constraints and invest in learning from each shortcoming (Feuerriegel et al., 2023; Raina et al., 2024).

Sections 4.2, 4.3 and 4.4 together paint a composite picture of the multifaceted challenges and ethical imperatives in deploying healthcare DTs within complex societal contexts. The hurdles span from incomplete digitization and shifting policy environments to the emotional resonance of patient data that demands a systematic approach that integrates technical engineering with social, moral, and legislative frameworks. The implication is that building a trustworthy DT for healthcare is neither a technological nor a policy matter. It requires an interdisciplinary coalition, bringing together software engineers, healthcare providers, ethicists, sociologists, legal experts, and the communities whose data fuels the system. Such an approach aligns with the notion of "co-design," where stakeholders are active participants in shaping data collection processes, calibrating predictive algorithms, and defining ethical guidelines. Societies themselves evolve—shifting demographics, governance changes, and realignments of social values—imply that the DT cannot be static. Much like the physical systems it models, the DT must be capable of self-reflection and transformation.

It is worth noting that embracing these ethical and operational complexities does not stifle innovation but rather strengthens it. As the global demand for equitable and efficient healthcare continues to grow, the role of technologies such as DTs will likely expand. Approached responsibly, such expansions can catalyze improved health outcomes, democratized data sharing, and more inclusive policymaking. The road to realizing these outcomes is undoubtedly winding.

4.6 Discussion and Conclusion

DTs hold remarkable promise as enablers of transformative change, particularly in the healthcare sector. This chapter has examined

DTs from their conceptual origins to their evolving applications in socio-technical contexts such as population health and urban planning. While industrial domains have demonstrated early successes where boundaries and data sources can be more strictly controlled, healthcare scenarios present distinct complexities. Cultural diversity, limited digitization of patient records, fluid governance structures, and the emotional sensitivities inherent to medical decision-making all intersect to shape how a healthcare-oriented DT may be realized. These layers of complexity, far from rendering DT inapplicable, underscore the need for inter-disciplinary strategies that blend engineering ingenuity with social, ethical, and policy-oriented frameworks. Central to the DT's effectiveness is the consistent and high-quality data. Yet, many societies still rely on paper-based records or inconsistent EHR systems, making large-scale digitization efforts both expensive and technologically challenging. OCR and advanced ML can partially bridge this gap, but practical issues such as model misreading and context-specific biases remain. In parallel, the notion of "equitable healthcare" necessitates that DTs capture and reflect the broad diversity of patient experiences, cultural practices, and local healthcare infrastructures. Socio-economic disparities, varying degrees of digital literacy, and differing access levels to networked devices pose additional hurdles. Likewise, the political environment in democratic societies introduces changeable mandates, requiring DT architectures to be flexible enough to accommodate new policy agendas and adapt to self-organizing local responses.

Given these challenges, trustworthiness becomes essential. DTs must incorporate robust mechanisms for privacy, security, and accountability, ensuring that data breaches or algorithmic missteps do not undermine confidence in the technology. Equally important are moral dimensions and emotional considerations—health data is intimate, and its usage must align with principles of informed consent, fairness, and respect for the diverse perspectives within a community. Anticipating patients' emotional responses to predictive analytics or digital intervention is crucial for maintaining a patient-centric approach. Recognizing that each healthcare ecosystem is unique, developers and policymakers can deploy pilot projects to tailor the DT's analytic techniques and user interfaces to specific local contexts.

The evolution of a successful DT in healthcare hinges on synergy among government agencies, healthcare professionals, data scientists, and the communities served. Co-design principles, where policy, technology, and societal stakeholders collaboratively shape the system, promise a balanced blend of innovation and inclusivity. Although no technology can eliminate every form of uncertainty and error, a well-governed DT can minimize risk through deliberate failsafes, audit mechanisms, and transparent communication strategies. In doing so, it becomes more than a high-tech mirror of the physical realm: it catalyzes targeted interventions, collaborative policymaking, and evidence-based healthcare delivery.

References

ABI Research. (2021). *The Use of Digital Twins for Urban Planning to Yield US$280 Billion in Cost Savings by 2030*. ABI Assessment Reports. https://www.abiresearch.com/press/use-digital-twins-urban-planning-yield-us280-billion-cost-savings-2030/?utm_source=chatgpt.com.

Aivaliotis, P., Georgoulias, K., Arkouli, Z., & Makris, S. (2019). Methodology for enabling digital twin using advanced physics-based modelling in predictive maintenance. *Procedia CIRP*, *81*, 417–422. https://doi.org/10.1016/J.PROCIR.2019.03.072.

Alla, S., Pazos, P., & DelAguila, R. (2017). The impact of requirements management documentation on software project outcomes in health care.

Alla, S., Soltanisehat, L., Tatar, U., & Keskin, O. (2018). Blockchain technology in electronic healthcare systems. In *IIE Annual Conference. Proceedings*, 901–906. Institute of Industrial and Systems Engineers (IISE).

Alla, S. (2024). *An Integrated Theoretical Socio-Technical Framework for Implementing Service Robots' Integration in Healthcare* (Doctoral dissertation, Old Dominion University).

Alla, S., Mohanty, J., Sriraman, H., & Chattu, V. K. (2025). Navigating the frontier: Integrating emerging biomedical technologies into modern healthcare. *Intelligent Biomedical Technologies and Applications for Healthcare 5.0*, 229–243. https://doi.org/10.1016/B978-0-443-22038-8.00015-5.

Asgari, E., Montaña-Brown, N., Dubois, M., Khalil, M. S., Balloch, M. J., & Pimenta, D. (2024). A framework to assess clinical safety and hallucination rates of LLMs for medical text summarisation. *MedRxiv*. https://doi.org/10.1101/2024.09.12.24313556.

Bhatt, U., Ravikumar, P., & Moura, J. M. F. (2019). *Building Human-Machine Trust via Interpretability*. www.aaai.org.

Bonnema, G. M., Veenvliet, K. T., & Broenink, J. F. (2017). *Systems Design and Engineering: Facilitating Multidisciplinary Development Projects* (1st ed.). CRC Publisher.

Bonney, M. S., de Angelis, M., Dal Borgo, M., & Wagg, D. J. (2023). Contextualisation of information in digital twin processes. *Mechanical Systems and Signal Processing, 184*. https://doi.org/10.1016/j.ymssp.2022.109657.

Boschert, S., & Rosen, R. (2016). Digital twin—The simulation aspect. *Mechatronic Futures: Challenges and Solutions for Mechatronic Systems and Their Designers*, 59–74. https://doi.org/10.1007/978-3-319-32156-1_5.

Centeio Jorge, C., Bouman, N. H., Jonker, C. M., & Tielman, M. L. (2023). Exploring the effect of automation failure on the human's trustworthiness in human-agent teamwork. *Frontiers in Robotics and AI, 10*. https://doi.org/10.3389/frobt.2023.1143723.

Chan, J. K. H., & Xiang, W. N. (2022). Fifty years after the wicked-problems conception: Its practical and theoretical impacts on planning and design. *Socio-Ecological Practice Research, 4*(1), 1. https://doi.org/10.1007/S42532-022-00106-W.

Cohen, J., Krishnamoorthy, G., & Wright, A. M. (2002). Corporate governance and the audit process. *Contemporary Accounting Research, 19*(4), 573–594. https://doi.org/10.1506/983M-EPXG-4Y0R-J9YK.

Conklin, J. (2005). Social complexity wicked problems. *Wicked Problems & Social Complexity in Dialogue Mapping: Building Shared Understanding of Wicked Problems*, 1–20. https://www.wiley.com/en-us/Dialogue+Mapping%3A+Building+Shared+Understanding+of+Wicked+Problems-p-9780470017685.

D'Amico, R. D., Erkoyuncu, J. A., Addepalli, S., & Penver, S. (2022). Cognitive digital twin: An approach to improve the maintenance management. *CIRP Journal of Manufacturing Science and Technology, 38*, 613–630. https://doi.org/10.1016/J.CIRPJ.2022.06.004.

Dhar, S., Tarafdar, P., & Bose, I. (2022). Understanding the evolution of an emerging technological paradigm and its impact: The case of Digital Twin. *Technological Forecasting and Social Change, 185,* 122098. https://doi.org/10.1016/J.TECHFORE.2022.122098.

J. P. Morgan Asset Management. (2025). *Diversity, Opportunity & Inclusion.* https://am.jpmorgan.com/us/en/asset-management/institutional/about-us/diversity-inclusion/.

Elmaraghy, W., Elmaraghy, H., Tomiyama, T., & Monostori, L. (2012). Complexity in engineering design and manufacturing. *CIRP Annals, 61*(2), 793–814. https://doi.org/10.1016/J.CIRP.2012.05.001.

Endsley, M. R., & Jones, D. G. (2012). *Designing for Situation Awareness: An Approach to User-Centered Design,* 363.

Ferrario, A., Loi, M., & Viganò, E. (2020). In AI we trust incrementally: A multi-layer model of trust to analyze human-artificial intelligence interactions. *Philosophy and Technology, 33*(3), 523–539. https://doi.org/10.1007/S13347-019-00378-3/TABLES/3.

Ferré-Bigorra, J., Casals, M., & Gangolells, M. (2022). The adoption of urban digital twins. *Cities, 131*(August 2021). https://doi.org/10.1016/j.cities.2022.103905.

Feuerriegel, S., Hartmann, J., Janiesch, C., & Zschech, P. (2023). Generative AI. *Business and Information Systems Engineering,* 1–16. https://doi.org/10.1007/S12599-023-00834-7/TABLES/2.

Ganguly, N., Fazlija, D., Badar, M., Fisichella, M., Sikdar, S.-P., Schrader, J., Wallat, J., Rudra, K., Koubarakis, M.-L., Patro, G. K., Zai, W., Amri, E. L., & Nejdl, W. (2023). *A Review of the Role of Causality in Developing Trustworthy AI Systems.* https://arxiv.org/abs/2302.06975v1.

Gebru, B., Zeleke, L., Blankson, D., Nabil, M., Nateghi, S., Homaifar, A., & Tunstel, E. (2022). A review on human-machine trust evaluation: Human-centric and machine-centric perspectives. In *IEEE Transactions on Human-Machine Systems, 52*(5), 952–962. Institute of Electrical and Electronics Engineers Inc. https://doi.org/10.1109/THMS.2022.3144956.

Gergen, K. J. (2011). The self as social construction. *Psychological Studies, 56*(1), 108–116. https://doi.org/10.1007/S12646-011-0066-1.

Glaessgen, E. H., & Stargel, D. S. (2012). The digital twin paradigm for future NASA and U.S. air force vehicles. *53rd Structures, Structural Dynamics, and Materials Conference: Special Session on the Digital Twin.*

Grieves, M., & Vickers, J. (2017). Digital twin: Mitigating unpredictable, undesirable emergent behavior in complex systems. *Transdisciplinary*

Perspectives on Complex Systems: New Findings and Approaches, 85–113. https://doi.org/10.1007/978-3-319-38756-7_4.

Hallam, C. R. A., & Contreras, C. (2018). Lean healthcare: Scale, scope and sustainability. *International Journal of Health Care Quality Assurance, 31*(7), 684–696. https://doi.org/10.1108/IJHCQA-02-2017-0023.

Jain, R. B. (2001). Towards good governance: A half century of India's administrative development. *International Journal of Public Administration, 24*(12), 1299–1334. https://doi.org/10.1081/PAD-100105941.

Khallouli, W., Pamie-George, R., Kovacic, S., Sousa-Poza, A., Canan, M., & Li, J. (2022). Leveraging transfer learning and GAN models for OCR from engineering documents. *2022 IEEE World AI IoT Congress,* 15–21. https://doi.org/10.1109/AIIOT54504.2022.9817319.

Kritzinger, W., Karner, M., Traar, G., Henjes, J., & Sihn, W. (2018). Digital twin in manufacturing: A categorical literature review and classification. *IFAC-PapersOnLine, 51*(11), 1016–1022. https://doi.org/10.1016/j.ifacol.2018.08.474.

Landini, L., Positano, V., Santarelli, M. F., & Celi, S. (2023). Digital twin technology: New frontiers for personalized healthcare. *Electronics, 12*(8), 1921. https://doi.org/10.3390/ELECTRONICS12081921.

Lehtola, V. V., Koeva, M., Elberink, S. O., Raposo, P., Virtanen, J.-P., Vahdatikhaki, F., & Borsci, S. (2022). Digital twin of a city: Review of technology serving city needs. *International Journal of Applied Earth Observation and Geoinformation*, 102915. https://doi.org/10.1016/J.JAG.2022.102915.

Lepore, S. M. (2023, April 17). Google CEO says he doesn't "fully understand" how new AI program Bard works | *Daily Mail Online*. Daily Mail. https://www.dailymail.co.uk/news/article-11980033/Google-CEO-says-doesnt-fully-understand-new-AI-program-Bard-works.html.

Li, H., Ma, W., Wang, H., Liu, G., Wen, X., Zhang, Y., Yang, M., Luo, G., Xie, G., & Sun, C. (2022). A framework and method for Human-Robot cooperative safe control based on digital twin. https://doi.org/10.1016/j.aei.2022.101701.

Macy, M. W., & Willer, R. (2002). From factors to actors: Computational sociology and agent-based modeling. *Annual Review of Sociology, 28*(1), 143–166. https://doi.org/10.1146/annurev.soc.28.110601.141117.

Mohanty, J. (2020). *A systems engineering approach to developing logistics architecture for the first crewed mission to Mars.* Skolkovo Institute of Science and Technology.

Mohanty, J., Alla, S., Vaishali, Bheesetty, N., Chidipudi, P., Chowdary Nandigam, S. P., Jmukhadze, M., Bheesetty, P., Lakshmana Gowda, N., Mohanty, J., Alla, S., Vaishali, Bheesetty, N., Chidipudi, P., Chowdary Nandigam, S. P., Jmukhadze, M., Bheesetty, P., & Lakshmana Gowda, N. (2025). Digital twin for smart societies: A catalyst for inclusive and accessible healthcare. *ArXiv*. https://doi.org/10.48550/ARXIV.2501.07570.

Mohanty, J., & Ivanov, A. (2020). Systems engineering and development of transport and logistics architecture in the vicinity of Mars to supply the future colony. *Proceedings of the International Astronautical Congress, IAC, 2020-October*, 12–14.

Mohanty, J., Nayak, S., Vaishali, Alla, S, Hazarika, A., & Shah, M. (2025). A meta-clustering framework for enhancing conversational AI in the healthcare sector. *20th Annual System of Systems Engineering Conference*. https://doi.org/10.1109/SoSE66311.2025.11083870.

Mohanty, J., & Vaishali. (2025). Digital twin for smart societies: A catalyst for inclusivity and growth. *Zenodo*. https://doi.org/10.5281/zenodo.14782378.

Mohanty, J., Vaishali, & Nayak, S. (2025). Meta-clustering for specialized language models: Enhancing contextual adaptation and mitigating hallucinations in diverse healthcare environments. *2nd Graduate Student Government Association (GSGA) Annual Research Conference*.

Mohanty, J., Yalim, C., Kovacic, S. F., & Handley, H. H. (2023). A natural language processing-based approach to automate the maintenance work order prioritization process: Understanding sentiments in context-aware systems. *26th Annual Systems & Mission Engineering Conference*. https://doi.org/https://doi.org/10.5281/zenodo.14767863.

Mullankandy, S., Venugopal, S. M., Gupta, A., & Mohanty, J. (2025). Enhancing document intelligence by mitigating hallucinations in large language models. *2025 IEEE International Conference on Data-Driven Social Change (ICDDSC-2025)*, 18–19.

Negri, E., & Abdel-Aty, T. A. (2023). Clarifying concepts of metaverse, digital twin, digital thread, and AAS for CPS-based production systems. *IFAC-PapersOnLine*, *56*(2), 6351–6357. https://doi.org/10.1016/J.IFACOL.2023.10.818.

Oppermann, L., Buchholz, F., & Uzun, Y. (2023). Industrial metaverse: Supporting remote maintenance with avatars and digital twins in collaborative XR environments. *Conference on Human Factors in Computing Systems - Proceedings*. https://doi.org/10.1145/3544549.3585835.

Pal, A., Umapathi, L. K., & Sankarasubbu, M. (2023). Med-HALT: Medical domain hallucination test for large language models. *CoNLL 2023 - 27th Conference on Computational Natural Language Learning, Proceedings,* 314–334. https://doi.org/10.18653/v1/2023.conll-1.21.

Rafiei, A., Moore, R., Jahromi, S., Hajati, F., & Kamaleswaran, R. (2024). Meta-learning in healthcare: A survey. *SN Computer Science, 5*(6), 1–34. https://doi.org/10.1007/S42979-024-03166-9.

Rahman, M. U., Baiardi, F., & Ricci, L. (2022). TACL: Trust-based and scalable access control for IoT using blockchain. *Lecture Notes in Networks and Systems, 358 LNNS,* 345–359. https://doi.org/10.1007/978-3-030-89906-6_24.

Raina, A., Mishra, P., Goyal, H., & Kumar, D. (2024). AI as a medical ally: Evaluating ChatGPT's usage and impact in Indian healthcare. *Proceedings of ACM CHI Conference on Human Factors in Computing Systems, 1.* https://arxiv.org/abs/2401.15605v1.

Rosen, R., Von Wichert, G., Lo, G., & Bettenhausen, K. D. (2015). About the importance of autonomy and digital twins for the future of manufacturing. *IFAC-PapersOnLine, 48*(3), 567–572. https://doi.org/10.1016/J.IFACOL.2015.06.141.

Sadri, N., Desir, J., Khallouli, W., Shahab Uddin, M., Kovacic, S., Sousa-Poza, A., Cannan, M., & Li, J. (2022). Image enhancement for improved OCR and deck segmentation in shipbuilding document images. *2022 IEEE 13th Annual Ubiquitous Computing, Electronics and Mobile Communication Conference, UEMCON 2022,* 45–51. https://doi.org/10.1109/UEMCON54665.2022.9965647.

Sharma, A., Kosasih, E., Zhang, J., Brintrup, A., & Calinescu, A. (2022). Digital twins: State of the art theory and practice, challenges, and open research questions. *Journal of Industrial Information Integration,* 100383. https://doi.org/10.1016/j.jii.2022.100383.

Shi, Y., Shen, W., Wang, L., Longo, F., Nicoletti, L., & Padovano, A. (2022). A cognitive digital twins framework for human-robot collaboration. *Procedia Computer Science, 200,* 1867–1874. https://doi.org/10.1016/J.PROCS.2022.01.387.

Singh, M., Gupta, P. K., & Srivastava, V. M. (2017). Key challenges in implementing cloud computing in Indian healthcare industry. *2017 Pattern Recognition Association of South Africa and Robotics and Mechatronics International Conference, PRASA-RobMech 2017, 2018-January,* 162–167. https://doi.org/10.1109/ROBOMECH.2017.8261141.

Singh, V., & Willcox, K. E. (2018). Engineering design with digital thread. *AIAA Journal, 56*(11), 4515–4528. https://doi.org/10.2514/1.J057255.

Tenhundfeld, N., Demir, M., & de Visser, E. (2022). Assessment of trust in automation in the "real world": Requirements for new trust in automation measurement techniques for use by practitioners. In *Journal of Cognitive Engineering and Decision Making, 16*(2), 101–118. SAGE Publications Inc. https://doi.org/10.1177/15553434221096261.

Thelen, A., Zhang, X., Fink, O., Lu, Y., Ghosh, S., Youn, B. D., Todd, M. D., Mahadevan, S., Hu, C., & Hu, Z. (2022a). A comprehensive review of digital twin – Part 1: Modeling and twinning enabling technologies. https://doi.org/10.48550/arxiv.2208.14197.

Thelen, A., Zhang, X., Fink, O., Lu, Y., Ghosh, S., Youn, B. D., Todd, M. D., Mahadevan, S., Hu, C., & Hu, Z. (2022b). A comprehensive review of digital twin – Part 2: Roles of uncertainty quantification and optimization, a battery digital twin, and perspectives. https://doi.org/10.48550/arxiv.2208.12904.

Van Bossuyt, D. L., Hale, B., Arlitt, R., & Papakonstantinou, N. (2023). Zero-trust for the system design lifecycle. *Journal of Computing and Information Science in Engineering, 23*(6). https://doi.org/10.1115/1.4062597/1163541.

van Dinter, R., Tekinerdogan, B., & Catal, C. (2022). Predictive maintenance using digital twins: A systematic literature review. *Information and Software Technology, 151*, 107008. https://doi.org/10.1016/J.INFSOF.2022.107008.

Wang, Y., Steinbach, T., Klein, J., & Anderl, R. (2021). Integration of model-based system engineering into the digital twin concept. *Procedia CIRP, 100*, 19–24. https://doi.org/10.1016/j.procir.2021.05.003.

Yalim, C., Mohanty, J., Kovacic, S. F., & Handley, H. H. (2023, September). Automated prioritization of maintenance work orders: A sentiment analysis approach using natural language processing. *Fleet Maintenance & Modernization Symposium*.

Yezdani, O., Sanzogni, L., & Poropat, A. (2015). Theory of emergence: Introducing a model-centred approach to applied social science research. *Prometheus, 33*(3). https://doi.org/10.1080/08109028.2016.1144669.

Zhang, Q., Liu, J., & Chen, X. (2024). A literature review of the digital thread: Definition, key technologies, and applications. *Systems, 12*(3), 70. https://doi.org/10.3390/SYSTEMS12030070.

Chapter 5

Toward Sustainable Care: Green Solutions for Managing Chronic Conditions

Berrak Itır Aylı

Hacettepe University, Graduate School of Health Sciences, Ankara, Turkey

itirayli@gmail.com

The intersection of healthcare, environmental sustainability, and non-communicable diseases (NCDs) presents a critical challenge in global public health. Healthcare systems must strike a balance between the ecological impact of their operations and the demands of treatment as the prevalence of NCDs increases due to aging populations, urbanization, and environmental factors. This chapter examines how healthcare practices affect the environment, including carbon emissions, greenhouse gas (GHG) emissions, waste production, and resource depletion, as well as how pollution and climate change contribute to the increased prevalence of NCDs. Potential remedies are investigated, including sustainable healthcare models, such as green hospital programs, sustainable pharmaceutical solutions, and ecologically friendly therapeutic

Environmentalism in Healthcare: Caring for Tomorrow Ecologically
Edited by Jacqueline A. Stagner and David S.-K. Ting

ISBN 978-981-5129-95-3 (Hardcover), 978-1-003-74869-4 (eBook)
www.jennystanford.com

DOI: 10.1201/9781003748694-5

approaches. This chapter, which takes a multidisciplinary approach, emphasizes the necessity of innovation, education, healthcare reforms, and behavioral change. To address the increasing burden of NCDs and reduce the environmental cost of healthcare.

5.1 Introduction

The idea of sustainability first gained attention with the Brundtland Report, titled *Our Common Future,* published in 1987 by the World Commission on Environment and Development (WCED). This report emphasized how deeply connected environmental, economic, and social challenges are. It called for a fresh approach to development—one that ensures a better, more sustainable future for everyone, whether in developing or industrialized nations. The report's definition of sustainability remains valid today, as "meeting the needs of the present without compromising the ability of future generations to meet their needs." In 1987, the United Nations Brundtland Commission indicated that many countries were grappling with the consequences of unsustainable practices, such as environmental degradation, poverty, and resource depletion. It stressed the need for a global commitment to sustainable development, which requires changes in policies and practices across all nations to address these interlinked crises effectively [1]. Since then, a number of initiatives have been put into effect to create a more sustainable world for everyone. However, despite the emphasis on the subject, the situation today is as grave or perhaps even graver than it was in 1987.

NCDs, often referred to as chronic diseases, are the leading cause of death and disability around the world. These long-term illnesses, although not contagious, are closely related to social, cultural, and environmental factors. They include some of the most serious health challenges, like heart disease, cancer, chronic respiratory conditions, diabetes, and strokes. NCDs tend to progress slowly, often requiring ongoing care and treatment throughout a person's life [2]. They are rarely fully curable, but they can usually be managed with proper medical care and lifestyle adjustments. They require frequent check-ups, close monitoring, and often, a number of drugs.

As of 2023, the World Health Organization (WHO) reports that NCDs are responsible for 74% of global deaths, which accounts for roughly 41 million lives lost every year [2]. What is even more concerning is that 77% of these deaths happen in low- and middle-income countries (LMICs), where access to healthcare can be limited. Among younger people under 70, this figure rises to 85%. On a positive note, it is estimated that 80% of these deaths could be prevented through early intervention, lifestyle changes, and better healthcare access [3].

NCDs also contribute significantly to disability, accounting for three out of every four years lived with a disability worldwide [4]. One disability adjusted life year (DALY) represents the loss of the equivalent of one year of full health. DALYs for a disease or health condition are the sum of the years of life lost due to premature mortality and the years lived with a disability due to prevalent cases of the disease or health condition in a population [5]. Looking at the top 10 DALYs of the 21st century, although DALYs from communicable diseases like diarrheal diseases and HIV have seen a significant fall, DALYs from NCDs have been on the rise, with an increase of almost 50% in Alzheimer's and Diabetes [6].

Due to their persistent nature, the management of NCDs is continuously dependent on several factors; the main ones being the healthcare system, the pharmaceutical industry, and medical technologies. However, the management of these diseases does not only rely on health and related systems, but also on people's ability to physically and economically access these systems, their intellectual capacity and health literacy to understand the systems, their diseases and management, environmental and climate factors, and their social life and status. And unfortunately, the cost of NCDs is not seen only on people but also on the ecosystem they inhabit.

Ecosystems are defined as complex networks of living organisms (plants, animals, and microorganisms) that interact with each other and their physical environment (soil, water, and air) to form a functional unit, providing various services essential for human well-being [7]. The idea of a relationship between human life and the ecosystem goes as far as Ancient Greece to Plato, who recognized the negative impacts of environmental degradation, such as deforestation, on the quality of life in Athens [8].

In modern times, the relationship between health, healthcare, and the environment first started to get attention after Rachel Carson, an environmental activist, gave a speech to 1500 physicians in the USA and spoke about "man against himself, the extraordinary unity that prevails between living organisms and the environment". Today, this relationship has a name: it is called "Ecosystem Services (ES)" and is defined as the benefits that humans derive from ecosystems. These services can be categorized into four main types: provisioning services (such as food and water), regulating services (such as climate regulation and flood control), cultural services (such as recreational and spiritual benefits), and supporting services (such as nutrient cycling and habitat provision). These services are crucial for sustaining human life, as they contribute to health, economic stability, and overall quality of life [9]. For the healthy continuity of human life, the ecosystem needs to remain intact and sustainable.

The best way of defining environmental sustainability is by making a small change in the definition provided by the United Nations Brundtland Report. Environmental sustainability can be defined as "meeting the resource and services needs of current and future generations without compromising the health of the ecosystems that provide them" or more specifically "a condition of balance, resilience, and interconnectedness that allows human society to satisfy its needs while neither exceeding the capacity of its supporting ecosystems to continue to regenerate the services necessary to meet those needs nor by our actions diminishing biological diversity" [10].

5.2 Burden of Non-Communicable Disease

Throughout human history, human life has been defined by several factors. Three centuries ago, the average life expectancy was no longer than 30 years, and communicable diseases were the major killers in every part of the world. At the end of the 19th century, life expectancy saw a significant rise to almost

50 years, following the Industrial Revolution and developments in both medicine and social determinants of health, communicable diseases finally became manageable. However, at the end of the 20th century, although life expectancy had reached almost 70 years in high-income countries (HICs), another major group of diseases became relevant: NCDs. The demographics of the population changed in tandem with this transition, as human life got longer; the birth rate started to lessen, and populations started to age. While only one in every 11 people in the world was older than 65 in 2021, estimations suggest that by 2050, one in every six people will be in this group. This complex set of changes in patterns of health, disease, and mortality is defined as the epidemiological transition and is the route that has been observed in most of the world, although with differences in timelines. In LMICs, populations remain younger and life expectancy is shorter, with communicable disease being more mortal than they are in HICs. Similarly, NCDs are more fatal and cause higher disability in LMICs [11–13].

NCDs account for more than half of the global disease burden, with cardiovascular conditions being the leading cause of NCD-related deaths. Most of these deaths occur in LMICs. Studies indicate that the rise in NCDs is partially linked to longer life expectancy resulting from reduced deaths from infectious and maternal illnesses. However, preventable factors, such as smoking, high blood pressure, unhealthy diets, air pollution, and excessive alcohol consumption, remain major contributors. The Global Burden of Disease (GBD) initiative continues to provide essential data, helping to track health losses and guide efforts to manage NCDs worldwide [14].

Urbanization, commercialization, and population aging are significant drivers of the increasing prevalence of NCDs, although these factors are not inevitable causes. Lifestyle changes, such as reduced physical activity and increased tobacco and alcohol use, are central contributors to conditions like cardiovascular diseases, cancer, obesity, and type 2 diabetes. Projections show tobacco-related deaths could reach up to 8 million annually by 2030. Similarly, obesity rates have surged, particularly in urban areas of countries like China, Malaysia, and South Africa, even as rural regions continue to face issues of undernutrition [13].

In 2005, NCDs were responsible for about 60% of global deaths, equating to nearly 34 million deaths, with the burden predominantly affecting developing countries. After almost two decades, NCDs are now responsible for almost every three out of four deaths globally, accounting for 41 million deaths in 2023, with 80% of these deaths occurring in LMICs. Compounding this, many developing countries face a double burden of communicable and non-communicable diseases, leading to both reduced life expectancy and prolonged periods of poor health [3, 4, 14].

Cardiovascular diseases, particularly heart attacks and strokes, are the primary causes of NCD-related deaths, claiming 17 million lives each year. Historically seen as problems of industrialized nations, these conditions are now rapidly growing in developing countries due to urbanization and industrialization. Diabetes also presents a costly challenge, with healthcare expenditures expected to reach over $300 billion annually in 2025 [15].

Cancer is another leading contributor to the NCD burden, with developing countries experiencing rapid increases in incidence and mortality. Lung cancer, strongly linked to smoking, is particularly prevalent and represents a major health concern in areas with high tobacco consumption. Similarly, respiratory diseases such as chronic obstructive pulmonary disease (COPD) affect hundreds of millions globally, with COPD being one of the five major causes of mortality worldwide.

The burden of NCDs also includes significant disabilities, such as blindness, amputations, and mobility impairments, which not only diminish quality of life but also strain social and healthcare systems. Disabilities caused by NCDs create a vicious cycle, increasing sedentary lifestyles and further elevating NCD risks. People with disabilities in LMICs often face worse socioeconomic and health outcomes [16]. Often, inverse care is especially prominent, with those in need of the highest amounts of healthcare receiving it the least. Strategies focusing on surveillance, health promotion, and primary prevention need to be developed and implemented globally to see a significant change in the effect of NCDs on life expectancy and quality.

NCDs are not only a health burden but also an economic one. According to Bloom et al. NCDs—like heart disease, lung disease, cancer, diabetes, and mental health issues—are already costing the global economy a great deal, and their impact is set to skyrocket by the end of the decade. Experts estimate these illnesses cost the world USD 47 trillion in lost economic output in 2010. To put that in perspective, that's about three-quarters of the entire global GDP in 2010 and could have funded poverty eradication (for those living on USD 2 a day) for over 50 years. Right now, wealthier nations bear the majority of the financial burden of NCDs. But as LMICs grow in population and economic activity, they are likely to face an even bigger share of this challenge. Business leaders around the world are also increasingly worried. About half of the executives surveyed by the World Economic Forum fear that at least one NCD will negatively affect their company's bottom line within the next five years. This concern is widespread across low-, middle-, and high-income countries, particularly in areas where healthcare quality or access is seen as poor [17].

NCDs impact the economy through several mechanisms. First, when individuals of working age pass away due to illness, there is a direct loss in economic output since human capital, which is essential to the production process, is lost and cannot be fully replaced by physical capital. This is especially prominent in jobs that are performed by highly educated individuals, as it is a rare commodity that is hard to replace. Second, even when individuals survive but live with chronic illnesses, their productivity often declines. Depending on the severity, they may work fewer hours, retire early, lose motivation, or struggle to contribute effectively to their work. Third, addressing NCDs through treatments and prevention demands substantial resources. These expenditures divert funds that could have been invested in other areas, such as infrastructure, education, or innovation, thereby reducing savings and slowing the accumulation of capital across the economy.

Altogether, the economic loss attributed to NCDs is staggering, estimated at nearly $94.9 trillion (in constant 2010 USD) from

2015 to 2050. Mental health conditions and cardiovascular diseases impose the greatest economic burden, followed by cancer, diabetes, and chronic respiratory illnesses. On a per-person basis, the global economic burden of NCDs during this period amounts to approximately $265,000. This highlights the profound and far-reaching economic burden of these diseases [18].

5.3 Healthcare Burden on the Environment

Healthcare systems worldwide, while essential to improving health outcomes and addressing diseases, have substantial environmental footprints. These systems contribute significantly to GHG emissions, air and water pollution, and other forms of environmental degradation. Below, we discuss key findings from studies analyzing healthcare's environmental effects, illustrating the global and local challenges this sector poses.

The healthcare sector accounts for 4.4% of global GHG emissions, with some national contributions exceeding 5% of total emissions. These emissions stem from energy-intensive operations, pharmaceutical manufacturing, and waste management processes [19]. In HICs, like the United States, healthcare contributes 8% of national GHG emissions, while in Canada, the sector represents 4.6% of the national total [20, 21].

In Canada, the healthcare system produces approximately 33 million tons of GHG emissions annually, with hospitals, pharmaceuticals, and physician services identified as primary contributors. Non-GHG pollutants, such as particulate matter (PM), account for a significant portion of the health damages linked to healthcare, highlighting the importance of addressing air quality in this sector [21]. Similarly, in the U.S., healthcare emissions were estimated at 546 $MMTCO_2Eq$ in 2007, with hospitals and prescription drugs contributing 39% and 14%, respectively [20]. These emissions have risen steadily over time, with healthcare's environmental impact growing by approximately 30% between 2003 and 2013 [22].

Beyond GHG emissions, the healthcare sector contributes significantly to air pollution through the release of PM, nitrogen oxides (NO_x), and sulfur dioxide (SO_2). For example, healthcare in Canada generates over 210,000 metric tons of pollutants, including ammonia, carbon monoxide, and methanol [21]. These emissions are linked to serious health outcomes, such as respiratory and cardiovascular diseases, resulting in the loss of 23,000 DALYs annually in Canada and 6.5 million DALYs annually in the U.S. due to air pollution [20, 22].

Healthcare also generates a substantial amount of hazardous waste, including infectious and toxic materials. Mercury, often used in medical equipment, poses a critical environmental concern, necessitating better management strategies. The incineration of medical waste further exacerbates air pollution and contributes to toxic emissions, highlighting the need for alternative waste management practices [23].

Indirect effects of healthcare operations, often overlooked, are equally significant. Upstream supply chains—such as those associated with medical devices, pharmaceuticals, and infrastructure—account for the majority of emissions. For instance, indirect activities contribute up to 90% of total healthcare-related GHG emissions in Canada [21]. These upstream impacts emphasize the interconnectedness of healthcare with other sectors, such as agriculture, which contributes to emissions through supply chain processes.

Efforts to mitigate the environmental impact of healthcare are increasingly recognized as essential for sustainable development. Strategies include adopting eco-friendly medical products, reducing energy consumption in hospitals, and implementing sustainable procurement practices. For example, initiatives to develop low-carbon inhalers and reduce waste in pharmaceutical production are gaining traction in HICs.

Moreover, healthcare systems must adopt a dual focus: improving patient care while minimizing their environmental footprint. This approach requires integrating environmental considerations into healthcare policies, investing in green technologies, and promoting public awareness about the sector's environmental impact.

The healthcare sector's environmental footprint represents a significant challenge that directly undermines public health.

The emissions and pollution generated by healthcare systems contribute to climate change and exacerbate health conditions such as respiratory and cardiovascular diseases. However, by adopting sustainable practices and prioritizing environmental stewardship, the healthcare sector can mitigate these impacts, ensuring a healthier future for both the people and the planet.

5.4 Rethinking Care Pathways

5.4.1 Prevention First

The most effective way of lessening the burden of NCDs is by preventing them. These prevention strategies relate closely to the determinants of health, which are classically categorized as behavioral factors, impacts of the natural environment, genetic determinants, and social determinants. The behavioral factors mainly consist of four major risk factors: use of tobacco products, harmful use of alcohol, physical inactivity, and unhealthy diet (Fig. 5.1). These factors are, in fact, avoidable.

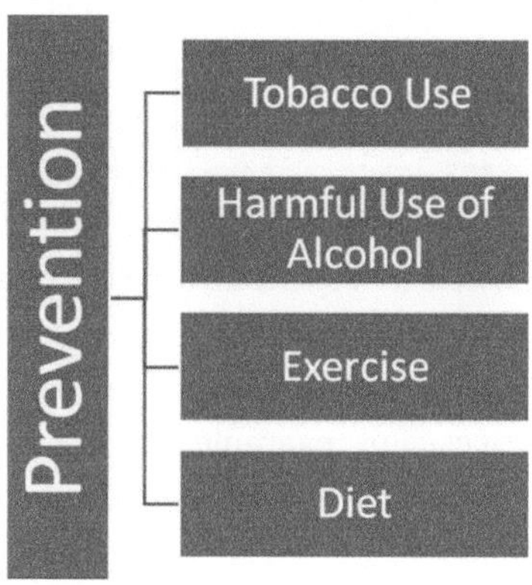

Figure 5.1 Prevention strategies [24].

Tobacco remains one of the greatest and most preventable public health challenges in the world. In the past century, it caused 100 million deaths, primarily in LMICs. If current trends continue, tobacco could be responsible for 1 billion deaths this century, with the majority occurring in LMICs, particularly in China. Right now, tobacco kills 5.4 million people annually—a figure expected to rise to 8 million per year by 2030, with 80% of those deaths occurring in developing countries. Among the 1 billion smokers alive today, around half—approximately 500 million—are projected to die from tobacco-related causes.

Despite this grim outlook, there's hope. Thanks to strong tobacco control measures, millions of lives have been saved since the 1960s, particularly in countries like the United States and the United Kingdom, which have led the way in implementing effective policies. Tobacco control is a shining example of global collaboration in public health. It even has its international treaty: the WHO Framework Convention on Tobacco Control (FCTC), ratified by 176 parties, representing 88% of the global population as of 2012 [25, 26].

To help countries combat tobacco use, WHO developed the MPOWER package, which outlines six key strategies [27] (Fig. 5.2).

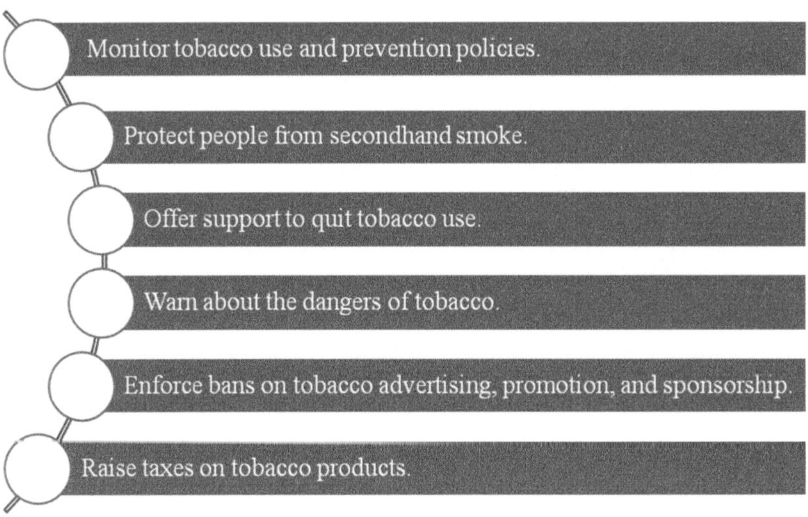

Figure 5.2 MPOWER [27].

By prioritizing these steps, governments and communities worldwide can work together to reduce the devastating impact of tobacco and save millions of lives. In HICs, many of these measures are already in place; several European nations have banned cigarette smoking in public areas while enforcing severe restrictions on their advertisement and sales. However, LMICs are severely behind in such campaigns, and tobacco products are not banned even in closed spaces in many of the countries where tobacco is a major risk factor.

Alcohol consumption has a wide range of harmful effects, both in the short term and long term. Acute effects are often tied to specific drinking events, where alcohol impairs physical coordination, cognition, and attention, leading to a higher risk of violence, accidents, and injuries. At higher levels of consumption, alcohol can impair judgment and intention, which may contribute to violent behavior and crime, though this relationship varies across cultures [28, 29]. Excessive alcohol intake can also result in a potentially fatal overdose by disrupting critical autonomic functions.

Chronic alcohol consumption, on the other hand, has long-term impacts on nearly every organ in the body. It is a significant cause of conditions such as liver cirrhosis, cancers of the upper digestive tract, liver, and breast, cardiomyopathy, gastritis, and pancreatitis [30]. Alcohol also plays a role in the development and progression of infectious diseases [31]. Sustained heavy drinking is associated with neurological disorders and mental health issues, including depression and affective disorders. Alcohol use disorder, previously termed alcoholism, reflects a loss of control over drinking along with psychological and physical consequences, as classified by DSM-5 and ICD-10 [24].

Studies on alcohol-related harm, such as drinking-driving incidents [32] and crimes like homicides [33], highlight its serious consequences, including death and injury. Evidence from large-scale studies shows that changes in alcohol consumption at the population level have substantial impacts on mortality. For example, in European societies, a 1-liter change in per capita alcohol consumption correlates with about a 1% change in overall mortality [34, 35]. Notably, the reduction in alcohol consumption during Russia's 1985–1988 restrictions led to a 2.7% decline in age-standardized mortality per 1-liter drop in per capita consumption [36, 37]. The annual global burden of alcohol-attributable NCDs is high, with more than 1.8 million deaths and 52 million years of life lost due to premature mortality and close to 29 million years of life lost due to disability [38, 39]. These findings underscore the importance of addressing alcohol consumption as a public health priority, particularly in societies with prevalent heavy drinking patterns.

Physical inactivity is another major modifiable risk factor for NCDs. A global WHO study across 122 countries, covering 88.9% of the world's population, revealed that 31.1% of adults are physically inactive. The highest inactivity rates were found in the Americas (43.2%), while the lowest were in Africa (27.5%) [40]. Physical inactivity is more common among low socioeconomic groups and is higher in individuals with lower educational status [41]. Urban populations are less active than rural ones. Overall, one in five adults worldwide is physically inactive [24].

Over 9% of all deaths globally can be attributed to physical inactivity [42]. A study in the United States estimated that by becoming active, the average 50-year-old person would gain 1.3–3.7 years of life [43, 44]. Another study among East Asians showed that at age 30, active individuals had a life expectancy 2.6 to 4.2 years longer than inactive peers [45]. In a study conducted by Lee et al., it was estimated that physical inactivity is responsible for 6% of the burden of disease from coronary heart disease, 7% of type 2 diabetes, and 10% each for breast cancer and colon cancer [46]. The WHO has outlined recommended levels of physical activity for different age groups to promote health and well-being [47]:

- **Children and Adolescents (5–17 years)**: At least 60 minutes of moderate to vigorous intensity physical activity every day.
- **Adults (18–64 years)**: A minimum of 150 minutes of moderate-intensity activity or 75 minutes of vigorous-intensity physical activity weekly, or a combination of the two.
- **Older Adults (65 years and above)**: At least 150 minutes of moderate-intensity activity or 75 minutes of vigorous-intensity activity weekly, or an equivalent mix. Additionally, exercises that improve balance and strengthen muscles are strongly recommended.

Diet is another modifiable behavioral risk factor that contributes to NCDs. Unhealthy diets are directly related to higher blood glucose levels and hyperlipidemia, and thus direct risk factors for metabolic syndrome, diabetes, and cardiovascular disease. Sodium intake is directly connected to blood pressure levels, which, in turn, are related to both cardiovascular disease, stroke, and kidney disease. In 2017, a study conducted across 195 countries determined that 11 million deaths and 255 million DALYs could be attributed to dietary risk factors. High intake of sodium, low intake of whole grains, and low intake of fruits and vegetables were found to be the leading dietary risk factors for deaths and DALYs globally [24, 48].

Healthy dietary habits should begin early in life. Breastfeeding supports healthy growth, better development of immunity systems, enhances cognitive development, and may provide long-term health benefits, including a reduced risk of overweight, obesity, and NCDs later in life [49, 50]. To maintain a healthy weight, energy and calorie intake should balance energy expenditure. Total fat intake should not exceed 30% of total energy, with saturated fats kept below 10% and trans-fats below 1%. Shifting from saturated and trans-fats to unsaturated fats is recommended, alongside efforts to eliminate industrially-produced trans-fats; this is believed to be the single most effective measure against hyperlipidemia [49, 51]. Limiting free sugar intake to less than 10% of total energy is also essential for a healthy diet, with further reductions to below 5% offering additional health benefits [52]. Reducing salt intake to under 5 grams per day can help prevent hypertension and lower the risk of heart disease and stroke [53]. WHO Member States have committed to reducing global salt intake by 30% and halting the rise of diabetes, obesity, and childhood overweight by 2025 [54].

Other prevention and management measures of NCDs are the integration of cost-effective interventions into primary healthcare systems, supported by innovative financing mechanisms such as taxes on tobacco and alcohol. Strengthening surveillance systems, including mortality registries and risk factor monitoring, is vital for tracking progress, while leveraging digital tools can enhance real-time data collection and response. Expanding access to affordable generic medicines and low-cost diagnostic technologies, alongside task-sharing with non-physician health workers, can address resource and workforce constraints. Scaling up high-impact screening programs and reorienting health systems toward continuous care are critical for early detection and management. Yearly blood glucose and blood pressure measurements are examples of easy, cheap, and acceptable methods for identifying patients in the early stages, even before the disease develops, and therefore providing a chance of avoiding the disease by behavioral changes. Drawing from HICs' successes, such as tobacco control and organized screening programs, LMICs can focus on prevention and primary care while addressing governance and infrastructure challenges. Achieving global goals will depend on translating evidence-based strategies into action through multisectoral collaboration and sustainable health policies.

Another vital aspect in the prevention and management of NCDs is health literacy. Empowering communities by enabling them to access, understand, and use health information, health literacy helps communities take part in life-saving prevention and make informed choices about their lifestyles. Such empowerment is particularly important, as generally, NCDs, such as cardiovascular diseases, diabetes, and cancers, are driven by behavioral factors and therefore require a knowledgeable public to modify risks [55]. Major health organizations emphasize that an improvement in health literacy is essential for effective public health intervention. When individuals are empowered with skills to understand their health conditions and resources available, they become more likely to be engaged in preventive behaviors and adhere to treatment plans, hence reducing the burden of NCDs within their communities. However, several challenges and barriers hinder the effective implementation of the health literacy program. Most health literacy initiatives focus on specific diseases, while socioeconomic disparities also pose other challenges for marginalized populations in accessing health information and resources [56, 57]. For this reason, policymakers, health professionals, and community organizations should work in tandem to design interventions that are more relevant to the diverse populations they serve and further health equity. A development strategy against NCD, health literacy not only helps create enabling opportunities in one's private judgment capabilities but also develops people-to-people associations and links medical services closer than hitherto, as these happen to play more fundamental roles in one's life, enhancing health for every individual through public health responses or diminished burdens from disparate incidence of NCD outcomes.

5.4.2 Digital Health

Digital health solutions are transforming healthcare delivery by improving efficiency, expanding access, and promoting sustainability. They are widely used in areas such as diagnosis, treatment, clinical decision support, and patient management, with over 300,000 health apps available globally [58]. These technologies enhance healthcare engagement, improve long-term outcomes, and facilitate informed decision-making, particularly in underserved communities [59]. Innovations like digital referrals, mobile health (mHealth), and decision support systems empower healthcare workers and optimize care delivery, contributing to the advancement of universal health coverage [60].

The One Digital Health (ODH) framework offers a structured approach to integrating human, animal, and environmental health through digital tools. It emphasizes the role of education, citizen engagement, and environmental monitoring in creating cohesive health ecosystems [61]. By incorporating diverse data sources, the ODH framework enhances disease detection, outbreak management, and health surveillance, while fostering interdisciplinary collaboration for sustainable solutions. This approach bridges the gap between public health needs and technological advancements, creating opportunities for equitable and efficient healthcare delivery.

Digital health solutions also have notable environmental benefits. By reducing the need for physical healthcare infrastructure and travel, they contribute to lower carbon emissions. For instance, mHealth and telemedicine minimize patient travel for consultations, while digital data sharing reduces paper waste and resource utilization [60]. These environmentally friendly practices align with broader goals of sustainability and public health equity.

Despite these benefits, challenges such as inadequate validation mechanisms, data privacy concerns, and inequitable access must be addressed [58, 59]. Establishing standardized frameworks, investing in digital infrastructure, and prioritizing equity-focused design can ensure the sustainable implementation of digital health solutions worldwide [60]. By leveraging these technologies effectively, we can create health systems that are not only efficient and equitable but also environmentally sustainable.

However, even though digital health solutions offer significant opportunities to improve healthcare delivery, their environmental impact at certain points requires critical evaluation and mitigation strategies. The environmental costs of digital health are primarily associated with device production, e-waste generation, energy consumption, and telecommunication infrastructure. The manufacturing and disposal of electronic devices such as smartphones, tablets, and wearables contribute to significant environmental degradation. Mining raw materials like iron, aluminum, and gold not only disrupts ecosystems and alters land use but also exposes workers to hazardous substances [61]. Furthermore, electronic devices account for approximately 8% of global energy consumption during production, while improper disposal leads to e-waste, with up to 40% ending up in landfills, releasing toxic chemicals into the environment [61].

Energy consumption is another critical factor. Data centers, required for storing large volumes of health data generated by digital health technologies, consume substantial electricity for operation and cooling. For example, storing data in cloud services consumes more energy compared to on-device storage. Telecommunication infrastructures that support digital health further add to the carbon footprint, especially for video conferencing in telehealth, which has a higher energy demand than simple phone consultations [62]. However, the environmental impact of digital health is not uniform. Simpler interventions, such as phone-based telehealth, generally have a smaller carbon footprint compared to more complex technologies. Despite this variability, a lack of standardized methods to evaluate the carbon footprint of these techniques remains a significant gap, making it challenging to compare or reproduce findings. The development of validated, robust tools to assess the life cycle impact of these technologies is crucial for sustainable implementation [61, 62].

According to a study on artificial intelligence (AI) use in health systems in the United Kingdom, AI offers significant environmental benefits in healthcare by improving operational efficiency, reducing emissions through optimized processes, and minimizing patient travel through telehealth services. The increasing reliance on renewable energy to power AI tools further lowers its carbon footprint, while AI-driven sustainable healthcare models contribute to climate adaptation efforts. However, challenges remain, including the substantial carbon emissions associated with AI development and deployment, the lack of standardized methods for measuring its climate impact, and insufficient tools for comprehensive environmental assessments. Additionally, AI's broader effects on land use, biodiversity, and water resources require attention. Addressing these challenges is critical to leveraging AI's potential while ensuring its implementation aligns with sustainability goals, such as achieving a net-zero healthcare system by 2040 [63].

To mitigate these environmental challenges, adopting practices like Green Information Technologies, ethical sourcing of materials, and promoting sustainability throughout the digital health life cycle is essential. Also, standardized methods for measuring the impact of AI, mobile health applications, and digital health devices need to be used. Collaboration among healthcare professionals, environmental scientists, engineers, and policymakers is needed to establish standardized methodologies and integrate environmentally sustainable practices into digital health systems. By addressing these gaps, digital health solutions can advance not only healthcare but also environmental sustainability, aligning with global goals to reduce carbon emissions and promote ecological health.

5.4.3 Waste Reduction

The issue of healthcare waste is a growing concern globally, particularly as the volume of waste generated by healthcare facilities continues to escalate. This waste includes a variety of materials such as infectious waste, hazardous substances, and non-hazardous materials, each of which poses distinct environmental and public health challenges if not managed effectively. Studies have consistently shown that inadequate waste management practices can result in soil and water contamination, air pollution from incineration, and the spread of infectious diseases among healthcare workers and the broader community [65, 66]. For the proper management of waste, first, categorization needs to be made clearly. Healthcare waste is categorized into several key types (Fig. 5.3) [64]:

Figure 5.3 Healthcare waste types [64].

- **Infectious Waste**: Includes materials contaminated with pathogens, such as used bandages, surgical waste, and laboratory specimens
- **Sharps Waste**: Items like needles, scalpels, and broken glass that pose injury and infection risks

- **Hazardous Waste**: Includes chemicals, pharmaceuticals, and other substances harmful to human health and the environment
- **Radioactive Waste**: Generated from medical procedures involving radioactive materials
- **General Waste**: Non-hazardous waste similar to municipal waste, which still requires proper disposal

Compounding these challenges is the increased generation of medical waste during crises such as the COVID-19 pandemic. Reports indicate that improper waste segregation and disposal, particularly in developing regions, have exacerbated environmental and health risks. For instance, approximately 2 billion people globally lacked access to basic waste collection services before the pandemic, and 3 billion had no controlled waste disposal systems [67]. These gaps in infrastructure and regulation lead to hazardous materials being mixed with municipal waste or openly burned, further harming ecosystems and human health. Improper healthcare waste disposal has several detrimental effects [68]:

- **Soil and Water Contamination**: Hazardous substances leach into groundwater, affecting ecosystems and public health
- **Air Pollution**: Incineration of waste releases harmful toxins, including dioxins and heavy metals
- **Public Health Risks**: Direct exposure to infectious waste increases the spread of diseases and drug-resistant micro-organisms
- **Financial and Systemic Burdens**: Wasteful spending on unnecessary procedures and administrative inefficiencies contributes to inefficiencies and higher healthcare costs

Lallemand estimates that approximately $700 billion in U.S. healthcare spending could be avoided through targeted interventions, such as payment reforms that incentivize quality care, comparative effectiveness research to eliminate redundant services, and the adoption of information technology to streamline administrative processes. Wasteful practices not only inflate costs but also divert resources from essential services, erode patient trust, and increase the risk of harm from unnecessary treatments [69]. According to Taylor et al., clinicians using pre-packaged procedure kits contribute significantly to waste generation. Clinicians using pre-packaged kits produced approximately 819.5 kg more waste annually than those selecting individual components [77].

Efforts to address these issues have focused on improving waste management practices and implementing policy reforms. Key recommendations include enhancing education and training for healthcare workers on waste segregation, investing in advanced treatment technologies such as autoclaving and chemical disinfection, and developing robust regulatory frameworks to enforce best practices. For instance, Jannik et al. emphasize the importance of inventory control and the adoption of physical waste treatment methods to minimize risks [68]. Similarly, Kenny highlights the need for international collaboration to share resources and expertise, particularly in low-resource settings [67].

Reducing waste requires a multifaceted approach that balances environmental sustainability, financial efficiency, and patient care. By integrating waste management strategies with systemic reforms, such as simplifying administrative processes and fostering international partnerships, healthcare systems can mitigate the harmful impacts of waste while enhancing the quality and accessibility of care. These efforts are essential for building resilient, sustainable healthcare systems capable of meeting the needs of diverse populations in an environmentally responsible manner.

5.4.4 Educational Changes

The relationship between environmental factors, communicable diseases, and health systems is multifaceted and multidirectional. Environmental risk factors and climate change increase the risk of NCDs. For example, air pollution is closely related to cardiovascular disease, respiratory disease, and certain cancers. Climate change, affects health directly, and indirectly rising temperatures and heat waves can trigger several conditions while disruptions to food and water sources, often exacerbate existing conditions and cause conditions to emerge. Environmental chains like natural disasters or extreme climate events affect health systems negatively and increase the vulnerability of risk groups while also impacting mental health in a negative way [70]. There is also an economic impact of these links. The economic burden of disease associated with environmental chemical exposure to seven chemicals, and only 10 held outcomes alone, was calculated to be 157 billion Euros by Woodruff, and unfortunately, the global chemical production is estimated to grow at a rate of 3.4% annually until 2030 [71].

The first step in creating an environmentally friendly healthcare system starts with education. Medical school curricula around the world should offer comprehensive knowledge about the relationship between climate change, the environment, and health. Surveys show that 86% of health professionals feel a responsibility to engage in advocacy related to climate change; however, almost half of them feel that they are hindered by their lack of knowledge. Around 89% of American medical students feel that education on climate change should be included in their medical curriculum. Currently, such programs are only available in a number of medical schools, like Stanford University [72]. Programs like this need to be incorporated into medical school curricula and be provided at healthcare facilities. Each healthcare facility could incorporate climate-conscious care into their orientations of new personnel and additionally offer seminars and courses for healthcare workers. The climate-conscious behavior of departments could be rated annually and rewarded by hospital managements to increase interest in both the education and the practice of environmentalism in healthcare.

Unfortunately, environmentally friendly behavior from only healthcare workers is not enough. Healthcare professionals could become communicators, educators, researchers, and climate leaders who work on raising awareness about climate change, its health implications in society, and lessening both our effects on the environment and the environment's effects on us. Each healthcare professional and provider would need to create their own action plan for this advocacy and education. Additionally, healthcare providers could conduct research on their carbon emissions and waste production to raise awareness about their environmental impact and, by sharing these results, could encourage sustainable behaviors, both in personal and professional life, such as decreasing plastic use, reducing meat consumption, and transitioning to renewable energy sources [73].

5.4.5 Sustainable Pharmaceutical Management

In a study performed in Australia on pharmacy students, the results showed that 98% of the students had some information about environmental sustainability, and 89% believed that pharmacists should incorporate sustainability efforts into their practices. However, less than 12% of the responders had knowledge about environmentally sustainable pharmaceutical practices [74]. This study shows that, like medical school curricula, pharmaceutical education needs to be updated to include environmentalism.

Although often perceived as less harmful, the pharmaceutical industry emits 13% more carbon emissions than the automobile industry. In the U.K., the carbon cost of medicines prescribed in primary care accounts for 65% of the total emissions related to primary care. Alarmingly, studies show that 10% of primary care prescriptions in the U.K. are unnecessary, while half of them go to waste [75].

These findings highlight the need to optimize medication use and avoid polypharmacy. By adopting a patient-centered care approach—where patients are actively involved in the decision-making process—unnecessary prescriptions can be reduced, and patients can be educated on proper drug disposal methods.

Unfortunately, the pharmaceutical industry is not transparent when it comes to environmental impacts. Of the over 200 global pharmaceutical companies participating in the market, only 25 of them consistently announced their GHG emissions between 2014 and 2019. This lack of information hinders the effects of monitoring the impact of the pharmaceutical industry on the environment, and similarly makes it harder to plan and implement interventions. However, there are a number of companies that have made environmental sustainability a priority. AstraZeneca announced in 2020 that 89% of its electricity use was from renewable sources. They aimed to reach carbon neutrality by 2025 and made significant progress in decreasing their emissions. Pfizer reduced their GHG emissions by 20% in four years by investing in energy preservation projects. GlaxoSmithKline has reduced waste sent to landfills by 78%, water consumption by 31%, and GHG emissions by 34% since 2010, and aims for zero emissions in its operations by 2030 [76].

5.4.6 GHG Emissions and Carbon Footprint

The healthcare sector is responsible for 4.4% of global GHG emissions. Studies indicate that transitioning healthcare systems to more sustainable models could reduce emissions by 32% to 80% by 2040, depending on the strategies implemented [78]. Although this transition is estimated to require an investment of $15 billion over the next 10 years, previous initiatives have demonstrated rapid returns on investment. For example, implementing effective carbon reduction measures could generate savings of £180 million across the NHS in England. Similarly, energy-saving initiatives have resulted in annual savings of £130,000 by reducing electricity and gas costs [79].

GHG emissions not only harm the environment but also pose serious risks to human health. Estimates suggest that GHG emissions from the U.S. healthcare sector contribute to substantial health damages, equivalent to 123,000 to 381,000 DALYs lost annually [80].

Several clinical initiatives have proven effective in reducing healthcare-related GHG emissions. For instance, the use of less harmful anesthetic gases and minimizing disposable materials in surgical settings have been shown to decrease the carbon footprint of surgical procedures by up to 80% [81]. Surgical operations not only contribute significantly to emissions but also generate large amounts of waste and consume substantial energy compared to other areas of healthcare. In the U.K., outpatient surgical centers produce an average of 1,758 grams of waste per patient, whereas in-clinic visits generate 379 grams per encounter [77]. Additionally, operating theaters have been identified as being three to six times more energy-intensive than entire hospitals [81, 82]. These findings highlight the need for surgical procedures and operating theaters to be a primary focus in achieving environmental sustainability in healthcare facilities, as they are among the most significant contributors to harmful emissions, waste production, and energy consumption.

5.5 Case Studies

There have been a number of environmentalist initiatives across the globe. The main focuses have been decreasing GHG emissions, lowering carbon footprints, decreasing energy consumption, and decreasing waste. Some of the initiatives can be listed as follows:

1. **BUND Label (Germany)**: This initiative recognizes hospitals for their energy-saving efforts by achieving the BUND "Energy Saving Hospital" label, which fosters a culture of sustainability [83].
2. **KLIK Project (Germany):** Various measures under the KLIK green framework were implemented, including the installation of combined heat and power plants to generate electricity, switching to LED lighting, and utilizing electric vehicles for hospital operations. In a collective effort, hospitals participating in this project reduced their CO_2 emissions by approximately 34,500 tons over three years, leading to a decrease in energy costs amounting to €9 million [83].
3. **Classification of Medicines (Sweden):** In this study, the environmental impact of active ingredients in human medicines marketed in Sweden was estimated, focusing on their risk assessment and hazard potential. The study intended to educate healthcare professionals and patients, promoting the use of less harmful pharmaceuticals and encouraging producers to consider environmental impact during drug development [84]. As NCD patients often use drugs from their diagnosis until their demise, it is especially important that these drugs are as environmentally friendly as possible, as

they will be in use for a long time. Allowing both the healthcare provider and the consumer to understand the impact of the products is therefore critical.

4. **Pharmaceutical Logistics Improvement (Italy):** In this case, the logistics within hospital pharmacies were improved, specifically focusing on warehouse centralization, automation of drug handling processes, and the implementation of department cabinets. The results indicated that these changes could lead to significant cost reductions, enhanced organization in drug management, and improved quality of service [85]. Patients with NCDs are a group of patients who use the highest number of drugs, with some patients using over four drugs for hypertension alone, whereas kidney disease patients sometimes take up to five medicines at every meal. Automated drug handling processes that minimize mistakes are therefore especially important in this group, as there can often be mistakes in drug handling because of the high number of drugs in use.
5. **Patient Electronic Management System (Portugal):** The PEM system was developed to enhance the electronic prescription process by integrating it with patient health records. This system allows physicians to access a patient's medication history and chronic medications, thereby preventing overdoses, reducing medication errors, and minimizing drug waste [86]. As most patients with NCDs visit multiple doctors and get prescriptions from all of them, systems that allow physicians to access records of drugs already in use are especially important.
6. **HVAC System Upgrade (USA):** Lewis County General Hospital improved its HVAC system to include four new variable frequency drives on the supply and return fans of the air handler. This upgrade aimed to reduce energy consumption and improve fan performance throughout the facility. The energy used by the HVAC system was reduced by 15%, resulting in a $7,500 annual savings in energy costs [87].
7. **Reducing Waste in Hemodialysis (Ireland):** The primary change was training the dialysis staff to use a function on the dialysis machines that allowed for the drainage of blood-

contaminated fluid from the dialysis circuit prior to the removal of the circuits for disposal. Through this application, 80 kg less clinical waste was generated weekly from the dialysis unit [88]. Chronic kidney disease is a top 10 cause of mortality worldwide; however, it is also costly in terms of finance and environmental burden. Lessening this burden is especially important as projections show that chronic kidney disease will show a significant rise in this decade.

8. **Optimization of Blood Collection (Argentina)**: The hospital's blood collection process was renewed at the medical laboratories. Technology was improved to be more efficient in energy consumption and the amount of blood volume necessary. The update resulted in 900 kg of biomedical waste avoided annually, and thus a reduction of more than 15,000 kg CO_2 emissions [89]. NCD patients are often in close control and have to have blood samples often. Minimizing blood draw volumes is critical to prevent anemia in patients undergoing frequent testing.
9. **On-site Treatment of Hazardous Waste (South Africa):** The hospital implemented an on-site Newster NW50 sterilizer to safely treat infectious and sharps waste, replacing outsourced incineration and transport. This transition led to a 99% reduction in transport emissions, a 75% decrease in waste volume, and a 45% cost savings ($70,000/year). The sterilized waste is now landfill-safe, reducing contamination risks and environmental impact [89].
10. **Telemedicine for Eye-Care (India):** The establishment of satellite-assisted telemedicine centers has expanded access to subsidized primary eye care for peri-urban populations, reducing the need for travel to distant tertiary hospitals. In 2021 alone, 8,553 trips were avoided, preventing 54.3 tCO_2e emissions while addressing preventable blindness and improving healthcare accessibility [89]. Diabetes patients, who require yearly check-ups, would especially benefit from these services. Many patients with NCDs, especially in advanced ages, have trouble visiting healthcare facilities, and accessible and easily usable telemedicine services are especially important for this group.

11. **Solar Panels (Singapore):** The hospital implemented an energy reduction plan by installing a photovoltaic system, securing clean energy at a 68% discount on national tariff rates with no maintenance costs. Since its commissioning in July 2021, the system has saved 154,722 kg CO_2 emissions and prevented the use of 368,504 kWh of fossil fuel-generated electricity, significantly reducing the hospital's carbon footprint [89].
12. **Electric Ambulances (Spain):** The Galician Health Service has introduced electric ambulances to reduce emissions and costs for non-urgent patient transfers. Compared to conventional ambulances, they used 97% less fuel, cutting CO_2 emissions by 80% and saving over €22 per 102 km [89].
13. **AstraZeneca Net-Zero Initiative:** The pharmaceutical company, which focuses mainly on medicines used in NCDs, has committed to environmental sustainability and has made it a priority in all its operations. With this approach, they have achieved a 67.6% reduction in GHG emissions, a 19.5% reduction in water use, and a 13.2% reduction in waste [90]. Additionally, because respiratory diseases like asthma and COPD are major NCDs, AstraZeneca has introduced low-carbon inhalers to replace traditional ones with high hydrofluorocarbon (HFC) emissions.
14. **Cork University Hospital Environment Program (Ireland):** The hospital established local maternity outpatient clinics to reduce patient travel costs and time for routine appointments. This initiative improved access to maternal care while simultaneously cutting down on transportation-related environmental impacts, such as vehicle emissions and traffic congestion. By bringing healthcare services closer to the community, the hospital enhanced patient convenience and reduced the carbon footprint associated with travel.

    The hospital additionally implemented "Kanban systems," which are aimed at optimizing inventory management and enhancing healthcare efficiency. This method ensures that resources are used based on actual demand, preventing overproduction and reducing waste caused by obsolescence. The system allows for real-time tracking and replenishment of supplies only when necessary, minimizing excess inventory and preventing materials from becoming outdated. This approach improved efficiency, reduced waste, and better aligned resources with patient needs [91].

15. **Queensland Hospitals 3Rs (Australia):** Queensland hospitals adopted a strategy named the "3Rs: Reduce, Reuse, and Recycle." The aim was to enhance waste management and sustainability. By refining procurement practices and promoting mindful material use, they minimized waste, cutting disposal costs. Reuse initiatives allowed for the sanitization and repurposing of non-hazardous materials, reducing landfill contributions and procurement expenses while fostering a culture of sustainability. A structured recycling program was implemented, with a strong focus on clear segregation guidelines and color-coded bins, and recycling rates saw significant improvements. The Royal Brisbane and Women's Hospital alone saved approximately $200,000 annually by implementing this strategy. Beyond environmental and financial benefits, this strategy also reduced occupational injuries related to waste management and increased staff awareness of sustainable practices [92].
16. **Pfizer's Sustainability Programs:** Between 2000 and 2014, Pfizer cut its GHG emissions by 50% and set a goal to reduce emissions by 20% by 2020 from their 2012 baseline. Since 2000, the company has completed around 3,300 energy projects, saving approximately $150 million annually and reducing CO_2 emissions by 814,000 tons. Investments in renewable energy included a second wind turbine in Puurs, Belgium, generating 3.3 million kilowatt-hours of clean energy. Pfizer also committed to ensuring 100% of key suppliers manage their environmental impacts by 2020, with 90% setting GHG reduction targets to address scope three emissions. Organizational initiatives included forming Site Sustainability teams and enhancing internal communications to promote energy efficiency awareness [93].
17. **National Health Service Net-Zero Goal (United Kingdom):** The U.K.'s NHS has set out to achieve two net-zero goals:

- by 2040 for the NHS Carbon Footprint (direct emissions) with an ambition for an 80% reduction (compared with a 1990 baseline) by 2032
- by 2045 for the NHS Carbon Footprint Plus (indirect emissions) with an ambition for an 80% reduction (compared with a 1990 baseline) by 2039

  By 2020, a reduction of 62% on carbon footprint and a reduction of 26% on carbon footprint plus has already been accomplished [94]. This program, which is the first of its kind in the world, is a standard that all countries and health services around the world should strive to reach.

18. **Novo Nordisk ReMed Program:** Novo Nordisk has committed to reaching net-zero CO_2 emissions in 2045 across its full value chain. In line with this goal, they have established their ReMed campaign, enabling diabetes patients who are dependent on daily insulin use to return their used insulin pens and thus enabling the pens to be safely recycled, instead of becoming hazardous waste [95].

19. **NYC's Plant-Based Prescriptions Program:** New York City public hospitals have started plant-based meal plans as a first-line treatment for NCDs like obesity, diabetes, and cardiovascular diseases, reducing reliance on emission-heavy meat production [96]. Similarly, some hospitals in the U.K. and Sweden have also introduced low-carbon, plant-based diets to reduce environmental impact while promoting better NCD prevention through healthier food choices.

5.6 Conclusion

Addressing the environmental impact of healthcare while managing the rising burden of NCDs poses a significant public health challenge globally. Reaching better outcomes in both areas requires a multidisciplinary paradigm shift toward sustainability. The current trajectory of healthcare systems—characterized by high resource consumption and significant waste production—

exacerbates ecological degradation and climate change, which, in turn, fuels the very diseases the systems aim to treat. Healthcare often treats disease while simultaneously harming the environment, creating a cycle that worsens both. This chapter has highlighted this bidirectional relationship between environmental sustainability and NCDs, emphasizing the need for systemic reforms. Green healthcare infrastructure, low-carbon medical technologies, pharmaceutical technology changes, educational reforms in medical schools and healthcare facilities, and policy-driven incentives for sustainable practices are crucial steps toward a more ecologically responsible health sector. Furthermore, interdisciplinary collaboration between public health professionals, policymakers, and environmental scientists is essential for implementing viable solutions. By integrating sustainability into healthcare policy and practice, we can create a future where health systems not only treat diseases but also contribute to planetary well-being, ensuring a healthier environment for generations to come. The concept of One Health, first proposed by Rudolf Virchow in the mid-19th century, has proven itself relevant one and a half centuries later, demonstrating that human health and environmental health are inextricably linked.

References

1. World Commission on Environment and Development. (1987). *Our Common Future*. Oxford University Press.
2. World Health Organization: WHO. (2019, June 12). Noncommunicable diseases. https://www.who.int/health-topics/noncommunicable-diseases.
3. Western Pacific Health Data Platform. (2018). Noncommunicable diseases. https://data.wpro.who.int/noncommunicable-diseases-2018.
4. NCDs. (2022, July 25). NCD Alliance. https://ncdalliance.org/why-ncds/NCDs.
5. WHO. (2020). Methods and data sources for country-level causes of death during 2000–2019 (Global Health Estimates Technical Paper WHO/DDI/DNA/GHE/2020.2).

27. World Health Organization. (2008). *WHO Report on the Global Tobacco Epidemic, 2008: The MPOWER Package*. Geneva. Available at: http://www.who.int/tobacco/mpower/mpower_report_full_2008.pdf.

28. Graham, K., Leonard, K.E., Room, R., et al. (1998). Current directions in research on understanding and preventing intoxicated aggression. *Addiction*, 93, 659–76.

29. Room, R., Schmidt, L., Rehm, J., & Mäkelä, P. (2008). International regulation of alcohol. *British Medical Journal*, 337, a236.

30. Rehm, J., Baliunas, D., Borges, G.L.G., et al. (2010). The relation between different dimensions of alcohol consumption and burden of disease: An overview. *Addiction*, 105(5), 817–43.

31. Parry, C., Rehm, J., Poznyak, V., & Room, R. (2009). Alcohol and infectious disease: An overlooked causal linkage. *Addiction*, 104(3), 331–2.

32. Perrine, M.W., Peck, R.C., & Fell, J.C. (1989). Epidemiologic perspectives on drunk driving. In *Surgeon General's Workshop on Drunk Driving: Background Papers*, 35–76. Washington, DC: US Department of Health and Human Services.

33. Wolfgang, M.E. (1958). *Patterns in Criminal Homicide*. Philadelphia, PA: University of Pennsylvania Press.

34. Her, M., & Rehm, J. (1998). Alcohol and all-cause mortality in Europe 1982–1990: A pooled cross-section time-series analysis. *Addiction*, 93, 1335–40.

35. Norström, T. (1996). Per capita consumption and total mortality: An analysis of historical data. *Addiction*, 91, 339–44.

36. Shkolnikov, V.M., & Nemtsov, A. (1997). The anti-alcohol campaign and variations in Russian mortality. In J.L. Bobadilla, C.A. Costello, and F. Mitchell (eds.) *Premature Death in the New Independent States*, 239–61. Washington, DC: National Academy Press.

37. Leon, D.A., Chenet, L., Shkolnikov, V.M., et al. (1997). Huge variation in Russian mortality rates 1984–94: Artefact, alcohol, or what? *The Lancet*, 350, 383–8.

38. Navarro, H.J., Doran, C.M., & Shakeshaft, A.P. (2010). Measuring costs of alcohol harm to others: A review of the literature. *Drug Alcohol Depend*, 114(2–3).

39. Connor, J., & Casswell, S. (2012). Alcohol-related harm to others in New Zealand: Evidence of the burden and gaps in knowledge. *N Z Med J.*, 125(1360), 11–27.

40. Hallal, P.C., Andersen, L.B., Bull, F.C., Guthold, R., Haskell, W., & Ekelund, U. (2012). Global physical activity levels: Surveillance progress, pitfalls, and prospects. *The Lancet*, 380(9838), 247–5.

41. Gupta, R., Deedwania, P.C., Sharma, K., et al. (2012). Association of educational, occupational and socioeconomic status with cardio-vascular risk factors in Asian Indians: A cross-sectional study. *PLoS One*, 7(8), e44098.

42. Lee, I.M., Shiroma, E.J., Lobelo, F., Puska, P., Blair, S.N., & Katzmarzyk, P.T. (2012). Effect of physical inactivity on major non-communicable diseases worldwide: An analysis of burden of disease and life expectancy. *The Lancet*, 219.

43. Franco, O.H., de Laet, C., Peeters, A., Jonker, J., Mackenbach, J., & Nusselder, W. (2005). Effects of physical activity on life expectancy with cardiovascular disease. *Arch Intern Med.*, 165, 2355–60.

44. Paffenbarger, R.S., Jr, Hyde R.T., Wing, A.L., & Hsieh, C.C. (1986). Physical activity, all-cause mortality, and longevity of college alumni. *N Engl J Med.*, 314, 605–13.

45. Wen, C.P., Wai, J.P.M., Tsai, M.K., Yang, Y.C., Cheng, T.Y.D., Lee, M-C, et al. (2011). Minimum amount of physical activity for reduced mortality and extended life expectancy: A prospective cohort study. *The Lancet*, 378, 1244–53.

46. Lee, I.M., Shiroma, E.J., Lobelo, F., Puska, P., Blair, S.N., Katzmarzyk, P.T., & Lancet Physical Activity Series Working Group. (2012). Effect of physical inactivity on major non-communicable diseases worldwide: An analysis of burden of disease and life expectancy. *The Lancet (London, England)*, 380(9838), 219–229. https://doi.org/10.1016/S0140-6736(12)61031-9.

47. World Health Organization. (2013b). *Global Recommendations on Physical Activity for Health*. [Online] Available at: http://www.who.int/dietphysicalactivity/factsheet_recommendations/en/.

48. GBD 2017 Diet Collaborators. (2019). Health effects of dietary risks in 195 countries, 1990–2017: A systematic analysis for the Global Burden of Disease Study 2017. *The Lancet (London, England)*, 393(10184), 1958–1972. https://doi.org/10.1016/S0140-6736(19)30041-8.

49. Hooper, L., Abdelhamid, A., Bunn, D., Brown, T., Summerbell, C.D., & Skeaff, C.M. (2015). Effects of total fat intake on body weight. *Cochrane Database Syst Rev.*, (8), CD011834.

50. World Health Organization. (2003). Diet, nutrition and the prevention of chronic diseases: Report of a Joint WHO/FAO Expert Consultation. *WHO Technical Report Series*, No. 916. Geneva.
51. Food and Agriculture Organization of the United Nations (2010). Fats and fatty acids in human nutrition: Report of an expert consultation. *FAO Food and Nutrition Paper 91*. Rome.
52. World Health Organization. (2015). Guideline: Sugars intake for adults and children. Geneva.
53. World Health Organization. (2012). Guideline: Sodium intake for adults and children. Geneva.
54. World Health Organization. (2013). Global action plan for the prevention and control of NCDs 2013–2020. Geneva.
55. Osborne, R.H., Elmer, S., Hawkins, M., Cheng, C.C., Batterham, R.W., Dias, S., Good, S., Monteiro, M.G., Mikkelsen, B. Nadarajah, R.G. & Fones, G. (2022). Health literacy development is central to the prevention and control of non-communicable diseases. *BMJ Global Health*, 7, e010362.
56. Fenta, E.T., Kidie, A.A., Tiruneh, M.G., et al. (2024). Exploring barriers of health literacy on non-communicable disease prevention and care among patients in North Wollo zone public hospitals, Northeast, Ethiopia, 2023: Application of socio-ecological model. *BMC Public Health*, 24, 971. https://doi.org/10.1186/s12889-024-18524-8.
57. Weiss, Barry D. (2007). Health Literacy and Patient Safety: Help Patients Understand. Manual for Clinicians. 2nd ed. Chicago, IL: American Medical Association Foundation.
58. Mathews, S.C., McShea, M.J., Hanley, C.L., Ravitz, A., Labrique, A.B., & Cohen, A.B. (2019). Digital health: A path to validation. *NPJ Digital Medicine*, 2, Article 38. https://doi.org/10.1038/s41746-019-0111-3.
59. Brewer, L.C., Fortuna, K.L., Jones, C., Walker, R., Hayes, S.N., Patten, C.A., & Cooper, L.A. (2020). Back to the future: Achieving health equity through health informatics and digital health. *JMIR mHealth and uHealth*, 8(1), e14512. https://doi.org/10.2196/14512.
60. Labrique, A., Vasudevan, L., Mehl, G., Rosskam, E., & Hyder, A.A. (2018). Digital health and health systems of the future. *Global Health: Science and Practice*, 6(Supplement 1), S1–S4. https://doi.org/10.9745/GHSP-D-18-00342.

61. Benis, A., Matz, S., & Tzafestas, A. (2021). One digital health: A unified framework for future health ecosystems. *Journal of Medical Internet Research,* 23(2), e22189. https://doi.org/10.2196/22189.
62. Thompson, M. (2021). The environmental impacts of digital health. *Digital Health,* 7, Article 20552076211033421. https://doi.org/10.1177/20552076211033421.
63. Zou, Z.L., et al. (2022). Evaluating the carbon footprint of digital health interventions: A scoping review. *Journal of the American Medical Informatics Association,* 29(12), 2128–2139. https://doi.org/10.1093/jamia/ocac196.
64. Bloomfield, P.S., Clutton-Brock, P., Pencheon, E., Magnusson, J., & Karpathakis, K. (2021). Artificial intelligence in the NHS: Climate and emissions. *The Journal of Climate Change and Health,* 4, 100056. https://doi.org/10.1016/j.joclim.2021.100056.
65. Thakur, R., & Ramesh, S. (2015). Healthcare waste management research: A structured analysis and review (2005–2014). *Waste Management & Research,* 33(10), 859–874.
66. Ananth, A.P., Prashanthini, V., & Visvanathan, C. (2009). Healthcare waste management in Asia. *Environmental Engineering and Management Journal,* 8(6), 1325–1332. https://doi.org/10.30672/eemj.2009.0211.
67. Kenny, C., & Priyadarshini, A. (2021). Review of current healthcare waste management methods and their effect on global health. *Healthcare,* 9, 284. http://doi.org/10.3390/healthcare9030284.
68. Janik-Karpinska, E., Brancaleoni, R., Niemcewicz, M., Wojtas, W., Foco, M., Podogrocki, M., & Bijak, M. (2023). Healthcare waste: A serious problem for global health. *Healthcare,* 11(2), 242. https://doi.org/10.3390/healthcare11020242.
69. Lallemand, N.C. (2012). Health policy brief: Reducing waste in health care. *Health Affairs.* Retrieved from https://www.healthaffairs.org/healthpolicybriefs.
70. Dhimal, M. (2021). Understanding linkages between environmental risk factors and noncommunicable diseases. *FASEB BioAdvances,* 3(5).
71. Woodruff, T.J. (2015). Making it real—The environmental burden of disease. *Journal of Clinical Endocrinology & Metabolism,* 100(4), 1241–1244. https://doi.org/10.1210/jc.2015-1622.

72. Kuijper, F.M. (2021). The urgent need of an ecological transition in medical training to address tomorrow's challenges: A medical student's perspective. *The Journal of Climate Change and Health,* 4, 100039. https://doi.org/10.1016/j.joclim.2021.100039.
73. Alexander, M. (2021). Climate change and health: The day for tomorrow. *The Journal of Climate Change and Health,* 4, 100062. https://doi.org/10.1016/j.joclim.2021.100062.
74. Singh, C., & Gurudiwan, P. (2024). Exploring pharmacy students' perceptions of environmental sustainability in pharmacy education. *Natural and Engineering Sciences,* 9(1), 452–460. https://doi.org/10.28978-nesciences.1575487-4323227.
75. Cussans, A., Harvey, G., Kemple, T., & Tomson, M. (2021). Interventions to reduce the environmental impact of medicines: A UK perspective. *The Journal of Climate Change and Health,* 4, 100079. https://doi.org/10.1016/j.joclim.2021.100079.
76. Okereke, M. (2021). How pharmaceutical industries can address the growing problem of climate change. *The Journal of Climate Change and Health,* 4, 100049. https://doi.org/10.1016/j.joclim.2021.100049.
77. Taylor, A.L., Levin, J., Chan, J., Lee, M., Kasitinon, D., Miller, E., & Fox, P. (2021). Improving environmental sustainability in outpatient clinics: Lessons from a waste audit. *The Journal of Climate Change and Health,* 4, 100070. https://doi.org/10.1016/j.joclim.2021.100070.
78. Health Care Without Harm, & Arup. (2023). Health care decarbonization: Road map.
79. King's Fund. (2012). Sustainable health and social care. Retrieved from https://www.kingsfund.org.uk/publications/sustainable-health-and-social-care.
80. Eckelman, M.J., & Sherman, J. (2016). Environmental impacts of the US health care system and effects on public health. *PLoS One,* 11(6), e0157014.
81. Thiel, C.L., Woods, N.C., & Bilec, M.M. (2018). Sustainability interventions in the operating room: A life cycle assessment study of laparoscopic hysterectomy. *American Journal of Public Health,* 108(S2), S158–S164. https://doi.org/10.2105/AJPH.2018.304397.
82. MacNeill, A.J, Lillywhite, R., & Brown, C.J. (2017). The impact of surgery on global climate: A carbon foot printing study of operating theatres in three health systems. *Lancet Planet Health.* 1(9), e381–e388. DOI: 10.1016/S2542-5196(17)30162-6.

83. Gaeta Hernández, A.-C. (2016). Reducing healthcare's climate footprint: Opportunities for European hospitals & health systems. *Health Care Without Harm (HCWH) Europe*. Retrieved from www.noharm-europe.org.

84. Wennmalm, Å., & Gunnarsson, B. (2009). Environmental risk assessment of human medicines in Sweden: A national classification system for human medicines. *Environment International*, 35(5), 775–777. https://doi.org/10.1016/j.envint.2008.11.001.

85. Ferretti, M., Favalli, F., & Zangrandi, A. (2014). Impact of a logistic improvement in a hospital pharmacy: Effects on the economics of a healthcare organization. *International Journal of Engineering Science and Technology*, 6(3), 85–95. https://doi.org/10.4314/ijest.v6i3.7S.

86. Patrao, L., Deveza, R., & Martins, H. (2013). PEM: A new patient centred electronic prescription platform. *Procedia Technology*, 9, 1313–1319. https://doi.org/10.1016/j.protcy.2013.12.147.

87. US Department of Energy. (2011). Hospitals save energy and money by optimizing HVAC performance. Available at: https://www1.eere.energy.gov/buildings/publications/pdfs/alliances/hea_hvac_fs.pdf.

88. Reidy, M. (2014). Reducing clinical waste in a haemodialysis clinic: Small change, big impact (Master's thesis). Royal College of Surgeons in Ireland.

89. Health Care Without Harm. (n.d.). Health Care Climate Learning Initiative. Health Care Climate Action. Retrieved on January 30, 2025, from https://healthcareclimateaction.org/learning-initiative.

90. AstraZeneca. (n.d.). Environmental protection. AstraZeneca. Retrieved on January 30, 2025, from https://www.astrazeneca.com/sustainability/environmental-protection.html.

91. Ryan-Fogarty, Y., O'Regan, B., & Moles, R. (2016). Greening healthcare: Systematic implementation of environmental programmes in a university teaching hospital. *Journal of Cleaner Production*, 126, 248–259. https://doi.org/10.1016/j.jclepro.2016.03.017.

92. Irianti, S. (2016). Hospital waste management in Queensland, Australia: Lessons and recommendations for Indonesian hospitals. *Media Litbangkes*, 26(2), 109–118.

93. Science Based Targets Case Study: Pfizer. Retrieved from www.sciencebasedtragets.org on 27/02/2025.

94. Delivering a 'Net Zero' National Health Service, 2022, NHS, England. Retrieved from www.england.nhs.uk/greenernhs/a-net-zero-nhs/on 27/02/2025.

95. Novo Nordisk. Recycling used devices. In Zero environmental impact. Retrieved February 27, 2025, from https://www.novonordisk.com/sustainable-business/zero-environmental-impact/recycling-used-devices.html
96. New York City Health + Hospitals. (n.d.). Lifestyle Medicine Program. Retrieved February 27, 2025, from https://www.nychealthandhospitals.org/services/lifestyle-medicine-program/.

Chapter 6

Eco-Friendly Practices: Reducing Healthcare's Carbon Footprint

Zulfkar Qadrie,[a] Humaira Ashraf,[b] Mudasir Maqbool,[a] and Mohd Altaf Dar[c]

[a]*Department of Pharmacology, Government Medical College, Baramulla, Jammu and Kashmir, India*
[b]*Department of Animal Nutrition, Sher-e-Kashmir University of Agricultural Sciences and Technology—Kashmir, Srinagar, Jammu and Kashmir, India*
[c]*Department of Pharmacology, CT Institute of Pharmaceutical Sciences, Punjab Technical University, Jalandhar, Punjab, India*

bhatmudasir92@gmail.com

Reducing healthcare's carbon footprint is imperative for a sustainable future, considering the sector's significant environmental impact. Adopting eco-friendly practices not only aligns with global sustainability goals but also promotes public health by minimizing pollution and resource depletion. One key strategy is the integration of renewable energy sources within healthcare facilities. Transitioning to solar, wind, or other sustainable energy options can significantly reduce carbon emissions associated with electricity consumption. Implementing energy-efficient

Environmentalism in Healthcare: Caring for Tomorrow Ecologically
Edited by Jacqueline A. Stagner and David S.-K. Ting

ISBN 978-981-5129-95-3 (Hardcover), 978-1-003-74869-4 (eBook)
www.jennystanford.com

DOI: 10.1201/9781003748694-6

technologies, such as LED lighting and smart HVAC systems, further contributes to a greener healthcare infrastructure. Promoting telehealth services is another impactful measure. Embracing virtual consultations reduces the need for patient travel, decreasing both carbon emissions from transportation and the overall demand on healthcare infrastructure. Remote monitoring and electronic health records (EHRs) also streamline operations, minimizing the carbon footprint of paperwork and administrative processes. Additionally, sustainable waste management practices play a vital role. Hospitals generate substantial amounts of waste, including hazardous materials. Implementing recycling programs, reducing single-use plastics, and proper disposal of medical waste through eco-friendly methods contribute to a more sustainable healthcare system. Supply chain management is crucial for a greener healthcare sector. Selecting suppliers with eco-friendly practices and sourcing products locally whenever possible can significantly reduce the carbon footprint associated with manufacturing and transportation.

6.1 Introduction

Climate change constitutes a crucial global health challenge of the twenty-first century. It transcends a mere environmental concern; it constitutes a grave public health catastrophe, having both direct and indirect ramifications for global human well-being. The World Health Organization (WHO) estimates that from 2030 to 2050, climate change may cause an additional 250,000 deaths annually due to malnutrition, malaria, diarrhea, and heat stress alone. As climate change progresses, health consequences will intensify, disproportionately affecting marginalized populations. Severe weather phenomena are among the most immediate consequences of climate change on human health [1]. Heatwaves, floods, storms, and wildfires are becoming common and severe, resulting in immediate physical damage and enduring health complications. Heatwaves significantly elevate the risk of heat-stroke, dehydration, and cardiovascular and respiratory ailments, particularly among the elderly and individuals with previous conditions. Recent instances encompass unprecedented heatwaves in Europe and North America, leading to thousands of fatalities attributable to heat [2]. Flooding and other extreme weather phenomena, like hurricanes and typhoons, pose significant health risks by causing injuries, displacing populations, and compromising essential infrastructure such as hospitals and clinics. Displaced populations are often susceptible to waterborne diseases like cholera, while stagnant water resulting from floods creates optimal breeding sites for mosquitoes that transmit malaria and dengue fever. Climate change exerts a significant indirect influence on health, alongside its direct consequences. Alterations in meteorological patterns are influencing the geographical distribution of infectious diseases [3]. Elevated temperatures facilitate the proliferation of mosquitoes in formerly cooler regions, enabling the dissemination of diseases such as malaria, dengue fever, and the Zika virus to novel locales. This proliferation poses substantial challenges for healthcare systems, especially in regions with minimal experience in managing these illnesses. Climate change affects agricultural productivity, hence heightening worries around food security. Droughts, erratic precipitation, and excessive temperatures diminish agricultural production, exacerbating hunger, especially in low-income countries dependent on subsistence agriculture. Malnutrition diminishes immune function, rendering children and other at-risk populations more susceptible to illness. This has been most apparent during prolonged droughts in East Africa, where extensive famine and malnutrition have jeopardized millions of lives [4].

Climate change is contributing to deteriorating air quality. Increasing temperatures and elevated concentrations of pollutants, including ground-level ozone and particulate matter, intensify respiratory ailments such as asthma, chronic obstructive pulmonary disease (COPD), and lung cancer. Wildfires, increasingly prevalent and intense, intensify air pollution and respiratory health problems. The consequences disproportionately impact marginalized populations, particularly low-income communities, indigenous peoples, and residents of small islands or coastal areas [5]. These communities often lack the resources necessary to adapt to or recover from climate-related health challenges, rendering them particularly susceptible to health risks. Increasing sea levels, for instance, pose existential threats to small island nations, endangering their populations with displacement, loss of livelihoods, and related mental health challenges. Climate change significantly affects mental health. Communities that have endured numerous climate-related disasters, displacement, or loss of livelihood are more susceptible to experiencing depression, anxiety, and post-traumatic stress disorder (PTSD) [6]. Moreover, apprehension and ambiguity regarding the enduring effects of climate change contribute to an escalating issue known as "eco-anxiety," especially among young people who are daunted by the magnitude of the catastrophe [7].

The healthcare sector is essential for preserving human health; nevertheless, it also plays a substantial role in environmental degradation via carbon emissions. Healthcare systems contribute more than 5% of worldwide carbon dioxide (CO_2) emissions, a startling figure considering the industry's objective to enhance health and well-being. As the world confronts escalating threats from climate change, healthcare institutions must acknowledge their involvement in the crisis and assume responsibility for reducing their carbon footprint. This is not merely an environmental need, but also a moral obligation, as climate change poses substantial health risks, especially to marginalized people [8]. The carbon footprint of healthcare arises from multiple aspects, including energy consumption in hospitals, the manufacturing and distribution of medical supplies and pharmaceuticals, waste creation, and the transportation of patients and staff. Hospitals, often functioning around the clock, are energy-intensive facilities requiring heating, cooling, lighting, and the operation of medical equipment. A multitude of hospitals depend on fossil fuels for energy, so they substantially contribute to greenhouse gas (GHG) emissions. Healthcare systems can significantly diminish their environmental impact by adopting energy-efficient technologies and utilizing renewable energy sources [9]. Certain hospitals have been utilizing solar, wind, and geothermal energy to operate, demonstrating that the move is both feasible and beneficial. Sustainable procurement and supply chain management are two significant domains in which healthcare can reduce its carbon footprint. The production and distribution of medical devices, pharmaceuticals, and other supplies substantially contribute to emissions. Healthcare systems can diminish their overall carbon footprint by choosing suppliers that adhere to sustainable standards, including reducing packaging, limiting transportation distances, and employing eco-friendly materials. Moreover, promoting the use of reusable medical devices, where safe and appropriate, can diminish the waste generated by single-use goods, which often end up in landfills or incinerators, releasing detrimental chemicals into the environment [10]. For example, the NHS in the UK and Gundersen Health System in the US have implemented solar and wind energy, achieving measurable reductions in carbon emissions while maintaining operational efficiency.

Waste management is a crucial component in reducing the carbon footprint of the healthcare industry. Hospitals produce substantial quantities of waste, a significant portion of which is hazardous and non-recyclable. Enhancing recycling systems, eradicating superfluous trash, and properly disposing of hazardous materials contribute to emission reduction. For instance, some healthcare systems have adopted measures to reduce plastic consumption, including substituting single-use plastic items with sustainable alternatives or reprocessing certain medical devices. The carbon footprint associated with patient and staff transportation contributes to the overall environmental impact of the healthcare sector. Promote telemedicine and remote consultations, especially for routine follow-ups or non-urgent care, to obviate the need for patients and staff to visit healthcare facilities, hence diminishing emissions [11].

Encouraging public transport, cycling, and carpooling for healthcare professionals and patients can help diminish the sector's reliance on fossil fuels. Certain healthcare facilities have offered incentives to staff who adopt eco-friendly modes of transportation, thereby promoting sustainability. Minimizing the carbon footprint of healthcare not only aids in combating climate change but also aligns with the sector's fundamental goal of preserving health. Climate change disproportionately impacts at-risk populations, including the elderly, economically disadvantaged communities, and individuals with preexisting health concerns. By reducing its emissions, the healthcare sector can directly mitigate these health risks [12]. Moreover, implementing sustainable practices can enhance health outcomes by promoting cleaner air, safer water, and healthier communities. The shift toward sustainability in healthcare can establish a benchmark for other enterprises, demonstrating that environmental preservation and superior treatment are not inherently incompatible. The connection between healthcare and environmental sustainability is complex, as the well-being of the planet and its inhabitants are fundamentally interconnected [13].

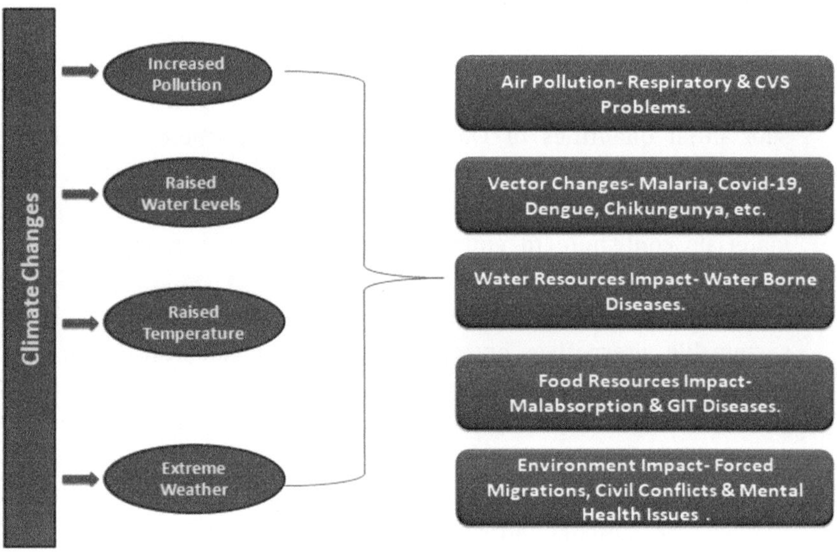

Figure 6.1 Human health and the effect of climate change.

Figure 6.1 highlights the impact of climate change on human health, focusing on four key areas: increased pollution, raised water levels, raised temperatures, and extreme weather. Increased pollution leads to respiratory and cardiovascular problems, while raised water levels contribute to waterborne diseases. Rising temperatures drive vector changes, spreading diseases like malaria,

COVID-19, dengue, and chikungunya. Extreme weather affects food resources, causing malabsorption and gastrointestinal issues, and creates environmental challenges like forced migrations, civil conflicts, and mental health problems. Overall, the image underscores the interconnectedness of climate change and its adverse effects on health and well-being. Although healthcare systems are designed to protect and enhance human health, their operations can significantly harm the environment, contributing to climate change, pollution, and resource depletion. Identifying and confronting this paradox is essential, as environmental degradation fundamentally opposes the long-term objective of safeguarding public health. Attaining equilibrium between healthcare provision and environmental sustainability is essential for protecting future human and ecological health. Healthcare systems are inherently resource-intensive, necessitating substantial quantities of energy, water, and materials to deliver services [14].

Hospitals, research laboratories, and pharmaceutical manufacturing facilities operate continuously, requiring substantial energy resources. Numerous institutions persist in their dependence on nonrenewable energy sources such as coal, natural gas, and oil, all of which significantly contribute to GHG emissions. These emissions not only exacerbate climate change but also degrade air quality, which is linked to respiratory disorders, cardiovascular issues, and early mortality. Healthcare institutions can significantly reduce their environmental footprint and improve health outcomes by transitioning to renewable energy sources, including solar, wind, and geothermal power, leading to cleaner air and a more stable climate [15]. Resource conservation constitutes a significant aspect of the healthcare-sustainability connection. Healthcare facilities and hospitals are significant consumers of water, particularly in regions experiencing water scarcity. Water is essential for maintaining hygiene, sterilizing instruments, and cooling medical technologies; yet, inefficient water usage can exacerbate environmental strain. Adopting water-conserving technologies, such as low-flow faucets, water-efficient sterilization methods, and water recycling and reuse systems, can help healthcare institutions diminish their water footprint while upholding superior care standards [16]. This degree of resource management is essential for ensuring the sustainable operation of healthcare services, particularly in areas already vulnerable to environmental fluctuations like droughts or declining water quality. The creation of waste is a critical issue at the intersection of healthcare and environmental sustainability. The healthcare sector produces a substantial volume of waste, encompassing hazardous substances, disposable plastics, pharmaceutical residues, and general medical waste. If improperly managed, these substances can harm ecosystems, contaminate water supplies, and exacerbate pollution. The transition to single-use products, although crucial for infection control, has led to a substantial rise in plastic waste within the sector [17]. For example, the NHS in the UK and Gundersen Health System in the US have implemented solar and wind energy, achieving measurable reductions in carbon emissions while maintaining operational efficiency.

Many healthcare companies are progressively exploring alternatives, including reusable medical equipment, biodegradable materials, and enhanced recycling operations. These waste-reduction strategies not only diminish the environmental impact of healthcare operations but also mitigate the long-term ecological repercussions of plastic pollution and landfill mismanagement. The environmental sustainability of healthcare directly influences public health, as environmental degradation leads to several health problems [18]. Climate change, driven by unsustainable practices across all sectors, is accelerating the proliferation of infectious diseases, exacerbating respiratory and cardiovascular ailments due to deteriorating air quality, and heightening the occurrence of extreme weather events that cause destruction and displacement. While healthcare organizations strive to mitigate the health effects of environmental changes, they concurrently exacerbate the very problems they want to resolve. The energy-intensive operations of hospitals and the trash produced by medical institutions may aggravate public health issues associated with climate change [19]. Mitigating the environmental impact of healthcare systems can disrupt the cycle by tackling the fundamental causes of environmental degradation while simultaneously enhancing public health. Sustainability in healthcare includes the advocacy of preventative care and healthy lifestyles, which can reduce the necessity for expensive medical interventions [20]. Healthcare systems that emphasize preventive measures, like vaccinations, health education, and chronic disease management, can enhance health outcomes while simultaneously reducing the environmental footprint associated with more complex and energy-demanding treatments. Advocating for a comprehensive approach to health that includes environmental wellness encourages healthcare organizations to transition from reactive care to proactive, sustainable practices that advantage both individuals and the planet [21]. The connection between healthcare and environmental sustainability illustrates a fundamental reality: human health and environmental health are inseparably intertwined. A contaminated environment leads to adverse health outcomes, whereas a cleaner environment fosters healthier populations. Emphasizing sustainability enables healthcare systems to reduce their environmental impact while simultaneously enhancing public health outcomes. Moreover, healthcare institutions can serve as a model for other industries and communities in implementing more sustainable practices. In light of the escalating challenges posed by climate change, resource depletion, and environmental degradation, it is imperative for the global health community to integrate sustainability into healthcare operations to secure a more favorable future for all [22].

6.2 Current Carbon Footprint of Healthcare Systems

The healthcare sector contributes substantially to global carbon emissions, a contradiction considering its objective to protect human health. Recent analyses reveal that healthcare accounts for approximately 5% of global GHG emissions, a significant statistic that positions it among the most carbon-intensive sectors. The global healthcare sector, if considered a nation, would rank as the fifth-largest CO_2 emitter, highlighting the imperative for immediate measures to mitigate its environmental impact. These emissions originate from multiple sources within the healthcare system, encompassing energy use in hospitals, pharmaceutical manufacturing, medical device production, and the transportation of patients and supplies. A significant factor in healthcare's carbon footprint is its reliance on energy, especially from fossil fuels [23]. Hospitals, functioning continuously, are among the most energy-intensive structures, utilizing substantial electricity for illumination, heating, cooling, and operating medical apparatus. In affluent nations, like the United States, healthcare accounts for around 8.5% of the total GHG emissions. The energy-intensive characteristics of contemporary healthcare indicate that even small efficiency improvements in hospitals can yield substantial environmental advantages. Notwithstanding progress in medical technology and healthcare provision, a significant portion of energy utilized in hospitals and clinics continues to derive from coal, oil, and natural gas, exacerbating climate change and its related health hazards. Pharmaceuticals and medical gadgets are a significant source of healthcare-associated emissions [24]. The worldwide pharmaceutical business constitutes around 55% of the emissions within the healthcare sector. This statistic encompasses the production, transportation, and disposal of pharmaceuticals, many of which need substantial energy for manufacturing. The production of pharmaceuticals necessitates significant consumption of chemicals, water, and energy, resulting in carbon emissions and environmental damage. Moreover, several medical gadgets and supplies are intended for single use, resulting in considerable waste production. This issue is especially concerning about plastics, extensively utilized in healthcare for applications ranging from packaging to syringes, resulting in carbon emissions during manufacture and enduring environmental harm upon disposal in landfills or incineration [25]. The carbon footprint of healthcare involves emissions from transportation, including patient travel, staff commuting, and the delivery of medical supplies and equipment. In remote or underserved regions, patients may traverse considerable distances to obtain medical care, thereby contributing to transportation-related emissions. Likewise, the distribution of medical supplies, especially during emergencies, contributes to the sector's carbon emissions [26].

Figure 6.2 highlights strategies to address climate change impacts, starting with monitoring early warnings to ensure timely preparations. It emphasizes reducing the burden on healthcare systems through prevention and proactive measures. Raising awareness and engaging communities is crucial, alongside educating them on the interconnection between health and climate issues. The figure also advocates integrating and adapting strategies discussed within communities to develop localized responses. Overall, it underscores a comprehensive, community-focused approach to managing climate challenges effectively.

Figure 6.2 Arbitration and straits for climate change.

Figure 6.3 outlines strategies to reduce carbon footprints in healthcare systems. It emphasizes the strategic construction of energy-efficient infrastructure and zero-emission transport to cut healthcare-related carbon emissions. Shifting to renewable energy sources, such as solar and wind, adopting zero-waste practices through local sourcing, and proper pharmaceutical prescribing are key measures. Effective circular waste management and digitalization further contribute to reducing environmental impact. These approaches highlight the importance of sustainable practices in healthcare to promote environmental and public health. For example, the NHS in the UK and Gundersen Health

System in the US have implemented solar and wind energy, achieving measurable reductions in carbon emissions while maintaining operational efficiency.

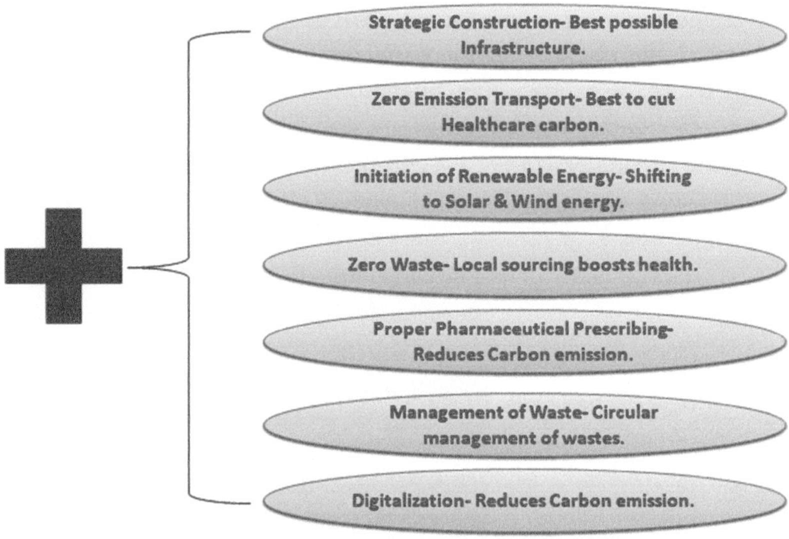

Figure 6.3 Advanced carbon footprints in the healthcare system.

In nations such as the United Kingdom, the NHS has projected that the transportation of patients and personnel constitutes approximately 4% of its overall carbon footprint. Mitigating these emissions via telemedicine, sustainable transportation alternatives, and localized care provision can substantially diminish healthcare's ecological footprint. The waste produced by the healthcare sector contributes to its total carbon emissions. Hospitals generate substantial quantities of waste, including dangerous substances, necessitating energy-intensive disposal techniques [27]. Medical waste, including used syringes, gloves, and medications, frequently requires incineration to avert contamination, resulting in the emission of detrimental chemicals and GHGs into the atmosphere. Estimates indicate that healthcare waste constitutes approximately 2% of worldwide healthcare-related emissions. Enhanced waste management is an integral part of the circular economy, which prioritizes the reuse, recycling, and reduction of waste materials.

Measures, including recycling initiatives, minimizing the use of single-use products, and investing in biodegradable materials, can help mitigate emissions linked to healthcare waste disposal [28].

The carbon footprint of the healthcare sector is alarming; however, there are positive indications of progress. Certain nations' healthcare systems have started to acknowledge their responsibility in addressing climate change and are implementing measures to decrease their emissions. The NHS in the UK has pledged to become the world's first net-zero health system by 2040, presenting a comprehensive strategy to diminish emissions from energy consumption, transport, and procurement. In the United States, numerous hospital systems have pledged to diminish their dependence on fossil fuels and shift toward renewable energy sources, including solar and wind. These efforts exemplify the capacity of healthcare to set a precedent in the worldwide struggle against climate change [29]. Nonetheless, considerable obstacles persist. The global demand for healthcare services is anticipated to increase due to aging populations, the growing prevalence of chronic diseases, and enhanced access to care in low- and middle-income nations. In the absence of coordinated initiatives to separate healthcare delivery from carbon emissions, the environmental effect of the sector may persist in its escalation. Formulating plans for sustainable healthcare delivery, encompassing energy efficiency, waste minimization, and environmentally friendly supply chains, is crucial for mitigating the sector's carbon footprint while upholding superior service standards. The healthcare sector significantly contributes to global carbon emissions, as its operations produce substantial GHGs from multiple sources [30]. Emissions in healthcare mostly stem from energy usage, transportation, medications, and waste management. Comprehending these sources is essential for formulating measures to mitigate healthcare's environmental impact while preserving care quality. Energy consumption constitutes the predominant source of carbon emissions in healthcare, principally attributable to the continuous operation of hospitals and healthcare institutions around the clock. Hospitals necessitate substantial energy for heating, cooling, illumination, and operating critical equipment such as ventilators,

MRIs, and surgical instruments. The predominant source of this energy continues to be fossil fuels, such as coal, oil, and natural gas, resulting in elevated emissions of CO_2 and other GHGs [31]. For example, the NHS in the UK and Gundersen Health System in the US have implemented solar and wind energy, achieving measurable reductions in carbon emissions while maintaining operational efficiency.

In nations such as the United States and the United Kingdom, energy consumption constitutes roughly 60–70% of the carbon footprint of the healthcare industry. Adopting energy-efficient technologies and renewable energy sources such as solar or wind power can markedly diminish emissions from this source. Transportation greatly contributes to the carbon footprint of healthcare. This encompasses the conveyance of patients, personnel, medical provisions, and apparatus. Ambulances, staff vehicles, and patient transportation to hospitals and clinics all entail fuel usage, especially in rural or remote regions where healthcare facilities are distantly located. Moreover, the transportation of medical supplies and equipment, frequently over extensive distances, contributes significantly to healthcare emissions. Estimates indicate that travel constitutes approximately 5% of the overall emissions within the healthcare industry in nations such as the UK [32]. For example, the NHS in the UK and Gundersen Health System in the US have implemented solar and wind energy, achieving measurable reductions in carbon emissions while maintaining operational efficiency.

Mitigating these emissions may entail enhancing telemedicine utilization, advocating for public or electric vehicle (EV) alternatives, and refining supply chain operations to minimize delivery distances. Pharmaceuticals and medical devices are a significant source of emissions within the healthcare sector. The manufacture of pharmaceuticals, encompassing the extraction of raw materials, chemical processing, and distribution, is exceedingly energy-intensive and resource-demanding [33]. This process produces substantial carbon emissions, especially due to the utilization of fossil fuels in production and logistics. The pharmaceutical sector contributes approximately 55% of emissions associated with healthcare worldwide. Moreover, the manufacturing and disposal of single-use medical devices, such as syringes, gloves, and surgical instruments, exacerbate emissions. Numerous technologies are constructed from plastics, which are derived from petroleum and possess an extended environmental lifecycle [34]. Mitigating emissions from drugs and devices can be accomplished by advocating for sustainable production techniques, employing biodegradable ingredients, and promoting the use of reusable or reprocessed medical apparatus. Waste management in healthcare contributes substantially to carbon emissions. Hospitals produce substantial amounts of waste, a significant portion of which is toxic and necessitates specialized treatment, such as burning, to mitigate contamination and infection hazards. Incineration, while essential for some categories of medical waste, emits CO_2 and other detrimental pollutants into the atmosphere. The increasing dependence on single-use medical supplies amplifies plastic waste, which predominantly accumulates in landfills, hence exacerbating emissions during its decomposition. Enhancing waste management is an integral part of the circular economy, which prioritizes the reuse, recycling, and reduction of waste materials. Practices such as recycling, minimizing single-use products, and investing in environmentally sustainable waste disposal technology can mitigate the carbon footprint of healthcare from this source [35].

6.3 Energy Efficiency and Renewable Energy in Healthcare Facilities

Implementing energy-efficient technology in healthcare facilities is a crucial technique for diminishing the sector's carbon footprint, while simultaneously reducing operational expenses and enhancing patient care surroundings. Hospitals and healthcare facilities, which function continually, utilize substantial energy for illumination, heating, cooling, and operating medical equipment. Adopting energy-efficient technology, such as LED lighting, sophisticated HVAC systems, and intelligent building management, can significantly decrease energy consumption while maintaining care quality. The installation of LED lighting is among the most straightforward and economical energy efficiency techniques. Conventional incandescent and fluorescent bulbs exhibit higher energy consumption and reduced longevity in comparison to LED lighting [36]. LEDs consume up to 75% less energy and have a lifespan 25 times greater, rendering them an optimal substitute in hospitals and clinics, where continuous lighting is essential. Furthermore, LEDs generate minimal heat, alleviating the burden on air conditioning systems, so facilitating additional energy savings. Numerous healthcare facilities have transitioned to LED lighting, substantially reducing their energy consumption while ensuring bright, high-quality illumination vital for medical settings. Enhancing heating, ventilation, and air conditioning (HVAC) systems is a vital measure for increasing the energy efficiency of healthcare facilities. HVAC systems account for a significant amount of a hospital's energy use, as they regulate indoor air quality, temperature, and humidity to guarantee comfort and safety [37]. Obsolete HVAC systems may exhibit significant inefficiency, resulting in excessive energy consumption and elevated GHG emissions. Enhancing energy-efficient HVAC systems, including those equipped with variable-speed motors, intelligent thermostats, and energy recovery ventilators (ERVs), can diminish energy use by 20–40%. Contemporary systems can regulate airflow and temperature in various areas of the hospital according to demand, enhancing energy efficiency while ensuring a comfortable atmosphere for patients, staff, and visitors. The implementation of smart building management systems (BMSs) can significantly improve energy efficiency in healthcare facilities [38].

BMSs utilize sensors, data analytics, and automation to oversee and regulate energy consumption in real-time. Sensors can autonomously modify lighting, heating, or cooling in empty spaces, thereby preventing energy wastage. Likewise, BMS can identify maintenance problems, such as leaks or defective equipment, prior to their escalation into significant energy losses. By centralizing the administration of energy-consuming systems such as lighting, HVAC, and medical equipment, a BMS can enhance energy efficiency throughout a facility and offer insights for potential improvements. This leads to significant energy conservation and a decrease in emissions, especially in extensive, intricate healthcare settings. Enhancements in insulation and the building envelope are essential for decreasing energy usage in healthcare facilities [39].

Numerous antiquated hospitals and clinics experience inadequate insulation, resulting in considerable energy loss through walls, windows, and roofs. Enhancing insulation and installing energy-efficient windows helps stabilize indoor temperatures, thereby diminishing the necessity for heating and cooling. Hospitals in colder regions can utilize high-performance insulation materials to limit heat loss, whilst facilities in warmer climates can decrease air conditioning demands by employing reflective roofing materials or window coatings that prevent heat ingress. These enhancements not only diminish energy use but also improve patient comfort by establishing more uniform interior temperatures. Moreover, renewable energy solutions, such as solar panels and geothermal heating and cooling, can be included in healthcare facilities to diminish dependence on fossil fuels. Solar panels offer a sustainable and renewable electricity source for hospitals, thereby decreasing energy expenses and carbon emissions [40]. For example, the NHS in the UK and Gundersen Health System in the US have implemented solar and wind energy, achieving measurable reductions in carbon emissions while maintaining operational efficiency.

Figure 6.4 illustrates the dimensions of sustained procurement, highlighting its environmental, societal, and economic impacts. It emphasizes renewable energy, waste disposal, and reducing harmful materials for environmental sustainability. Societal benefits include health and safety equality, job security, self-employment, and learning opportunities. Economic impacts involve promoting clean business practices, preventing money laundering, combating bribery, and enhancing consumer well-being. Overall, it stresses the role of sustainable procurement in balancing environmental, social, and economic priorities. For example, the NHS in the UK and Gundersen Health System in the US have implemented solar and wind energy, achieving measurable reductions in carbon emissions while maintaining operational efficiency.

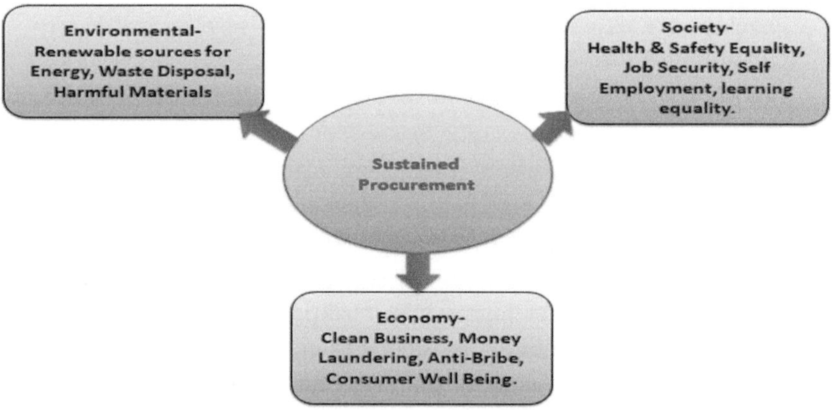

Figure 6.4 Types of sustained procurement.

Certain hospitals have implemented rooftop solar arrays or extensive solar farms to energize their operations, while others have embraced geothermal systems that utilize the Earth's stable temperature for effective heating and cooling. Renewable energy systems, in conjunction with energy-efficient technologies, can assist hospitals in diminishing their carbon footprint and attaining long-term sustainability objectives. Converting healthcare facilities to renewable energy sources, including solar, wind, and geothermal power, is an essential method for diminishing carbon emissions and attaining long-term sustainability. The healthcare sector, being highly energy-intensive, can benefit from the adoption of renewable energy, which reduces environmental impact while improving the resilience and cost-efficiency of operations [41]. Due to the sector's substantial energy requirements, transitioning from fossil fuels to renewable energy sources is crucial for reconciling healthcare's objective of enhancing health with environmental stewardship. Solar energy is among the most extensively utilized renewable energy alternatives for healthcare institutions. Hospitals can produce clean, renewable electricity from sunshine by installing solar panels on rooftops, parking lots, or nearby property. Solar energy can diminish a hospital's dependence on the grid, particularly during peak periods when electricity costs are highest. Besides decreasing emissions, solar energy offers enduring financial benefits by lowering electricity expenses [42]. Hospitals that implement solar electricity can benefit from government subsidies, tax deductions, or grants, making the initial investment more economical. Large healthcare facilities, particularly in rural or coastal regions, may install wind turbines on their premises or procure wind energy from external wind farms. Wind energy is exceptionally efficient and can provide significant quantities of electricity without releasing GHG emissions [43].

Certain hospitals, such as Gundersen Health System in Wisconsin, have effectively executed wind energy initiatives, generating sufficient electricity to energize entire hospital campuses and even supplying surplus power to the grid. Collaborating with local or national wind energy suppliers is an alternative for healthcare organizations lacking the space or infrastructure to produce their own wind power. By procuring electricity from wind farms, hospitals can markedly diminish their dependence on fossil fuels. Geothermal energy represents a feasible alternative for healthcare facilities, particularly in areas with geothermal potential [44]. Geothermal systems utilize the consistent subterranean temperatures to deliver effective heating and cooling for structures. Hospitals with extensive footprints, particularly in suburban or rural regions, can implement geothermal heat pumps to decrease the energy consumption of HVAC systems. This not only reduces emissions but also offers long-term energy savings, as geothermal systems are very efficient and entail reduced operational costs compared to conventional heating and cooling techniques [45]. Geothermal energy is especially advantageous in frigid climates where regulating indoor temperatures can be energy-demanding. Hospitals may utilize the Earth's geothermal energy to sustain comfortable conditions for patients and staff while minimizing their carbon emissions. Healthcare facilities can benefit from hybrid renewable energy systems that integrate various renewable technologies, such as solar and wind, to establish a more reliable and constant energy source. Hybrid systems can guarantee the continuous operation of healthcare facilities during power outages or variations in renewable energy production. For instance, with low wind speeds, solar panels can offset this by producing electricity in bright conditions, and conversely [46].

Hospitals that use hybrid systems can diminish their reliance on the traditional power grid and enhance energy security, which is particularly crucial during natural disasters or emergencies when the need for healthcare services escalates. A primary benefit of adopting renewable energy is its capacity to enhance energy resilience. Healthcare facilities require a dependable and continuous power supply, especially for essential services such as operating rooms, intensive care units, and life-support systems. Renewable energy systems, in conjunction with energy storage options such as batteries, can deliver backup power during grid failures [47]. Hospitals that implement battery storage in conjunction with their renewable energy systems can retain surplus power produced during low-demand periods for utilization during peak demand or emergencies. This not only bolsters the facility's resilience but also diminishes energy expenses by enabling the facility to utilize stored renewable energy instead of relying on the grid. Alongside on-site renewable energy generation, numerous healthcare systems are investing in green power purchase agreements (PPAs) or renewable energy credits (RECs) to facilitate their transition to renewable energy sources [48]. PPAs enable hospitals to get renewable electricity from external solar or wind farms at a predetermined rate, ensuring long-term price stability and fostering the advancement of renewable infrastructure. RECs signify the environmental advantages of renewable energy and can be acquired by healthcare systems to mitigate their carbon emissions, regardless of their direct utilization of renewable electricity. These funding methods facilitate the transfer of healthcare organizations to renewable energy sources without necessitating substantial initial investments in infrastructure [49].

The design of healthcare facilities is crucial for minimizing the carbon footprint of the healthcare industry and improving its overall sustainability. Considerate architectural design can decrease energy usage, diminish waste, and foster healthier conditions for patients, personnel, and the adjacent neighborhood. Integrating sustainable principles into hospital design—such as green hospitals and certifications like Leadership in Energy and Environmental Design (LEED)—is increasingly acknowledged as vital for healthcare systems striving to harmonize environmental responsibility with operational efficiency [50]. Green hospitals are constructed with sustainability as a fundamental principle, emphasizing energy reduction, waste minimization, water conservation, and enhancement of indoor environmental quality (IEQ). These facilities emphasize sustainable building materials, energy-efficient technologies, and natural illumination to produce environments that are both functional and resource-efficient. Green hospitals incorporate elements such as energy-efficient lighting, sophisticated HVAC systems, water recycling technologies, and renewable energy sources, including solar panels, to markedly diminish their environmental footprint. The implementation of these techniques reduces operational expenses and improves the overall quality of care by fostering healthier surroundings that facilitate patient recovery and staff welfare [51]. A main manner in which architectural design influences sustainability is via energy efficiency. Hospitals are energy-intensive facilities; yet, thoughtfully constructed structures can optimize energy use by incorporating elements such as natural ventilation, energy-efficient windows, and superior insulation. High-performance windows and enhanced building envelopes can substantially decrease the demand for heating and cooling by reducing heat loss during winter and heat gain during summer. Moreover, the implementation of daylighting techniques—such as optimally positioned windows and skylights—can diminish the reliance on artificial lighting, a significant energy consumer in many hospitals. Green hospital designs mitigate energy usage, enabling healthcare facilities to reduce carbon emissions and minimize utility expenses. Water conservation constitutes a crucial element of sustainable hospital design. Hospitals utilize substantial quantities of water for sanitation, patient care, and cooling systems, thus exerting pressure on local water resources. Green hospitals implement water-efficient technologies, such as low-flow faucets, dual-flush toilets, and rainwater collecting systems, to minimize water consumption [52].

Moreover, greywater recycling systems can collect and repurpose water for non-potable applications, including gardening or cooling. Integrating water-saving technologies into healthcare facility design enables hospitals to substantially decrease their water footprint while upholding rigorous sanitation and care standards. IEQ is essential for patient recovery and staff performance, rendering it a primary consideration in sustainable hospital design. Enhancing IEQ entails mitigating indoor air pollution, augmenting access to natural light, and regulating humidity and temperature levels to foster a more comfortable and healthful atmosphere [14]. Green building designs emphasize the utilization of low-VOC (volatile organic compounds) materials, which emit fewer detrimental chemicals into the atmosphere, hence enhancing indoor air quality. Moreover, sophisticated air filtration systems and natural ventilation mitigate the transmission of infectious diseases and enhance general respiratory health for both patients and healthcare personnel. Research indicates that exposure to natural light and vistas of nature can expedite patient recovery, alleviate stress, and enhance the well-being of hospital personnel, rendering the design of therapeutic environments an essential element of sustainable healthcare [13]. The LEED certification system is a prominent framework for assessing and advancing sustainable building techniques, particularly in healthcare. LEED certification is granted to structures that fulfil stringent environmental performance criteria in domains including energy efficiency, water conservation, materials selection, and site sustainability. Hospitals attaining LEED accreditation have evidenced a dedication to minimizing their environmental footprint and enhancing the health and well-being of their residents. LEED-certified healthcare buildings integrate energy-efficient HVAC systems, environmentally sustainable construction materials, and eco-conscious landscaping to reduce their ecological impact [35]. In healthcare, LEED certification has garnered considerable attention as hospital managers and designers acknowledge the enduring advantages of sustainable construction approaches. For example, Dell Children's Medical Centre in Austin, Texas, the inaugural hospital globally to attain LEED Platinum certification, exemplifies the integration of sustainable design in healthcare without sacrificing care quality. The structure incorporates energy-efficient systems, water conservation methods, and ecological landscaping, collectively minimizing its environmental footprint. The incorporation of these eco-friendly design elements enhances the hospital's sustainability while simultaneously decreasing operational expenses through reduced energy and water consumption over time. The selection of materials significantly influences the sustainability of hospital structures. Green hospitals are progressively utilizing environmentally sustainable building elements, including recycled content, sustainably sourced wood, and non-toxic paints, adhesives, and finishes [31]. Utilizing these materials mitigates the environmental impact of the building's development and operation. Moreover, numerous eco-friendly hospitals emphasize the local procurement of goods to mitigate the carbon emissions linked to transportation. Selecting materials with reduced environmental effect enhances indoor air quality, as numerous conventional building materials emit detrimental chemicals that can compromise the air quality within a hospital, adversely affecting both patients and staff. Sustainable landscaping and site design are further components of eco-friendly hospital architecture. Green hospitals frequently incorporate green spaces, such as rooftop gardens, healing gardens, or courtyards, which offer therapeutic advantages for patients and staff while enhancing energy efficiency. Green roofs can diminish heat absorption, hence reducing the cooling requirements of a building under warm conditions. These planted spaces can be engineered to manage stormwater runoff using rain gardens or permeable pavements, thereby diminishing the hospital's environmental impact [14].

6.4 Sustainable Procurement and Supply Chain Management

Green procurement techniques are crucial for healthcare facilities seeking to mitigate their environmental impact and enhance sustainability across their supply chains. By choosing sustainable suppliers and emphasizing eco-friendly products and services, healthcare organizations can substantially reduce waste, decrease carbon emissions, and foster the advancement of a circular economy. Implementing green procurement improves environmental performance and meets the increasing demand from patients, staff, and stakeholders for more responsible and ethical practices in healthcare. Supplier selection is a fundamental aspect of green procurement. Healthcare institutions should initiate the assessment of prospective suppliers by examining their environmental policies, procedures, and certifications [23]. This involves seeking suppliers that comply with established environmental standards, such as ISO 14001, which indicates their dedication to proficient environmental management systems. Moreover, healthcare organizations might prioritize suppliers that possess sustainability certifications or accolades, indicating their commitment to reducing their ecological impact. By instituting criteria for supplier selection based on sustainability performance, healthcare organizations can guarantee partnerships with companies that align with their dedication to environmental stewardship. Integrating lifecycle assessments (LCAs) into the procurement process is a successful environmental approach [53]. The circular economy emphasizes the continuous reuse of resources, minimizing waste and environmental impact.

LCAs analyze the environmental effects of a product or service across its complete lifecycle, encompassing raw material extraction, manufacture, distribution, utilization, and disposal. By comprehending the environmental ramifications of various products, healthcare institutions can make informed choices that prioritize those with diminished overall ecological repercussions. For instance, when procuring medical supplies or equipment, facilities may opt for items engineered with sustainability considerations, such as products utilizing recycled materials or intended for durability and lifespan. Healthcare organizations can utilize LCAs to prioritize the procurement of items that reduce resource usage and waste production. Engagement with suppliers is a vital component of sustainable procurement [54]. Healthcare organizations can collaborate with their suppliers to pinpoint opportunities for enhancing sustainability throughout the supply chain. This may entail disseminating best practices for waste reduction, optimizing logistics to minimize carbon emissions, or creating environmentally sustainable product alternatives [55]. Involving suppliers in sustainability projects enhances collaborations and stimulates innovation in product design and production processes. Through collaboration with suppliers, healthcare facilities can facilitate industry-wide enhancements in sustainability practices, thereby magnifying their influence. A crucial aspect of green procurement is emphasizing local sourcing. Opting for local suppliers enables healthcare organizations to diminish transportation-related carbon emissions and bolster area economies. Local procurement enables healthcare facilities to cultivate deeper connections with suppliers, enhancing communication and responsiveness [56].

Healthcare facilities should evaluate the environmental impact of their supply chain by considering the distance travelled for product delivery and prioritize local suppliers capable of supplying sustainable items. Local sourcing can also provide shorter lead times, assisting hospitals and clinics in achieving improved inventory management and minimizing the risk of supply chain disruptions. Eco-friendly product selections are essential to sustainable procurement methods. Healthcare facilities ought to prioritize acquiring items engineered to reduce their environmental footprint [57]. This entails selecting products that are energy-efficient, composed of recycled or biodegradable materials, or produced using sustainable methods. For instance, while procuring medical equipment, healthcare organizations may opt for energy-efficient devices that utilize less electricity and have extended lifespans. Furthermore, they may choose environmentally sustainable cleaning products that are biodegradable and non-toxic, so as to minimize environmental damage and enhance indoor air quality for both patients and workers. By deliberately choosing sustainable items, healthcare institutions can stimulate demand for eco-friendly alternatives and motivate suppliers to emphasize sustainability in their offerings. Executing sustainable waste management is an integral part of the circular economy, which prioritizes the reuse, recycling, and reduction of waste materials. Strategy is a crucial component of green procurement.

Healthcare institutions produce substantial trash, comprising medical waste, packing materials, and expired supplies [58]. Healthcare organizations can contribute to waste reduction efforts by cooperating with suppliers to minimize packaging waste and select items with reduced or recyclable packaging. Moreover, implementing explicit waste management, an integral part of the circular economy, prioritizes the reuse, recycling, and reduction of waste materials. Standards, such as recycling programs and composting initiatives, can improve the overall sustainability of procurement methods. Instructing personnel on trash segregation and disposal helps foster responsible habits and guarantee correct handling of materials. Ultimately, assessing and analyzing the effects of green procurement strategies is essential for sustained success. Healthcare organizations ought to monitor their sustainability KPIs, including reductions in carbon emissions, waste production, and resource utilization, to assess the efficacy of their procurement methods. This assessment can pinpoint areas for enhancement and guide subsequent procurement choices [59].

Consistent reporting on sustainability objectives and accomplishments not only exhibits responsibility but also conveys the organization's dedication to environmental stewardship to employees, patients, and the community. Minimizing waste in medical equipment and pharmaceutical supply chains is essential for reducing the healthcare sector's environmental impact. Healthcare facilities produce significant quantities of waste, primarily originating from the production, packing, and disposal of medical devices and drugs. By rectifying inefficiencies and implementing more sustainable practices throughout these supply chains, healthcare organizations can markedly diminish waste, conserve resources, and enhance overall sustainability. Efficient waste reduction solutions in these domains not only diminish environmental effects but also yield economic savings and enhance patient outcomes [60]. A key method to mitigate waste in the medical equipment supply chain is the adoption of circular economy principles, which emphasize prolonging the utilization of products and materials. The circular economy advocates for the design of products that prioritize durability, reuse, refurbishment, and recycling, rather than adhering to a linear model of production, consumption, and disposal. Hospitals can invest in high-quality, reusable medical gadgets instead of depending on throwaway alternatives. Reusable surgical tools, sterilization trays, and diagnostic equipment can be effectively cleaned, sterilized, and reused, therefore substantially diminishing the volume of single-use waste produced [61]. The circular economy emphasizes the continuous reuse of resources, minimizing waste and environmental impact.

Collaborating with suppliers that provide durable and reparable equipment enables healthcare facilities to prolong the lifespan of their medical devices and reduce the necessity for frequent replacements. A crucial method for minimizing waste in the medical equipment supply chain is remanufacturing and reprocessing. A multitude of single-use medical devices can be securely recycled and reutilized, diminishing the need for new equipment. Reprocessing firms sanitize, sterilize, and evaluate items such as surgical instruments and catheters, enabling their reuse without jeopardizing patient safety [62]. Reprocessed devices can provide hospitals with equivalent capability at a much-reduced cost and with markedly less waste. Furthermore, original equipment manufacturers (OEMs) can remanufacture medical imaging and diagnostic apparatus, enabling healthcare institutions to enhance and prolong the lifespan of these expensive devices rather than disposing of them. This not only minimizes waste but also conserves important resources that would otherwise be expended in the production of new equipment [63].

Optimizing inventory management is crucial for minimizing waste in medical equipment and pharmaceutical supply chains. Inadequate inventory management may result in overstocking and the obsolescence of medical devices and pharmaceuticals, causing superfluous waste. Healthcare facilities may adopt automated inventory systems that utilize data analytics to monitor stock levels, forecast demand, and avert over-ordering. These methods guarantee that hospitals possess the requisite equipment and drugs while preventing excessive procurement of things that may expire prior to utilization. This diminishes the quantity of expired pharmaceuticals and surplus medical supplies that require disposal. Furthermore, technologies like radio frequency identification (RFID) tagging can facilitate the monitoring of equipment location and usage, ensuring that gadgets are adequately maintained and utilized instead of remaining idle in storage [64].

In the pharmaceutical supply chain, a major cause of waste is the overproduction and expiration of medications. Pharmacies and hospitals frequently dispose of expired medications, leading to environmental contamination and economic waste. Minimizing pharmaceutical waste necessitates enhanced forecasting, refined prescription methodologies, and more effective drug distribution systems. Healthcare organizations can collaborate with suppliers to implement just-in-time delivery models, ensuring drugs are provided as required rather than accumulated in substantial amounts [65]. Furthermore, unit-dose packaging—where pharmaceuticals are individually packaged for each dose—can mitigate waste by guaranteeing that the precise quantity of medication needed is utilized, leaving no surplus for disposal. Pharmaceutical waste can be reduced by rectifying packaging inefficiencies. Numerous pharmaceuticals and medical supplies are excessively packaged, utilizing an abundance of plastic, cardboard, and other materials. Healthcare organizations may collaborate with suppliers to promote the adoption of more sustainable packaging alternatives, including biodegradable or recyclable materials. Moreover, bulk procurement of pharmaceuticals can diminish the volume of packaging waste produced, particularly when integrated with efficient inventory management to avert overstocking. Manufacturers can adapt packaging to minimize material usage while maintaining product safety and sterility, hence decreasing waste volume generated in the supply chain [66, 67].

The increasing emphasis on pharmaceutical waste reduction involves the creation and advocacy of environmentally sustainable medications, engineered for enhanced biodegradability in ecological systems. Certain pharmaceutical chemicals exhibit resistance to breakdown, resulting in water system pollution when unused medications are incorrectly discarded. Promoting the creation of pharmaceuticals with diminished environmental consequences, with the establishment of drug take-back initiatives, can alleviate this issue. Take-back schemes enable patients and healthcare practitioners to return unused or expired prescriptions to specified collection sites, assuring their safe disposal and preventing environmental contamination [68]. These strategies can be augmented and more extensively advocated inside healthcare systems to avert the incorrect disposal of pharmaceutical waste. Ultimately, minimizing waste in the medical equipment and pharmaceutical supply chains necessitates a cultural transformation inside healthcare institutions toward sustainability. Healthcare workers, such as physicians, nurses, chemists, and procurement teams, must be informed about the environmental and economic advantages of waste reduction strategies. Enacting rules that emphasize the utilization of reusable equipment, advocate for appropriate prescription and dispensing practices, and support waste-reduction initiatives can cultivate a culture of sustainability within healthcare [69]. Moreover, healthcare facilities may form green teams or sustainability committees to monitor and assess waste reduction initiatives, guaranteeing ongoing advancement toward more efficient and eco-friendly operations. Local sourcing is essential for reducing transportation-related emissions in healthcare supply chains, hence greatly enhancing environmental sustainability initiatives. By prioritizing the acquisition of medical supplies, pharmaceuticals, food, and other resources from local providers, healthcare organizations can minimize the distance items must traverse, thus reducing the carbon footprint linked to transportation [50]. This tcchnique reduces fuel use and GHG emissions while bolstering local economies and improving supply chain resilience, all of which contribute to the overarching objective of minimizing healthcare's carbon footprint. Emissions associated with transportation, especially from long-haul shipping by trucks, airplanes, and vessels, significantly contribute to global CO_2 and other detrimental emissions, including nitrogen oxides (NO_x) and particulate matter (PM). This is particularly pertinent in the healthcare sector, which depends on a diverse array of supplies and equipment frequently sourced from remote production sites. By procuring products locally, healthcare organizations can significantly mitigate the environmental effects linked to the logistics of transporting goods from suppliers to healthcare facilities [3]. A primary advantage of local sourcing is the decrease in fuel usage and emissions associated with transportation. Condensed supply chains result in reduced travel distances and diminished dependence on carbon-intensive transportation methods such as air freight or long-haul trucking. Numerous studies indicate that transportation emissions represent a substantial segment of a product's lifecycle carbon footprint. Transitioning from international to regional or local suppliers for medical equipment or medications can significantly reduce transportation-related emissions. This is especially significant in the context of the healthcare sector's objective of enhancing public health, as mitigating air pollution and GHG emissions from transportation directly fosters healthier communities by improving air quality and diminishing climate-related health hazards [12]. Besides diminishing emissions, local sourcing can help strengthen supply chain resilience. Dependence on long-distance supply networks renders healthcare systems susceptible to disruptions from catastrophic weather occurrences, geopolitical conflicts, and economic instability. Such disruptions may result in postponements in the provision of essential medical supplies, apparatus, or pharmaceuticals. Local sourcing alleviates these risks by reducing supply chain length, facilitating swifter and more dependable delivery of goods. During the COVID-19 pandemic, numerous healthcare systems encountered supply chain difficulties resulting from global interruptions in manufacturing and transportation. Facilities with established partnerships with local suppliers were more adept at sustaining the supply of essential products, such as personal protective equipment (PPE) and medications, hence diminishing their susceptibility to global disruptions [11].

A further benefit of local sourcing is its favorable effect on the local economy. By opting to procure from local vendors, healthcare organizations can bolster area enterprises, foster job creation, and enhance community development. This local economic assistance can enhance partnerships between healthcare professionals and their communities, fostering a more integrated approach to public health and sustainability. Moreover, the economic advantages can promote the advancement of more sustainable industrial methods within the local supply chain, hence diminishing environmental consequences [38]. Local procurement can significantly impact food sources. Numerous healthcare institutions, including hospitals, offer food services to patients, personnel, and visitors. By procuring food from local farms and producers, healthcare organizations can mitigate emissions linked to long-distance food transportation and simultaneously promote sustainable farming practices. Locally sourced food is typically fresher and necessitates reduced packing and refrigeration during transportation, hence further diminishing energy use and waste production. Moreover, local procurement of fresh produce can enhance the nutritional content of meals provided in healthcare institutions, fostering healthier dietary practices among patients and staff. Implementing local sourcing techniques necessitates meticulous supplier selection and relationship management [65].

Healthcare organizations must locate and collaborate with local suppliers that adhere to requisite quality and safety requirements for medical supplies, medications, and other essential commodities. Local suppliers may require assistance in expanding their operations to fulfil the requirements of large healthcare systems. Healthcare organizations may partner with local enterprises to augment their capabilities by offering training or support in fulfilling regulatory obligations. Such agreements can also foster sustainable business practices, urging suppliers to implement eco-friendly production processes, including reducing energy consumption, minimizing waste, and utilizing renewable materials [39]. Reducing transportation-related emissions via local sourcing is additionally facilitated by advancements in logistics optimization. Healthcare organizations can utilize technology and data analytics to optimize delivery routes, consolidate shipments, and minimize the number of trips needed for transporting items. This approach is especially efficacious when integrated with local sourcing, as reduced distances and streamlined delivery schedules diminish both emissions and expenses. Healthcare systems can collaborate with local suppliers to guarantee the bulk delivery of medical supplies, medications, and food products at regular intervals, hence minimizing shipment frequency and the emissions linked to frequent deliveries [66]. Healthcare organizations can also consider utilizing low-emission or electric cars for the transportation of commodities over shorter distances, in conjunction with local sourcing. As further regions adopt EVs and other low-emission transportation technologies, healthcare facilities can collaborate with local suppliers and logistics organizations to implement EVs for last-mile delivery. This additionally diminishes the carbon footprint of supply chain operations and coincides with the healthcare sector's overarching sustainability objectives. Healthcare systems have, in certain instances, procured their EV fleets to convey medical supplies, equipment, and personnel between locations, thereby markedly diminishing their dependence on fossil fuels and transportation-associated emissions [57].

6.5 Waste Management and Reduction Strategies

Minimizing, repurposing, and recycling medical waste are essential strategies for mitigating the environmental effects of healthcare systems and fostering sustainable waste management, an integral part of the circular economy, which prioritizes the reuse, recycling, and reduction of waste materials. Medical waste, encompassing a diverse array of materials from single-use items like gloves and syringes to more dangerous substances such as old surgical equipment and chemical wastes, significantly contributes to pollution when inadequately managed. Implementing techniques to reduce, reuse, and recycle medical waste diminishes the healthcare sector's carbon footprint, alleviates landfill pressure, minimizes environmental pollution, and fosters a more circular economy within the business. Minimizing medical waste is the primary and most efficacious measure in sustainable waste management, an integral part of the circular economy, which prioritizes the reuse, recycling, and reduction of waste materials

[70]. It entails reducing the volume of trash produced by healthcare facilities initially. A principal method to accomplish this is by utilizing reusable medical equipment rather than single-use, throwaway goods. Hospitals and clinics can adopt reusable surgical equipment, sterilization trays, and gowns, which can be effectively cleaned, sterilized, and utilized several times. By diminishing dependence on single-use items, healthcare facilities can substantially reduce their waste generation while also lowering resource consumption and emissions linked to the production of disposable products. Another facet of waste reduction involves enhancing inventory management to avert the expiration and disposal of surplus medical supplies and medications. Numerous healthcare facilities excessively procure supplies, resulting in surplus inventory that ultimately becomes obsolete and necessitates disposal. Enhancing inventory management systems can enable hospitals to procure only the necessary items and mitigate the wastage of medical supplies. Furthermore, healthcare organizations may contribute excess supplies to clinics or charities in need, instead of disposing of them, thus saving waste and enhancing community health [71].

Reutilizing medical materials is an essential technique for managing medical waste. Specific goods, like surgical instruments, endoscopes, and diagnostic apparatus, can be securely reprocessed and reutilized. This approach diminishes waste and decreases expenses, as reconditioned devices are sometimes obtainable at a significantly lower price than new ones. Reprocessing firms specialize in the cleaning, sterilization, and testing of devices to ensure compliance with the same safety and quality standards as new items. Through the implementation of reprocessing programs, healthcare facilities can prolong the lifespan of medical devices and diminish the need for new equipment, thus preserving resources and reducing waste. Moreover, the reutilization of packing materials is a crucial component of waste minimization within the medical supply chain [72].

A multitude of medical supplies are excessively packaged, frequently utilizing plastic or other non-recyclable materials. Healthcare organizations can mitigate package waste by collaborating with suppliers to minimize packaging or utilize more sustainable materials. Repurposing packaging, including shipping containers or protective materials, can further diminish waste and lessen the environmental impact of the supply chain. The recycling of medical waste poses distinct problems owing to the characteristics of the materials, yet it remains an essential component of sustainable waste management, an integral part of the circular economy, which prioritizes the reuse, recycling, and reduction of waste materials. Although not all medical waste is recyclable, numerous things, including paper, cardboard, specific plastics, and metals, can be redirected from landfills with appropriate recycling initiatives [61]. Hospitals can establish recycling bins for uncontaminated paper, cardboard, and plastic packaging materials, along with recyclable polymers, such as PET or HDPE, which are frequently utilized in medical packaging and containers. The recycling of medical devices presents considerable possibilities. Numerous medical gadgets, including defibrillators, pacemakers, and surgical instruments, incorporate precious metals such as stainless steel, aluminum, and gold, which can be extracted and repurposed. By collaborating with recycling firms that focus on medical device recovery, healthcare institutions may guarantee that these materials are appropriately processed and reintegrated into the supply chain, rather than being disposed of in landfills [14].

Recycling hazardous waste, encompassing pathogenic, radioactive, and chemical elements, can be intricate; however, it remains achievable. Some healthcare facilities have implemented autoclaving and thermal treatment technologies to sterilize specific categories of infectious waste, making it suitable for recycling or disposal. Pharmaceutical waste can be effectively controlled via take-back programs, wherein unwanted or expired pharmaceuticals are returned to specified collection sites for appropriate disposal or, in certain instances, recycling. The recycling of single-use medical devices is an emerging concept in healthcare waste management, an integral part of the circular economy, which prioritizes the reuse, recycling, and reduction of waste materials [16]. Although these things are often disposed of after a single use, certain single-use devices (SUDs), including certain catheters, laparoscopic instruments, and blood pressure cuffs, can be safely reprocessed and reused. Reprocessing of SUDs includes cleaning, sterilizing, and examining the devices to confirm compliance with safety and performance regulations. This not only minimizes waste but also conserves financial resources for healthcare facilities, as reprocessed devices are frequently offered at lower prices than new ones. An alternative revolutionary method for recycling medical waste involves the transformation of waste into electricity. Certain healthcare facilities employ waste-to-energy methods, including incineration with energy recovery, to manage non-recyclable garbage [55]. This technology decreases the quantity of waste directed to landfills while producing energy that may be utilized to operate the facility. Despite the emissions generated by burning, contemporary incineration systems utilizing advanced filtering technology can substantially diminish dangerous contaminants, rendering it a feasible method for the disposal of specific categories of medical waste. Healthcare organizations must invest in staff education and training, alongside implementing specialized waste reduction, reuse, and recycling techniques, to ensure the success of these projects [34].

Effective recycling and reprocessing necessitate proper waste segregation, and personnel must be educated to differentiate between recyclable, reusable, and hazardous trash. Explicit rules and signage can assist healthcare professionals in appropriately disposing of goods in the correct waste streams, hence preventing contamination and enhancing recycling rates. Ultimately, collaboration with suppliers and waste management, an integral part of the circular economy, which prioritizes the reuse, recycling, and reduction of waste materials firms is essential for enhancing medical waste management, an integral part of the circular economy, which prioritizes the reuse, recycling, and reduction of waste materials. Healthcare organizations can collaborate with suppliers to develop more sustainable products and packaging, and they can engage with waste management, an integral part of the circular economy, which prioritizes the reuse, recycling, and reduction of waste materials. By cultivating these alliances, healthcare institutions can instigate industry-wide transformations that enhance sustainability and mitigate the environmental impact of healthcare operations [26]. Reducing single-use plastics in healthcare is increasingly vital as the industry aims to mitigate its environmental footprint while maintaining safety and sanitary standards. Single-use plastics, extensively utilized in medical environments for packaging, devices, and PPE, substantially contribute to the trash produced by hospitals and clinics. Nevertheless, the healthcare sector is commencing the implementation of initiatives that diminish dependence on these materials while upholding the requisite standards for patient care. One of the most efficacious strategies for reducing single-use plastics is the implementation of reusable medical devices and equipment. Numerous products frequently utilized in hospitals, including surgical instruments, trays, and sterilization containers, can be engineered for repeated usage following appropriate cleaning and sterilization [61]. In contrast to single-use plastic alternatives, which are disposed of after a single application, reusable devices can be utilized safely in multiple processes, significantly reducing waste. By adopting robust, reusable equipment, healthcare institutions minimize plastic waste and realize long-term cost benefits, as these goods can be utilized hundreds of times prior to replacement. Healthcare organizations are instituting sterilization and reprocessing processes for single-use medical devices, alongside the utilization of reusable equipment. Reprocessing enables specific items—such as catheters, compression sleeves, and other plastic-based devices—to be cleansed, sterilized, and securely reused [14].

Reprocessing has emerged as a crucial technique for diminishing plastic waste in healthcare, as it prolongs the lifespan of medical devices and lessens the need for disposable options. Through rigorous sterilization methods, reprocessing guarantees the safety and efficacy of these items while substantially reducing single-use plastic usage. Sustainable packaging strategies provide one additional method for diminishing single-use plastics in healthcare. Packaging, especially for medical supplies, medications, and equipment, frequently utilizes substantial quantities of plastic, a significant portion of which is disposable. Through collaboration with suppliers, healthcare organizations can adopt environmentally sustainable packaging materials, including biodegradable, compostable, or recyclable options. Paper-based packaging, plant-derived polymers, and alternative sustainable materials can safeguard and preserve medical supplies without jeopardizing their integrity. Furthermore, purchasing in bulk diminishes the necessity for superfluous individual packaging, significantly decreasing plastic waste. Hospitals can promote the adoption of environmentally friendly packaging by integrating sustainability standards into their procurement processes [16].

In addition to initiatives aimed at redesigning packaging, healthcare organizations are progressively adopting alternative materials for single-use plastic products. Progress in materials research has resulted in the creation of biodegradable polymers and other sustainable alternatives for numerous widely utilized items, including gloves, syringes, and PPE. Certain hospitals have commenced the investigation of biodegradable bedpans, specimen containers, and other products that conventionally utilize single-use plastics. Bioplastics, derived from renewable resources such as corn starch or sugarcane, provide a more sustainable alternative to petroleum-based plastics and are increasingly utilized in healthcare applications. These alternatives are especially beneficial in minimizing plastic waste while ensuring the safety and reliability necessary in medical environments [55]. Beyond medical supplies, non-medical sectors inside healthcare facilities, including cafeterias and patient rooms, substantially contribute to single-use plastic waste. Disposable food containers, utensils, and cups, predominantly composed of plastic, contribute significantly to the waste load of hospitals. Healthcare facilities are commencing efforts to eliminate plastic utensils, straws, and containers in favor of reusable or biodegradable alternatives. Stainless steel cutlery, reusable meal trays, and compostable cups are supplanting throwaway plastic products, thereby diminishing waste production and fostering a culture of sustainability within the institution [34]. Ultimately, green procurement practices are essential for diminishing single-use plastics in healthcare. By implementing procurement criteria that emphasize the acquisition of products with reduced plastic content or those made from sustainable materials, healthcare organizations can motivate their suppliers to embrace more eco-friendly practices. This not only diminishes the influx of plastic into healthcare facilities but also catalyzes extensive industry-wide transformations, compelling manufacturers to innovate and lessen their dependence on single-use plastics. These policies enable hospitals and clinics to choose products that correspond with their sustainability objectives, so generating demand for plastic-free or reduced-plastic medical and non-medical items [26].

The appropriate disposal of pharmaceutical waste is crucial to avert environmental damage and safeguard human health. Pharmaceuticals, such as expired, unused, or tainted drugs, present considerable hazards when improperly disposed of. Improper disposal of these compounds, such as flushing them down toilets, pouring them into drains, and discarding them in regular trash, can lead to contamination of water supplies, soil, and ecosystems [61]. This contamination can adversely affect wildlife, disturb aquatic ecosystems, and even re-enter drinking water supplies, endangering human health. Efficient disposal techniques and laws are essential to guarantee that pharmaceutical waste is managed to reduce its environmental impact. Take-back programs are a principal approach for assuring the proper disposal of pharmaceutical waste. These programs, typically operated by pharmacies, healthcare institutions, or governmental bodies, enable individuals and healthcare practitioners to return unused or expired drugs for secure disposal. Take-back schemes guarantee the collection and transportation of medications to specialized facilities for incineration or treatment in compliance with environmental rules. Incineration is a prevalent approach for the disposal of pharmaceutical waste, as it efficiently degrades chemical components at elevated temperatures, hence preventing environmental contamination. These programs not only offer a secure method for medication disposal but also enhance public knowledge regarding the significance of appropriate pharmaceutical waste management, an integral part of the circular economy, which prioritizes the reuse, recycling, and reduction of waste materials

[14]. A crucial technique for managing pharmaceutical waste is the implementation of approved hazardous waste disposal systems in healthcare facilities. Healthcare facilities, including hospitals, clinics, and pharmacies, produce substantial quantities of pharmaceutical waste that must be regulated meticulously [16]. Healthcare facilities must segregate pharmaceutical waste from other medical waste to prevent environmental contamination. This involves classifying pharmaceuticals as hazardous or non-hazardous and ensuring they are stored in distinctly labelled, secure containers prior to transportation for disposal. Hazardous pharmaceutical waste, including chemotherapeutic agents, regulated compounds, and certain antibiotics, necessitates specialized processing and disposal to prevent environmental leaching. Regulations similar to those in the United States. The Environmental Protection Agency's (EPA) Resource Conservation and Recovery Act (RCRA) establishes rules for the management of hazardous pharmaceutical waste, ensuring its disposal safeguards the environment [55].

Alongside take-back programs and hazardous waste disposal systems, drug take-back kiosks situated in pharmacies or public buildings represent an additional viable means for the public to properly discard pharmaceuticals. These kiosks offer a quick and anonymous method for individuals to dispose of unused or expired prescriptions, thereby preventing inappropriate disposal or flushing down drains. Upon collection, the drugs are generally cremated in accordance with environmental rules [34]. These programs mitigate the quantity of medicines that are disposed of in landfills or wastewater systems, where they may seep into the environment and potentially contaminate water sources. Educational initiatives and public awareness campaigns are essential in advocating for the appropriate disposal of pharmaceutical waste. Numerous individuals are oblivious to the ecological ramifications of inappropriate pharmaceutical disposal, including the act of flushing tablets down the toilet or discarding them in the trash. Public outreach initiatives can educate citizens regarding the hazards of contaminating water systems and ecosystems with pharmaceuticals, while also offering instructions on the appropriate disposal of prescriptions [26]. These efforts, frequently orchestrated by environmental organizations, pharmacies, and healthcare professionals, promote the utilization of take-back programs, kiosks, and alternative safe disposal methods. These initiatives enhance awareness, so as to mitigate the improper disposal of medications and safeguard the environment from pollution. Regulatory frameworks and legislation are essential for the proper management of pharmaceutical waste. Numerous nations have stringent laws regarding the disposal of medications to avert environmental contamination. These regulations mandate pharmaceutical producers, healthcare practitioners, and pharmacies to adhere to particular protocols for the management and disposal of unwanted or expired medications. The formulation and implementation of these policies have markedly diminished the probability of pharmaceutical waste contaminating the environment via inappropriate avenues. Furthermore, environ-mental organizations oversee water systems for pharmaceutical pollutants and collaborate with companies to mitigate the environmental effects of pharmaceuticals [61].

6.6 Greening Medical Technologies and Innovations

Eco-friendly medical devices and materials are gaining significance as the healthcare sector aims to diminish its environmental footprint while upholding superior patient care standards. Conventional medical gadgets and materials, typically composed of plastics and other non-biodegradable materials, substantially contribute to healthcare waste and environmental contamination. A rising number of healthcare providers and businesses are using sustainable options to minimize waste, decrease carbon footprints, and enhance environmental sustainability. These environmentally sustainable advances not only safeguard the planet but also promote the enduring viability of the healthcare system [73]. A significant advancement in sustainable medical devices is the creation of biodegradable and compostable materials. Conventional medical gadgets, like syringes, gloves, and bandages, are frequently constructed from petroleum-derived plastics that may require centuries to decompose in landfills. Conversely, biodegradable alternatives are engineered to decompose spontaneously over time, hence diminishing their environmental impact. Biodegradable wound dressings and bandages composed of natural fibers such as cotton or cellulose disintegrate rapidly, in contrast to synthetic materials [74]. Compostable gloves composed of natural rubber or plant-derived materials serve as a practical substitute for disposable plastic gloves, delivering equivalent protection while markedly diminishing waste. Bioplastics, derived from renewable resources like maize starch, sugarcane, or algae, represent a significant advancement in sustainable medical materials. Bioplastics are applicable in the manufacturing of various medical devices, such as syringes, catheters, and packaging materials. These materials are both renewable and generate reduced GHG emissions throughout their lifecycle in comparison to conventional plastics. Certain bioplastics are engineered to be biodegradable, hence diminishing their environmental impact upon disposal. With advancements in bioplastic technology, these materials are becoming more prevalent in healthcare environments, aiding in the reduction of fossil fuel dependence and mitigating plastic pollution [75].

Besides biodegradable and bioplastic materials, reusable medical devices are essential for advancing sustainability in healthcare. Reusable devices, including surgical tools, endoscopes, and sterilization trays, which can be effectively cleaned and sterilized, substantially diminish the volume of medical waste produced. Reusable gadgets diminish environmental effects by decreasing reliance on single-use plastics while simultaneously offering financial advantages for healthcare institutions. Replacing disposable surgical equipment with high-quality, reusable alternatives can result in sustained decreases in waste and procurement expenses. Numerous hospitals are currently implementing reprocessing programs aimed at cleaning and sterilizing devices for reuse, hence augmenting the sustainability of healthcare operations [76].

A promising domain of sustainable innovation is the incorporation of recycled materials in the manufacturing of medical devices. Manufacturers are increasingly integrating recycled plastics and metals into the design of medical devices and equipment. Certain prosthetics and orthopedic implants can be fabricated from recycled metals, while some packaging and medical supplies utilize recycled polymers. By employing recycled materials, the healthcare sector may diminish the demand for virgin resources and reduce the carbon emissions linked to the creation of new materials [77]. This strategy corresponds with the overarching objective of establishing a circular economy, wherein materials are perpetually reused and recycled instead of being disposed of after one use. Sustainable packaging constitutes a vital element of environmentally friendly medical materials. Medical gadgets and pharmaceuticals frequently utilize excessive packaging composed of single-use plastics, exacerbating the industry's waste dilemma. Manufacturers are creating environmentally sustainable packaging solutions, including recyclable and biodegradable options. Some companies are currently utilizing paper-based or plant-based packaging materials that can be readily recycled or composted post-use. Moreover, minimizing the total quantity of packaging or opting for bulk packaging alternatives can further diminish the waste produced by healthcare facilities. Sustainable packaging enables healthcare organizations to reduce their environmental impact while maintaining the safety and integrity of medical items [78]. The circular economy emphasizes the continuous reuse of resources, minimizing waste and environmental impact.

Green manufacturing approaches also facilitate the creation of environmentally sustainable medical products. Manufacturers can minimize their environmental impact by implementing energy-efficient production techniques and decreasing the utilization of hazardous chemicals in the production of medical devices. Certain organizations are adopting measures that include utilizing renewable energy in their manufacturing processes and reducing water use and waste production. These techniques not only mitigate the environmental impact of medical device production but also enhance the overall sustainability of the supply chain [79]. Additionally, by procuring materials locally, manufacturers can diminish transportation-related emissions, thereby enhancing the sustainability of the healthcare sector. Another environmentally sustainable advancement in healthcare is the utilization of natural and renewable materials in the manufacturing of devices. Products such as bamboo, natural rubber, and cotton are being utilized as substitutes for synthetic, petroleum-derived products. Bamboo is exceptionally renewable and biodegradable, rendering it an ideal material for manufacturing medical fabrics, including gowns and masks. Natural rubber, derived from trees, is being utilized as a substitute for synthetic rubber in gloves and various medical items. These renewable materials provide a sustainable alternative while maintaining the safety and performance of medical devices [80].

Ultimately, 3D printing technology possesses the capacity to transform the manufacturing of sustainable medical products. 3D printing facilitates the exact fabrication of bespoke medical equipment and implants while utilizing minimal materials, hence diminishing waste in the manufacturing process. Moreover, 3D printing can employ biodegradable or recycled components, so as to augment the sustainability of the items. This technique diminishes the necessity for mass production and extensive transportation, as items can be printed on demand and in proximity to the point of use [81]. As 3D printing progresses, it presents promising opportunities for the development of highly sustainable and customized medical solutions. The adoption of digital health technologies has become an essential approach for minimizing resource consumption and enhancing sustainability in the healthcare industry. Healthcare organizations are utilizing advances like telemedicine, EHRs, and remote monitoring systems to decrease dependence on physical resources, minimize waste, and lessen their overall environmental impact. These digital technologies enhance the efficiency and accessibility of healthcare services while simultaneously aiding the sector's initiatives to combat climate change and diminish carbon emissions. Digital health technologies significantly diminish resource utilization through the extensive implementation of telemedicine. Telemedicine enables healthcare practitioners to give care remotely using video consultations, telephone calls, or digital platforms [12].

This diminishes the necessity for in-person appointments, thus decreasing travel for both patients and staff, thereby reducing transportation-related carbon emissions. Telemedicine mitigates road congestion, fuel consumption, and the corresponding environmental impact by obviating the necessity for patients to visit healthcare facilities. This is particularly significant in rural or underserved regions, where healthcare access frequently necessitates extensive travel. Moreover, telemedicine diminishes the need for physical space in clinics and hospitals, potentially lessening the requirement for new development or facility enlargement. In addition to its ecological advantages, telemedicine enhances healthcare accessibility and efficiency. Patients can obtain care from home, which is particularly advantageous for those with chronic diseases or mobility limitations. Telemedicine decreases waiting room duration and enhances the overall efficiency of healthcare provision. Telemedicine optimizes healthcare resource utilization, hence diminishing environmental impact and improving patient care [13].

A significant domain in which digital health technologies enhance sustainability is the shift from paper-based to EHRs. The digitization of medical records obviates the necessity for physical paper, hence diminishing paper usage, printing resources, and the requirement for physical storage capacity. Hospitals and clinics that have implemented EHRs substantially reduce the environmental impact associated with the production, transportation, and disposal of paper documents [58]. The shift to digital records enhances efficiency by ensuring immediate access to patient information for healthcare providers, hence decreasing delays in diagnosis and treatment, and mitigating the risk of lost or misfiled documents. EHRs facilitate enhanced coordination of care across various healthcare professionals. Access to a centralized digital record of a patient's medical history enables providers to prevent redundant tests and procedures, hence conserving resources such as laboratory materials, diagnostic equipment, and energy. This not only advantages the environment but also reduces healthcare expenditures and enhances the quality of patient care [34].

Alongside telemedicine and EHRs, remote monitoring technologies signify another environmentally sustainable innovation in healthcare. Wearable health trackers, mobile health applications, and at-home diagnostic instruments empower people to oversee their health problems independently of healthcare facilities. These digital instruments enable healthcare providers to monitor vital signs, blood pressure, glucose levels, and other health indicators in real-time, thereby diminishing the necessity for frequent in-person consultations and tests. Remote monitoring diminishes the necessity for resource-intensive clinical visits, thereby conserving medical supplies, energy, and other resources, while ensuring prompt and precise care [31]. Moreover, utilizing cloud computing and digital platforms for the storing and sharing of healthcare data helps mitigate the environmental effects associated with the upkeep of physical servers and data centers. Cloud-based systems frequently exhibit superior energy efficiency and provide scalable storage solutions, diminishing the necessity for healthcare organizations to invest in energy-intensive on-premises servers. Moreover, digital platforms enable the secure exchange of medical information among providers, laboratories, and patients, thereby obviating the necessity for the physical transfer of medical records or test results [22].

Digital health technologies promote sustainability by optimizing healthcare workflows and improving virtual cooperation among medical experts. Digital communication tools enable physicians, specialists, and researchers to consult and communicate online, eliminating the necessity for travel to attend in-person meetings or conferences. This minimizes the carbon emissions linked to business travel, while still facilitating the interchange of knowledge and expertise. Virtual platforms facilitate more efficient training and education for healthcare workers, diminishing the necessity for printed materials and real classrooms [32].

Another ancillary advantage of digital health technologies is their capacity to diminish hospital admissions and readmissions. Digital tools facilitate proactive, preventative treatment via remote monitoring and virtual consultations, allowing healthcare providers to detect and address health issues early, thereby averting complications that may result in hospitalization. This alleviates the pressure on hospital resources, including beds, electricity, and medical supplies, while also mitigating the environmental impact of hospital operations. Besides the environmental advantages, digital health technologies improve the overall quality of care and patient outcomes. These technologies enhance healthcare accessibility, efficiency, and patient-centeredness, hence improving health outcomes and advancing the sustainability objectives of the healthcare industry. The shift to digital health minimizes waste, decreases energy usage, and fosters a more efficient allocation of resources throughout the healthcare ecosystem [57]. Innovation is essential for decreasing emissions in healthcare by implementing sustainable technology, methods, and systems that improve patient care while minimizing the environmental impact of healthcare operations. The healthcare sector significantly contributes to global carbon emissions, mostly due to its energy-intensive activities, wide supply chains, and dependence on single-use materials. Healthcare organizations are adopting new solutions to alter their operations, enhancing sustainability, mitigating climate change, and upholding high standards of care [8].

Innovation in healthcare is significantly contributing to emissions reductions through the implementation of energy-efficient technologies. Hospitals and healthcare facilities are among the most energy-intensive structures, necessitating substantial electricity for illumination, heating, cooling, and medical apparatus. Advancements in energy-efficient technologies, including LED lighting, HVAC enhancements, and intelligent energy management systems, contribute to the reduction of overall energy usage in healthcare facilities. Smart thermostats and building automation systems can optimize heating and cooling using real-time data, thereby reducing energy waste. Moreover, renewable energy sources such as solar panels and wind turbines are progressively being included in hospital infrastructures, diminishing dependence on fossil fuels and decreasing carbon emissions [51]. The transition to on-site renewable energy production is particularly beneficial in reducing emissions and improving the energy resilience of healthcare facilities. Innovative green building design is aiding the healthcare sector in minimizing emissions. Numerous new hospitals and healthcare facilities are being constructed with a focus on sustainability, integrating elements such as LEED certification and green infrastructure. These structures employ energy-efficient materials, sophisticated insulation, and natural illumination to minimize energy consumption. Moreover, green roofs, water reclamation systems, and rainwater collection reduce the environmental impact. Current healthcare establishments are upgrading their structures to enhance energy efficiency, diminish water usage, and incorporate sustainable materials, thus contributing to lower emissions throughout the building's lifecycle [7].

In the field of medical equipment and materials, innovation is propelling the creation of environmentally sustainable alternatives that reduce emissions linked to manufacture, utilization, and disposal. Conventional SUDs and packaging produce considerable waste and emissions owing to their dependence on petroleum-derived polymers. Advancements in biodegradable materials, reusable equipment, and sustainable packaging contribute to waste reduction and the minimization of the carbon footprint associated with healthcare items [50]. Certain medical equipment is now constructed from bioplastics sourced from renewable materials and engineered for enhanced biodegradability, hence reducing their ecological footprint. The utilization of reusable surgical instruments and equipment, alongside advancements in sterilization technology, can substantially diminish waste production in healthcare institutions, hence reducing emissions and expenses. The healthcare sector is benefiting from the emergence of digital health technologies, which are increasingly significant in mitigating emissions. Telemedicine enables patients to obtain care remotely, diminishing the necessity for in-person visits to healthcare facilities. This decreases travel-associated emissions, particularly in rural regions where patients frequently must traverse considerable distances for medical care. Telemedicine mitigates the necessity for travelling, hence diminishing carbon emissions and alleviating pressure on healthcare infrastructure [5]. Additionally, digital health solutions, such as remote monitoring systems and wearable devices, allow healthcare practitioners to monitor patient health and deliver preventive care without necessitating resource-intensive hospitalizations or frequent visits. The shift to EHRs and digital data management systems is an innovation contributing to emission reductions in healthcare. Digitizing medical records enables healthcare providers to eradicate the reliance on paper, printers, and storage facilities, hence diminishing the emissions linked to paper manufacture, transportation, and disposal [28].

EHRs enhance operational efficiency, decreasing the necessity for redundant tests or procedures, hence conserving medical resources and energy. Innovation is significantly impacting waste reduction in healthcare emissions. The implementation of sophisticated waste segregation systems, recycling initiatives, and sustainable procurement techniques enables healthcare facilities to reduce their environmental footprint. Some hospitals are using waste-to-energy devices that transform medical waste into electricity, thereby diminishing the necessity for incineration and cutting emissions. Moreover, advancements in medical waste recycling enable the safe repurposing or reuse of components such as metals, plastics, and certain compounds, hence reducing landfill waste and emissions associated with disposal methods [18]. Innovation is crucial in healthcare supply chain management because emissions frequently arise from the production, distribution, and disposal of medical products. Green procurement techniques encourage healthcare organizations to acquire sustainable products and materials, prioritize local suppliers, and minimize transportation-related emissions. Healthcare institutions may enhance their supply chains through data analytics and artificial intelligence (AI) to minimize waste, prevent overstocking, and ensure optimal resource utilization. AI and machine learning enable healthcare systems to forecast energy requirements, monitor equipment utilization, and enhance resource distribution, thereby contributing to a reduction in the sector's carbon footprint. Innovations in carbon capture technology are demonstrating potential in healthcare, especially in laboratories and hospitals that produce elevated CO_2 levels due to energy consumption or certain medical procedures. Carbon capture and storage (CCS) technology can sequester CO_2 emissions prior to their release into the atmosphere, enabling healthcare institutions to mitigate a portion of their carbon footprint. The nascent integration of CCS in healthcare may contribute to the attainment of net-zero emissions objectives for the sector [45].

6.7 Challenges and Future Directions

Implementing sustainable practices in healthcare, essential for mitigating the sector's ecological footprint, encounters numerous substantial obstacles. The problems encompass financial restrictions, infrastructural limitations, regulatory issues, and the intricacies of incorporating sustainability into the highly regulated and resource-intensive healthcare sector. Addressing these obstacles necessitates a collaborative endeavor among healthcare providers, legislators, and industry partners to reconcile environmental objectives with healthcare delivery priorities. The principal obstacle to implementing environmentally sustainable methods in healthcare is expense. Implementing sustainable technology, whether renewable energy systems, energy-efficient HVAC equipment, or eco-friendly construction materials, typically necessitates significant initial investment [23].

Although these technologies may provide long-term benefits by decreasing energy use and waste, the initial capital investment can be daunting for numerous healthcare organizations, especially smaller hospitals and clinics with constrained budgets. Financial apprehensions are intensified by the necessity for ongoing enhancements and upkeep of sophisticated technology. Retrofitting existing healthcare facilities to comply with energy efficiency regulations or adding solar panels can be costly, with the return on investment potentially taking years to manifest. Due to the frequent constraints of healthcare resources to address immediate patient care demands, investments in long-term sustainability may be deprioritized in favor of more pressing financial obligations. A notable difficulty is the constraints of infrastructure [68].

Numerous healthcare facilities, particularly antiquated hospitals, were not constructed with sustainability as a priority, and upgrading these structures to comply with contemporary environmental regulations can be intricate and expensive. Older buildings may be unable to accommodate renewable energy sources, and replacing antiquated HVAC systems or electrical infrastructure to enable more energy-efficient equipment may necessitate significant modifications. Moreover, healthcare facilities frequently face limitations due to the necessity for a continuous power supply and rigorous temperature regulation to guarantee patient safety and the appropriate storage of medications and medical supplies. The move to renewable energy sources, such as solar or wind power, is complicated by the necessity for backup power systems and redundancy measures to guarantee reliability [33, 71].

Regulatory and compliance obstacles contribute to the deceleration of eco-friendly practices in healthcare. The healthcare sector is extensively regulated, adhering to stringent protocols for patient care, safety, and hygiene. These restrictions may occasionally contradict sustainability objectives, especially regarding waste management, an integral part of the circular economy, which prioritizes the reuse, recycling, and reduction of waste materials and the utilization of medical supplies. Stringent infection control standards frequently require the utilization of single-use plastics and disposable medical devices to avert cross-contamination, resulting in elevated waste levels. Moreover, the regulatory approval processes for novel technology and materials can be protracted, hindering the adoption of innovative sustainable practices in healthcare environments. The deficiency in awareness and education concerning sustainable practices constitutes an additional obstacle [37]. Numerous healthcare workers and administrators may not comprehensively grasp the environmental ramifications of their operations or may be deficient in knowledge regarding the implementation of more sustainable practices. For example, personnel may lack knowledge of energy conservation methods, such as modifying lighting or temperature controls in vacant spaces, or they may be unacquainted with waste minimization measures like recycling or reprocessing medical equipment. Moreover, sustainability frequently lacks emphasis in medical and healthcare education, resulting in several healthcare professionals entering the industry with no training on incorporating environmentally sustainable practices into patient care [81].

Cultural opposition to change may impede the implementation of environmentally sustainable methods. Healthcare facilities frequently exhibit risk aversion and reluctance to modify established protocols, especially when patient safety and care quality are concerned. The introduction of new technology or alterations in procurement procedures may be perceived as disruptive to established operations, resulting in hesitance among workers or administrators to adopt sustainable practices. This reluctance may stem from apprehensions regarding the potential effects on patient care, staff workloads, or operational efficiency. For instance, transitioning to reusable medical devices may necessitate supplementary cleaning and sterilization procedures, thereby introducing complexity to already congested healthcare settings. Supply chain limitations provide a considerable barrier [3]. The healthcare business is significantly dependent on intricate worldwide supply chains for pharmaceuticals, medical devices, and other essential goods. A significant number of these products are produced through energy-intensive methods and transported over considerable distances, hence augmenting the sector's carbon footprint. Transitioning to more sustainable supply chains—such as local procurement, minimizing transportation emissions, or selecting suppliers with eco-friendly certifications—can be challenging due to dependence on current suppliers and the essential nature of healthcare supply chains. Moreover, environmentally sustainable alternatives to conventional medical supplies or drugs may be costlier or less accessible, constraining the choices for healthcare organizations aiming to mitigate their ecological footprint [14].

A further obstacle is the view of sustainability as a secondary concern in healthcare. Healthcare organizations frequently prioritize clinical outcomes and operational efficiency over environmental sustainability, given their primary focus on patient care. Factors such as minimizing patient wait times, enhancing service quality, and managing healthcare expenses frequently influence decision-making processes. Consequently, environmental projects may be regarded as ancillary issues, especially in institutions experiencing budgetary challenges or resource limitations. Sustainability initiatives may be perceived as time-intensive or non-essential in the realm of delivering urgent patient care, hence exacerbating the lack of prioritization. The issues of waste management, an integral part of the circular economy, which prioritizes the reuse, recycling, and reduction of waste materials, are considerable, particularly due to the toxic and infectious characteristics of many medical wastes. Healthcare facilities produce substantial amounts of garbage, encompassing single-use plastics, packaging, and biomedical waste that necessitate specialized management [19].

The expenses and intricacies associated with sustainably handling this waste—through methods such as recycling, re-processing, or waste-to-energy technologies—can be substantial. The necessity to adhere to stringent rules on hazardous waste disposal sometimes supersedes initiatives aimed at material reduction or recycling, thereby constraining the potential for environmentally sustainable waste management, an integral part of the circular economy, which prioritizes the reuse, recycling, and reduction of waste materials. The absence of standardized criteria and frameworks for assessing and reporting sustainability in healthcare hinders the adoption and monitoring of environmentally friendly activities. In contrast to other sectors, where carbon accounting and sustainability reporting are increasingly prevalent, healthcare organizations frequently lack the necessary tools or skills to effectively assess their environmental impact. In the absence of explicit benchmarks or universal criteria for sustainability, healthcare organizations may struggle to establish objectives, track advancements, or convey the significance of sustainability programs to stakeholders [2].

Figure 6.5 outlines the aims of green technology through a circular approach to sustainability. It emphasizes recycling to minimize waste, refusing non-sustainable practices, and renewing resources by adopting renewable alternatives. It also highlights reducing resource consumption and responding proactively to environmental challenges. Together, these actions promote a responsible and resource-efficient framework to achieve environmental sustainability.

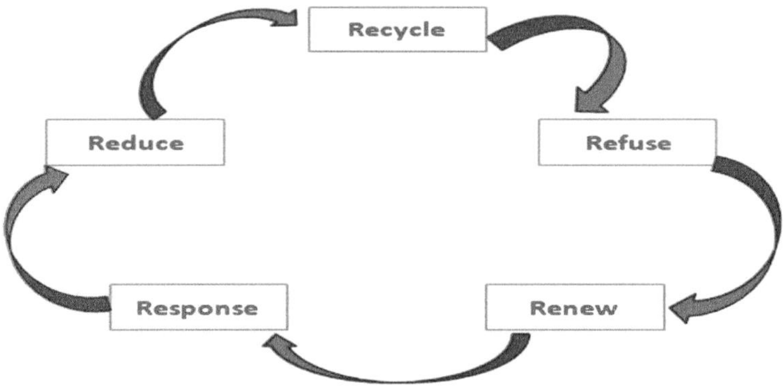

Figure 6.5 Aims of green technology.

Confronting legislative and institutional obstacles is crucial for advancing the implementation of sustainable practices in healthcare. These issues frequently stem from the intricate and heavily regulated characteristics of the healthcare sector, where patient safety and care quality are prioritized, and occasionally, at the expense of environmental sustainability. Surmounting these challenges necessitates a unified strategy encompassing legislative reform, institutional leadership, and the incorporation of sustainability into healthcare policies and practices [79]. A significant regulatory difficulty is the discord between infection control standards and environmental sustainability. Stringent hygiene and infection control measures in healthcare frequently require the utilization of single-use plastics, disposable medical instruments, and substantial quantities of cleaning chemicals and disinfectants, all of which produce considerable waste and emissions. Regulators and healthcare institutions must collaborate to create adaptable rules that reconcile infection control with sustainability. This may entail the implementation of sustainable alternatives, such as reusable medical devices and environmentally friendly sterilization technologies, while guaranteeing compliance with the same rigorous standards of patient safety and infection control. Regulatory frameworks may promote the utilization of biodegradable or recyclable materials in medical supplies and packaging, hence diminishing the environmental impact of disposables. Integrating sustainability into regulatory standards is an alternative approach to tackle these difficulties [24]. Governments and healthcare authorities could impose energy efficiency criteria for new healthcare facilities or offer incentives for hospitals to obtain green building certifications such as LEED. This would guarantee that healthcare facilities incorporate sustainability into their infrastructure development and renovation initiatives. Regulators might establish waste reduction targets or mandate healthcare providers to monitor and report their carbon emissions, fostering responsibility and encouraging organizations to embrace more sustainable practices [15].

Optimizing the approval process for sustainable technologies is an additional method to mitigate regulatory obstacles. Medical devices, medications, and other healthcare items must undergo stringent testing and approval procedures prior to their utilization in healthcare environments. This may impede the implementation of environmentally sustainable developments, such as biodegradable medical devices or renewable energy technology for healthcare facilities. Regulators may provide expedited procedures for the approval of sustainable technology that exhibits environmental advantages and ensures patient safety. Furthermore, cooperative initiatives among healthcare entities, innovators, and regulators could facilitate the establishment of standardized standards for assessing the sustainability of medical items, thereby simplifying the introduction of environmentally friendly alternatives to the market [30]. Addressing issues on the institutional level necessitates robust leadership and a commitment to sustainability from the highest echelons of healthcare administration. Institutional inertia may provide a considerable obstacle, as healthcare organizations frequently exhibit risk aversion and prioritize fast therapeutic results. Healthcare executives must include sustainability in the fundamental mission and operations of their institutions to address this issue. This may involve designating sustainability officers or green teams in hospitals and clinics, tasked with promoting eco-friendly projects and enforcing adherence to environmental rules. Board-level supervision and dedication to sustainability can facilitate the prioritization of these initiatives, connecting them with overarching institutional objectives. Institutional transformation necessitates the cultivation of a sustainable culture inside healthcare organizations. Sustainability can be integrated into training and educational programs for healthcare workers [23].

Medical schools and healthcare training programs must incorporate courses addressing the environmental ramifications of healthcare, as well as instruct on optimal methods for waste reduction, energy conservation, and the promotion of sustainable alternatives. By equipping healthcare professionals with the knowledge and resources to adopt sustainable practices, institutions may cultivate a culture of environmental accountability throughout all tiers of care. A significant institutional problem is the incorporation of sustainability into procurement procedures. Healthcare organizations frequently depend on long-standing supply chains and supplier partnerships, many of which may not emphasize sustainability. Healthcare institutions must implement sustainable procurement strategies by selecting vendors that provide environmentally friendly products and services. This necessitates a modification of procurement rules to emphasize sustainable materials, local sourcing, and products with less environmental impact. Through collaboration with authorities, healthcare organizations can guarantee that procurement contracts incorporate environmental standards, so as to generate a ripple effect across the supply chain [67].

Healthcare facilities encounter the difficulty of reconciling sustainability with budgetary limitations. Numerous eco-friendly solutions, including energy-efficient systems, renewable energy installations, and waste reduction initiatives, necessitate initial investment, which can be challenging to substantiate in the context of constrained healthcare budgets. Institutional leaders should investigate financial options and incentives that facilitate the implementation of sustainable practices. Governments, private foundations, and international organizations frequently provide grants or subsidies to healthcare organizations that implement green technologies. Moreover, public-private partnerships can facilitate the financing of sustainability initiatives in healthcare, distributing the financial responsibility among many stakeholders while guaranteeing enduring advantages [49]. Data openness and benchmarking are crucial for tackling regulatory and institutional concerns. Healthcare facilities require explicit criteria and reporting systems to assess their advancements in emission reduction and sustainability enhancement. Governments and healthcare organizations can contribute by establishing standardized sustainability reporting criteria for hospitals and clinics. These rules mandate institutions to monitor and report essential environmental metrics, including energy usage, waste production, and carbon emissions. This data can subsequently be utilized to build standards and compare the performance of other healthcare organizations, fostering competition and the exchange of best practices. Collaborative networks across healthcare institutions, governments, and industry stakeholders are crucial for addressing regulatory and institutional difficulties. Through collaboration, these entities can exchange information, resources, and innovations that foster sustainability. Public policy measures that promote green practices in healthcare, along with industry collaborations that facilitate access to sustainable technologies and resources, can expedite the implementation of eco-friendly practices throughout the sector. Collaboration aids healthcare organizations in navigating intricate regulatory frameworks, ensuring that sustainability objectives coincide with patient care standards and environmental considerations [6].

The future of sustainable healthcare is influenced by rising trends and technologies, presenting a significant opportunity to mitigate the sector's environmental footprint. Nonetheless, acknowledging these improvements entails considerable obstacles. As healthcare progresses toward a sustainable future, it will encounter challenges in cost, technological integration, infrastructure constraints, legal frameworks, and the cultural transformations necessary for widespread adoption [9]. Confronting these difficulties is essential to guarantee that upcoming technologies and trends provide both environmental and healthcare advantages. A primary obstacle to the adoption of innovative eco-friendly technology in healthcare is expense. Numerous emerging sustainable technologies, like renewable energy systems, biodegradable medical gadgets, and sophisticated waste management solutions, necessitate substantial initial investment [11]. Despite the potential for long-term cost savings via less energy usage and waste, the initial financial outlay might be prohibitive for some healthcare organizations, particularly in developing nations or smaller facilities with constrained resources. Moreover, the continual expenses associated with the maintenance and enhancement of modern green technologies may dissuade organizations from their adoption. Governments and corporate entities must establish financial incentives, grants, or subsidies to facilitate the transition to sustainable practices, especially for resource-constrained organizations [47]. A further difficulty is the technological integration of sustainable solutions into current healthcare infrastructures. Numerous hospitals and clinics are constructed on antiquated systems, hindering the seamless integration of new, energy-efficient technology or sustainable materials without substantial modification. Installing renewable energy sources, such as solar panels or wind turbines, may be impractical in older properties with restricted roof space or insufficient electrical infrastructure. Moreover, the integration of smart energy management systems, which utilize real-time data to enhance energy efficiency, can be intricate, necessitating staff training and enhancements to the building's IT infrastructure. Adopting digital health technology such as telemedicine and electronic records necessitates strong cybersecurity protocols and dependable internet connectivity, which are often deficient in numerous areas. Healthcare facilities must confront infrastructural and technical challenges while adopting these advances, frequently under constraints of time and finances [75].

Regulatory concerns provide substantial impediments to the future of sustainable healthcare. The healthcare industry is extensively regulated to guarantee patient safety, hygiene, and quality of care; yet, these rules frequently conflict with sustainable objectives. Stringent regulations concerning sterilization, packaging, and SUDs, intended to avert illness and cross-contamination, can hinder the adoption of more sustainable alternatives like reusable medical instruments or biodegradable packaging. Regulatory authorities must identify methods to reconcile the healthcare sector's necessity for safety and compliance with the demand for enhanced sustainability practices [65]. This may necessitate the reassessment of rules to establish more adaptable regulatory frameworks that promote innovation while upholding superior standards of care. Moreover, the clearance procedures for novel eco-friendly technologies, including biodegradable medical equipment or sustainable building materials, are frequently protracted, hindering their extensive use. Data and measurement difficulties present obstacles for the future of sustainable healthcare. As the sector endeavors to diminish its carbon footprint, healthcare institutions must precisely evaluate and monitor their environmental impact. Many healthcare organizations, however, lack standardized measurements and reporting methods to evaluate their carbon emissions, energy usage, and waste generation [48]. In the absence of explicit benchmarks, assessing progress or comparing performance among other institutions becomes challenging. The healthcare sector must implement uniform sustainability measurements and reporting systems, potentially necessitating the development of new technologies for monitoring and reporting environmental data. Moreover, hospitals and clinics may require investment in AI and data analytics to enhance resource utilization and decrease energy use, thereby introducing further complexity and expense. The cultural and behavioral transformations necessary for the adoption of eco-friendly technologies in healthcare present an additional obstacle. The healthcare sector frequently exhibits a reluctance to adopt change, prioritizing the preservation of the status quo to guarantee patient safety and care quality [54]. The implementation of new technologies and processes, such as minimizing single-use plastics or shifting to digital health records, may encounter resistance from healthcare professionals accustomed to conventional ways. Furthermore, personnel may lack comprehensive awareness of the environmental consequences of their actions or the methods to adopt more sustainable practices. Surmounting this opposition necessitates education, training, and leadership from institutional management to cultivate a culture of sustainability inside healthcare organizations. Altering entrenched habits and procedures will need time, and leadership must prioritize sustainability within the overarching goal of healthcare organizations [4].

Disruptions in the supply chain provide a significant obstacle to the future of sustainable healthcare. The healthcare industry depends on intricate global supply chains to procure medications, medical devices, and other vital goods. Adopting sustainable procurement strategies, such as procuring from environmentally friendly vendors or selecting local materials, may not always be practical, particularly if it escalates costs or causes delays in the delivery of essential supplies. Moreover, supply chain interruptions, exemplified by the COVID-19 epidemic, might intensify the challenges of procuring sustainable resources. Healthcare facilities may find it challenging to reconcile their requirement for dependable, cost-effective supplies with the aspiration to minimize their environmental footprint [27]. A transition to local sourcing and sustainable supply chain management needs meticulous preparation, investment, and coordination with suppliers to guarantee that patient care remains uncompromised. The rapid advancement of innovation and the intricacy of healthcare systems present an additional barrier. Innovative technologies are perpetually arising, ranging from energy-efficient construction systems to AI-enhanced trash management. Nevertheless, the healthcare sector may find it challenging to adapt to these swift changes due to the intrinsic complexity of its operations. Simultaneously implementing many new systems, while maintaining uninterrupted patient care, can be daunting for hospital administrators and healthcare providers [76].

Moreover, healthcare professionals may require continuous education to remain informed on the latest technologies and sustainable practices, which can be resource-demanding. Ultimately, there are issues about equity in the implementation of environmentally sustainable healthcare solutions. A multitude of rising trends and ideas are cultivated in high-income nations, where healthcare systems possess greater resources for investment in sustainability. Nevertheless, low- and middle-income nations may encounter difficulties in obtaining these technologies owing to budgetary limitations, inadequate infrastructure, or insufficient regulatory assistance. This may result in an expanding disparity between healthcare systems regarding environmental impact, with affluent nations profiting from more sustainable methods while impoverished countries remain neglected. Overcoming this challenge necessitates international collaboration and initiatives to guarantee that sustainable healthcare technologies are accessible and affordable for all nations, irrespective of their economic conditions [52].

6.8 Conclusion

The healthcare sector is at a critical juncture when minimizing its carbon footprint has evolved into both a practical need and an ethical imperative. The healthcare sector accounts for almost 5% of global carbon emissions; hence, it is imperative for the business to contribute to climate change mitigation and safeguard public health. Focusing on critical sectors such as energy consumption, transportation, pharmaceuticals, and waste management will be essential for reducing emissions. Transitioning to renewable energy sources, deploying energy-efficient technologies, optimizing architectural design, and adopting sustainable procurement techniques are all critical measures in this process. Similarly, minimizing waste in medical equipment, pharmaceuticals, and single-use plastics, while advocating for recycling and the utilization of environmentally sustainable medical technologies, can provide a significant impact. Nonetheless, the trajectory ahead is fraught with obstacles. Substantial obstacles include the expense of adopting sustainable technologies, legislative limitations, and the necessity to modernize current infrastructures. Cultural resistance to change within healthcare organizations can impede progress, necessitating a determined effort to enhance knowledge and cultivate a culture of sustainability. The ethical need for the healthcare sector to take the lead in environmental stewardship is paramount. The industry is responsible for safeguarding human health; nevertheless, its environmental repercussions exacerbate issues like air pollution, climate change, and water contamination, which adversely affect public health. By assuming a leading position in minimizing its environmental impact, healthcare may accord with its fundamental objective of "do no harm" within a broader global framework. Going forward, emphasis should be placed on cooperative initiatives among governments, healthcare institutions, private sector entities, and international organizations. Regulatory frameworks must promote sustainability, while innovation and technical progress must be utilized to mitigate the sector's environmental impact. Through robust leadership, institutional dedication, and a transformation in organizational culture, the healthcare sector may markedly diminish its carbon emissions. Ultimately, these initiatives will solve environmental issues and enhance public health, thereby satisfying the sector's ethical obligation to safeguard both individuals and the Earth.

References

1. C. Ray, X. Ming, Climate change and human health: A review of allergies, autoimmunity and the microbiome, *Int. J. Environ. Res. Public Health*, 17 (2020).
2. S.I. Zandalinas, F.B. Fritschi, R. Mittler, Global warming, climate change, and environmental pollution: Recipe for a multifactorial stress combination disaster, *Trends in Plant Science*, 26 (2021) 588–599.
3. D. Campbell-Lendrum, T. Neville, C. Schweizer, M. Neira, Climate change and health: Three grand challenges, *Nat. Med.*, 29 (2023) 1631–1638.
4. K.L. Ebi, S.B. Fawcett, J. Spiegel, H. Tovalin, Carbon pollution increases health inequities: Lessons in resilience from the most vulnerable, *Rev. Panam. Salud Publica*, 40 (2016) 181–185.
5. K.L. Ebi, J.J. Hess, P. Watkiss, Health risks and costs of climate variability and change, in: C.N. Mock, R. Nugent, O. Kobusingye, K.R. Smith (Eds.) *Injury Prevention and Environmental Health*, The International Bank for Reconstruction and Development / The World Bank, Washington (DC), 2017.
6. C. Bezirtzoglou, K. Dekas, E. Charvalos, Climate changes, environment and infection: Facts, scenarios and growing awareness from the public health community within Europe, *Anaerobe*, 17 (2011) 337–340.
7. J.A. Patz, P.R. Epstein, T.A. Burke, J.M. Balbus, Global climate change and emerging infectious diseases, *JAMA*, 275 (1996) 217–223.

8. A.R. Pearson, K.E. White, L.M. Nogueira, N.A. Lewis, D.J. Green, J.P. Schuldt, D. Edmondson, Climate change and health equity: A research agenda for psychological science, *Am. Psychol.*, 78 (2023) 244–258.
9. R. Boekels, C. Nikendei, E. Roether, H.C. Friederich, T.J. Bugaj, Climate change and health in international medical education: A narrative review, *GMS Journal for Medical Education*, 40 (2023) Doc37.
10. J. Sheather, K. Littler, J.A. Singh, K. Wright, Ethics, climate change and health: A landscape review, *Wellcome Open Research*, 8 (2023) 343.
11. E. National Academies of Sciences, Medicine, E. Division on, S. Life, I. Environmental Health Matters, The National Academies Collection: Reports Funded by National Institutes of Health, in: A. Reich, A. Ulman, C. Berkower (Eds.) *Communities, Climate Change, and Health Equity: Proceedings of a Workshop—in Brief*, National Academies Press (US), Washington (DC), 2022.
12. C.D. Butler, I.C. Hanigan, Anthropogenic climate change and health in the Global South, *Int. J. Tuberc. Lung Dis.*, 23 (2019) 1243–1252.
13. M. Romanello, C. Di Napoli, P. Drummond, C. Green, H. Kennard, P. Lampard, D. Scamman, N. Arnell, S. Ayeb-Karlsson, L.B. Ford, K. Belesova, K. Bowen, W. Cai, M. Callaghan, D. Campbell-Lendrum, J. Chambers, K.R. van Daalen, C. Dalin, N. Dasandi, S. Dasgupta, M. Davies, P. Dominguez-Salas, R. Dubrow, K.L. Ebi, M. Eckelman, P. Ekins, L.E. Escobar, L. Georgeson, H. Graham, S.H. Gunther, I. Hamilton, Y. Hang, R. Hänninen, S. Hartinger, K. He, J.J. Hess, S.C. Hsu, S. Jankin, L. Jamart, O. Jay, I. Kelman, G. Kiesewetter, P. Kinney, T. Kjellstrom, D. Kniveton, J.K.W. Lee, B. Lemke, Y. Liu, Z. Liu, M. Lott, M.L. Batista, R. Lowe, F. MacGuire, M.O. Sewe, J. Martinez-Urtaza, M. Maslin, L. McAllister, A. McGushin, C. McMichael, Z. Mi, J. Milner, K. Minor, J.C. Minx, N. Mohajeri, M. Moradi-Lakeh, K. Morrissey, S. Munzert, K.A. Murray, T. Neville, M. Nilsson, N. Obradovich, M.B. O'Hare, T. Oreszczyn, M. Otto, F. Owfi, O. Pearman, M. Rabbaniha, E.J.Z. Robinson, J. Rocklöv, R.N. Salas, J.C. Semenza, J.D. Sherman, L. Shi, J. Shumake-Guillemot, G. Silbert, M. Sofiev, M. Springmann, J. Stowell, M. Tabatabaei, J. Taylor, J. Triñanes, F. Wagner, P. Wilkinson, M. Winning, M. Yglesias-González, S. Zhang, P. Gong, H. Montgomery, A. Costello, The 2022 report of the Lancet countdown on health and climate change: Health at the mercy of fossil fuels, *Lancet*, 400 (2022) 1619–1654.
14. A. Colao, G. Muscogiuri, P. Piscitelli, Environment and health: Not only cancer, *Int. J. Environ. Res. Public Health*, 13 (2016).
15. L. Frehlich, C.D. Christie, P.E. Ronksley, T.C. Turin, P. Doyle-Baker, G.R. McCormack, The neighbourhood built environment and health-

related fitness: A narrative systematic review, *Int. J. Behav. Nutr. Phys. Act.*, 19 (2022) 124.

16. G. Scally, C. Perkins, Environment and health, *Hosp. Med.*, 59 (1998) 872–876.
17. E.L. Bird, J.O. Ige, P. Pilkington, A. Pinto, C. Petrokofsky, J. Burgess Allen, Built and natural environment planning principles for promoting health: An umbrella review, *BMC Public Health*, 18 (2018) 930.
18. A. Mousavi, A. Ardalan, A. Takian, A. Ostadtaghizadeh, K. Naddafi, A.M. Bavani, Climate change and health in Iran: A narrative review, *Journal of Environmental Health Science & Engineering*, 18 (2020) 367–378.
19. D. Acosta, A. Barrow, I.S. Mahamadou, V.S. Assuncao, M.E. Edwards, S.L. McKune, Climate change and health in the Sahel: A systematic review, *Royal Society Open Science*, 11 (2024) 231602.
20. P. The Lancet regional health-western, water, climate change, and health in the Western Pacific Region, *The Lancet Regional Health. Western Pacific*, 32 (2023) 100753.
21. J.I. Levy, Climate change and health justice: New perspectives on pressing challenges, *Am. J. Public Health*, 110 (2020) 1718.
22. Y.S. Khader, M. Abdelrahman, N. Abdo, M. Al-Sharif, A. Elbetieha, H. Bakir, R. Alemam, Climate change and health in the Eastern Mediterranean countries: A systematic review, *Rev. Environ. Health*, 30 (2015) 163–181.
23. A.L. Soares, S.C. Buttigieg, B. Bak, S. McFadden, C. Hughes, P. McClure, J.G. Couto, I. Bravo, A review of the applicability of current green practices in healthcare facilities, *International Journal of Health Policy and Management*, 12 (2023) 6947.
24. M. Chan, J. Mutimer, Reducing carbon footprint of disposable pulse lavage systems in total hip and knee arthroplasty, *Cureus*, 16 (2024) e52195.
25. S. McAlister, R.L. Morton, A. Barratt, Incorporating carbon into health care: Adding carbon emissions to health technology assessments, *The Lancet. Planetary Health*, 6 (2022) e993–e999.
26. P. Ten Have, P. van Hal, I. Wichers, J. Kooistra, P. Hagedoorn, E.A. Brakema, N. Chavannes, P. de Heer, H.C. Ossebaard, Turning green: The impact of changing to more eco-friendly respiratory healthcare – A carbon and cost analysis of Dutch prescription data, *BMJ Open*, 12 (2022) e055546.
27. S.C. Walpole, M.N. Eii, T. Lyons, C. Aldridge, Improving antimicrobial use to protect the environment: What is the role of infection specialists?, *Antibiotics* (Basel, Switzerland), 12 (2023).

28. B. Chinene, L.S. Mudadi, O. Bwanga, P. Nyawani, L. Mutandiro, S. Kafwimbi, W. Matika, B. Ohene-Botwe, Sustainability in radiography: Knowledge, practices, and barriers among radiographers in Zimbabwe and Zambia, *Journal of Medical Imaging and Radiation Sciences*, 55 (2024) 101438.
29. C.A. Sánchez Zavaleta, Evolution of the climate change concept and its impact in the public health of Peru, *Rev. Peru. Med. Exp. Salud Publica*, 33 (2016) 128–138.
30. S. Desmond, Health service planning and sustainable development: Considering what, where and how care is delivered through a pro-environmental lens, *Aust. Health Rev.*, 42 (2018) 140–145.
31. M.R. Cummins, S. Shishupal, B. Wong, N. Wan, J. Han, J.D. Johnny, A. Mhatre-Owens, R. Gouripeddi, J. Ivanova, T. Ong, H. Soni, J. Barrera, H. Wilczewski, B.M. Welch, B.E. Bunnell, Travel distance between participants in US telemedicine sessions with estimates of emissions savings: Observational study, *J. Med. Internet Res.*, 26 (2024) e53437.
32. L. Rodríguez-Jiménez, M. Romero-Martín, T. Spruell, Z. Steley, J. Gómez-Salgado, The carbon footprint of healthcare settings: A systematic review, *J. Adv. Nurs.*, 79 (2023) 2830–2844.
33. I. Tennison, S. Roschnik, B. Ashby, R. Boyd, I. Hamilton, T. Oreszczyn, A. Owen, M. Romanello, P. Ruyssevelt, J.D. Sherman, A.Z.P. Smith, K. Steele, N. Watts, M.J. Eckelman, Health care's response to climate change: A carbon footprint assessment of the NHS in England, *The Lancet. Planetary Health*, 5 (2021) e84–e92.
34. S. González-García, X. Esteve-Llorens, M.T. Moreira, G. Feijoo, Carbon footprint and nutritional quality of different human dietary choices, *Sci. Total Environ.*, 644 (2018) 77–94.
35. B. Pradere, R. Mallet, A. de La Taille, F. Bladou, D. Prunet, S. Beurrier, F. Bardet, X. Game, G. Fournier, E. Lechevallier, P. Meria, X. Matillon, T. Polguer, N. Abid, B. De Graeve, D. Kassab, A. Mejean, V. Misrai, U. Pinar, Climate-smart actions in the operating theatre for improving sustainability practices: A systematic review, *Eur. Urol.*, 83 (2023) 331–342.
36. D. Ueda, S.L. Walston, S. Fujita, Y. Fushimi, T. Tsuboyama, K. Kamagata, A. Yamada, M. Yanagawa, R. Ito, N. Fujima, M. Kawamura, T. Nakaura, Y. Matsui, F. Tatsugami, T. Fujioka, T. Nozaki, K. Hirata, S. Naganawa, Climate change and artificial intelligence in healthcare: Review and recommendations towards a sustainable future, *Diagn. Interv. Imaging*, (2024).

37. R. Zhong, X. Ren, M.W. Akbar, Z. Zia, R. Sroufe, Striving towards sustainable development: How environmental degradation and energy efficiency interact with health expenditures in SAARC countries, Environ. *Sci. Pollut. Res. Int.*, 29 (2022) 46898–46915.

38. X. Xue, R. Marappan, S.K. Raju, R. Raghavan, R. Rajan, O.I. Khalaf, G.M. Abdulsahib, modelling and analysis of hybrid transformation for lossless big medical image compression, *Bioengineering* (Basel, Switzerland), 10 (2023).

39. J. Yeo, M.H. Ryu, Y. Yang, Energy harvesting from upper-limb pulling motions for miniaturized human-powered generators, *Sensors* (Basel, Switzerland), 15 (2015) 15853–15867.

40. S. McCarney, J. Robertson, J. Arnaud, K. Lorenson, J. Lloyd, Using solar-powered refrigeration for vaccine storage where other sources of reliable electricity are inadequate or costly, *Vaccine*, 31 (2013) 6050–6057.

41. H. Saleem, M.B. Khan, M.S. Shabbir, G.Y. Khan, M. Usman, Nexus between non-renewable energy production, CO_2 emissions, and healthcare spending in OECD economies, *Environ. Sci. Pollut. Res. Int.*, 29 (2022) 47286–47297.

42. M. Moner-Girona, G. Kakoulaki, G. Falchetta, D.J. Weiss, N. Taylor, Achieving universal electrification of rural healthcare facilities in sub-Saharan Africa with decentralized renewable energy technologies, *Joule*, 5 (2021) 2687–2714.

43. H. Burch, F. McGain, Victorian public healthcare Chief Executive Officers' views on renewable energy supply, *Aust. Health Rev.*, 45 (2021) 7–11.

44. P. Slathia, A. Vashishtha, P.K. Jena, P.K. Sahu, Examining the dynamic impact of carbon emissions, renewable energy and economic growth on healthcare expenditure in Asian countries, *Heliyon*, 10 (2024) e30136.

45. J.M. Polimeni, M. Simionescu, R.I. Iorgulescu, Energy poverty and personal health in the EU, *Int. J. Environ. Res. Public Health*, 19 (2022).

46. H. Liu, K. Zhong, Relationship between health spending, life expectancy and renewable energy in China: A new evidence from the VECM approach, *Frontiers in Public Health*, 10 (2022) 993546.

47. E.E. Wadhwani, The impact of environmental factors on credit ratings in healthcare, *Front. Health Serv. Manage.*, 39 (2022) 26–32.

48. C.S. Ramos-Meza, J.P. Flores-Arocutipa, J. Jinchuña-Huallpa, E.E. Corzo-Palomo, V.K. Gamero-Huarcaya, Y. Gutiérrez-Acuña, J.C.

Valencia-Martinez, Does environment quality affect the health care spending? Nexus among CO_2 emissions, non-renewable energy production, financial development, and health care spending, *Environ. Sci. Pollut. Res. Int.*, 30 (2023) 48903–48910

49. A. Anwar, S. Hyder, R. Bennett, M. Younis, Impact of environmental quality on healthcare expenditures in developing countries: a panel data approach, *Healthcare* (Basel, Switzerland), 10 (2022).
50. A.A. Alola, D. Kirikkaleli, The nexus of environmental quality with renewable consumption, immigration, and healthcare in the US: Wavelet and gradual-shift causality approaches, *Environ. Sci. Pollut. Res. Int.*, 26 (2019) 35208–35217.
51. M. Aydin, T. Degirmenci, O. Bozatli, D. Balsalobre-Lorente, Fresh evidence of the impact of economic complexity, health expenditure, natural resources, plastic consumption, and renewable energy in air pollution deaths in the USA? An empirical approach, *Sci. Total Environ.*, 921 (2024) 171127.
52. G. Sánchez-Barroso, J. González-Domínguez, J. García-Sanz-Calcedo, Potential savings in DHW facilities through the use of solar thermal energy in the Hospitals of Extremadura (Spain), *Int. J. Environ. Res. Public Health*, 17 (2020).
53. K. Vanderwee, L. Demarré, S. Malfait, E. Kieckens, P. De Waegemaeker, V. Duprez, N. Fraeyman, How to choose between single-use and reusable medical materials for sustainable nursing: Methodological lessons learned from a national study, *J. Adv. Nurs.*, (2024).
54. N. Al-Hadithy, K. Knight, A. Gopfert, M. Van Hove, X. Villa Garcia, Vital role of clinicians in reducing the NHS carbon footprint through smarter procurement decisions, *BMJ Leader*, 8 (2024) 43–48.
55. A. Lyne, P. Ashley, S. Saget, M. Porto Costa, B. Underwood, B. Duane, Combining evidence-based healthcare with environmental sustainability: Using the toothbrush as a model, *Br. Dent. J.*, 229 (2020) 303–309.
56. V.L. Collada Sánchez, E. Villamañán Bueno, M. Ayllón Morales, M. Ruano Encinar, C. Sobreino Jimenez, C. Lara Catedra, E. Perez Andreu, A. Herrero Ambrosio, Green hospital pharmacy: A sustainable approach to the medication use process in a tertiary hospital, *Farmacia hospitalaria: organo oficial de expresion cientifica de la Sociedad Espanola de Farmacia Hospitalaria*, 47 (2023) T196–T200.
57. P. Bedouch, M. Baudrant, M. Detavernier, C. Rey, E. Brudieu, L. Foroni, B. Allenet, J. Calop, Drug supply chain safety in hospitals: Current

data and experience of the Grenoble University Hospital, *Ann. Pharm. Fr.*, 67 (2009) 3–15.

58. R.A. Leather, M. Gardner, M.S. Green, K. Kavanagh, L. Macle, K. Ahmad, C. Gray, F. Ayala-Paredes, P.G. Guerra, G. O'Hara, V. Essebag, M. Sturmer, A. Baranchuk, T. Hruczkowski, I. Lahevsky, P. Novak, S. Chakrabarti, L. Harris, L.J. Gula, C. Morillo, S. Sanatani, R.M. Hamilton, R.M. Gow, A.D. Krahn, Charting a course for cardiac electrophysiology training in Canada: The vital role of fellows in advanced cardiovascular care, *Can. J. Cardiol.*, 29 (2013) 1527–1530.
59. W. Zeng, A.E. Finlayson, S. Shankar, W. de Bruyn, B. Godman, Prescribing efficiency of proton pump inhibitors in China: Influence and future directions, *BMC Health Serv. Res.*, 15 (2015) 11.
60. H.M. Edwards, R. Sarwar, P. Mahmud, S. Emmanuel, K. Maxwell, J.K. Tibenderana, The impact of the private sector co-payment mechanism (PSCM) on the private market for ACT in Nigeria: Results of the 2018 cross-sectional outlet and household market surveys, *Malar. J.*, 21 (2022) 42.
61. M. Chatzipavlou, D. Karayiannis, S. Chaloulakou, E. Georgakopoulou, K.A. Poulia, Implementation of sustainable food service systems in hospitals to achieve current sustainability goals: A scoping review, *Clinical Nutrition ESPEN*, 61 (2024) 237–252.
62. A. Malakahmad, M.S. Abualqumboz, S.R.M. Kutty, T.J. Abunama, Assessment of carbon footprint emissions and environmental concerns of solid waste treatment and disposal techniques: Case study of Malaysia, *Waste Management* (New York), 70 (2017) 282–292.
63. K. Rouhi, M. Shafiepour Motlagh, F. Dalir, Developing a carbon footprint model and environmental impact analysis of municipal solid waste transportation: A case study of Tehran, Iran, *J. Air Waste Manag. Assoc.*, 73 (2023) 890–901.
64. K. Crider, J. Williams, Y.P. Qi, J. Gutman, L. Yeung, C. Mai, J. Finkelstain, S. Mehta, C. Pons-Duran, C. Menéndez, C. Moraleda, L. Rogers, K. Daniels, P. Green, Folic acid supplementation and malaria susceptibility and severity among people taking antifolate antimalarial drugs in endemic areas, *Cochrane Database Syst. Rev.*, 2 (2022).
65. S.B. Park, J.M. Cha, Gastrointestinal endoscopy's carbon footprint, *Clinical Endoscopy*, 56 (2023) 263–267.
66. S. Sonaiya, R. Marino, K. Agollari, P. Sharma, M. Desai, Environmentally sustainable gastroenterology practice: Review of current state and future goals, *Dig. Endosc.*, 36 (2024) 406–420.

67. E.B. Parker, A. Bluman, J. Pruneski, W. Soens, A. Bernstein, J.T. Smith, E.M. Bluman, American orthopaedic foot and ankle society annual meeting all-in-person attendance results in immense carbon expenditure, *Clin. Orthop. Relat. Res.*, 481 (2023) 2469–2480.

68. P.J. Landrigan, H. Raps, M. Cropper, C. Bald, M. Brunner, E.M. Canonizado, D. Charles, T.C. Chiles, M.J. Donohue, J. Enck, P. Fenichel, L.E. Fleming, C. Ferrier-Pages, R. Fordham, A. Gozt, C. Griffin, M.E. Hahn, B. Haryanto, R. Hixson, H. Ianelli, B.D. James, P. Kumar, A. Laborde, K.L. Law, K. Martin, J. Mu, Y. Mulders, A. Mustapha, J. Niu, S. Pahl, Y. Park, M.L. Pedrotti, J.A. Pitt, M. Ruchirawat, B.J. Seewoo, M. Spring, J.J. Stegeman, W. Suk, C. Symeonides, H. Takada, R.C. Thompson, A. Vicini, Z. Wang, E. Whitman, D. Wirth, M. Wolff, A.K. Yousuf, S. Dunlop, The Minderoo-Monaco Commission on Plastics and Human Health, *Annals of Global Health*, 89 (2023) 23.

69. J.R. Lewy, C.D. Patnode, P.J. Landrigan, J.C. Kolars, B.C. Williams, Quantifying the climate benefits of a virtual versus an in-person format for an international conference, *Environ. Health*, 21 (2022) 71.

70. C. Dias-Ferreira, T. Santos, V. Oliveira, Hospital food waste and environmental and economic indicators: A Portuguese case study, *Waste Management* (New York), 46 (2015) 146–154.

71. A.E. Lim, A. Perkins, J.W. Agar, The carbon footprint of an Australian satellite haemodialysis unit, *Aust. Health Rev.*, 37 (2013) 369–374.

72. B. McPherson, M. Sharip, T. Grimmond, The impact on life cycle carbon footprint of converting from disposable to reusable sharps containers in a large US hospital geographically distant from manufacturing and processing facilities, *PeerJ*, 7 (2019) e6204.

73. X. Chen, F. Wu, F. Fan, Q. Wu, D. Zhu, Green biosynthesis of chiral pharmaceutical chemicals, *Sheng wu gong cheng xue bao = Chinese Journal of Biotechnology*, 38 (2022) 4240–4262.

74. N. Ribeiro, G.C. Soares, V. Santos-Rosales, A. Concheiro, C. Alvarez-Lorenzo, C.A. García-González, A.L. Oliveira, A new era for sterilization based on supercritical CO_2 technology, *J. Biomed. Mater. Res. B Appl. Biomater.*, 108 (2020) 399–428.

75. H. Shokrani, A. Shokrani, M. Jouyandeh, F. Seidi, F. Gholami, S. Kar, M.T. Munir, D. Kowalkowska-Zedler, P. Zarrintaj, N. Rabiee, M.R. Saeb, Green polymer nanocomposites for skin tissue engineering, *ACS Applied Bio Materials*, 5 (2022) 2107–2121.

76. S. Pina, J.M. Oliveira, R.L. Reis, Natural-based nanocomposites for bone tissue engineering and regenerative medicine: A review, *Advanced Materials* (Deerfield Beach, Fla.), 27 (2015) 1143–1169.

77. J. Nandhini, E. Karthikeyan, S. Rajeshkumar, Eco-friendly bio-nanocomposites: Pioneering sustainable biomedical advancements in engineering, *Discover Nano*, 19 (2024) 86.

78. K.R. Aadil, A. Nathani, A. Rajendran, C.S. Sharma, N. Lenka, P. Gupta, Investigation of human hair keratin-based nanofibrous scaffold for skin tissue engineering application, *Drug Delivery and Translational Research*, 14 (2024) 236–246.

79. J. Dharmaraja, S. Shobana, S. Arvindnarayan, R.R. Francis, R.B. Jeyakumar, R.G. Saratale, V. Ashokkumar, S.K. Bhatia, V. Kumar, G. Kumar, Lignocellulosic biomass conversion via greener pretreatment methods towards biorefinery applications, *Bioresour. Technol.*, 369 (2023) 128328.

80. Y. Dong, M. Ghasemzadeh, Z. Khorsandi, R. Sheibani, M. Nasrollahzadeh, Starch-based hydrogels for environmental applications: A review, *Int. J. Biol. Macromol.*, 269 (2024) 131956.

81. S. Ahmad, M. Ahmad, K. Manzoor, R. Purwar, S. Ikram, A review on latest innovations in natural gums-based hydrogels: Preparations & applications, *Int. J. Biol. Macromol.*, 136 (2019) 870–890.

Chapter 7

Recent Advances in Energy-Saving Technologies for Hospital Heating, Ventilation, and Air Conditioning Systems

Xi Wang, Rupp Carriveau, and David S.-K. Ting

Turbulence and Energy Laboratory, University of Windsor, Windsor, Ontario, Canada

Wang1st@uwindsor.ca

Heating, ventilation, and air conditioning (HVAC) systems play a critical role in the healthcare sector, particularly in hospitals, clinics, and long-term care facilities, where ensuring optimal indoor air quality, temperature, and humidity is essential for patient comfort, health, and safety. At the same time, HVAC systems are among the largest contributors to energy consumption and carbon emissions in healthcare buildings, presenting significant environmental and economic challenges that must be addressed to achieve sustainability goals. To tackle these challenges, the integration of energy-saving technologies into HVAC systems has become a primary focus, aimed at enhancing energy efficiency and reducing environmental impact. This chapter provides an in-

Environmentalism in Healthcare: Caring for Tomorrow Ecologically
Edited by Jacqueline A. Stagner and David S.-K. Ting

ISBN 978-981-5129-95-3 (Hardcover), 978-1-003-74869-4 (eBook)
www.jennystanford.com

DOI: 10.1201/9781003748694-7

depth review of advanced energy management strategies, including artificial intelligence (AI) and machine learning (ML), which have been increasingly applied to optimize the performance of HVAC systems. These technologies play a vital role in minimizing energy waste, enhancing operational efficiency, and improving system adaptability to meet varying operational demands. Additionally, this chapter discusses the integration of renewable energy sources—such as solar power, geothermal energy, air source, and biomass—into HVAC systems, emphasizing their potential to reduce dependence on conventional energy sources and improve sustainability in healthcare facilities. By combining intelligent energy management strategies with renewable energy solutions, HVAC systems can achieve substantial improvements in efficiency, cost-effectiveness, and environmental performance, contributing to more sustainable healthcare infrastructure.

7.1 Introduction

The HVAC system plays a pivotal role in the healthcare industry, not only by providing a comfortable environment for patients and staff but also by significantly influencing infection rates in intensive care units (ICUs) [1]. With the rapid growth of the global population, the demand for HVAC systems within the healthcare sector has experienced a notable increase over the past decades. As of 2022, the global market for hospital HVAC systems was valued at approximately USD 9.55 billion and is expected to expand at a compound annual growth rate (CAGR) of 7.2% from 2023 to 2030 [2].

However, it is essential to highlight that HVAC systems are among the primary contributors to energy consumption and carbon emissions worldwide. They account for approximately 40% of the global energy consumption and 36% of CO_2 emissions each year [3–5]. A significant portion of the energy supply for HVAC systems is derived from fossil fuel combustion. For instance, nearly half of the heating systems sold globally in 2020 relied directly on fossil fuels, including oil, natural gas, and propane—fuels commonly obtained through oil and natural gas refining processes [6].

Additionally, the use of coal stoves for heating remains widespread in many developing countries, further contributing to environmental concerns [7]. Therefore, developing and implementing advanced HVAC control strategies is increasingly recognized as one of the most effective measures to achieve substantial energy savings and reduce carbon emissions within the healthcare industry.

With the advancement of data-driven model technologies, smart control strategies have emerged as effective tools for enhancing both comfort and energy efficiency in HVAC systems. A smart control strategy is characterized by its ability to perceive interactions between users and their environment while autonomously processing and understanding contextual data to respond effectively to users' needs [8]. In healthcare buildings, Reijula et al. [9] emphasize that implementing smart HVAC systems should be a top priority for ensuring the well-being of hospital users while also supporting the transition to a low-carbon economy.

In the past decades, limitations in computer science technology restricted the use of sophisticated algorithms for HVAC energy management. As a result, simple algorithms like multiple linear regression (MLR) were commonly applied to predict and control energy consumption in HVAC equipment [10]. However, predicting and controlling energy use in real healthcare environments is highly complex. Traditional methods are insufficient to handle intricate and dynamic interactions involving various occupancy types, specific indoor environment requirements, and diverse weather conditions.

Recently, advanced algorithms powered by AI and ML have attracted significant attention from engineers seeking to improve energy consumption prediction and control in HVAC systems [11–13]. Selecting an appropriate algorithm involves balancing accuracy and computational efficiency. Among various methods, ensemble techniques and hybrid models have shown exceptional potential in achieving this balance, making them popular choices for HVAC energy management systems. Achieving optimal accuracy, efficiency, and interpretability remains essential for promoting sustainable energy management and efficient operations across key industries. Future research is expected to prioritize enhancing parameter tuning and refining algorithms within ensemble and hybrid models to improve forecasting and control accuracy [14]. Additionally, improving model interpretability will be crucial for effectively conveying AI-driven insights to healthcare stakeholders, facilitating more efficient and sustainable energy management in healthcare facilities.

Beyond HVAC energy management strategies, integrating alternative energy sources has become a fundamental aspect of developing a low-carbon healthcare economy. In the HVAC sector, various renewable energy solutions, including solar, geothermal, air source, and biomass, have been increasingly adopted in different types of buildings to enhance sustainability and reduce environmental impacts [4].

Firstly, Solar technology is a promising renewable energy source known for its cost-effectiveness and high efficiency. Governments worldwide are increasingly investing in solar devices to reduce HVAC energy consumption. According to the International Energy Agency (IEA), around 250 million dwellings utilized solar thermal technology for water heating by 2020, with projections of 290 million installations needed by 2050 to achieve net-zero emissions [15]. China leads in solar technology adoption, contributing over 70% of global solar collector capacity, mainly through affordable evacuated tube collectors used in rural areas [16]. Additionally, countries like Denmark are developing large-scale solar thermal plants integrated with district heating networks, with approximately 300 systems providing a total capacity of 1,140 MWth by the end of 2017 [17]. The integration of solar photovoltaic (PV) technology with building facades to meet HVAC energy demands is also growing, with a global market size of 2.3 GW, of which Europe holds 42%, due to favorable policies in France, Italy, and Germany [18].

Except for solar energy, other advanced heat pump technologies, such as geothermal and air-source systems, have also been incorporated into HVAC systems to enhance energy efficiency and promote environmental sustainability. Geothermal energy is typically extracted from the Earth's subsurface and can be utilized for various applications, including heating, cooling, and energy storage, making it a versatile option for HVAC systems [19]. The current global geothermal capacity stands at around 30 gigawatts, with approximately 75% of geothermal energy production coming from four countries: China, Iceland, Japan, and Turkey [20]. Notably, geothermal energy is predominantly used for water heating purposes, such as providing hot water for baths and swimming pools, which accounts for more than 40% of the total thermal energy generated [20]. While the full potential of geothermal technology has yet to be fully explored, its usage is expected to grow significantly due to the implementation of supportive policies. For instance, geothermal energy became the largest single source of energy production in New Zealand, achieving an output of 204 PJ in 2021—an impressive 37% increase compared to 2011 [21]. However, differing from the geothermal technology, air source heat pumps (ASHPs) primarily extract thermal energy from indoor and outdoor air [22]. Due to their excellent cost-effectiveness, ASHPs have gained increasing attention from the public. According to an overview of the heat pump market in the U.S., ASHP shipments saw a significant rise in 2018 compared to 2017, reaching nearly 3 million units [23]. A similar trend is evident in the Chinese market. Driven by policy incentives, ASHPs accounted for approximately 30% of the space heating market during the first half of 2018 [24]. Notably, air source heating systems accounted for 12.5% of the commercial space heating sector [24].

In addition, biomass energy has emerged as a valuable complement to energy-saving technologies within HVAC systems. Biomass energy is derived from organic materials, such as wood pellets, agricultural residues, and other biodegradable resources [25]. Biomass heaters can effectively replace traditional fossil fuel-based devices, contributing to significant reductions in oil consumption and greenhouse gas emissions [25]. According to the Biomass Thermal Energy Council (BTEC), biomass heating systems can lower greenhouse gas emissions by up to 96% compared to conventional fossil fuels, demonstrating their potential as a cleaner energy alternative [26, 27]. Biomass energy continues to play an increasingly important role in the global energy market, currently accounting for more than 10% of the world's primary energy supply [28]. Projections from the Department of Energy and Climate Change in the UK suggest that by 2050, biomass energy could potentially meet more than 40% of the nation's heating and cooling demands, underscoring its viability as a long-term solution for achieving sustainability in HVAC systems [29].

The primary motivation of this chapter is to present a comprehensive review of recent advancements in energy-saving technologies within hospital HVAC systems. To achieve this goal, it is essential to first illustrate the energy flow in a typical HVAC system, covering aspects such as energy demand, energy conversion, and distribution processes. Following this, the chapter highlights the critical role of data-driven models in enhancing energy management and control of hospital HVAC equipment, emphasizing how AI and ML have been applied to improve operational efficiency and adaptability. Furthermore, the integration of renewable energy resources within HVAC systems is examined, as it plays a pivotal role in promoting a low-carbon economy within the healthcare industry. This chapter provides an in-depth review of recent progress related to the utilization of solar, geothermal, air source, and biomass energy technologies in HVAC systems, underscoring their potential to reduce carbon emissions and enhance energy efficiency. Overall, this chapter offers readers a valuable and detailed summary of the latest advancements in renewable energy technologies for HVAC systems, contributing to the development of more sustainable and energy-efficient healthcare facilities.

7.2 Energy Flow of a General HVAC System

The main purpose of an HVAC system is to provide thermal comfort by supplying or removing heat. Before delving into recent advancements in energy-saving technologies related to HVAC systems, it is essential to have a clear understanding of the fundamental aspects of energy demand and energy conversion that occur during the operation of an HVAC system. This understanding serves as the basis for evaluating and improving the efficiency of HVAC systems, as well as identifying areas where energy-saving measures can be effectively applied to enhance overall performance and sustainability.

7.2.1 Energy Demand

Buildings can be regarded as passive systems where thermal comfort services are provided through HVAC systems [30]. To achieve a specific level of thermal comfort service quality, it is essential to quantify the useful energy that is either added to or extracted from the building space. Typically, thermal demand is employed as a critical metric to evaluate the amount of thermal energy required to maintain comfortable indoor conditions [31]. This thermal demand is determined by calculating the integral of the thermal load over a specified time interval $(t_1,\ t_2)$, as represented by Eq. (7.1) [31].

$$D = \int_{t_1}^{t_2} Q(t)dt \tag{7.1}$$

where D and Q denote the thermal demand and thermal load, respectively.

Accurately assessing the thermal demand of a building requires a clear definition of the specific thermal services provided, including heating, cooling, ventilation, and humidification, along with the duration of these services. Generally, thermal demand is classified into two distinct categories: ideal demand and actual demand on an HVAC system [31].

The actual demand involves considering various real-world factors such as system inefficiencies, environmental fluctuations, and operational constraints. Due to the constantly changing conditions, accurately predicting the actual energy demand of HVAC systems remains a challenging task. In contrast, the ideal demand represents the theoretical energy required to achieve desired thermal conditions based on certain reasonable assumptions. This ideal demand serves as a useful benchmark for evaluating system performance and identifying opportunities for potential improvements. Understanding the distinction between ideal and actual demand is essential for optimizing energy management strategies and enhancing HVAC efficiency.

7.2.2 Ideal Thermal Demand Evaluation

The ideal demand refers to the theoretical amount of thermal energy that an ideal system would add or remove from a conditioned space, such as a building or room, to maintain specified thermal comfort conditions [31]. This ideal demand is determined based on a thermodynamic model, which involves establishing an energy balance within the various subsystems of the HVAC system at the space level. By accurately modeling these energy interactions, the ideal demand provides a benchmark for assessing HVAC performance and identifying areas for efficiency improvement.

Figure 7.1 illustrates a typical HVAC system comprising heating and cooling water generation components. A conventional HVAC system generally includes a boiler, chiller, cooling tower, water supply devices, and ventilation equipment. Based on the functional roles of these components, the HVAC system can be categorized into four distinct subsystems: heating generation, cooling generation, water transport, and air transport, as shown in Fig. 7.2. Therefore, to accurately evaluate the ideal thermal demand, it is essential to establish the energy balance within each of these subsystems. This detailed analysis ensures a comprehensive understanding of energy flow throughout the entire HVAC system.

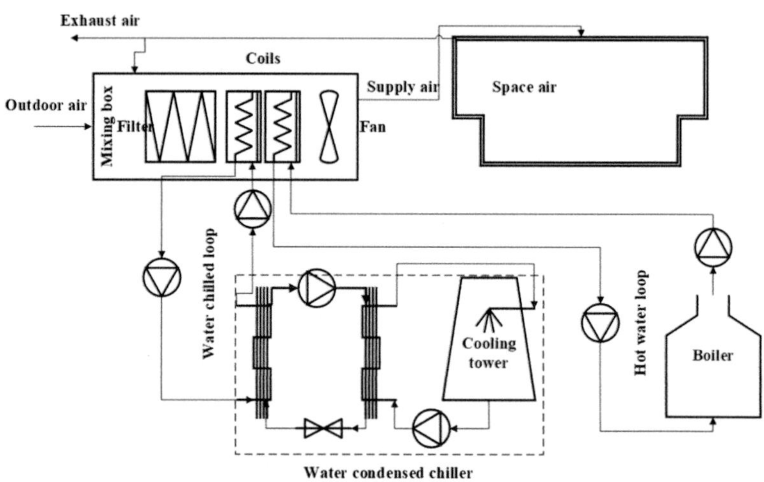

Figure 7.1 Schematic diagram of a HVAC system [31].

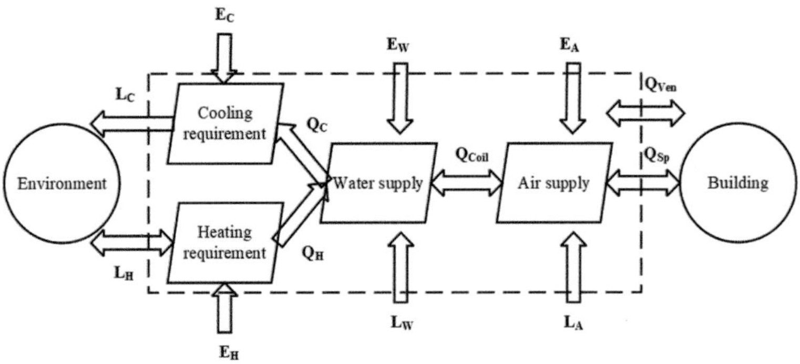

Figure 7.2 Core components of a HVAC system [31].

In a heating subsystem, the primary objective is to consume energy to increase the temperature of air or water. However, during this process, heat losses are inevitable due to various factors, such as unburned fuel, exhaust gases, and system inefficiencies [31]. According to the first law of thermodynamics, the energy consumed in the heating process (E_H) is the sum of the desired thermal load (Q_H) and the associated heat losses (L_H), as expressed in Eq. (7.2) [31].

$$E_H = Q_H + L_H \tag{7.2}$$

Similarly, the cooling subsystem extracts thermal energy from the hot side and transfers it to the cold side by consuming other forms of energy, such as electricity. When accounting for heat losses during the cooling process (L_C), the energy balance can be expressed as shown in Eq. (7.3) [31].

$$E_C = Q_C + L_C \tag{7.3}$$

where E_C represents the energy consumption in the cooling subsystem. Typically, this includes the energy used for refrigerant compression, the condensing fan, and the condensing water loop [31]. Q_C refers to the thermal load extracted from the conditioned space during the cooling process.

The water transport subsystem is responsible for supplying water to the heat exchanger through hydraulic equipment, such as water pumps and pipes. During this process, heat exchange (either adding or extracting heat) occurs between the water and the generation subsystems. Additionally, thermal losses are generated due to the water distribution network and inefficiencies in the pumping devices. Therefore, the heating or cooling generation load ($Q_{H/C}$) is the algebraic sum of the heat added or extracted by the water (Q_{Coil}), energy losses (L_W), and energy usage (E_W), as expressed in Eq. (7.4) [31].

$$Q_{H/C} = Q_{\text{Coil}} + L_W - W_W \tag{7.4}$$

The air transport subsystem utilizes fans to facilitate air distribution and exchange. This process mainly consists of external and internal loops. Both loops contribute to the energy load due to changes in air mass and temperature. Therefore, the mass and energy balance can be established as shown in Eq. (7.5) [31].

$$Q_A = Q_{Sp} + Q_{Ven} + L_A - E_A \tag{7.5}$$

Where E_A, L_A, and Q_A represent the energy usage of fans, energy losses in air transportation, and heat exchange between the air and water, respectively. Q_{Sp} denotes the energy change due to the internal air loop, which can be calculated using Eq. (7.6). The energy change caused by the air transportation is represented by Q_{Ven}, which can be evaluated using Eq. (7.7) [31].

$$Q_{Sp} = \dot{m}_{SA} (h_{SA} - h_{RA}) \tag{7.6}$$

$$Q_{Ven} = \dot{m}_{OA} (h_{RA} - h_{OA}) \tag{7.7}$$

In this equation, the supply and outdoor air mass flow rates are represented by $\dot{m}_{SA}$ and $\dot{m}_{OA}$, respectively. h denotes air enthalpy. The subscripts *SA*, *RA*, and *OA* refer to the space air, return air, and outdoor air, respectively.

7.3 Energy Management and Control in HVAC Equipment

In the energy management and control of HVAC systems, accurately determining thermal demand is essential, as it significantly impacts overall system performance and efficiency. Proper assessment of thermal demand involves analyzing heat transfer processes occurring within various system components that either supply or remove heat to maintain the desired indoor environment, as described in the previous section. This section presents two prominent approaches for energy management and control in HVAC systems: the physics-based model and the data-driven model. The physics-based model is grounded in fundamental thermodynamic and heat transfer principles, providing a comprehensive understanding of system behavior. In contrast, the data-driven model utilizes historical data combined with advanced ML techniques to enhance performance optimization, predict energy consumption, and improve control strategies.

7.3.1 Physical-Based Model

Numerical simulation is widely regarded as one of the most effective methods for accurately determining the thermal demand of HVAC systems. In recent years, the most commonly used commercial simulation software for HVAC systems includes EnergyPlus, TRNSYS, and IDA-ICE, among others [32, 33].

Boyano et al. [34] employed an EnergyPlus model to evaluate energy consumption in an office building situated within three different areas: Tallinn, London, and Madrid. Their study demonstrated that HVAC energy demand constitutes a significant proportion of the total energy consumption across all three zones. Moreover, the simulation results helped them formulate various energy-saving strategies. For example, their findings indicated that altering the building's orientation could lead to average energy savings in HVAC systems ranging from 3% to

6%, primarily due to changes in solar gains. Besides, Seo et al. [35] constructed a building model using TRNSYS to estimate the energy demand associated with heating and cooling. To enhance efficiency, they applied a multi-island genetic algorithm combined with energy demand data to optimize HVAC system operations, achieving a considerable reduction in energy consumption. Likewise, Jylhä et al. [33] assessed the energy demand of HVAC systems for a typical detached house in Finland and predicted how future climate conditions would influence energy consumption trends. Their study revealed that global warming could potentially decrease the energy requirements for heating and ventilation by 20% to 40% by the year 2100. However, it was also found that the energy demand for cooling could experience a substantial increase, ranging from 40% to 80%, due to rising temperatures.

7.3.2 Data-Driven Model

Building energy simulation tools are commonly developed based on various assumptions and simplifications; as a result, there is often a noticeable discrepancy between simulation results and actual measured data, referred to as the energy gap [36]. Reducing this gap and achieving accurate energy demand evaluation and management are significant challenges that require continuous improvement of prediction models. With the advancement of sensor technology and measurement techniques, data-driven models have increasingly attracted the attention of thermal engineers due to their potential for higher accuracy and reliability. Unlike conventional simulation tools, data-driven models or ML approaches are constructed based on historical datasets, enabling them to capture complex patterns and relationships that are difficult to model through traditional simulation methods. Therefore, predictions made by data-driven models are generally closer to real-world energy demands, providing more accurate assessments and optimization strategies [37].

Figure 7.3 illustrates the general structure of a data-driven model applied to HVAC systems. Typically, a data-driven model comprises three essential layers: the input layer, the hidden layer, and the output layer [38, 39]. The input layer serves as the foundation of the model, where historical data variables are collected and defined. These variables commonly include indoor temperature, outdoor temperature, humidity, solar gains, occupancy patterns, and other influential factors related to HVAC performance [38]. The hidden layer, which is responsible for processing and analyzing the input data, involves several steps such as data training, pattern recognition, and dimensionality reduction. Dimensionality reduction techniques are often applied to simplify the data structure and extract essential features that effectively represent the complex relationships within the dataset. Moreover, nonlinear transformations are introduced to enhance the model's ability to learn and generalize from high-dimensional and nonlinear problems, thereby improving prediction accuracy [38]. The output layer then stores the results obtained from the hidden layer, which are subsequently compared with historical data to refine and optimize the data-driven model. Through continuous updating and retraining processes within the hidden layer, the model's accuracy and robustness can be progressively enhanced, making it a powerful tool for energy demand evaluation and control in HVAC systems.

Recently, there has been a growing interest among researchers in developing data-driven models for building energy management, aimed at accurately estimating and optimizing thermal demand for HVAC systems. One notable approach is the artificial neural network (ANN)-based model proposed by Mugnini et al. [38], which was designed to estimate a building's thermal energy demand. Their study demonstrated that the data-driven model possesses a remarkable capability to replicate the reference building's energy behavior when provided with identical input conditions, thereby confirming its reliability and accuracy. In addition, Godinho et al. [40] developed a data-driven model utilizing support vector machines to predict heating and cooling energy demand in an office building situated in Lisbon, Portugal. To further enhance prediction accuracy, they incorporated the Simulated Annealing algorithm, resulting in significant improvements in the model's performance. Additionally, Zhang et al. [41] employed a light gradient boosting machine (LightGBM) combined with the

Shapley Additive exPlanations (SHAP) algorithm to construct a sophisticated data-driven model. This model effectively integrates building characteristics, geometric features, and urban morphology, providing a comprehensive framework for forecasting energy usage and greenhouse gas emissions of residential buildings with high accuracy and interpretability.

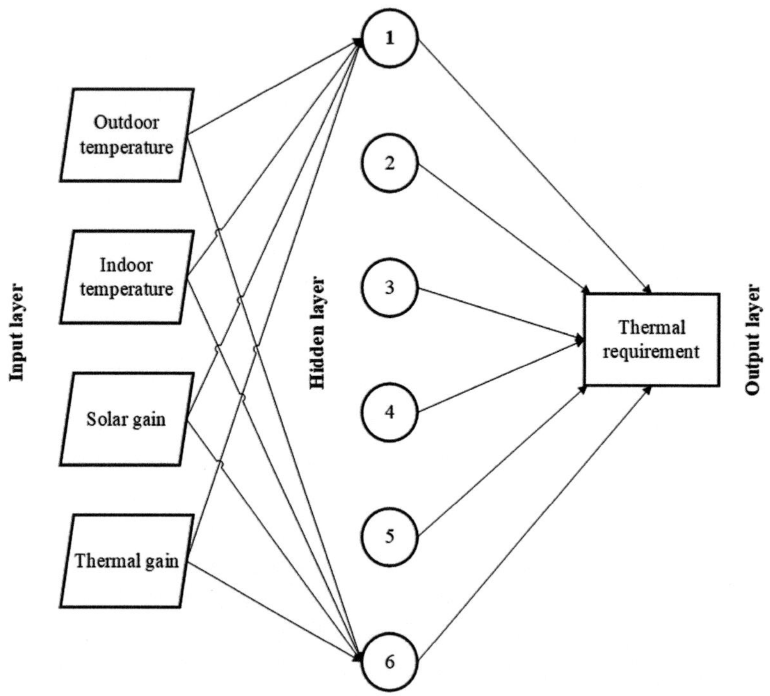

Figure 7.3 Working principle of a data-driven model [38].

7.3.3 Role of Data-Driven Models in Energy-Saving of Hospitals' HVAC Systems

It is well acknowledged that data-driven model technology is highly suitable for energy management and control in HVAC systems within hospitals, offering the potential to significantly reduce energy consumption and operational costs. Ahmed et al. [42] emphasized that hospital administrators can leverage data-driven predictive models to enhance energy efficiency and decrease operational expenses. By analyzing essential variables such as patient admission patterns, daily usage fluctuations, and seasonal trends, hospitals can achieve more accurate estimations of energy requirements. This enables administrators to optimize energy utilization by allowing heating, cooling, and lighting systems to adapt dynamically to real-time needs, rather than continuously operating at maximum capacity.

Furthermore, Dulce-Chamorro and Martinez-de-Pison [43] developed a data-driven model composed of a weighted combination of ANN and support vector regression (SVR) methods. Implementing this model within a building management system allowed hospitals to achieve annual energy savings of approximately 7–10%. Additionally, to address the heightened occupancy rates and indoor air quality demands during the COVID-19 pandemic, the energy service provider Edison collaborated with Enerbrain to upgrade the HVAC equipment of a hospital in Northern Italy [44]. They developed HVAC control software based on an ML algorithm that integrated Internet of Things (IoT) and ICT technologies. This retrofit achieved a 5% reduction in natural gas consumption related to HVAC operation during the pandemic without compromising indoor environmental quality.

Clearly, improving energy efficiency in hospitals requires innovative solutions, with AI technologies playing a crucial role in optimizing energy consumption. By analyzing large datasets generated by IoT-enabled devices, ML can reveal patterns that enhance the accuracy of energy demand predictions. Future research should focus on developing predictive models capable of adjusting energy usage in real-time while integrating renewable energy sources such as solar and wind power [42]. An important research direction involves creating adaptable frameworks that enable hospitals to seamlessly balance conventional and renewable energy resources, achieving both environmental sustainability and economic benefits [42]. Moreover, the establishment of smart hospitals is becoming a public concern. With the advent of smart home products, such as smart curtains, smart windows, and smart air-conditioners, IoT technology enables HVAC modules to form an integrated sensor network. In this context, integrating IoT and AI-based energy management can significantly enhance real-time control of HVAC systems by accurately monitoring indoor and outdoor environments [45]. In the future, optimizing sensor measurements will be essential to improve the reliability of energy prediction and management in smart hospitals [45]. Additionally, hospitals consist of multiple zones and accommodate various individuals with differing thermal comfort preferences [46]. The diverse functions of these zones and personal comfort requirements add complexity to the energy management system [46]. To address this challenge, decentralized technology can be integrated into the smart control model of HVAC systems. This approach effectively mitigates the coupling effects between different zones and individual comfort preferences, enabling real-time optimization of energy demand and efficiency throughout the entire building [45].

7.4 Renewable Energy Resources

Based on the building's energy demand, the HVAC system must consume appropriate amounts of energy to ensure the operation of thermal generators and thermal medium movers. Traditionally, fossil fuels such as coal, natural gas, and oil derivatives have been the primary energy sources used in HVAC systems [31]. However, in response to the escalating environmental crisis and the push for a low-carbon economy, a growing number of renewable energy sources, including solar, geothermal, air source, and biomass energy, have been increasingly integrated into HVAC systems over the past decade. The following subsections will primarily focus on the recent advancements and developments in various renewable energy technologies applied to HVAC systems.

7.4.1 Solar Power Technology

Due to its excellent cost-effectiveness and reliability, solar energy technology has found widespread applications in HVAC systems for both residential and commercial buildings. Firstly, it is widely acknowledged that directly harnessing solar light and irradiation is one of the most efficient approaches in various solar technologies. Utilizing natural sunlight effectively can significantly regulate indoor temperatures, thereby reducing the reliance on HVAC systems. Additionally, sufficient natural daylight plays a critical role in creating a healing environment, as it improves indoor air quality and helps alleviate stress for both patients and medical staff. To achieve these benefits, hospitals need to optimize lighting and shading performance through well-designed room layouts. Wagdy et al. [47] employed Rhinoceros modeling software to enhance daylighting performance for two types of patient rooms: inboard and outboard bathroom designs. Their results demonstrated that adjusting the cut-off angle and tilt angle of shading devices effectively enhances natural daylight while minimizing discomfort glare in both room types [47].

In addition, solar energy can be converted into thermal and electrical forms, which can be utilized to power HVAC systems. Based on their working principles, the solar technologies available in the market are generally categorized into two types: solar collectors and solar PV panels [48].

Solar collectors are designed to convert solar radiation into thermal energy by transferring it to a working fluid, such as air or water, which flows through the collectors [49]. Figure 7.4 illustrates a typical HVAC system integrated with solar collectors, where these collectors serve as the core components responsible for capturing and converting solar radiation into usable thermal energy. The collected thermal energy can then be supplied directly to heating or cooling devices, enhancing system efficiency and reducing reliance on conventional energy sources.

In contrast to solar collectors that capture thermal energy, solar panels operate on the principle of the photoelectric effect, converting sunlight directly into electricity, as illustrated in Fig. 7.5 [50, 51]. A standard PV cell is composed of two thin semiconductor layers that form a P-N junction. When sunlight strikes the PV cell, photons with sufficient energy excite electrons from the valence band to the conduction band, generating free electrons [51]. These electrons are then driven by the internal electric field within the PV material, resulting in a direct current (DC) flow through an external circuit. The electrical energy generated by this process can be utilized to power various building systems, including HVAC systems, lighting, and other operational requirements. This technology provides a clean, efficient, and sustainable alternative to conventional energy sources, significantly contributing to reducing carbon emissions and promoting energy independence.

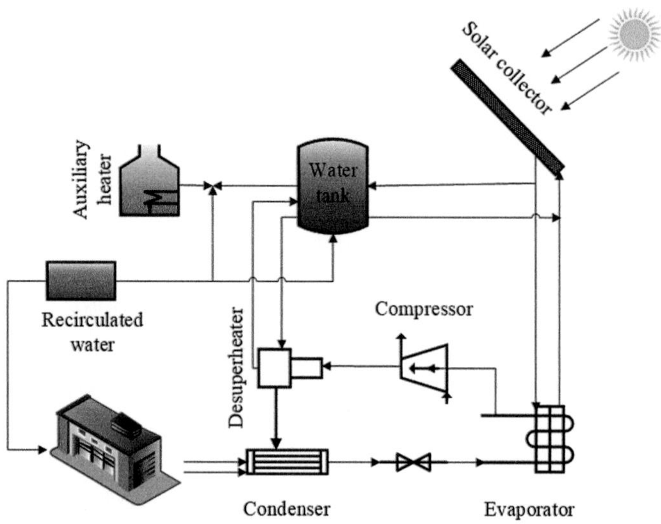

Figure 7.4 Schematic diagram of a HVAC system driven by a solar collector [4].

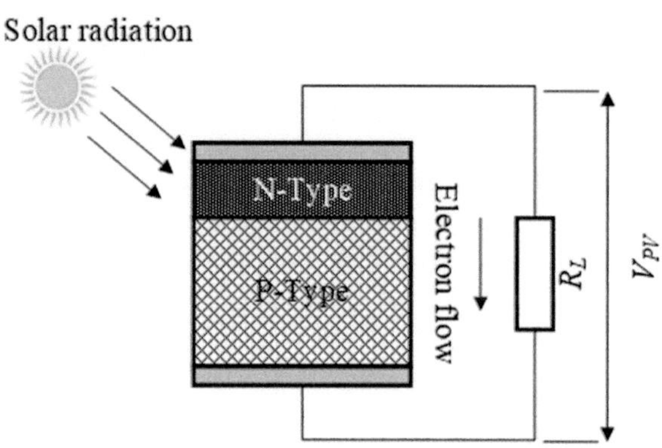

Figure 7.5 Schematic diagram of a PV cell [51].

Currently, solar power technology has been increasingly applied to transform energy supply systems for HVAC systems in hospitals. For example, Bakheet [52] developed a solar PV system for a hospital in Saudi Arabia, where the total power consumption for HVAC equipment, lighting, and medical facilities amounted to around 162 kWh/day. The PV system was equipped with 49 PV panels and six lead-acid batteries, capable of providing about 72 kWh/day. In a real-world case study conducted at a hospital located in southern Italy, which has a total volume of 88,000 m^3, Regno et al. [53] used numerical models to evaluate the performance of various HVAC system upgrades, including a PV system, an electric heat pump, a solar energy-driven absorption heat pump, and cogeneration. Their findings indicated that the combination of a solar thermal-powered absorption heat pump and a cogeneration system performed the best, achieving an impressive energy savings of 20%. Additionally, Refahi et al. [54] assessed the feasibility of installing PV panels on both the roof and windows of a five-story hospital building with a total area of 5,000 m^2 in Iran. Using EnergyPlus for simulations, they concluded that this solar PV setup could result in an 18% reduction in annual energy consumption, specifically for cooling demands. Similarly, Siow et al. [55] used the PVsyst model to explore the application of solar PV technology across 42 hospitals in Malaysia. They confirmed that in two of the hospitals, the solar PV system was able to fully satisfy the power requirements for HVAC systems and medical facilities. For the remaining 40 hospitals, the solar PV system played a crucial role in energy savings, contributing to reductions in energy consumption by 38.76%, 37.48%, and 52.58% in large, medium, and small hospitals, respectively.

7.4.2 Geothermal Technology

Geothermal energy, alongside solar power, is recognized as one of the most reliable and energy-efficient renewable energy technologies. This energy is produced and stored underground due to gravitational pressures and the decomposition of radioactive elements deep within the Earth's crust [56]. The fundamental principle of geothermal technology is to harness this stored thermal energy to maintain thermal comfort in buildings throughout the entire year. It is well-known that, when a specific depth is reached, the temperature underground remains relatively constant throughout the year, as illustrated in Fig. 7.6. This stable temperature can be utilized effectively for heating and cooling purposes, providing a sustainable solution for energy management in buildings.

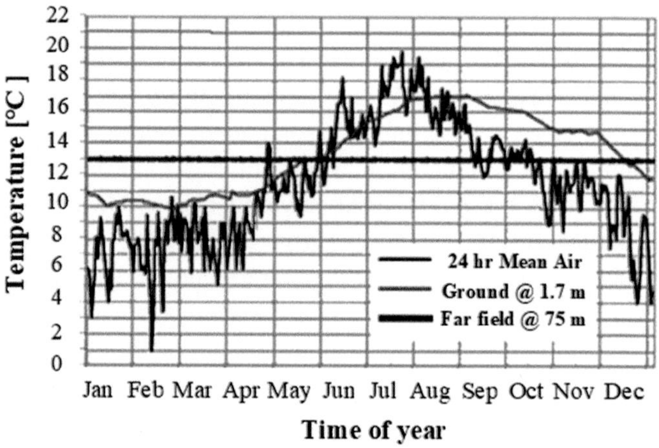

Figure 7.6 Temperature variations of the ground with different depths [56].

Due to the principle of thermal inertia, geothermal systems are capable of maintaining a consistent temperature difference between the underground and the surrounding air. In winter, the temperature underground tends to be higher than that of the surrounding air, while in summer, the temperature underground is typically lower. This natural temperature differential allows geothermal systems to function efficiently as both a heat sink during the summer months and a heat source in the winter.

Figure 7.7 illustrates the core components of a geothermal heat pump system, which typically includes three main parts: the heat exchanger unit, the secondary unit, and the heat pump unit [56]. The heat exchanger unit consists of a network of closed-loop pipes that are installed underground. These pipes facilitate the transfer of thermal energy between the ground and the fluid circulating within the system. The heat pump unit, which is the heart of the system, contains four essential components: the evaporator, condenser, compressor, and expansion valve. During the heating process, thermal fluid is circulated through the heat exchanger unit, where it absorbs heat from the ground. The fluid then carries this thermal energy to the heat pump unit, which extracts the heat and transfers it to the secondary unit through a cyclic process of evaporation, compression, condensation, and expansion. In contrast to the heating mode, the cooling process operates in the opposite direction. In this mode, the secondary unit acts as the heat source, while the heat exchanger unit functions as the heat sink, transferring unwanted heat from the building to the ground.

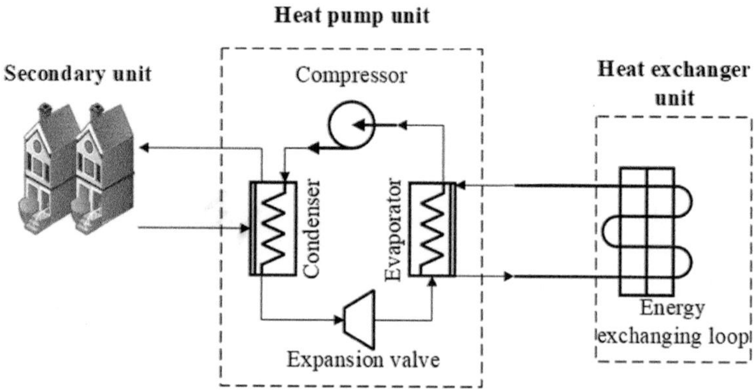

Figure 7.7 Schematic diagram of a geothermal heat pump [56].

Geothermal technology has been increasingly applied across various industries over the past few decades. As shown in Fig. 7.8, more than 50% of geothermal technology installations have been utilized for providing HVAC services [57]. Recent reports indicate a growing trend among hospitals to refurbish their HVAC systems with geothermal technology, highlighting its effectiveness in improving energy efficiency and sustainability in healthcare facilities.

A hospital in Rotorua Township, New Zealand, is strategically located to harness geothermal energy, as it sits atop one of the natural upflows of a geothermal reservoir [58]. Since 1977, the hospital has operated a doublet geothermal heating system, which consists of 18 counterflow heat exchangers, each 4 meters in length and connected in series [58]. Years of operational experience have shown that this geothermal system is fully capable of meeting the hospital's heating demands, providing a reliable and efficient source of energy [58]. Similarly, in another New Zealand hospital located in Taupo Township, two coal-fired boilers were originally used, consuming approximately 340 tons of coal per year [59]. However, in 2010, the hospital transitioned to a geothermal system, which has been running steadily for over four years. This switch has significantly reduced fuel and maintenance costs, while achieving zero emissions [59].

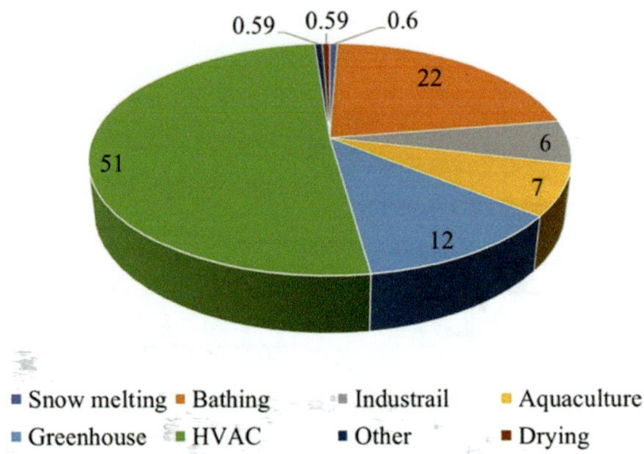

Figure 7.8 Global distribution of geothermal technology [57].

Additionally, Massachusetts General Hospital (MGH), one of the leading hospitals in the United States, has historically consumed large amounts of energy for heating and cooling. Zyvith et al. [60] proposed the implementation of a geothermal vertical closed-loop system for the Gray Building at MGH. Their analysis revealed that the energy consumption and associated costs for heating and cooling would decline substantially with the adoption of this geothermal system. In fact, this system allows the hospital to save approximately 60% on annual heating and cooling costs [60]. Furthermore, Serbia has been actively advancing its geothermal energy technologies, capitalizing on its unique geological features. In Vranjska Banja Spa, about two-thirds of the region's total geothermal potential (approximately 62.4 MWt) has been developed to provide heating for various public buildings, including hospitals, hotels, and schools [61]. Notably, the geothermal system can provide up to 1350 kW of heating to the local special hospital each month [61].

7.4.3 Air Source Technology

Unlike geothermal heat pumps, ASHPs utilize ambient air as their heat source and heat sink. Industrial applications have demonstrated that ASHPs offer better cost-effectiveness compared to geothermal heat pumps [62]. The fundamental operating principle of an ASHP is based on the reverse Carnot cycle. As illustrated in Fig. 7.9, an ASHP typically consists of a compressor, evaporator, condenser, and expansion valve [63].

During cooling operation, the heat pump extracts heat from indoor air and releases it to the outdoor environment through the reverse Carnot cycle [63]. In heating mode, this process is reversed, where heat is absorbed from the outside air and transferred indoors [63].

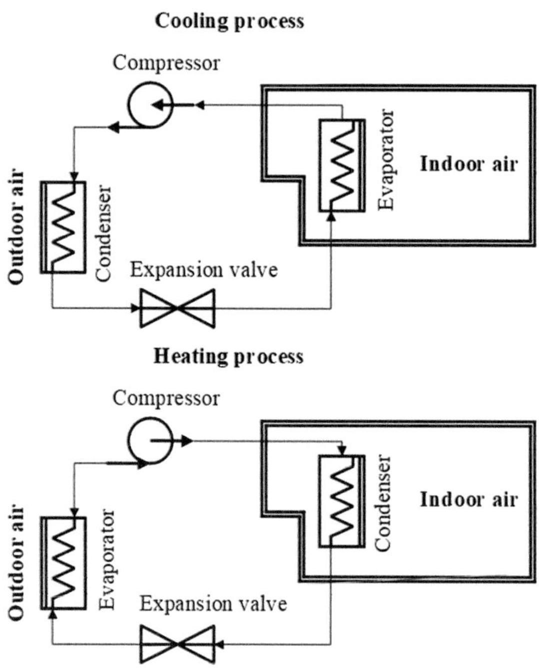

Figure 7.9 Schematic diagram of an ASHP [63].

ASHP technology has been increasingly implemented to upgrade HVAC systems, contributing to energy savings and emissions reduction in buildings. For instance, Hen et al. [64] conducted an energy audit and field tests on a building equipped with ASHPs, revealing that its energy use intensity (EUI) was significantly lower, averaging 126 kWh/m^2, compared to conventional buildings with EUIs ranging from 130 kWh/m^2 to 292 kWh/m^2 [64].

Furthermore, Kcalin Inc., a prominent heat pump manufacturer, emphasizes the considerable potential of ASHPs in healthcare facilities [65]. By harnessing natural energy, ASHPs can significantly reduce energy consumption and operating costs compared to traditional boilers or electric heaters [65]. When integrated with filtration, disinfection, and sterilization modules, ASHPs can rapidly regulate temperature while enhancing air quality, providing a comfortable and healthy environment for patients and staff [65]. Recently, Queen's Medical Centre in Nottingham announced plans to acquire advanced heat pumps, including both air-source and ground-source systems, to upgrade its HVAC systems [66]. This initiative aims to reduce carbon emissions by approximately 10,000 tons per year [66]. Additionally, Yan et al. [67] conducted a MATLAB simulation analyzing the performance of a steam sterilization system powered by ASHPs in a hospital setting. The study confirmed that the sterilization efficiency of ASHPs is significantly higher than that of electric and gas-fired boilers [67]. From an economic perspective, the ASHP-based sterilization system offers superior long-term performance, achieving annual cost savings of approximately CNY 750,000 compared to electric boilers and CNY 1,145,000 compared to gas-fired boilers [67].

7.4.4 Biomass Technology

Furthermore, it is important to recognize the significant role that biomass technology plays in supporting the low-carbon economy of hospitals. Currently, biomass technology accounts for approximately 10% to 15% of global energy demand [68]. In industrialized nations, biomass contributes an average of 9–14% of energy demand, while in developing countries, this figure can reach around 25% [68].

Biomass technology can be utilized both directly and indirectly to convert solid waste into liquid and gas fuels. One of the primary methods used is pyrolysis, where biomass is heated to over 500 °C in the absence of air [68, 69]. During this process, liquid bio-oil and gas, which can serve as alternatives to fossil fuels, are produced by vaporizing the volatile components of solid carbonaceous material [69].

Another common biomass technology is direct combustion, which is the most widely implemented method for generating bioenergy. Approximately 95% of bioenergy is derived from biomass combustion. In the context of buildings, thermal or electrical energy can be generated through biomass combustion to power HVAC systems. Among various biomass technologies, cogeneration systems stand out for their efficiency [68]. As shown in Fig. 7.10, a typical biomass cogeneration system includes combustion chambers, steam boilers, turbines, power generators, and heat distribution systems that provide heating through the condenser [68]. The working principle of these systems is similar to that of the Rankine cycle, with the driving force coming from high-pressure and high-temperature steam produced by the combustion of biomass.

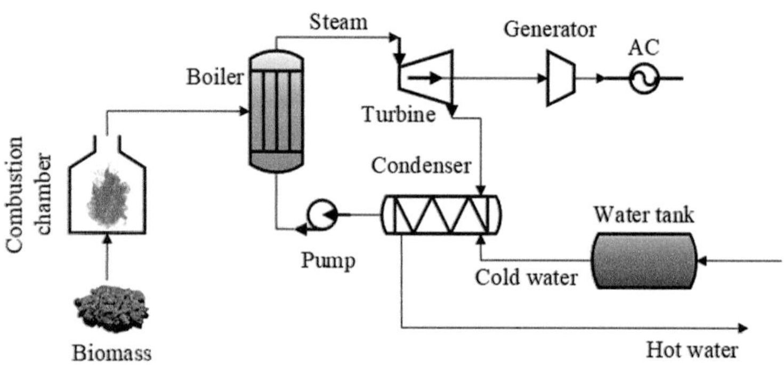

Figure 7.10 Schematic diagram of a biomass cogeneration system [68].

Over the past few decades, several reports have highlighted the adoption of biomass technology in the refurbishment of HVAC systems in hospitals, underscoring its potential in advancing a low-carbon economy. For instance, in a hospital located in Crete,

Greece, a biomass burning system was integrated with solar PV panels and a geothermal heat pump to upgrade the energy system, aiming for zero CO_2 emissions [70]. The hospital, with a building area of 15,000 m^2 and 300 beds, was able to reduce its net carbon emissions by 10.9 tons per bed per year through the use of this renewable energy system [70]. Among its subsystems, the biomass burner alone produced 2,278 MWh of energy annually, which was used to provide heating and hot water for the hospital [70]. Similarly, Vourdoubas [71] explored the feasibility of biomass systems to meet the heating demands of two other hospitals. The estimated cost for upgrading their HVAC systems with biomass boilers ranged from €1.7 to €2.1 million. These upgrades could generate annual savings in fuel costs ranging from approximately €1,963 to €2,328 per bed, depending on the system. Additionally, the biomass boilers in these two hospitals would reduce net CO_2 emissions by 8.8 and 10.4 tons per bed per year, respectively [71].

Moreover, Sanz-Calcedo [72] emphasized the excellent cost-effectiveness of biomass technology compared to traditional heating systems in hospitals. For a hospital with 100 beds, using a biomass boiler fueled by olive stones could lead to cost savings of 20%, 41%, and 50% compared to coal, natural gas, and oil, respectively [72]. Furthermore, the net carbon emissions from using olive stone are significantly lower than those of traditional fuels, as the plants absorb large amounts of CO_2 during their life cycle. Pina et al. [73] also confirmed that replacing part of the natural gas boilers with biomass boilers in a Brazilian hospital could result in an annual 9% reduction in net CO_2 emissions. In their proposed system, the primary heating demand is provided by the biomass boilers, while the natural gas boilers are used only during peak demand periods.

7.5 Conclusion

Unlike other public buildings, such as hotels and schools, HVAC systems in hospitals are not only critical for ensuring a comfortable environment, but they are also indispensable for the proper functioning of healthcare operations. Specifically, hospital HVAC systems must maintain a stable environment with specific temperature settings and excellent ventilation, which are vital to meet the unique needs of specialized healthcare areas, such as operating rooms, medical freezers, and isolation wards. In addition to providing thermal comfort, it is essential to emphasize the significant role HVAC systems play in controlling bacterial content and improving air quality. This is crucial in safeguarding the health of both medical staff and patients. Therefore, hospital HVAC systems are subject to highly reliable and diverse demands, necessitating continuous improvements in both their performance and energy efficiency. Given the high energy consumption of HVAC systems, it is essential to integrate energy-saving technologies that can significantly contribute to reducing the overall carbon footprint and fostering a low-carbon economy within the healthcare sector.

This chapter has primarily focused on reviewing the energy-saving technologies employed in hospital HVAC systems from two major aspects: energy management strategies and alternative energy solutions. First, compared to conventional methods, the integration of AI and ML algorithms in energy management systems allows for more precise and efficient operation. Hybrid AI and ML models can optimize the HVAC system by taking into account dynamic variables, such as changing user needs and environmental factors like weather fluctuations. This approach enables HVAC systems to meet temperature and ventilation requirements while minimizing energy wastage, ultimately enhancing overall energy efficiency. Furthermore, case studies from various hospitals have demonstrated that renewable energy sources, such as solar, geothermal, air-source, and biomass, can replace traditional fossil fuels in powering HVAC systems. The long-term implementation of renewable energy in hospital HVAC systems has the potential not only to drastically reduce carbon emissions but also to result in considerable cost savings when compared to conventional fossil fuel-based systems.

However, the development of energy-saving technologies is still ongoing, and many advancements are needed to optimize these systems further. Future research should focus on utilizing deep learning to improve real-time energy management models, making them more responsive to real-world fluctuations. Additionally, there is a need to enhance AI- and ML-based energy management models through continuous refinement and parameter tuning to strike an ideal balance between prediction accuracy and computational load. Moreover, addressing the inherent challenges of renewable energy, such as intermittency and low efficiency, requires technological breakthroughs in areas like novel energy materials, energy storage systems, and structural optimizations. Another important area for future research is the integration of AI with renewable energy technologies in hospital HVAC systems. By leveraging deep learning techniques, it is possible to design an optimal framework that balances traditional fuel consumption with renewable energy integration, allowing hospitals to achieve both economic savings and meet their environmental targets.

Nomenclature

AI	Artificial intelligence	L_C	Heat losses in the cooling process
ANN	Artificial neural network	L_H	Heat losses in the heating process
ASHP	Air source heat pump	LightGBM	Light Gradient Boosting Machine
BTEC	Biomass Thermal Energy Council	L_W	Energy losses in water transportation
CAGR	compound annual growth rate	MGH	Massachusetts general hospital
D	Thermal demand	ML	Machine learning
DC	Direct current	MLR	Multiple linear regression
E_A	Energy usage of fans	$\dot{m}_{OA}$	Outdoor air mass rates
E_C	Consumed energy in the cooling process	$\dot{m}_{SA}$	Supply air mass rates
E_H	Consumed energy in the heating process	PV	Photovoltaic
EUI	Energy use intensity	Q	Thermal load
E_W	Energy usage in water transportation	Q_A	Heat exchange between the air and water

h_{OA}	Outdoor air enthalpy	Q_C	Thermal load in the cooling process
h_{RA}	Return air enthalpy	Q_{Coil}	Adding or extracting heat to water
h_{SA}	Space air enthalpy	Q_H	Thermal load in the heating process
HVAC	Heating, ventilation, and air conditioning	$Q_{H/C}$	Heating or cooling generation load
ICU	Intensive care unit	Q_{Sp}	Energy changes due to the internal air loop
IEA	International Energy Agency	Q_{Ven}	Energy changes caused by the external air loop
IoT	Internet of Things	SHAP	Shapley Additive exPlanations
L_A	Energy losses in the air transportation	SVR	Support vector regression

Acknowledgment

This work was made possible by funding from the Natural Sciences and Engineering Research Council of Canada.

References

1. S. Saran, M. Gurjar, A. Baronia, and V. Sivapurapu et al., (2020). 'Heating, ventilation and air conditioning (HVAC) in intensive care unit,' *Critical Care*, vol. 24 (194), pp. 1–11.
2. Grand View Research, [Online], 'Hospital HVAC systems market size, share & trends analysis report by product (heating, ventilation, cooling), by end use (intensive care unit, operating rooms, airborne infection isolation rooms), by region, and segment forecasts, 2023–2030,' Hospital HVAC Systems Market Size & Share Report, 2030. Accessed 16, March 2025.
3. M. M. Andronache and C. Teodosiu, (2021). 'Studies on geothermal energy utilization: A review,' *IOP Conference Series: Earth and Environmental Science*, vol. 664 (1), p. 012072.
4. X. Yuan, Z. Chen, Y. Liang, and Y. Pan et al., (2021), 'Heating energy-saving potentials in HVAC system of swimming halls: A review,' *Building and Environment*, vol. 205, p. 108189.

5. D. Kolokotsa, D. Rovas, E. Kosmatopoulos, and K. Kalaitzakis, (2011). 'A roadmap towards intelligent net zero- and positive-energy buildings,' *Solar Energy*, vol. 85 (12), pp. 3067–3084.
6. Climate Portal, [Online], 'Heating and cooling,' Heating and Cooling | MIT Climate Portal. Accessed 16, March 2025.
7. A. Kerimray, L. Rojas-Sol—rzano, M. Amouei Torkmahalleh, and P. K. Hopke et al., (2017). 'Coal use for residential heating: Patterns, health implications and lessons learned,' *Energy for Sustainable Development*, vol. 40, pp. 19–30.
8. J. Reijula, M. Gröhn, K. Müller, and K. Reijula et al., (2011). 'Human well-being and flowing work in an intelligent work environment,' *Intelligent Buildings International*, vol. 3 (4), pp. 223–237.
9. J. Reijula, R. Holopainen, E. Kähkönen, and K. Reijula et al., (2013). 'Intelligent HVAC systems in hospitals,' *Intelligent Buildings International*, vol. 5 (2), pp. 101–119.
10. Y. Yao, Z. Lian, Z. Hou, and W. Liu, (2006). 'An innovative air-conditioning load forecasting model based on RBF neural network and combined residual error correction,' *International Journal of Refrigeration*, vol. 29 (4), pp. 528–538.
11. M. Sahu and S. Majee, (2025). 'A systematic analysis of AI-based methods for thermal control and energy-efficiency in sustainable buildings,' *AIS-Architecture Image Studies*, vol. 6 (1), pp. 36–45.
12. M. Arun, D. Barik, S. S. R. Chandran, and S. Praveenkumar et al., (2025). 'Economic, policy, social, and regulatory aspects of AI-driven smart buildings,' *Journal of Building Engineering*, vol. 99, p. 111666.
13. R. S. Ghoneim, M. Arabasy, and A. N. Abdulhadi, (2025). 'AI-driven optimization of indoor environmental quality and energy consumption in smart buildings: A bio-inspired algorithmic approach,' *Journal of Asian Architecture and Building Engineering*, pp. 1–25.
14. M. Fatehijananloo, H. Stopps, and J. J. McArthur, (2024). 'Exploring artificial intelligence methods for energy prediction in healthcare Facilities: An in-depth extended systematic review,' *Energy and Buildings*, vol. 320, p. 114598.
15. International Energy Agency, [Online], 'Solar thermal technologies deployed in around 400 million dwellings by 2030,' Solar thermal technologies deployed in around 400 million dwellings by 2030 – Analysis - IEA. Accessed 16, March 2025.
16. J. Huang, Z. Tian, and J. Fan, (2019). 'A comprehensive analysis on development and transition of the solar thermal market in China

with more than 70% market share worldwide,' *Energy*, vol. 174, pp. 611–624.

17. International Energy Agency, [Online], 'Renewables 2018,' Market Report Series: Renewables 2018 – Analysis - IEA. Accessed 16, March 2025.
18. F. J. W. Osseweijer, L. B. P. van den Hurk, E. J. H. M. Teunissen, and W. G. J. H. M. van Sark, (2018). 'A comparative review of building integrated photovoltaics ecosystems in selected European countries,' *Renewable and Sustainable Energy Reviews*, vol. 90, pp. 1027–1040.
19. R. A. Almasri and M. S. Alshitawi, (2021). 'Electricity consumption indicators and energy efficiency in residential buildings in GCC countries: Extensive review,' *Energy and Buildings*, vol. 255, p. 111664.
20. International Energy Agency, [Online], 'Renewable energy policies in a time of transition: Heating and cooling,' Renewable Energy Policies in a Time of Transition: Heating and Cooling – Analysis - IEA. Accessed 16, March 2025.
21. International Energy Agency, [Online], 'New Zealand 2023,' https://www.iea.org/reports/new-zealand-2023. Accessed 16, March 2025.
22. A. C. Violante, F. Donato, G. Guidi, and M. Proposito et al., (2022). 'Comparative life cycle assessment of the ground source heat pump vs air source heat pump,' *Renewable Energy*, vol. 188, pp. 1029–1037.
23. J. Joe, M. Malhotra, M. V. Lapsa, and V. Baxter, (2021). 'US heat pump market overview – 2020,' *Oak Ridge National Laboratory (ORNL)*, Oak Ridge, TN (United States).
24. Y. Zhang, G. Zhang, A. Zhang, and Y. Jin et al., (2018). 'Frosting phenomenon and frost-free technology of outdoor air heat exchanger for an air-source heat pump system in China: An analysis and review,' *Energies*, vol. 11 (10), p. 2642.
25. U.S. Energy Information Administration, [Online], 'Biomass explained,' Biomass explained - U.S. Energy Information Administration (EIA). Accessed 16, March 2025.
26. U.S. Department of Energy, [Online], 'Biomass basics: The facts about bioenergy,' Biomass Basics: The Facts About Bioenergy. Accessed 16, March 2025.
27. Biomass Magazine, [Online], 'Time for Federal Tax Policy to Recognize Biomass Thermal,' Time for Federal Tax Policy to Recognize Biomass Thermal | Biomass Magazine. Accessed 16, March 2025.
28. W. V. Reid, M. K. Ali, and C. B. Field, (2020). 'The future of bioenergy,' *Global Change Biology*, vol. 26 (1), pp. 274–286.

29. Climate Home News, [Online], 'Biomass could provide 44% of UK energy by 2050 – Study,' Biomass could provide 44% of UK energy by 2050 - study. Accessed 16, March 2025.
30. J. M. Cullen, J. M. Allwood, and E. H. Borgstein, (2011). 'Reducing energy demand: What are the practical limits?,' *Environmental Science & Technology*, vol. 45 (4), pp. 1711–1718.
31. L. Perez-Lombard, J. Ortiz, and I. R. Maestre, (2011). 'The map of energy flow in HVAC systems,' *Applied Energy*, vol. 88 (12), pp. 5020–5031.
32. X. Wang, T. Li, Y. Yu, and Q. Liu et al., (2024). 'Performance simulation and energy efficiency analysis of multi-energy complementary HVAC system based on TRNSYS,' *Applied Thermal Engineering*, vol. 257, p. 124378.
33. K. Jylhä, J. Jokisalo, K. Ruosteenoja, and K. Pilli-Sihvola et al., (2015). 'Energy demand for the heating and cooling of residential houses in Finland in a changing climate,' *Energy and Buildings*, vol. 99, pp. 104–116.
34. A. Boyano, P. Hernandez, and O. Wolf, (2013). 'Energy demands and potential savings in European office buildings: Case studies based on EnergyPlus simulations,' *Energy and Buildings*, vol. 65, pp. 19–28.
35. J. Seo, R. Ooka, J. T. Kim, and Y. Nam, (2014). 'Optimization of the HVAC system design to minimize primary energy demand,' *Energy and Buildings*, vol. 76, pp. 102–108.
36. D. Coakley, P. Raftery, and M. Keane, (2014). 'A review of methods to match building energy simulation models to measured data,' *Renewable and Sustainable Energy Reviews*, vol. 37, pp. 123–141.
37. T. Ahmad, H. Chen, Y. Guo, and J. Wang, (2018). 'A comprehensive overview on the data driven and large scale-based approaches for forecasting of building energy demand: A review,' *Energy and Buildings*, vol. 165, pp. 301–320.
38. A. Mugnini, G. Coccia, F. Polonara, and A. Arteconi, (2020). 'Performance assessment of data-driven and physical-based models to predict building energy demand in model predictive controls,' *Energies*, vol. 13 (12), p. 3215.
39. D. Zhuang, V. J. L. Gan, Z. Duygu Tekler, and A. Chong et al., (2023). 'Data-driven predictive control for smart HVAC system in IoT-integrated buildings with time-series forecasting and reinforcement learning,' *Applied Energy*, vol. 338, p. 120936.

40. X. Godinho, H. Bernardo, J. C. de Sousa, and F. T. Oliveira, (2021). 'A data-driven approach to forecasting heating and cooling energy demand in an office building as an alternative to multi-zone dynamic simulation,' *Applied Sciences*, vol. 11 (4), p. 1356.

41. Y. Zhang, B. K. Teoh, M. Wu, and J. Chen et al., (2022). 'Data-driven estimation of building energy consumption and GHG emissions using explainable artificial intelligence,' *Energy*, vol. 262, p. 125468.

42. A. Ahmed, T. Jakir, M. N. H. Mir, and M. D. A. F. Zeeshan et al., (2025). 'Predicting energy consumption in hospitals using machine learning: A data-driven approach to energy efficiency in the USA,' *Journal of Computer Science and Technology Studies*, vol. 7 (1), pp. 199–219.

43. E. Dulce-Chamorro and F. J. Martinez-de-Pison, (2021). 'An advanced methodology to enhance energy efficiency in a hospital cooling-water system,' *Journal of Building Engineering*, vol. 43, p. 102839.

44. R. Frassanito, T. Buso, S. Aumann, and J. Toniolo et al., (2022). 'How IoT and artificial intelligence can improve energy efficiency in hospitals: A North Italian case study,' In *E3S Web of Conferences*, vol. 343, p. 02001.

45. R. Carli, G. Cavone, S. Ben Othman, and M. Dotoli, (2020). 'IoT based architecture for model predictive control of HVAC systems in smart buildings,' *Sensors*, vol. 20 (3), p. 781.

46. D. S-K. Ting and J. A. Stagner, (2025). 'Adaptive heating, ventilation, and air conditioning: Energy-efficient thermal comfort for tomorrow,' In *Adaptive Engineering*, pp. 197–211, Woodhead Publishing.

47. A. Wagdy, A. Sherif, H. Sabry, and R. Arafa et al., (2017). 'Daylighting simulation for the configuration of external sun-breakers on south oriented windows of hospital patient rooms under a clear desert sky,' *Solar Energy*, vol. 149, pp. 164–175.

48. Q. Al-Yasiri, M. Szabó, and M. Arýcý, (2022). 'A review on solar-powered cooling and air-conditioning systems for building applications,' *Energy Reports*, vol. 8, pp. 2888–2907.

49. P. Upadhyay, P. Kuchhal, and S. Mondal, (2024). 'A review of the use of different technologies/methods for the transmission of solar radiation for lighting purposes using optical fibers,' *Renewable Energy Focus*, vol. 50, p. 100614.

50. A. S. Al-Ezzi and M. N. M. Ansari, (2022). 'Photovoltaic solar cells: A review,' *Applied System Innovation*, vol. 5 (4), p. 67.

51. S. A. Kalogirou, (2014). *Solar Energy Engineering: Processes and Systems*, 2nd Ed. (Elsevier: Oxford, UK).

52. M. A. Bakheet, (2023). 'Design and modelling of solar energy system for electrification for a hospital in Saudi Arabia,' *European Journal of Energy Research*, vol. 3 (2), pp. 1–12.

53. N. Del Regno, A. Gigante, S. Ruggiero, and F. Tariello et al., (2023). 'Energy efficiency in hospitals: Comparative analysis of different HVAC configurations,' *Advances in Building Energy Research*, vol. 17 (5), pp. 554–577.

54. A. Refahi, H. Talkhabi, A. Rostami, and A. H. Aghdam, (2024). 'Technical feasibility study of the integration of the solar photovoltaic system for a hospital: A case study of Qom City, Iran,' *Future Energy*, vol. 3 (1), pp. 1–12.

55. C. L. Siow, H. Y. Leao, and A. Panneerselvem, (2025). 'Techno-economic study of solar energy implementation in hospitals in Malaysia,' *International Journal of Energy Economics and Policy*, vol. 15 (2), pp. 583–590.

56. M. E. Haj Assad, M. Nooman AlMallahi, A. Ramadan, and M. A. Awad et al., (2022). 'Geothermal heat pumps: principles and applications,' In *2022 Advances in Science and Engineering Technology International Conferences (ASET), IEEE*, pp. 1–8.

57. M. Soltani, F. M. Kashkooli, A. R. Dehghani-Sanij, and A. R. Kazemi et al., (2019). 'A comprehensive study of geothermal heating and cooling systems,' *Sustainable Cities and Society*, vol. 44, pp. 793–818.

58. C. Steins and S. J. Zarrouk, (2012). 'Assessment of the geothermal space heating system at Rotorua Hospital, New Zealand,' *Energy Conversion and Management*, vol. 55, pp. 60–70.

59. R. Febrianto, I. Thain, and S. J. Zarrouk, (2016). 'The geothermal heating system at Taupo Hospital, New Zealand,' *Geothermics*, vol. 59, pp. 347–356.

60. Z. Zyvith, M. T. Trevena, A. Yong, and R. Lamantia et al., (2018). 'Geothermal heating/cooling in Massachusetts general hospital,' In *2018 ASEE Mid-Atlantic Section Spring Conference*.

61. A. Milanović Pešić, J. Brankov, S. Denda, and Ž. Bjeljac et al., (2022). 'Geothermal energy in Serbia: Current state, utilization and perspectives,' *Renewable and Sustainable Energy Reviews*, vol. 162, p. 112442.

62. The HVAC service solutions, [Online], 'How much does it cost to install a heat pump in Canada,' Heat Pump Installation Cost: Average Price in Canada 2023. Accessed 20, March 2025.

63. R. Wu, (2009). 'Energy efficiency technologies: Air source heat pump vs. ground source heat pump,' *Journal of Sustainable Development*, vol. 2 (2), pp. 14–23.

64. X. Han, J. Chen, C. Huang, and W. Weng et al., (2014). 'Energy audit and air-conditioning system renovation analysis on office buildings using air-source heat pump in Shanghai,' *Building Services Engineering Research and Technology*, vol. 35 (4), pp. 376–392.

65. Kalin, [Online], 'Application of air source heat pump in hospital heating,' Application of air source heat pump in hospital heating. Accessed 20, March 2025.

66. The Guardian Labs, [Online], 'Healing people and the planet: everyone wins when the NHS cuts its carbon footprint,' Healing people and the planet: everyone wins when the NHS cuts its carbon footprint | Urban Energy Innovation | The Guardian. Accessed 20, March 2025.

67. H. Yan, B. Hu, and R. Wang, (2021). 'Air-source heat pump heating-based water vapor compression for localized steam sterilization applications during the COVID-19 pandemic,' *Renewable and Sustainable Energy Reviews*, vol. 145, p. 111026.

68. T. Abbas, M. Issa, and A. Ilinca, (2020). 'Biomass cogeneration technologies: A review,' *Journal of Sustainable Bioenergy Systems*, vol. 10 (1), pp. 1–15.

69. T. Kan, V. Strezov, and T. J. Evans, (2016). 'Lignocellulosic biomass pyrolysis: A review of product properties and effects of pyrolysis parameters,' *Renewable and Sustainable Energy Reviews*, vol. 57, pp. 1126–1140.

70. J. Vourdoubas, (2015). 'Creation of zero CO_2 emissions hospitals due to energy use a case study in Crete-Greece,' *Journal of engineering and Architecture*, vol. 3 (2), pp. 79–86.

71. J. Vourdoubas, (2016). 'Possibilities of using solid biomass for covering the heating needs in hospitals in Crete, Greece,' *Studies in Engineering and Technology*, vol. 3 (1), pp. 124–131.

72. J. Sanz-Calcedo, (2016). 'Analysis of the use of thermal biomass on healthcare centers in Extremadura (Spain),' *J Archit Eng Tech*, vol. 5 (182), p. 2.

73. E. A. Pina, M. A. Lozano, and L. M. Serra (2018). 'Opportunities for the integration of solar thermal heat, photovoltaics and biomass in a Brazilian hospital,' In *EuroSun 2018 Conference Proceedings*.

Chapter 8

The Effect of Social Capital on Eco-Friendly Behavior

Loghman Abbasi,[a] Hamed Sheykhi,[b] Mohammad Shokati Amghani,[c] and Moslem Savari[d]

[a]*Agriculture and Natural Resources Research and Education Center of Mazandaran Province, Agricultural Research, Education, and Extension Organization, Sari, Iran*
[b]*Department of Agriculture, Water and Energy Governance, Faculty of Governance, University of Tehran, Tehran, Iran*
[c]*Department of Agricultural Extension and Education, College of Agriculture, Tarbiat Modares University, Tehran, Iran*
[d]*Department of Agricultural Extension and Education, Agricultural Sciences and Natural Resources University of Khuzestan, Mollasani, Iran*

m.shokati@modares.ac.ir

In the past, environmental psychologists have sought to understand people's behaviors to improve environmental conditions. Researchers initially focused on pro-environmental behaviors from a psychological perspective, often overlooking the role of social factors. However, most current researchers emphasize the influence of social factors on the adoption of environmentally friendly behaviors, viewing social capital as a valuable resource to

Environmentalism in Healthcare: Caring for Tomorrow Ecologically
Edited by Jacqueline A. Stagner and David S.-K. Ting

ISBN 978-981-5129-95-3 (Hardcover), 978-1-003-74869-4 (eBook)
www.jennystanford.com

DOI: 10.1201/9781003748694-8

mitigate environmentally harmful actions. This approach can enhance residents' sense of belonging and trust within their communities, promoting a pro-environmental generation. Social capital is a crucial factor in facilitating collective action and encouraging residents to take on environmental responsibility. In this chapter of the book, we will review the literature to identify the key dimensions of social capital that affect pro-environmental behaviors. Additionally, we will discuss the most important theories related to these behaviors. The results of this study indicate that social capital, with its various components and at different levels, can significantly influence the adoption of environmentalist behaviors. Therefore, this study makes a significant contribution to the field of environmental psychology by emphasizing the critical role of social factors, particularly social capital, in promoting pro-environmental behaviors.

8.1 Introduction

The convergence on environmental issues related to global warming, including pollution and rising CO_2 levels, has compelled human societies to adopt eco-friendly environmental practices aimed at reducing adverse impacts on the ecosystem (Abunyewah et al., 2023; Savari & Khaleghi, 2024). Environmental injustices, climate change, ethical concerns regarding environmental stewardship, social responsibility, the marginalization of environmental issues, the emergence of influential stakeholder groups, radicalism, and anti-capitalist protests have collectively heightened environmental awareness within society (Ahmad et al., 2021; Maleknia et al., 2024). Furthermore, key environmental challenges arising from human activities include biodiversity loss, rangeland degradation, depletion of water resources, deforestation, and the excessive use of chemical pesticides (Thondhlana & Hlatshwayo, 2018; Dornhoff et al., 2019; Behl et al., 2022; Savari et al., 2022a), along with soil erosion and land-use change (Akintunde, 2017; Bleys et al., 2018; Khanpae et al., 2020). Consequently, many environmental problems stem from irresponsible human behavior towards nature (Vicente-Molina et al., 2013). Understanding and modifying individual behavior is thus recognized as a fundamental prerequisite for sustainable environmental management programs (Janmaimool & Denpaiboon, 2016). In other words, assessing how individuals perceive and value natural resources, along with their willingness to take action for conservation, is essential in addressing environmental crises (Akter et al., 2018). Therefore, researchers and policymakers assert that environmental issues can be alleviated by promoting eco-friendly behaviors within society (Akintunde, 2017; Thondhlana & Hlatshwayo, 2018; Bleys et al., 2018; Dornhoff et al., 2019).

Eco-friendly behaviors encompass actions that modify resource and energy consumption in ways that preserve the structure and dynamics of ecosystems, thereby minimizing harm and, where possible, benefiting the environment (Steg & Vlek, 2009; Choobchian et al., 2024). Alternatively, these behaviors can be defined as conscious efforts by individuals to mitigate the negative impact of human activities on the environment (Tang et al., 2017). In previous decades, environmental psychologists investigated individual behaviors to improve environmental conditions (Abrahamse & Steg, 2013). Initially, researchers studied eco-friendly behaviors from a psychological perspective, often overlooking the influence of social factors (Savari et al., 2022b). However, more recent studies emphasize the importance of social factors in fostering eco-friendly behaviors (Cai & Zhu, 2015; Alcock et al., 2020) and have identified social capital as a potent and accessible resource for mitigating environmentally harmful behaviors (Abrahamse & Steg, 2013; Liu et al., 2014; Vesely et al., 2020). Social capital can enhance residents' sense of belonging and trust in their communities, thereby promoting a pro-environmental generation (Cai & Zhu, 2015; Alcock et al., 2020). It is generally regarded as a significant factor in facilitating collective action (Ostrom, 2000) and guides residents toward embracing environmental responsibility (Ostrom, 2000; Li et al., 2019).

The concepts of social capital and social norms aim to guide individuals toward desirable personal and social behaviors, thereby reducing environmentally destructive actions (Dorigoni & Bonini, 2023). Studies indicate that social networks enhance the flow of information among people, which subsequently curbs individual opportunism in collective behavior (Cai & Zhu, 2015). Social capital helps minimize actions that undermine collective well-being (Dai et al., 2023), functioning as a mechanism for intrinsic regulation and order that directs individuals' activities toward environmental protection (Shi et al., 2018). To some extent, individuals' pro-environmental attitudes are shaped by perceived pressure from social norms regarding environmental conservation (Savari et al., 2022b). Specifically, social capital operates through the influence of peer monitoring (Guo et al., 2018). It represents a set of actual or potential resources inherent within social relationships or networks (Nahapiet & Ghoshal, 1998; Yildiz et al., 2015). At the local level, social cohesion is characterized by mutual trust among neighbors and relationships that foster support, which, in turn, affects their capacity to protect resources (Savari et al., 2023a). In other words, social capital can help resolve many natural resource issues, provided residents have greater influence in local planning and development decisions (Matthew & Nicholas, 2013). The key dimensions of social capital that can influence eco-friendly behaviors include social norms, social awareness, social networks, social participation, and social trust (Cai & Zhu, 2015; Savari & Khaleghi, 2023).

Several researchers have examined the effects of social capital across various fields, highlighting its significant role in these areas. For instance, social capital has been shown to influence environmental governance behaviors in agriculture (De Krom, 2017), waste sorting (Ling & Xu, 2020), carbon sequestration and storage (Moon et al., 2020), water conservation (Aprile & Fiorillo, 2017), and forest protection (Ling & Xu, 2020). Moreover, social capital components have been identified as drivers of eco-friendly and sustainable activities. Examples include the impact of social norms (Ling & Xu, 2020), shared social identity (Mouw, 2006), trust (Yun & Lee, 2015; Frederiks et al., 2015), and relationships and social identity (Lede et al., 2019) on pro-environmental and sustainable behaviors. Accordingly, the aim of this research is to study the effect of social capital on eco-friendly behavior.

8.2 Social Capital

Previous studies in this area reveal that sociologists and psychologists engaged in environmental protection view social capital as a crucial factor in promoting eco-friendly behaviors within society. Alongside human, economic, and natural capital, social capital has emerged as an influential resource (Li et al., 2024). Social capital, the intangible dimension of a community, is a historical legacy that fosters cooperation and participation in social interactions, helping to address various social issues, particularly environmental challenges. This resource enables progress toward accelerated economic, political, cultural, and environmental development. Social capital is primarily regarded as a valuable asset based on interpersonal relationships (Abdul-Rahaman et al., 2021). It is closely connected to material and human capital, encompassing social networks, norms, social authority, consensus on action, social ethics, social trust, and other related aspects (Villalonga-Olives & Kawachi, 2015). Furthermore, connections among individuals, organizations, and communities significantly influence behaviors (Portes, 1995; Teshome et al., 2016). Therefore, individuals with higher levels of social capital can access more information and opportunities, thereby gaining specific advantages (Wu, 2018). In addition, social capital can foster cooperation among farmers and support collective actions (Compton & Beeton, 2012; Chen et al., 2014; Barnes-Mauthe et al., 2015; Zhang et al., 2023).

Bourdieu (1986a) and Coleman (1988) provided some of the earliest definitions of social capital. Bourdieu described it as the aggregate of resources acquired by an individual or group through stable social networks, while Coleman portrayed social capital as a productive social network. Later, social capital was characterized by social attributes such as trust, norms of interaction, and membership in groups that facilitate collective action (Putnam, 1994; Kawachi, 1999). Similarly, Fukuyama (2001) and Healy and Cote (2001) defined social capital as an informal norm or network that fosters connections among individuals and groups. Overall, common terms used to define social capital include social networks, participation in social activities, trust and interaction, shared norms and values, attachment, and a sense of belonging (Mepparambath et al., 2024). Putnam's view of social capital emphasizes the organizational features of the social group underlying it, which can enhance social efficiency through participatory behaviors. Social capital is typically regarded as a public resource (Zhang, 2003).

In another definition provided by the World Bank, social capital is considered an asset for environmental protection, as it holds the potential to mobilize communities, stimulate organizations for development, and facilitate the sharing of critical information (World Bank, 1998). This concept has been further explored by various sociologists (Davis et al., 2005; Dunlap & York, 2008; Pampel & Hunter, 2012) and is primarily composed of two aspects: (a) Individual Social Capital and (b) Collective Social Capital. These aspects focus on how individuals invest in social relationships to access and utilize resources within social networks (Bian, 2012). Collective social capital emphasizes the formation of group trust, group participation, and group interaction. It also focuses on how a specific group develops or maintains social capital as a public good, enhancing the quality of life for its members (Bian, 2018). These two types of social capital differ in their functions across various social contexts. Therefore, it is important to identify their distinct effects in studies on eco-friendly behaviors.

8.2.1 Social Capital Elements

Social capital has a multidimensional nature, as documented in the works of various scholars (Van Oorschot & Arts, 2005; Rostila, 2007; Tahlyan et al., 2022). The strength of social relationships among citizens (Burt, 2000; MacGillivray, 2018; Yaqi et al., 2023), the frequency of social resource exchanges (Koopman et al., 2015), perceptions of fairness and social justice (Kawachi et al., 1998; Veenstra, 2000), and levels of mutual trust and solidarity (Lyon, 2000; Kant & Vertinsky, 2022) are central to the concept of social capital. Based on this analysis, we propose that social capital generally comprises social networks, social trust, and social equity. First, social networks are defined as sets of social actors and their relationships (MacGillivray, 2018). These networks emphasize interaction, connectivity, and communication among individuals, influencing their social behaviors (Siegel, 2009). In other words, the frequency and extent of an individual's interactions with relatives, neighbors, and colleagues determine the socioeconomic and environmental benefits of their actions. For instance, neighborhood effects can influence residents' decisions regarding relocation (Helms, 2012) and their "green" travel habits, helping to mitigate the adverse impacts of air pollution (Jansson et al., 2017). A robust social network can transform individual environmental expectations into group environmental expectations (Gunningham et al., 2004). As a result, individuals may reduce the costs of certain eco-friendly actions by engaging with relatives, neighbors, or colleagues. Consequently, environmental conservation activities can generate positive external effects, encouraging other community members to adopt similar behaviors for shared benefits.

On the other hand, social equity reflects human and social contact and is used to examine various dimensions of social life, such as education and environmental protection (Guy & McCandless, 2012). It connects with other priorities, including social, cultural, spatial, political, and structural inequalities (Perrin & Nougaredes, 2020). Social justice perspectives have proven beneficial in addressing environmental issues. For example, the equitable distribution of environmental facilities or resources fosters residents' trust in environmental conservation (Atshan et al., 2020; Lliso et al., 2021). Additionally, considering the social needs of residents and providing fair economic opportunities can establish a material foundation for their participation in eco-friendly behaviors (Dempsey et al., 2011). Thus, social justice can play a critical role in environmental protection. Ultimately, social trust is the psychological inclination of community members to trust one another. In a society with a higher level of social trust, individuals' eco-friendly behaviors have a greater impact on the broader public. Furthermore, building social trust can enhance the accuracy of shared information (Chow & Chan, 2008). In conclusion, following a literature review on social capital and its relationship with eco-friendly behaviors, the components and subcomponents of social capital that can influence individuals' eco-friendly behaviors are presented in Table 8.1.

Table 8.1 Components of social capital influencing eco-friendly behavior

Component	Sub-components
Social participation	I want to express my opinions on programs and initiatives promoting environmentally friendly activities.
	I enjoy participating in activities that support environmental preservation.
	I encourage and mobilize local communities to engage in eco-friendly activities.
	Community members can contribute to environmental protection by forming organizations dedicated to conservation.
Social trust	Community members collaborate to address environmental issues.
	I feel I can trust those around me without needing to be cautious.
	I believe that others are unlikely to harm me.
	Others are trustworthy people.
Social awareness	I obtain information on environmental protection through both formal and informal channels.
	Members of society are consistently aware of the impor-tance and benefits of environmental preservation for their livelihoods.
	The people of the society recognize the significance of eco-friendly behaviors.
Social norms	Environmental destruction in any form is unacceptable to society.
	My friends and neighbors encourage me to adopt eco-friendly behaviors.
	Embracing caring behaviors in society is regarded as a social value.
Social networks	I am a member of environmental protection organizations and NGOs.
	I regularly engage with experts and environmental specialists.
	I frequently connect with friends and neighbors, as I believe they share valuable knowledge with me.

52. M. A. Bakheet, (2023). 'Design and modelling of solar energy system for electrification for a hospital in Saudi Arabia,' *European Journal of Energy Research*, vol. 3 (2), pp. 1–12.

53. N. Del Regno, A. Gigante, S. Ruggiero, and F. Tariello et al., (2023). 'Energy efficiency in hospitals: Comparative analysis of different HVAC configurations,' *Advances in Building Energy Research*, vol. 17 (5), pp. 554–577.

54. A. Refahi, H. Talkhabi, A. Rostami, and A. H. Aghdam, (2024). 'Technical feasibility study of the integration of the solar photovoltaic system for a hospital: A case study of Qom City, Iran,' *Future Energy*, vol. 3 (1), pp. 1–12.

55. C. L. Siow, H. Y. Leao, and A. Panneerselvem, (2025). 'Techno-economic study of solar energy implementation in hospitals in Malaysia,' *International Journal of Energy Economics and Policy*, vol. 15 (2), pp. 583–590.

56. M. E. Haj Assad, M. Nooman AlMallahi, A. Ramadan, and M. A. Awad et al., (2022). 'Geothermal heat pumps: principles and applications,' In *2022 Advances in Science and Engineering Technology International Conferences (ASET), IEEE*, pp. 1–8.

57. M. Soltani, F. M. Kashkooli, A. R. Dehghani-Sanij, and A. R. Kazemi et al., (2019). 'A comprehensive study of geothermal heating and cooling systems,' *Sustainable Cities and Society*, vol. 44, pp. 793–818.

58. C. Steins and S. J. Zarrouk, (2012). 'Assessment of the geothermal space heating system at Rotorua Hospital, New Zealand,' *Energy Conversion and Management*, vol. 55, pp. 60–70.

59. R. Febrianto, I. Thain, and S. J. Zarrouk, (2016). 'The geothermal heating system at Taupo Hospital, New Zealand,' *Geothermics*, vol. 59, pp. 347–356.

60. Z. Zyvith, M. T. Trevena, A. Yong, and R. Lamantia et al., (2018). 'Geothermal heating/cooling in Massachusetts general hospital,' In *2018 ASEE Mid-Atlantic Section Spring Conference*.

61. A. Milanović Pešić, J. Brankov, S. Denda, and Ž. Bjeljac et al., (2022). 'Geothermal energy in Serbia: Current state, utilization and perspectives,' *Renewable and Sustainable Energy Reviews*, vol. 162, p. 112442.

62. The HVAC service solutions, [Online], 'How much does it cost to install a heat pump in Canada,' Heat Pump Installation Cost: Average Price in Canada 2023. Accessed 20, March 2025.

connections that span across other groups, thereby benefiting a wider population" (Payne et al., 2011).

Social capital at the individual level emphasizes the importance of individuals and their relationships with others. This level of social capital is often considered a private good belonging to individuals (Bhandari & Yasunobu, 2009). Research on social capital at the collective level typically focuses on specific social groups (Akram et al., 2016; Jia et al., 2020). Consequently, analyses of social capital may center on internal social capital, external social capital, or both. However, the research literature lacks consensus regarding which level of social capital has a greater impact on individuals' adoption of eco-friendly behaviors (Onyx & Bullen, 2003; Mignone et al., 2008). For instance, Meyer (2018) argued in favor of collective social capital in the context of disasters, while other studies suggest that these external effects are determined by individual social capital (Fukuyama, 2002; Dasgupta, 2000). In addition to categorizing social capital based on individual versus collective dimensions, social capital can also be classified into bonding and bridging types, based on intra-group and inter-group connections, respectively. Bonding social capital refers to relationships within organizations or communities and is inward-looking, facilitating resource aggregation and knowledge transfer. Bridging social capital represents connections between groups and organizations, offering actors the potential to fill 'structural holes,' thereby helping them acquire new information (Redondo & Camarero, 2019).

Individuals can build their social capital by investing in personal relationships, participating in networking events, joining associations or interest-based groups, or volunteering their time within their communities. These activities enable individuals to meet new people and establish new relationships. They can form supportive friendships, provide assistance, show kindness, and be trustworthy and compassionate. Such behaviors foster goodwill and build a positive reputation. By engaging with their network connections, individuals can share experiences and perspectives on shared interests. These actions foster aspects of social capital such as networks, trust, reciprocity, and shared language and understanding. In other words, it encompasses all three dimensions of social capital: structural, relational, and cognitive. On the other hand, social capital examined at the community level is regarded as a public good, a collective rather than an individual asset. Thus, it is a community-level resource or 'collectively-owned capital' (Bourdieu, 1986b). At this level, social capital changes gradually over time and is deeply embedded in history and culture. Collective social capital tends to focus on trust, civic norms, association memberships, and volunteer activities. Measuring collective social capital is challenging due to the difficulty in gathering data from a significant proportion of the population. Researchers often rely on 'best-fit' indicators, which may not align precisely with social capital theory, as the data are often not collected to examine social capital. This difficulty stems from the high costs associated with obtaining data from a substantial portion of the community (Claridge, 2018).

8.3 Eco-Friendly Behavior

In recent years, increased energy consumption in developed countries has led to significant environmental degradation. As a result, these countries have implemented environmental policies, stringent regulations, and economic instruments to address this issue (Savari et al., 2023b; Xu et al., 2024). Despite these efforts, the environmental crisis remains a persistent challenge due to the continued exploitation of natural resources in these regions (Roscoe et al., 2019; Su et al., 2023). Therefore, developed societies must be encouraged to adopt eco-friendly initiatives (Tirno et al., 2023). In particular, embracing environmentally conscious behaviors aimed at minimizing the impact of products and production processes on the environment is considered an effective means to achieve not only environmental but also economic and social objectives (Savari et al., 2023c; Liao et al., 2023). Additionally, eco-friendly behavior enhances competitive advantage, as an environmental mindset aligns with the requirements of various stakeholder groups (Kneipp et al., 2019). Nevertheless, the environmental performance of a society depends heavily on the knowledge, attitudes, and behaviors of its individuals (Piwowar-

Sulej et al., 2024). Thus, environmental protection is a critical issue of the present century (Kim & Lee, 2023).

Eco-friendly behavior, often referred to as the eco-friendly approach, encompasses actions that demonstrate environmental responsibility accessible to individuals in society (Fawehinmi et al., 2020). It is further defined as conscious environmental behavior, which includes both role-prescribed and extra-role behaviors (Aboramadan et al., 2019). Extra-role behavior, in particular, refers to voluntary green actions that fall outside an individual's formal job description and are not explicitly evaluated in their performance assessments (Aboramadan & Karatepe, 2021). Consequently, eco-friendly behavior may also be described as environmental preservation behavior. Stern (2000) defined it as community activities aimed at protecting or preventing damage to the environment. Similarly, Kollmuss and Agyeman (2002) characterized eco-friendly behavior as actions by individuals intended to minimize the negative impact of human activities on the environment. Rice (2006) categorized most environmentally supportive behaviors into individual and collective environmental behaviors. Individual environmental behavior involves personal or family-centered actions closely linked to daily life, such as waste sorting and resource reuse, while collective environmental behavior encompasses participation in environmental campaigns and acceptance of environmental policies.

Various studies indicate that environmental threats currently exist and are rapidly increasing, primarily driven by human activities (Hansen & Sato, 2012). The behaviors contributing to these threats are modifiable. However, despite the apparent scientific consensus regarding the imminent and permanent effects of environmental threats (Intergovernmental Panel on Climate Change, 2014), organized social actions to prevent further harmful changes remain largely insufficient. Thompson (2010) presented three potential responses to environmental threats, such as climate change: reducing climate change, adapting to new environments, or enduring its effects. For humanity to survive and thrive, reducing behaviors that contribute to climate change and adapting to expected climatic changes are essential. Nevertheless, consumers respond tardily to this pressing issue (Alavosius et al., 2015).

Environmental threats stemming from human activities are problems that arise from human behavior and can be mitigated through behavioral changes. To alter human behavior in significant and sustainable ways, we require a scientific understanding of the motivations behind behavior change. One area of psychology that provides the precision, breadth, and depth necessary to comprehend human behavior is the focus on social capital within human societies (Hayes et al., 2012). The relationship between social capital and pro-environmental beliefs and behaviors has been well documented in recent times (Masoom, 2024).

Thompson (2010) asserts that three responses are available for addressing climate change: reducing climate change, adapting to new environments, or enduring its effects. If humanity wishes to survive and grow, responses that include reduction (e.g., minimizing behaviors that lead to climate change) and adaptation (i.e., adjusting to expected climate changes) are essential. However, consumers, both at the individual and organizational levels, react slowly to this urgent matter (Alavosius et al., 2015). In essence, climate change is a problem arising from human behavior, and it can be addressed through behavioral changes. To enact significant and sustainable behavioral change, we need a scientific understanding of the motivations behind behavior change. One domain within psychology that provides the necessary precision, breadth, and depth for understanding human behavior is contextual behavioral science (CBS) (Hayes et al., 2012).

Overall, most environmentally conscious individuals support eco-friendly products. However, their support does not always translate into actual purchasing behavior (Schuitema & De Groot, 2015). According to Procter & Gamble (2021), among 4,000 South Korean consumers surveyed about eco-friendly product purchases, 82.2% indicated a willingness to buy environmentally friendly products. Nevertheless, only 25.5% of respondents purchased such products. These results suggest that the intention to buy eco-friendly products is unlikely to lead to actual purchases. Moreover, the findings indicate that despite having environmental goals, consumers exhibit hesitance when purchasing eco-friendly products. In other words, individuals concerned about the environment do not necessarily purchase and consume eco-friendly products. Previous studies have measured the behavioral aspect of eco-friendly product purchasing in terms of purchase intention (Hanss et al., 2016; Liu et al., 2017). Studies on consumer behavior typically consider intention as either synonymous with or closely related to actual behavior (Ajzen et al., 2005). The area of purchase intention and the behavioral gaps in consumers' purchasing of eco-friendly products has been extensively explored in the literature (Kim & Choi, 2005; Morwitz et al., 2007; Carrington et al., 2014; Joshi & Rahman, 2015; Park et al., 2018; Kaur & Bhardwaj, 2021). Nonetheless, a gap still exists between intention and actual behavior. Therefore, it is evident that an individual's intention and will alone cannot guarantee the adoption of eco-friendly behavior. Instead, a more robust component is necessary to guide individuals toward adopting environmentally friendly practices and create a lasting and significant impact on their behavior.

8.4 Social Capital and Eco-Friendly Behavior

Today, environmental issues have garnered the attention of organizations, communities, and governmental bodies (Siyambalapitiya et al., 2018; Michaelowa et al., 2022; Tirno et al., 2023). Consequently, the implementation of appropriate environmental programs is on the rise, and human societies are increasingly responsive to the environmental issues arising from their activities (Jabbour, 2013; Koberg & Longoni, 2019). These operations encompass the unsustainable use of natural resources and improper waste disposal (Singh & Singh, 2017; Siyambalapitiya et al., 2018). Examples of environmental issues include global warming, ozone layer depletion, air pollution, and the generation of medical hazardous waste (Kaza & Yao, 2018; Soutter & Mõttus, 2020; Neale et al., 2021). Various approaches have been adopted by different communities to address and mitigate environmental challenges, such as green operations (Zhu et al., 2008) and green supply chains (Jabbour et al., 2016). However, among the various approaches utilized by communities, eco-friendly behavior is considered a critical endpoint for successfully implementing green strategies and environmental management practices, as adopting appropriate behaviors enhances individuals' roles in environmental protection (Renwick et al., 2013; Jabbour & Renwick, 2018; Malik et al., 2021). Although various researchers conceptualize eco-friendly behavior in different ways, they all emphasize the active participation of individuals in preventing or resolving environmental issues through social actions. Haynes defines eco-friendly behaviors as "conscious actions based on responsibility and personal values, aimed at avoiding or addressing environmental problems from an individual perspective" (Granovetter, 1985). While Kolmous views eco-friendly behavior as actions taken by individuals to minimize the negative impacts of their activities on the environment (Yang & Cheng, 2021). Besides, Stern (2000) initially distinguished three types of eco-friendly behavior: private eco-friendly behavior, radical public eco-friendly behavior, and non-radical public eco-friendly behavior (Coleman, 1988). Similarly, Hunter merged the latter two categories, categorizing eco-friendly behaviors into private eco-friendly behaviors and public eco-friendly behaviors (Burt, 2018). Private eco-friendly behaviors include green consumption, energy conservation in buildings, and so on, while public eco-friendly behaviors involve donating to environmental organizations and raising awareness of environmental issues (Shi et al., 2022).

Eco-friendly behaviors are a combination of social motivations and individual benefits (Lucas et al., 2008; Capstick et al., 2022) and always have spillover effects. In the context of eco-friendly behaviors, spillover refers to the encouragement, obligation, promotion, education, and policy of specific eco-friendly behaviors to influence other non-specific eco-friendly behaviors (Gneezy et al., 2012). Research has shown that positive spillover effects play a significant role in the eco-friendly behaviors of local populations, such as recycling, green consumption (Truelove et al., 2014), energy conservation (Maki et al., 2019), and natural resource protection (Tobler et al., 2012). Although environmental policies can encourage and guide people to adopt eco-friendly behaviors, their guiding effects are not significant, and the level of collective eco-friendly behaviors remains less than ideal. This is because government policies primarily regulate community eco-friendly behaviors at the macro level (Zhang et al., 2013). Social capital serves as an important informal regime and a micro-level factor that significantly influences people's decision-making. It can enhance the vigor and cohesion of the public in environmental governance and promote the collective participation of residents in managing public affairs, thereby improving the performance and effectiveness of environmental governance (Hartlieb et al., 2020). Therefore, the environment and social groups are phenomena that are affected by the interactions and communications between individuals (Sawyer, 2005; Aureli & Schino, 2019), which influence each other in response to the impacts they receive. Often, these interactions collectively exhibit complex behaviors that were never the original goals of individuals. These emergent features are prevalent across social sciences, from physics to biology and environmental studies, or even management (Cropanzano & Mitchell, 2005; Aziz-Alaoui & Bertelle, 2009; Mantica, Stoop, & Stramaglia, 2017). Notably, these complex and sometimes unpredictable behaviors arise from simple interactions among their components. Scientists have long recognized how such interactions lead to complex yet structured and stable behaviors in adopting eco-friendly practices. Understanding the mechanisms of social group formation and social behaviors (Stadtfeld, Takács, & Vörös, 2020) is a significant challenge in sociology, resulting in various hypotheses in this area (Turner, 1987; Baumeister & Leary, 1995; Cartwright & Zander, 1966; Berkman, Glass, Brissette, & Seeman, 2000; Kadushin, 2002; George Homans, 2013). Some of these theories attempt to theorize the fundamental principles of the formation of these social institutions from human interactions using a bottom-up approach. However, one concern among sociologists has been that many sociological theories have evolved in a way that lacks specific empirical references (Hedström, 2005). Presenting these seemingly stable theories resembles describing how a complex machine theoretically operates based on its components. We often do not recognize the flaws and shortcomings until we assemble these components in practice.

Today, with the increase in computational power and the development of various methods such as Agent-Based Modeling (ABM) (Railsback, 2019) and Computational Social Science (Keuschnigg et al., 2018; Anzola, 2019; Edelmann et al., 2020), researchers have been able to study these laws, strengths, and weaknesses by constructing artificial societies in a computer environment (Macy & Willer, 2002; Bruch & Atwell, 2015), albeit in a simple and detailed manner.

Various theories have been proposed regarding the impact of social capital on individual behavior. In 1961, George Casper Homans, the founder of behavioral sociology, published the book "Social Behavior: Its Elementary Forms" (Homans, 1961), introduced social exchange theory. His inspiration stemmed from a desire to view sociology from a psychological perspective. The main concern of this book is to explain social structures based on the actions of individuals that do not require the creation of these structures (Ritzer, 2011). As he discusses in the framework of social exchange theory, his notion of action refers to the exchange between individuals in society. Exchange is a broad term. Hence, Homans proposes fundamental propositions to explain these structures, focusing on individuals' psychological behaviors (Enayat et al., 2022). Social exchange theory is one of the most influential conceptual paradigms for understanding individuals' environmental behaviors (Cropanzano & Mitchell, 2005). Although different perspectives on social exchange have emerged, theorists agree that social exchange involves a series of interactions that create commitments (Emerson, 1976). The type of interaction that humans have with the environment (whether collaborative or antagonistic) can generate a series of commitments within individuals. Specifically, in a collaborative context, it ultimately leads to the emergence of eco-friendly behaviors. Notably, these interactions are usually seen as interdependent and conditional on the actions of others in social exchange theory (Blau, 1964). Therefore, this theory suggests that behaviors can be viewed as the result of a cost-benefit analysis by individuals attempting to engage with society and the environment (Cook et al., 2013). In other words, exchange theory is essentially an effort to integrate behavioral principles, blend them with other ideas, and apply them to topics such as environmental conservation (Cropanzano & Mitchell, 2005).

A review of related theoretical foundations regarding social capital and related theories showed that this capital always has a key impact on the development of societies, both socially and culturally, economically, and environmentally. Therefore, in the following, we introduce a model that has been presented to study the role of social capital in protecting the environment through eco-friendly behaviors. For example, Savari & Khaleghi (2023), by investigating the role of social capital in forest conservation, presented a model in which these components affect protective measures through a specific mechanism, which means that they can affect protective behaviors by influencing the cognition of policies and increasing the awareness of rural communities.

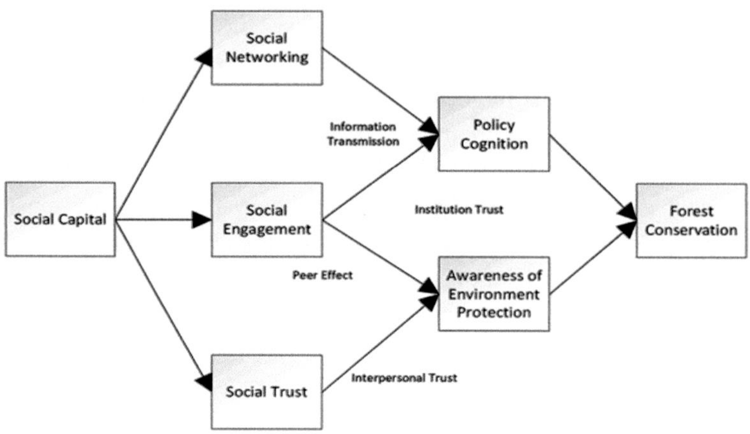

Figure 8.1 The conceptual framework of the research derived from Dai et al., 2023.

8.5 Literature Review

Various studies have been conducted on the impact of social capital on environmental protection and natural resources, guiding environmental planners in different communities to invest in social capital (Mepparambath et al., 2024). To better stimulate eco-friendly behaviors, researchers have undertaken numerous studies on the factors influencing behavior at the micro level. For instance, earlier research has demonstrated that socioeconomic characteristics of communities (Fan et al., 2019), environmental awareness (Liu et al., 2020), and environmental responsibility (Yang et al., 2021) are key factors affecting eco-friendly behaviors in different societies. Thus, it is clear that identifying the factors influencing collective eco-friendly behavior and finding ways to promote such behavior is essential. Existing studies categorize the influencing factors on eco-friendly behavior into cognitive, demographic, structural social, and cultural factors. Cognitive factors (Gao et al., 2019; Díaz-Siefer et al., 2020; Poirier-Pocovi & Bailey, 2020) primarily focus on the one-way output state of the public towards the environment, ranging from logical environmental knowledge to individual sensory experiences. These factors concentrate on individuals' environmental benefits and the individual-environment pathway to analyze their eco-friendly behaviors. Demographic factors mainly include social characteristics of individuals, such as gender, income, and other aspects (Nisbet & Gick, 2008; Otto et al., 2016; Vicente-Molina et al., 2018; Enzler & Diekmann, 2019), to study the impact of social benefits on public environmental tendencies. In comparison to cognitive factors, demographic factors can be viewed as external factors at the individual level (Wan & Du, 2022). A study in China concerning factors influencing the reduction of chemical fertilizer consumption concluded that, in addition to individual characteristics of farmers, social capital is a significant factor in this context (Zheng et al., 2022). Another study investigated the interplay between social capital, social needs, and environmental concerns in sustainable social action and found that social capital and its components (cognitive, relational, and structural) can facilitate collective activities toward achieving sustainable development (Broska, 2021). Besides, in a study examining the impact of social capital (with components of social networks, collective trust, and social participation) on forest conservation behaviors (including forest maintenance, protection, and restoration), it was found that social capital components significantly affect forest conservation and restoration efforts (Dai et al., 2023) (Fig. 8.1). Additionally, research on social capital's influence on farmers' participation in ecological watershed management concluded that social networks and social participation have a positive and significant impact on farmers' willingness to engage in ecological watershed management. A strong communication network positively and significantly influenced the level of farmers' participation, while public trust also positively and significantly impacted farmers' willingness and level of participation (Shi et al., 2018). Research findings on the effect of social capital on the adoption of green inputs among farmers revealed that social capital components have a positive and significant influence in this area (Ren et al., 2022). Savari and Shahidzadeh (2023) investigated the role of social capital in the environmental protection of agricultural lands in arid regions. They found that the behaviors of "using minimum tillage to reduce soil erosion" and "using organic and animal fertilizers in farms" ranked higher in priority among farmers. Moreover, structural equation modeling results indicated that the dimensions of social capital (social norms, social awareness, social networks, social participation, and social trust) significantly affect the environmental protection of agricultural lands in arid regions, explaining 73% of the variance in the dependent variable of environmental protection in these areas.

Miller and Buys (2008) conducted a study titled "The Role of Social Capital in Predicting and Promoting Responsibility for Environmental Issues in Local Australian Communities,". They found that different types of social capital enhance the understanding and prediction of sustainable environmental actions. The elements of social capital were involved in both reducing and enhancing feelings of responsibility regarding environmental issues within the local Australian community.

Similarly, Liu et al. (2014) explored the role of social capital in encouraging eco-tourism behaviors based on individual actions. They emphasized that strengthening the components of social capital, particularly social trust, can significantly influence the environmental behaviors of community members.

Moreover, Krasny et al. (2015) measured social capital among youth through environmental education programs utilizing Putnam's theories. They found that social capital improves active youth participation in environmentally friendly initiatives.

Additionally, Stapleton et al. (2022) investigated how to promote eco-friendly behaviors and concluded that messaging, advertising, and social marketing are effective methods for encouraging eco-friendly behaviors.

Shi et al. (2022) examined the effects of social capital on eco-friendly behaviors in China, concluding that collective social capital has a significantly lower impact on eco-friendly behaviors compared to individual social capital. Furthermore, women engage in individual eco-friendly behaviors more than men. Furthermore, they argued that social capital should be actively used to promote civic participation in China's environmental protection processes.

Wan and Du (2022) explored the relationship between social capital, environmental knowledge, and eco-friendly behavior. They measured social capital from four dimensions: social trust, social norms, social networks, and social participation. Furthermore, they empirically tested its impact on both individual and collective eco-friendly behaviors. The results indicated that social capital contributes to promoting eco-friendly behavior. Specifically, the greater the adherence to social norms among the public, the higher the social participation and the stronger the inclination to adopt individual and collective eco-friendly behaviors. However, enhancing social trust significantly affects only individual environmental behaviors, while expanding the social network scale only influences collective environmental support behaviors. Our results revealed that the increased social capital strengthens environmental knowledge and promotes eco-friendly behaviors. Furthermore, mediation analysis revealed that environmental knowledge plays a mediating role in the pathway through which social capital affects individuals' eco-friendly behavior.

In a study conducted by Kim and Lee (2023) to identify factors influencing eco-friendly behavior, they found that consumers' environmental knowledge and perceived effectiveness significantly impact the intention to purchase environmentally friendly products.

Additionally, Xu et al. (2024) examined the relationship between eco-friendly behaviors and social capital in China. They discovered that expanding social networks has a substantial positive impact on all three types of eco-friendly behaviors. Conversely, social trust and social equality are only associated with behavior focused on environmental payment. This study highlighted cognitive environmental variables as mediators to test the mechanism through which social capital influences eco-friendly behaviors. They noted that, overall, environmental knowledge, concerns, and attitudes play a crucial role in how social networks affect the eco-friendly behaviors of residents.

8.6 Discussion

Social researchers have established a significant direct relationship between various types of social capital and eco-friendly behaviors (Wan & Du, 2022). However, the mere existence of social capital is not a sufficient condition for improving individuals' environmental preferences or government policies. This type of social capital, and the outcomes derived from it, can differ, leading to varied overall impacts on individuals' environmental preferences and governmental policies (Pretty & Ward, 2001; Jones, 2010; Dulal et al., 2011; Cho & Kang, 2016). Accordingly, this review highlights insights into the influence of social capital on eco-friendly behavior. A comprehensive examination of theoretical and empirical literature regarding social capital, along with its components and levels (both individual and collective), revealed that numerous studies have investigated the impact of this capital on eco-friendly behavior. Collectively, they affirm a consistently positive and significant relationship between social capital and eco-friendly behavior across different communities (Zhang & Shih, 2023). Consequently, social capital has garnered significant attention from researchers and policymakers in the environmental sector due to its predictive effects on preparedness, risk management, recovery, and resilience at both community and individual levels (Adger, 2010; Aldrich, 2012). A crucial aspect of this capital is its potential to remain latent in some human societies. By raising awareness and promoting social capital, it can be activated within individuals, thereby encouraging appropriate behaviors regarding environmental protection and natural resource management. This activation can only occur through social empowerment, which enhances the social capacities of individuals within these communities. Empowerment is a fundamental concept in developing social capital for environmental protection. Capacity building and empowering local communities and organizations are prerequisites for sustainable development (Ghorbani et al., 2016). One of the most successful approaches to empowering local communities and achieving sustainable development is the participatory management approach based on adaptability. This approach emphasizes that achieving sustainable management in local communities requires considering the social concerns, interests, and benefits of all individuals affected within the community. Therefore, recognizing and analyzing the complexities of social systems becomes imperative. Additionally, this approach highlights the importance of engaging local stakeholders in the decision-making process and executing management projects tailored to the social and ecological context of each area (Bodin & Prell, 2011). Overall, environmental issues and challenges remain a serious global concern. Understanding the determinants of various eco-friendly behaviors, especially social capital, is essential to guide targeted actions aimed at enhancing individuals' eco-friendly behaviors and improving people's quality of life. The findings of this study indicate that social capital significantly impacts individuals' environmental behaviors. Social networks foster interaction, communication, and collaboration among residents, positively influencing private, public, and environmentally focused behaviors. However, social trust and equality showed a closer relationship only with environmentally focused behaviors related to financial aspects. Moreover, social networks profoundly influence individuals' environmental knowledge, concerns, and attitudes. Notably, social trust is closely linked to environmental knowledge and concerns. In summary, environmental knowledge, concerns, and attitudes greatly influence eco-friendly behaviors.

8.7 Conclusion

This study makes a significant contribution to the field of environmental psychology by emphasizing the critical role of social factors, particularly social capital, in promoting pro-environmental behaviors. Unlike earlier research that primarily focused on psychological aspects, this work acknowledges and explores the profound influence of social dynamics and community trust on environmentally friendly actions. By examining the key dimensions of social capital, this chapter provides valuable insights into how collective action and social responsibility can be harnessed to foster a more sustainable and environmentally conscious generation. Through an extensive literature review, this study not only identifies the most impactful elements of social capital but also delves into the theories and behaviors that underpin effective environmental stewardship. Therefore, based on the results of this study, several practical policies are suggested for planners. The most important of these are as follows:

1. **Community Engagement Programs**

   (i) **Organize community events and workshops:** Facilitate regular gatherings focused on environmental awareness and sustainable practices to strengthen community bonds and educate residents.

   (ii) **Foster local environmental groups:** Support the formation of local groups dedicated to environmental stewardship, allowing residents to collaborate on green initiatives.

2. **Education and Awareness Campaigns**

   (i) **Develop educational materials:** Create and distribute resources that explain the importance of social capital in environmental conservation and the specific actions individuals can take.

   (ii) **Implement school programs:** Integrate environmental education into school curricula, emphasizing the role of community and social responsibility.

3. **Incentive-Based Initiatives**

   (i) **Offer incentives for green behaviors:** Provide rewards or recognition for residents who actively participate in environmentally friendly activities, such as recycling programs or community clean-up events.

   (ii) **Promote green certifications:** Encourage local businesses and organizations to adopt sustainable practices by offering green certifications and publicizing their efforts.

4. **Policy and Infrastructure Development**

   (i) **Enhance green spaces:** Invest in the development and maintenance of parks and community gardens to create spaces where residents can connect and engage in environmental activities.

   (ii) **Support sustainable infrastructure:** Promote the use of eco-friendly building materials and energy-efficient systems in new developments and renovations.

5. **Collaborative Partnerships**

   (i) **Form partnerships with local organizations:** Collaborate with NGOs, educational institutions, and businesses to pool resources and expertise for environmental initiatives.

   (ii) **Engage with government agencies:** Work with municipal and regional authorities to align local policies with broader environmental goals and secure funding for community projects.

6. **Measurement and Evaluation**

   (i) **Organize (i) Monitor and evaluate progress:** Regularly assess the effectiveness of implemented policies and programs through surveys, focus groups, and other feedback mechanisms.

   (ii) **Adjust strategies based on feedback:** Use collected data to refine and improve policies, ensuring they remain relevant and impactful.

In conclusion, it is recommended that policymakers and planners involved in environmental and natural resource protection consider implementing the following policies and programs to enhance the role of social capital in eco-friendly behaviors:

- Emphasizing the importance of social networks and empowering individuals within communities
- Providing political and logistical support for NGOs and civil society organizations active in environmental and natural resource conservation
- Fostering corporate social responsibility among manufacturers of industrial products and companies in the service sector
- Monitoring and enforcing the implementation of projects impacting the environment and natural resources, with a requirement for environmental impact assessments conducted by specialists
- Building public trust in the government's positive and essential role in environmental and natural resource protection
- Involving the public at various levels of decision-making, implementation, monitoring, and evaluation of infrastructure, industrial, service, and agricultural projects, and so on

Every research has its set of limitations. Some limitations are inherent to the nature of the research itself, such as those found in review studies, while others are specific to the particular study in question. This research is no exception and has a series of limitations, the most important of which are as follows:

(i) The review might be limited by the availability and scope of existing literature, potentially leading to gaps in coverage of certain topics or areas.

(ii) The study might be influenced by publication bias, where only studies with positive or significant results are published and included, while negative or null results are underrepresented.

(iii) The inclusion and exclusion criteria used to select studies for the review might introduce bias and affect the overall findings.

(iv) Limiting the review to studies published in certain languages might result in the exclusion of relevant research conducted and published in other languages.

(v) Also, since review studies do not involve primary data collection, they rely entirely on the existing literature, which might limit the ability to address certain research questions or gaps.

References

Abdul-Rahaman, A., Issahaku, G., & Zereyesus, Y. A. (2021). Improved rice variety adoption and farm production efficiency: Accounting for unobservable selection bias and technology gaps among smallholder farmers in Ghana. *Technology in Society*, 64, 101471.

Aboramadan, M., & Karatepe, O. M. (2021). Green human resource management, perceived green organizational support and their effects on hotel employees' behavioral outcomes. *International Journal of Contemporary Hospitality Management*, 33(10), 3199–3222.

Aboramadan, M., Albashiti, B., Alharazin, H., & Dahleez, K. A. (2019). Human resources management practices and organizational commitment in higher education: The mediating role of work engagement. *International Journal of Educational Management*, 34(1), 154–174.

Abrahamse, W., & Steg, L. (2013). Social influence approaches to encourage resource conservation: A meta-analysis. *Global Environmental Change*, 23(6), 1773–1785.

Abunyewah, M., Erdiaw-Kwasie, M. O., Okyere, S. A., Thayaparan, G., Byrne, M., Lassa, J. & Maund, K. (2023). Influence of personal and collective social capital on flood preparedness and community resilience: Evidence from Old Fadama, Ghana. *International Journal of Disaster Risk Reduction*, 94, 103790.

Adger, W. N. (2010). Social capital, collective action, and adaptation to climate change. *Der Klimawandel: Sozialwissenschaftliche Perspektiven*, 327–345.

Ahmad, S., Islam, T., Sadiq, M., & Kaleem, A. (2021). Promoting green behavior through ethical leadership: A model of green human resource management and environmental knowledge. *Leadership & Organization Development Journal*, 42(4), 531–547.

Ajzen, I., Fishbein, M., Albarracín, D., Johnson, B. T., & Zanna, M. P. (2005). *The Handbook of Attitudes*. Mahwah, NJ, US: Lawrence Erlbaum Associates Publishers, 173–221.

Akintunde, E.A. (2017). Theories and concepts for human behavior in environmental preservation. *J. Environ. Sci. Public Health*, 1(2), 120e133. https://doi.org/10.26502/JESPH.012.

Cai, Q., & Zhu, Y. (2015). Social trust, income level and farmers participating in provision of rural public goods. *Journal of Nanjing Agricultural University (Social Sciences Edition)*, 15(1), 41–50.

Capstick, S., Nash, N., Whitmarsh, L., Poortinga, W., Haggar, P., & Brügger, A. (2022). The connection between subjective wellbeing and pro-environmental behaviour: Individual and cross-national characteristics in a seven-country study. *Environmental Science & Policy*, 133, 63–73.

Carrington, M. J., Neville, B. A., & Whitwell, G. J. (2014). Lost in translation: Exploring the ethical consumer intention–behavior gap. *Journal of Business Research*, 67(1), 2759–2767.

Cartwright, D., & Zander, A. (1966). Group dynamics, research and theory. *Sociological Review*, 2(1), 131–131.

Chen, H., Wang, J., & Huang, J. (2014). Policy support, social capital, and farmers' adaptation to drought in China. *Global Environmental Change*, 24, 193–202.

Cho, S., & Kang, H. (2016). Putting behavior into context exploring the contours of social capital influences on environmental behavior. *Environment and Behavior*, 1–31.

Choobchian, S., Ghorbannejad, M., Amghani, M. S., & Azadi, H. (2024). Barriers to the deployment of renewable energy technologies. In *Reclaiming Eden*, 111–144, Jenny Stanford Publishing.

Chow, W. S., & Chan, L. S. (2008). Social network, social trust and shared goals in organizational knowledge sharing. *Information & Management*, 45(7), 458–465.

Claridge, T. (2018). Explanation of the different levels of social capital: Individual or collective. *Social Capital Research*, 17.

Coleman, J. S. (1988). Social capital in the creation of human capital. *American Journal of Sociology*, 94, S95–S120.

Compton, E., & Beeton, R. B. (2012). An accidental outcome: Social capital and its implications for Landcare and the "status quo". *Journal of Rural Studies*, 28(2), 149–160.

Cook, K. S., Cheshire, C., Rice, E. R., & Nakagawa, S. (2013). Social exchange theory. *Handbook of Social Psychology*, 61–88.

Cropanzano, R., & Mitchell, M. S. (2005). Social exchange theory: An interdisciplinary review. *Journal of Management*, 31(6), 874–900. doi:10.1177/0149206305279602.

Dai, J., Chen, J., Luo, Z., & Zhou, W. (2023). Coping with giant panda nature reserve protection dilemmas in China: Social capital's role in forest conservation. *Global Ecology and Conservation*, 42, e02379.

Dasgupta, P. (2000). Economic progress and the idea of social capital. *Social Capital: A Multifaceted Perspective/World Bank.*

Davis, G. F., McAdam, D., Scott, W. R., & Zald, M. N. (Eds.). (2005). *Social Movements and Organization Theory.* Cambridge University Press.

De Krom, M. P. (2017). Farmer participation in agri-environmental schemes: Regionalisation and the role of bridging social capital. *Land Use Policy,* 60, 352–361.

Dempsey, N., Bramley, G., Power, S., & Brown, C. (2011). The social dimension of sustainable development: Defining urban social sustainability. *Sustainable Development,* 19(5), 289–300.

Díaz-Siefer, P., Neaman, A., Salgado, E., Celis-Diez, J. L., & Otto, S. (2015). Human-environment system knowledge: A correlate of pro-environmental behavior. *Sustainability,* 7(11), 15510–15526.

Dorigoni, A., & Bonini, N. (2023). Water bottles or tap water? A descriptive-social-norm based intervention to increase a pro-environmental behavior in a restaurant. *Journal of Environmental Psychology,* 86, 101971.

Dornhoff, M., Sothmann, J. N., Fiebelkorn, F., & Menzel, S. (2019). Nature relatedness and environmental concern of young people in Ecuador and Germany. *Frontiers in Psychology,* 10, 453.

Dulal, H. B., Foa, R., & Knowles, S. (2011). Social capital and cross-country environmental performance. *The Journal of Environment & Development,* 20(2), 121–144.

Dunlap, R. E., & York, R. (2008). The globalization of environmental concern and the limits of the postmaterialist values explanation: Evidence from four multinational surveys. *The Sociological Quarterly,* 49(3), 529–563.

Edelmann, A., Wolff, T., Montagne, D., & Bail, C. A. (2020). Computational social science and sociology. *Annual Review of Sociology,* 46.

Emerson, R. M. (1976). Social exchange theory. *Annual Review of Sociology,* 2, 335–362.

Enayat, T., Ardebili, M. M., Kivi, R. R., Amjadi, B., & Jamali, Y. (2022). A computational approach to Homans social exchange theory. *Physica A: Statistical Mechanics and its Applications,* 597, 127263.

Enzler, H. B., & Diekmann, A. (2019). All talk and no action? An analysis of environmental concern, income and greenhouse gas emissions in Switzerland. *Energy Research & Social Science,* 51, 12–19.

Erickson, B. H. (2004). The distribution of gendered social capital in Canada. In *Creation and Returns of Social Capital,* 27–50, Routledge, New York.

Fan, Y., Fang, C., & Zhang, Q. (2019). Coupling coordinated development between social economy and ecological environment in Chinese provincial capital cities: Assessment and policy implications. *Journal of Cleaner Production*, 229, 289–298.

Fawehinmi, O., Yusliza, M. Y., Mohamad, Z., Noor Faezah, J., & Muhammad, Z. (2020). Assessing the green behaviour of academics: The role of green human resource management and environmental knowledge. *International Journal of Manpower*, 41(7), 879–900.

Flap, H. (2002). No man is an island: The research programme of a social capital theory. In O. Favereau & E. Lazega (Eds.), *Conventions and Structures in Economic Organization: Markets, Networks and Hierarchies*, 29–59, London: Edward Elgar.

Frederiks, E. R., Stenner, K., & Hobman, E. V. (2015). Household energy use: Applying behavioural economics to understand consumer decision-making and behaviour. *Renewable and Sustainable Energy Reviews*, 41, 1385–1394.

Fukuyama, F. (1995). *Trust: The Social Virtues and the Creation of Prosperity.* London: Hamish Hamilton.

Fukuyama, F. (2001). Social capital, civil society and development. *Third World Quarterly*, 22(1), 7–20.

Fukuyama, F. (2002). Social capital and development: The coming agenda. *SAIS Review*, 22(1), 23–37.

Gao, S., Li, W., Ling, S., Dou, X., & Liu, X. (2019). An empirical study on the influence path of environmental risk perception on behavioral responses in China. *International Journal of Environmental Research and Public Health*, 16(16), 2856.

Ghorbani, M., Avazpour, L., & Rasekhi, S. (2016). Social capital analysis of rural women network in line with empowerment of local. *Quarterly of Social Studies and Research in Iran*, 5(2), 273–294. doi: 10.22059/jisr.2016.59243 (In Persian).

Glaeser, E. L., Laibson, D., & Sacerdote, B. (2002). An economic approach to social capital. *The Economic Journal*, 112(483), 437–458.

Gneezy, A., Imas, A., Brown, A., Nelson, L. D., & Norton, M. I. (2012). Paying to be nice: Consistency and costly prosocial behavior. *Management Science*, 58(1), 179–187.

Granovetter, M. (1985). Economic action and social structure: The problem of embeddedness. *American Journal of Sociology*, 91(3), 481–510.

Gunningham, N., Kagan, R. A., & Thornton, D. (2004). Social license and environmental protection: Why businesses go beyond compliance? *Law & Social Inquiry*, 29(2), 307–341.

Guo, Q. H., Li, S. P., & Li, H. (2018). Adoption behaviors of farmers' chemical fertilizer reduction measures based on the perspective of social norms. *J. Arid Land Resour. Environ*, 32, 50–55.

Guy, M. E., & McCandless, S. A. (2012). Social equity: Its legacy, its promise. *Public Administration Review*, 72(s1), S5–S13.

Hansen, J. E., & Sato, M. (2012). Paleoclimate implications for human-made climate change. In *Climate Change: Inferences from Paleoclimate and Regional Aspects*, 21–47, Vienna: Springer Vienna.

Hanss, D., Böhm, G., Doran, R., & Homburg, A. (2016). Sustainable consumption of groceries: The importance of believing that one can contribute to sustainable development. *Sustainable Development*, 24(6), 357–370.

Hartlieb, S., Loy, T. R., & Eierle, B. (2020). Does community social capital affect asymmetric cost behaviour? *Management Accounting Research*, 46, 100640.

Hayes, S. C., Barnes-Holmes, D., & Wilson, K. G. (2012). Contextual behavioral science: Creating a science more adequate to the challenge of the human condition. *Journal of Contextual Behavioral Science*, 1(1–2), 1–16.

Healy, T., & Côté, S. (2001). The well-being of nations: The role of human and social capital, education and skills. Organisation for Economic Cooperation and Development, 2 rue Andre Pascal, F-75775 Paris Cedex 16, France.

Hedström, P. (2005). *Dissecting the Social: On the Principles of Analytical Sociology*. Cambridge, UK.; New York: Cambridge University Press.

Helms, A. C. (2012). Keeping up with the Joneses: Neighborhood effects in housing renovation. *Regional Science and Urban Economics*, 42(1–2), 303–313.

Henrich, J., Boyd, R., Bowles, S., Camerer, C., Fehr, E., Gintis, H., & McElreath, R. (2001). Cooperation, reciprocity and punishment in fifteen small-scale societies.

Homans, G. C. (1961). *Social Behavior: Its Elementary Forms*. New York: Harcourt.

Homans, G. C. (2013). *The Human Group*, Routledge.

Intergovernmental Panel on Climate Change. Summary for policymakers. In *Climate Change 2014: Mitigation of Climate Change*. Contribution of Working Group III to the Fifth Assessment Report of the Intergovernmental Panel on Climate Change. Cambridge University Press: Cambridge, UK, 2014.

Jabbour, C. J. C. (2013). Environmental training in organisations: From a literature review to a framework for future research. *Resources, Conservation and Recycling*, 74, 144–155.

Jabbour, C. J. C., & Renwick, D. W. S. (2018). The soft side of environmentally-sustainable organizations. *RAUSP Management Journal*, 53, 622–627.

Jabbour, C. J. C., & de Sousa Jabbour, A. B. L. (2016). Green human resource management and green supply chain management: Linking two emerging agendas. *Journal of Cleaner Production*, 112, 1824–1833.

Janmaimool, P., & Denpaiboon, C. (2016). Evaluating determinants of rural villagers' engagement in conservation and waste management behaviors based on integrated conceptual framework of pro-environmental behavior. *Life Sciences, Society and Policy*, 12(1), 12.

Jansson, J., Pettersson, T., Mannberg, A., Brännlund, R., & Lindgren, U. (2017). Adoption of alternative fuel vehicles: Influence from neighbors, family and coworkers. *Transportation Research Part D: Transport and Environment*, 54, 61–73.

Jia, X., Chowdhury, M., Prayag, G., & Chowdhury, M. M. H. (2020). The role of social capital on proactive and reactive resilience of organizations post-disaster. *International Journal of Disaster Risk Reduction*, 48, 101614.

Jones, N. (2010). Environmental activation of citizens in the context of policy agenda formation and the influence of social capital. *The Social Science Journal*, 47(1), 121–136.

Joshi, Y., & Rahman, Z. (2015). Factors affecting green purchase behaviour and future research directions. *International Strategic Management Review*, 3(1–2), 128–143.

Kadushin, C. (2002). The motivational foundation of social networks. *Journal of Social Networks*, 24(1), 77–91.

Kant, S., & Vertinsky, I. (2022). The anatomy of social capital of a Canadian indigenous community: Implications of social trust field experiments for community-based forest management. *Forest Policy and Economics*, 144, 102822.

Kaur, J., & Bhardwaj, N. (2021). Their control will make or break the sustainable clothing deal: A study of the moderating impact of actual behavioural control on the purchase intention-behaviour gap for sustainable clothing in India. *Australasian Accounting, Business and Finance Journal*, 15(5), 59.

Kawachi, I. (1999). Social capital and community effects on population and individual health. *Annals of the New York Academy of Sciences*, 896(1), 120–130.

Kawachi, I., Kennedy, B. P., Lochner, K., & Prothrow-Stith, D. (1997). Social capital, income inequality, and mortality. *American Journal of Public Health*, 87(9), 1491–1498.

Kaza, S., Yao, L., Bhada-Tata, P., & Van Woerden, F. (2018). What a waste 2.0: A global snapshot of solid waste management to 2050. World Bank Publications.

Keuschnigg, M., Lovsjö, N., & Hedström, P. (2018). Analytical sociology and computational social science. *Journal of Computational Social Science*, 1, 3–14.

Khanpae, M., Karami, E., Maleksaeidi, H., & Keshavarz, M. (2020). Farmers' attitude towards using treated wastewater for irrigation: The question of sustainability. *Journal of Cleaner Production*, 243, 118541.

Kim, Y., & Choi, S. M. (2005). Antecedents of green purchase behavior: An examination of collectivism, environmental concern, and PCE. *Advances in Consumer Research*, 32, 592.

Kim, N., & Lee, K. (2023). Environmental consciousness, purchase intention, and actual purchase behavior of eco-friendly products: The moderating impact of situational context. *International Journal of Environmental Research and Public Health*, 20(7), 5312.

Kneipp, J. M., Gomes, C. M., Bichueti, R. S., Frizzo, K., & Perlin, A. P. (2019). Sustainable innovation practices and their relationship with the performance of industrial companies. *Revista de Gestão*, 26(2), 94–111.

Koberg, E., & Longoni, A. (2019). A systematic review of sustainable supply chain management in global supply chains. *Journal of Cleaner Production*, 207, 1084–1098.

Kollmuss, A., & Agyeman, J. (2002). Mind the gap: Why do people act environmentally and what are the barriers to pro-environmental behavior? *Environmental Education Research*, 8(3), 239–260.

Koopman, J., Matta, F. K., Scott, B. A., & Conlon, D. E. (2015). Ingratiation and popularity as antecedents of justice: A social exchange and social capital perspective. *Organizational Behavior and Human Decision Processes*, 131, 132–148.

Korea P&G, Korea Zero Waste Movement Network, Consumer Sustainability Survey 24 June 2020. [(accessed on 24 June 2020)]. Available online: https://m.waste21.or.kr/board/board_content.asp?menu=2&sub=5&idx=7500&b_type=BOARD5&page=3&b_kinds=&b_word=.

Krasny, M. E., Kalbacker, L., Stedman, R. C., & Russ, A. (2015). Measuring social capital among youth: Applications in environmental education. *Environmental Education Research*, 21(1), 1–23.

Lede, E., Meleady, R., & Seger, C. R. (2019). Optimizing the influence of social norms interventions: Applying social identity insights to motivate residential water conservation. *Journal of Environmental Psychology*, 62, 105–114.

Li, D., Zhao, L., Ma, S., Shao, S., & Zhang, L. (2019). What influences an individual's pro-environmental behavior? A literature reviews. *Resources, Conservation and Recycling*, 146, 28–34.

Li, L., Dingyi, S., Fengluan, S., Xiujun, T., & Noor, H. (2024). Effects of social capital and technology cognition on farmers' adoption of soil and water conservation tillage technology in the Loess Plateau of China. *Heliyon*, 10(5).

Liao, Z., Liu, X., & Sun, Y. (2023). Can corporate background characteristics predict environmental innovation? Evidence from a meta-analysis. *European Management Journal*, 41(6), 1047–1055.

Lin, Nan. 2001. Building a network theory of social capital, In N. Lin, K. S. Cook, and R. Burt (eds.), *Social Capital: Theory and Research*, 3–30, New York: Aldine de Gruyter.

Ling, M., & Xu, L. (2020). Relationships between personal values, micro-contextual factors and residents' pro-environmental behaviors: An explorative study. *Resources, Conservation and Recycling*, 156, 104697.

Liu, J., Qu, H., Huang, D., Chen, G., Yue, X., Zhao, X., & Liang, Z. (2014). The role of social capital in encouraging residents' pro-environmental behaviors in community-based ecotourism. *Tourism Management*, 41, 190–201.

Liu, P., Teng, M., & Han, C. (2020). How does environmental knowledge translate into pro-environmental behaviors? The mediating role of environmental attitudes and behavioral intentions. *Science of the Total Environment*, 728, 138126.

Liu, Y., Qu, Y., Lei, Z., & Jia, H. (2017). Understanding the evolution of sustainable consumption research. *Sustainable Development*, 25(5), 414–430.

Lliso, B., Pascual, U., & Engel, S. (2021). On the role of social equity in payments for ecosystem services in Latin America: A practitioner perspective. *Ecological Economics*, 182, 106928.

Lucas, K., Brooks, M., Darnton, A., & Jones, J. E. (2008). Promoting pro-environmental behaviour: Existing evidence and policy implications. *Environmental Science & Policy*, 11(5), 456–466.

Lyon, F. (2000). Trust, networks and norms: The creation of social capital in agricultural economies in Ghana. *World Development*, 28(4), 663–681.

MacGillivray, B. H. (2018). Beyond social capital: The norms, belief systems, and agency embedded in social networks shape resilience to climatic and geophysical hazards. *Environmental Science & Policy*, 89, 116–125.

Macy, M. W., & Willer, R. (2002). From factors to actors: Computational sociology and agent-based modeling. *Annual Review of Sociology*, 28(1), 143–166.

Maki, A., Carrico, A. R., Raimi, K. T., Truelove, H. B., Araujo, B., & Yeung, K. L. (2019). Meta-analysis of pro-environmental behaviour spillover. *Nature Sustainability*, 2(4), 307–315.

Maleknia, R., Heindorf, C., Rahimian, M., & Saadatmanesh, R. (2024). Do generational differences determine the conservation intention and behavior towards sacred trees? *Trees, Forests and People*, 16, 100591.

Malik, S. Y., Hayat Mughal, Y., Azam, T., Cao, Y., Wan, Z., Zhu, H., & Thurasamy, R. (2021). Corporate social responsibility, green human resources management, and sustainable performance: Is organizational citizenship behavior towards environment the missing link? *Sustainability*, 13(3), 1044.

Mantica, G., Stoop, R., & Stramaglia, S. (2017). *Emergent Complexity from Nonlinearity, in Physics, Engineering and the Life Sciences* (Vol. 191). Springer International Publishing.

Masoom, M. R. (2024). Social capital and health beliefs: Exploring the effect of bridging and bonding social capital on health locus of control among women in Dhaka. *Heliyon*, e28932. https://doi.org/10.1016/j.heliyon.2024.e28932.

Matthew, D. M., & Nicholas L. (2013). Social capital, type of crime, and social control. *Journal Research in Crime & Delinquency*, 62, 728–747.

Mepparambath, R. M., Le, D. T. T., Oon, J., Song, J., & Huynh, H. N. (2024). Influence of the built environment on social capital and physical activity in Singapore: A structural equation modelling analysis. *Sustainable Cities and Society*, 103, 105259.

Meyer, M. A. (2018). Social capital in disaster research. *Handbook of Disaster Research*, 263–286.

Michaelowa, A., & Sacherer, A. K. (Eds.). (2022). *Handbook of International Climate Finance*. Edward Elgar Publishing.

Mignone, J., Henley, H., Brown, J., O'Neil, J., & Ross, W. (2008). Information and communication technology in Aboriginal communities in Canada: Increasing Aboriginal social capital: A discussion paper. Faculty of Human Ecology, University of Manitoba.

Miller, E., & Buys, L. (2008). Retrofitting commercial office buildings for sustainability: Tenants' perspectives. *Journal of Property Investment & Finance*, 26(6), 552–561.

Moon, W. K., Kahlor, L. A., & Olson, H. C. (2020). Understanding public support for carbon capture and storage policy: The roles of social capital, stakeholder perceptions, and perceived risk/benefit of technology. *Energy Policy*, 139, 111312.

Morwitz, V. G., Steckel, J. H., & Gupta, A. (2007). When do purchase intentions predict sales? *International Journal of Forecasting*, 23(3), 347–364.

Mouw, T. (2006). Estimating the causal effect of social capital: A review of recent research. *Annu. Rev. Sociol.*, 32, 79–102.

Nahapiet, J., & Ghoshal, S. (1998). Social capital, intellectual capital, and the organizational advantage. *Academy of Management Review*, 23(2), 242–266.

Neale, R. E., Barnes, P. W., Robson, T. M., Neale, P. J., Williamson, C. E., Zepp, R. G., ... & Zhu, M. (2021). Environmental effects of stratospheric ozone depletion, UV radiation, and interactions with climate change: UNEP Environmental Effects Assessment Panel, Update 2020. *Photochemical & Photobiological Sciences*, 20(1), 1–67.

Newton, K. (2001). Trust, social capital, civil society, and democracy. *International Political Science Review*, 22(2), 201–214.

Nisbet, E. K., & Gick, M. L. (2008). Can health psychology help the planet? Applying theory and models of health behaviour to environmental actions. *Canadian Psychology/Psychologie Canadienne*, 49(4), 296.

Onyx, J., & Bullen, P. (2003). The different faces of social capital in NSW Australia. In *Social Capital and Participation in Everyday Life*, 45–58, Routledge.

Ostrom, E. (2000). Collective action and the evolution of social norms. *Journal of Economic Perspectives*, 14(3), 137–158.

Otto, S., Neaman, A., Richards, B., & Marió, A. (2016). Explaining the ambiguous relations between income, environmental knowledge, and environmentally significant behavior. *Society & Natural Resources*, 29(5), 628–632.

Pampel, F. C., & Hunter, L. M. (2012). Cohort change, diffusion, and support for environmental spending in the United States. *American Journal of Sociology*, 118(2), 420–448.

Park, K., Ewing, R., Scheer, B. C., & Tian, G. (2018). The impacts of built environment characteristics of rail station areas on household travel behavior. *Cities*, 74, 277–283.

Payne, G. T., Moore, C. B., Griffis, S. E., & Autry, C. W. (2011). Multilevel challenges and opportunities in social capital research. *Journal of Management*, 37(2), 491–520.

Perrin, C., & Nougaredes, B. (2022). An analytical framework to consider social justice issues in farmland preservation on the urban fringe. Insights from three French cases. *Journal of Rural Studies*, 93, 122–133.

Piwowar-Sulej, K., Iqbal, Q., Dagar, V., & Singh, S. (2024). Employees' eco-friendly innovative behaviors: Examining the role of individual and situational factors. *European Management Journal.* https://doi.org/10.1016/j.emj.2024.04.005.

Poirier-Pocovi, M., & Bailey, B. N. (2020). Sensitivity analysis of four crop water stress indices to ambient environmental conditions and stomatal conductance. *Scientia Horticulturae*, 259, 108825.

Portes, A. (1995). Economic sociology and the sociology of immigration: A conceptual overview. *The Economic Sociology of Immigration*, 1–41.

Portes, A. (2000). The two meanings of social capital. In *Sociological Forum*, 15, 1–12, Kluwer Academic Publishers–Plenum Publishers.

Pretty, J., & Ward, H. (2001). Social capital and the environment. *World Development*, 29, 209–227.

Putnam, R. D. (1994). Social capital and public affairs. *Bulletin of the American Academy of Arts and Sciences*, 5–19.

Putnam, R. R. D. (1995). Bowling alone: America's declining social capital. *Journal of Democracy*, 6(1), 65–78.

Railsback, S. F. (2019). *Agent-Based and Individual-Based Modeling: A Practical Introduction* (2nd edition). Princeton, NJ: Princeton University Press.

Redondo-Carretero, M. & Camarero-Izquierdo, C. (2017). Relationships between entrepreneurs in business incubators: An exploratory case study. *Journal of Business-to-Business Marketing*, 24(1), 57–74.

Ren, Z., Fu, Z., & Zhong, K. (2022). The influence of social capital on farmers' green control technology adoption behavior. *Frontiers in Psychology*, 13, 1001442.

Renwick, D. W., Redman, T., & Maguire, S. (2013). Green human resource management: A review and research agenda. *International Journal of Management Reviews*, 15(1), 1–14.

Rice, G. (2006). Pro-environmental behavior in Egypt: Is there a role for Islamic environmental ethics? *Journal of Business Ethics*, 65, 373–390.

Ritzer, G. (2011). Exchange, networks, and rational choice theories. In *Sociological Theory*, 8th ed., 416–453, New York: McGraw-Hill.

Roscoe, S., Subramanian, N., Jabbour, C. J., & Chong, T. (2019). Green human resource management and the enablers of green organisational culture: Enhancing a firm's environmental performance for sustainable development. *Business Strategy and the Environment*, 28(5), 737–749.

Rostila, M. (2007). Social capital and health in European welfare regimes: A multilevel approach. *Journal of European Social Policy*, 17(3), 223–239.

Savari, M., & Khaleghi, B. (2023). The role of social capital in forest conservation: An approach to deal with deforestation. *Science of the Total Environment*, 896, 165216.

Savari, M., & Khaleghi, B. (2024). Factors influencing the application of forest conservation behavior among rural communities in Iran. *Environmental and Sustainability Indicators*, 21, 100325.

Savari, M., & Shehitzadeh, S. (2023). The role of social capital in the environmental protection of agricultural lands in dry areas (Case study: Bavi County). *Journal of Arid Biome*, 13(2), 53–69. doi: 10.29252/aridbiom.2024.20672.1958.

Savari, M., Sheheytavi, A., & Amghani, M. S. (2023a). Promotion of adopting preventive behavioral intention toward biodiversity degradation among Iranian farmers. *Global Ecology and Conservation*, 43, e02450.

Savari, M., Damaneh, H. E., Damaneh, H. E., & Cotton, M. (2023b). Integrating the norm activation model and theory of planned behaviour to investigate farmer pro-environmental behavioural intention. *Scientific Reports*, 13(1), 5584.

Savari, M., Sheheytavi, A., & Amghani, M. S. (2023c). Factors underpinning Iranian farmers' intention to conserve biodiversity at the farm level. *Journal for Nature Conservation*, 73, 126419.

Savari, M., Mombeni, A. S., & Izadi, H. (2022a). Socio-psychological determinants of Iranian rural households' adoption of water consumption curtailment behaviors. *Scientific Reports*, 12(1), 13077.

Savari, M., Naghibeiranvand, F., & Asadi, Z. (2022b). Modeling environmentally responsible behaviors among rural women in the forested regions in Iran. *Global Ecology and Conservation*, 35, e02102.

Sawyer, R. K. (2005). *Social Emergence: Societies as Complex Systems.* Cambridge; New York: Cambridge University Press.

Schuitema, G., & De Groot, J. I. (2015). Green consumerism: The influence of product attributes and values on purchasing intentions. *Journal of Consumer Behaviour*, 14(1), 57–69.

Shi, H., Sui, D., Wu, H., & Zhao, M. (2018). The influence of social capital on farmers' participation in watershed ecological management behavior: Evidence from Heihe Basin. *China Rural Economy*, (1).

Shi, J., Lu, C., & Wei, Z. (2022). Effects of social capital on pro-environmental behaviors in Chinese residents. *Sustainability*, 14(21), 13855.

Siegel, D. A. (2009). Social networks and collective action. *American Journal of Political Science*, 53(1), 122–138.

Singh, R. L., & Singh, P. K. (2017). Global environmental problems. *Principles and Applications of Environmental Biotechnology for a Sustainable Future*, 13–41.

Siyambalapitiya, J., Zhang, X., & Liu, X. (2018). Green human resource management: A proposed model in the context of Sri Lanka's tourism industry. *Journal of Cleaner Production*, 201, 542–555.

Slangen, L. H., van Kooten, G. C., & Suchanek, P. (2004). Institutions, social capital and agricultural change in central and eastern Europe. *Journal of Rural Studies*, 20(2), 245–256.

Soutter, A. R. B., & Mõttus, R. (2020). "Global warming" versus "climate change": A replication on the association between political self-identification, question wording, and environmental beliefs. *Journal of Environmental Psychology*, 69, 101413.

Stadtfeld, C., Takács, K., & Vörös, A. (2020). The emergence and stability of groups in social networks. *Social Networks*, 60, 129–145.

Stapleton, A., McHugh, L., & Karekla, M. (2022). How to effectively promote eco-friendly behaviors: Insights from contextual behavioral science. *Sustainability*, 14(21), 13887.

Steg, L., & Vlek, C. (2009). Encouraging pro-environmental behaviour: An integrative review and research agenda. *Journal of Environmental Psychology*, 29(3), 309–317.

Stern, P. C. (2000). New environmental theories: Toward a coherent theory of environmentally significant behavior. *Journal of Social Issues*, 56(3), 407–424.

Su, W., Bataa, B., & Hahn, J. (2024). Does green human resources management (GHRM) promote employee environmental performance? A multilevel time-lagged study from Mongolia. *Journal of Environmental Planning and Management*, 67(10), 2135–2156.

Tahlyan, D., Stathopoulos, A., & Maness, M. (2022). Disentangling social capital: Understanding the effect of bonding and bridging on urban activity participation. *Transportation Research Interdisciplinary Perspectives*, 15, 100629.

Tang, Y., Geng, L., Schultz, P. W., Zhou, K., & Xiang, P. (2017). The effects of mindful learning on pro-environmental behavior: A self-expansion perspective. *Consciousness and Cognition*, 51, 140–148.

Teshome, A., de Graaff, J., & Kessler, A. (2016). Investments in land management in the north-western highlands of Ethiopia: The role of social capital. *Land Use Policy*, 57, 215–228.

Thompson, L. G. (2010). Climate change: The evidence and our options. *The Behavior Analyst*, 33, 153–170.

Thondhlana, G., & Hlatshwayo, T. N. (2018). Pro-environmental behaviour in student residences at Rhodes University, South Africa. *Sustainability*, 10(8), 2746.

Tirno, R. R., Islam, N., & Happy, K. (2023). Green HRM and ecofriendly behavior of employees: Relevance of proecological climate and environmental knowledge. *Heliyon*, 9(4).

Tobler, C., Visschers, V. H., & Siegrist, M. (2012). Addressing climate change: Determinants of consumers' willingness to act and to support policy measures. *Journal of Environmental Psychology*, 32(3), 197–207.

Truelove, H. B., Carrico, A. R., Weber, E. U., Raimi, K. T., & Vandenbergh, M. P. (2014). Positive and negative spillover of pro-environmental behavior: An integrative review and theoretical framework. *Global Environmental Change*, 29, 127–138.

Turner, J. C. (1987). *Rediscovering the Social Group: Self-Categorization Theory*. Oxford, UK; New York, NY, USA: B. Blackwell.

Van Oorschot, W., & Arts, W. (2005). The social capital of European welfare states: The crowding out hypothesis revisited. *Journal of European Social Policy*, 15(1), 5–26.

Veenstra, G. (2000). Social capital, SES and health: An individual-level analysis. *Social Science & Medicine*, 50(5), 619–629.

Vesely, S., Klöckner, C. A., & Brick, C. (2020). Pro-environmental behavior as a signal of cooperativeness: Evidence from a social dilemma experiment. *Journal of Environmental Psychology*, 67, 101362.

Vicente-Molina, M. A., Fernández-Sainz, A., & Izagirre-Olaizola, J. (2018). Does gender make a difference in pro-environmental behavior?

The case of the Basque Country University students. *Journal of Cleaner Production*, 176, 89–98.

Vicente-Molina, M. A., Fernández-Sáinz, A., & Izagirre-Olaizola, J. (2013). Environmental knowledge and other variables affecting pro-environmental behaviour: Comparison of university students from emerging and advanced countries. *Journal of Cleaner Production*, 61, 130–138.

Villalonga-Olives, E., & Kawachi, I. (2015). The measurement of social capital. *Gaceta Sanitaria*, 29(1), 62–64.

Wan, Q., & Du, W. (2022). Social capital, environmental knowledge, and pro-environmental behavior. *International Journal of Environmental Research and Public Health*, 19(3), 1443.

World Bank (1998). Social capital: The missing link? https://documents1.worldbank.org/curated/zh/902971468764409654/pdf/multi0page.pdf.

Wu, Y. F. (2018). Social class, social capital, and commercial insurance purchase behavior of urban and rural residents in my country: Based on the survey data of CGSS2015. *China Soft Sci*, 23, 56–66.

Xu, Z., Li, Y., Wang, C., & Shan, J. (2024). Social capital and environmentally friendly behaviors. *Environmental Science & Policy*, 151, 103612.

Yang, K. (2007). Individual social capital and its measurement in social surveys. *Survey Research Methods*, 1(1), 19–27.

Yang, R., Wong, C. W., & Miao, X. (2021). Analysis of the trend in the knowledge of environmental responsibility research. *Journal of Cleaner Production*, 278, 123402.

Yang, X. Y., & Cheng, Y. (2021). Can social networks enhance residents' environmental behavior? — An empirical study based on CGSS 2013 data. *J. Hefei Univ. Technol. (Soc. Sci. Ed.)*, 35, 1–11.

Yaqi, C., Xiao, H., Xiaoning, Z., & Mei, Q. (2023). Influence of social capital on rural household garbage sorting and recycling behavior: The moderating effect of class identity. *Waste Management*, 158, 84–92.

Yildiz, Ö., Rommel, J., Debor, S., Holstenkamp, L., Mey, F., Müller, J. R., ... & Rognli, J. (2015). Renewable energy cooperatives as gatekeepers or facilitators? Recent developments in Germany and a multi-disciplinary research agenda. *Energy Research & Social Science*, 6, 59–73.

Yun, S., & Lee, J. (2015). Advancing societal readiness toward renewable energy system adoption with a socio-technical perspective. *Technological Forecasting and Social Change*, 95, 170–181.

Zhang, L., & Shih, T. (2023). Collective and individual social capital and the impact on incubator tenants' graduation. *Journal of the Knowledge Economy*, 14(3), 2692–2722.

Zhang, L., He, G., Mol, A. P., & Zhu, X. (2013). Power politics in the revision of China's Environmental Protection Law. *Environmental Politics*, 22(6), 1029–1035.

Zhang, W. H. (2003). Social capital: Theoretical discussion and empirical studies. *Sociological Studies*, 4, 23–35.

Zhang, Z., Yang, A., & Wang, Y. (2023). How do social capital and village-level organizational trust affect farmers' climate-related disaster adaptation behavior? Evidence from Hunan Province, China. *International Journal of Disaster Risk Reduction*, 99, 104083.

Zheng, S., Yin, K., & Yu, L. (2022). Factors influencing the farmer's chemical fertilizer reduction behavior from the perspective of farmer differentiation. *Heliyon*, 8(12).

Zhu, Q., Sarkis, J., & Lai, K. H. (2008). Confirmation of a measurement model for green supply chain management practices implementation. *International Journal of Production Economics*, 111(2), 261–273.

Chapter 9

Measures to Manage the Urban Water Quality for Public Health

Shashikant Nishant Sharma,[a] **Kavita Dehalwar,**[a] **and Ashutosh Kumar Pandey**[b]

[a]*Maulana Azad National Institute of Technology, Bhopal, Madhya Pradesh, India*
[b]*Jaipur School of Mass Communication, Jaipur, Rajasthan, India*

urp2025@gmail.com

Urban water quality management is paramount for promoting good public health in urban areas. The rapid urbanization and increasing population density pose significant challenges to maintaining clean and safe water supplies. This chapter focuses on the strategies and approaches employed in urban water quality management to ensure safe drinking water and protect public health. Community engagement and public awareness campaigns are essential in fostering responsible water use, pollution prevention, and adopting sustainable practices. It also examines the role of urban planning and infrastructure development in minimizing pollution sources and protecting water resources. Case studies from urban areas in Delhi are presented to illustrate water quality management practices and highlight lessons learned.

Environmentalism in Healthcare: Caring for Tomorrow Ecologically
Edited by Jacqueline A. Stagner and David S.-K. Ting

ISBN 978-981-5129-95-3 (Hardcover), 978-1-003-74869-4 (eBook)
www.jennystanford.com

DOI: 10.1201/9781003748694-9

The chapter concludes by emphasizing the need for integrated and holistic urban water quality management approaches. This involves addressing not only the treatment of contaminated water but also the prevention of pollution at its source through sustainable urban planning, wastewater management, and pollution control measures. In conclusion, urban water quality management is critical in promoting good public health in urban areas.

9.1 Introduction

India is projected to need 1.5 trillion cubic meters of water by 2030. However, only 16.8% of the sewage generated in the country is currently treated. This substantial disparity between water demand and treated water supply underscores the importance of recycling and reusing treated wastewater. According to data from the Central Pollution Control Board (CPCB), less than 5% of the treated wastewater is currently being reused domestically (Somnath Pal, 2023). Urban areas are characterized by a high population density, extensive infrastructure, and various sources of pollution, making water quality management a critical concern for maintaining public health. Access to clean and safe water is vital for human well-being, as it directly impacts drinking water supplies, recreational activities, and the overall environment of cities. Urban water quality management aims to protect, preserve, and enhance water resources in urban settings, explicitly promoting good public health (Xiang et al., 2021). In recent years, rapid urbanization and population growth have placed significant pressure on water resources and infrastructure in urban areas. Industrial activities, domestic wastewater, stormwater runoff, and other human-induced factors contribute to the deterioration of water quality. Pollution sources such as improper waste disposal, agricultural runoff, and industrial discharges introduce harmful contaminants into water bodies, posing severe health risks to urban communities (Roy, 2016).

Effective water quality management strategies are essential to mitigate these risks and protect public health. These strategies involve monitoring and assessing the quality of water resources, implementing appropriate treatment processes, and enforcing regulatory measures to prevent pollution. Education and awareness programs can also be crucial in promoting responsible water use and reducing contamination at the source (Jamwal et al., 2008). Waterborne diseases are a significant concern in urban environments where densely populated areas can quickly become breeding grounds for pathogens. Contaminated water can transmit various diseases, including gastrointestinal infections, cholera, typhoid fever, and hepatitis A. These illnesses can lead to severe health consequences and even fatalities, particularly among vulnerable populations such as children, the elderly, and individuals with compromised immune systems (Verma et al., 2022).

Urban water quality management strives to address these challenges by establishing robust water treatment systems, implementing disinfection protocols, and enforcing strict water quality standards. By ensuring the provision of safe drinking water, urban communities can experience improved public health outcomes, reduced disease burden, and enhanced quality of life (Acharya et al., 2018). Furthermore, an integrated approach to water management is crucial for achieving sustainable urban development. Urban planners, policymakers, water authorities, and public health agencies must collaborate to develop comprehensive strategies that address water quality concerns holistically. This approach involves considering the entire water cycle, including source protection, wastewater treatment, stormwater management, and water reuse, to optimize resource efficiency, minimize pollution, and safeguard public health (Bidhuri & Khan, 2020).

Stormwater management plays a crucial role in maintaining urban water quality and safeguarding public health. Uncontrolled stormwater runoff carries pollutants such as heavy metals, sediments, nutrients, and pathogens into urban water bodies, leading to water contamination and increased risks of waterborne diseases (Hatt et al., 2006). Traditional drainage systems, which prioritize rapid removal of stormwater, often exacerbate pollution by directly channeling untreated runoff into surface water bodies (Fletcher et al., 2013).

Modern stormwater management approaches, including green infrastructure, low-impact development, and best management practices, offer sustainable solutions to mitigate pollution while improving urban resilience (Patel et al., 2024). Green infrastructure methods such as bioretention systems, permeable pavements, constructed wetlands, and green roofs help filter contaminants, enhance groundwater recharge, and reduce peak flow rates (Ahiablame et al., 2012). Low-impact development strategies focus on maintaining natural hydrological processes and minimizing impervious surfaces to reduce stormwater runoff at the source (Dietz, 2007). Studies suggest that best management practices, including detention basins and vegetative swales, are effective in capturing pollutants and improving the quality of urban stormwater before it reaches municipal water supplies (Trowsdale & Simcock, 2011).

Furthermore, integrated stormwater management approaches emphasize the need for regulatory frameworks, community engagement, and technological innovations to enhance water quality management (Roy et al., 2008). Monitoring programs and real-time data collection have proven effective in identifying contamination hotspots and optimizing stormwater treatment interventions (Shuster et al., 2005). As urbanization continues to grow, implementing holistic stormwater management strategies is essential to reducing public health risks associated with poor water quality.

By incorporating evidence-based stormwater management measures, cities can achieve sustainable urban water systems, ensuring cleaner water resources and better public health outcomes.

Urban water quality management plays a vital role in safeguarding public health within rapidly growing urban environments. By prioritizing the protection of water resources, implementing effective treatment processes, and enforcing stringent regulations, urban communities can access clean and safe water, thereby reducing the risks of waterborne diseases and promoting the well-being of their residents. A holistic and integrated approach to water management is crucial for sustainable urban development and ensuring a healthy future for urban populations.

This study explores effective measures to manage urban water quality to safeguard public health. Key research questions include: What are the primary sources of urban water pollution, and how do they impact public health? What regulatory frameworks and management strategies are currently in place to ensure safe urban water quality? How effective are existing water treatment and monitoring systems in mitigating health risks? What role do community participation and technological advancements play in improving urban water quality management? How can integrated urban planning contribute to sustainable water quality management for public health protection? These questions guide the investigation into policies, technologies, and practices essential for maintaining clean and safe urban water.

9.2 Methodology

Studying urban water quality management for good public health requires a rigorous research methodology to investigate the complex interactions between water quality, public health, and urban environments. The following research methodology was undertaken:

- **Research Objectives:** The study began by clearly defining the research objectives and questions. These objectives aimed to understand the current state of urban water quality, assess its impact on public health, and identify effective management strategies for promoting good public health outcomes.
- **Literature Review:** A comprehensive literature review was conducted to gather existing knowledge and theories related to urban water quality management and its impact on public health, as shown in Fig. 9.1. This step provided a foundation for the research, helped identify research gaps, and guided the development of the research framework (Dehalwar & Sharma, 2023).

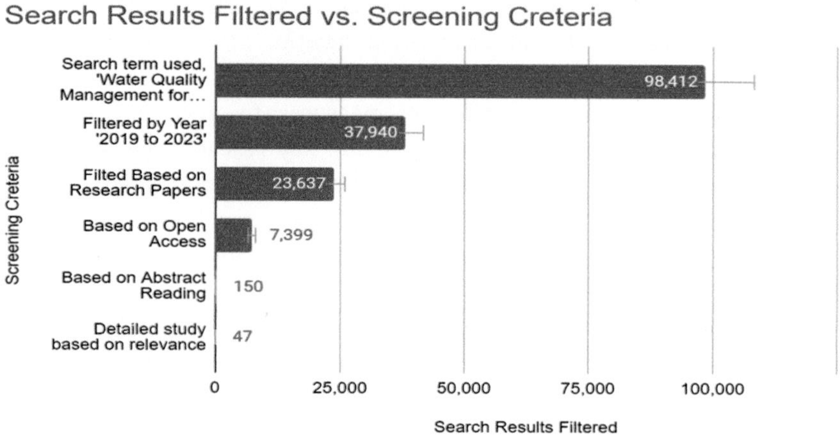

Figure 9.1 Systematic literature review conducted for the study.

The initial search yielded many search results, with 98,412 articles related to "Water Quality Management for Good Public Health." The search results were filtered based on the publication year, focusing on research conducted between 2019 and 2023. This reduced the number of relevant articles to 37,940, indicating a more recent and up-to-date selection of studies, as shown in Fig. 9.1. Among the filtered results, 23,637 articles were identified as research papers. This indicates a substantial number of scholarly studies on water quality management and its impact on public health. From the research papers, 7,399 articles were classified as open access, meaning they are freely available to the public. The availability of open-access articles enhances accessibility and allows for a broader dissemination of knowledge on the subject. A subset of 150 articles was selected for further examination based on abstract reading. Abstracts provide a concise summary of the research article and help assess the relevance of the study to the specific topic of water quality management for good public health. Out of the subset of 150 articles, 47 were identified for a more detailed study based on their relevance to the research objectives. These selected articles are likely to provide valuable insights and in-depth analysis of water quality management practices and their implications for public health.

This study is based on the findings of field studies, surveys, and experimental analyses conducted by the CPCB of India in Delhi. The methodology follows a secondary data analysis approach, where officially published reports and datasets from CPCB have been reviewed and interpreted to assess urban water quality management measures and their impact on public health.

9.3 Finding

The CPCB in India offers categorizations for water quality, utilizing a range of parameters for evaluation. These classifications serve as a valuable tool for gauging the appropriateness of water for diverse applications. For instance, they assist in determining whether water is suitable for drinking, recreational activities, industrial use, or agricultural purposes. The specifics of these classifications, including the parameters considered and the corresponding suitability for various uses, are outlined in detail in Table 9.1. This information aids stakeholders, policymakers, and the general public in making informed decisions regarding water usage and management practices.

Drinking Water Standard (Class A)

- Water suitable for human consumption without conventional treatment, but after disinfection.
- The highest quality standard for water intended for direct human consumption.

Bathing Water Standard (Class B)

- Water suitable for outdoor bathing purposes.
- Parameters may be less stringent than drinking water standards, but still ensure safety for recreational activities.

Water for Fisheries (Class C)

- Water quality is suitable for protecting and propagating fish and other aquatic organisms.
- Parameters are defined to support aquatic life and maintain a healthy ecosystem.

Table 9.1 Classification of surface water based on quality

Sr. No.	Designated-best-use	Drinking water source without conventional treatment but after disinfection	Outdoor bathing (organised)	Drinking water source after conventional treatment and disinfection	Propagation of wildlife and fisheries	Irrigation, industrial cooling, controlled waste disposal
1	Class of water	A	B	C	D	E
2	Total coliform organisms (MPN/100 ml)	≤ 50	≤ 500	≤ 5000	N/A	N/A
3	pH range	6.5–8.5	6.5–8.5	6.5–8.5	6.5–8.5	6–8.5
4	Dissolved oxygen (mg/l)	≥ 6	≥ 5	≥ 4	≥ 4	N/A
5	Biochemical oxygen demand (mg/l, 5 days at 20 °C)	≤ 2	≤ 3	≤ 3	N/A	N/A
6	Free ammonia (as N) (mg/l)	N/A	N/A	N/A	≤ 1.2	N/A
7	Electrical conductivity (μmhos/cm at 25 °C)	N/A	N/A	N/A	N/A	≤ 2250
8	Sodium absorption ratio	N/A	N/A	N/A	N/A	≤ 26
9	Boron (mg/l)	N/A	N/A	N/A	N/A	≤ 2
10	Turbidity (NTU)	≤ 1	≤ 5	≤ 10	N/A	N/A
11	Total dissolved solids (mg/l)	≤ 500	≤ 1000	≤ 2000	N/A	≤ 2100
12	Hardness (mg/l as $CaCO_3$)	≤ 300	≤ 500	≤ 600	N/A	N/A
13	Lead (mg/l)	≤ 0.01	≤ 0.05	≤ 0.1	N/A	N/A
14	Arsenic (mg/l)	≤ 0.01	≤ 0.05	≤ 0.1	N/A	N/A

Source: Central Pollution & Control Board, 2008

Irrigation Water Quality (Class D)

- Water suitable for agricultural purposes, including irrigation.
- Standards consider factors that may affect soil quality and crop health.

Industrial Water Quality (Class E)

- Water quality is suitable for industrial processes.
- Standards account for parameters that may impact industrial operations without causing significant harm to the environment. Each category is defined by distinct criteria and permissible thresholds for a variety of physical, chemical, and biological factors, including pH, dissolved oxygen (DO), biochemical oxygen demand (BOD), and total coliform levels.

The data in Table 9.2 indicates that most water treatment plants operate close to or exceed their peak production capacities, with Bhagirathi (106.5 MGD) and Nangloi (42 MGD) surpassing their limits. Wazirabad and Haiderpur are key contributors, producing 124 MGD and 210 MGD, respectively. The primary raw

Table 9.2 Daily water production from different sources for drinking water

Water treatment plant	Peak production capacity (MGD)	Raw water source	Average production per day
Chandrawal	98	Wazirabad Pond	93.5
Wazirabad	124	-Do-	124
Haiderpur	220	WJC Canal	210
Nangloi	40	-Do-	42
Okhla	20	Recycled process waste from Chandrawal & R.W.	21
Dwarka	–	WJC Canal	46.5
Bawana	–	WJC Canal	18.5
Bhagirathi	100	Upper Ganga Canal	106.5
Sonia Vihar	144	-Do-	141

Source: Delhi Jal Board, Delhi, 2023

water sources are the Wazirabad Pond and the Western Yamuna Canal (WJC), while Bhagirathi and Sonia Vihar rely on the Upper Ganga Canal. Notably, the Okhla plant contributes 21 MGD using recycled process waste, showcasing water reuse potential. Some plants, like Dwarka and Bawana, lack specified peak capacities but still contribute significantly. Overall, the data highlights efficient utilization, reliance on major sources, and the importance of expanding recycling initiatives.

9.3.1 Analysis of Water Production in Delhi

1. **Water Treatment Plants:**
   - **Chandrawal:** With a peak production capacity of 98 MGD, utilizing raw water from Wazirabad Pond, the average daily production is 93.5 MGD.
   - **Wazirabad:** This plant has a peak capacity of 124 MGD, drawing water from Wazirabad Pond, and consistently produces 124 MGD.
   - **Haiderpur:** Operating at a peak capacity of 220 MGD, it draws water from the WJC Canal, providing an average daily production of 210 MGD.
   - **Nangloi:** With a capacity of 40 MGD, the plant draws water from the WJC Canal, producing an average of 42 MGD.
   - **Okhla:** Utilizing recycled process waste from Chandrawal and raw water, this plant has a capacity of 20 MGD and produces 21 MGD on average.
   - **Dwarka:** Drawing water from the WJC Canal, this plant has an unspecified peak capacity and produces an average of 46.5 MGD.
   - **Bawana:** With an unspecified peak capacity, this plant draws water from the WJC Canal and produces an average of 18.5 MGD.
   - **Bhagirathi:** Operating at a peak capacity of 100 MGD and drawing water from the Upper Ganga Canal, the average production is 106.5 MGD.

- **Sonia Vihar:** With a peak capacity of 144 MGD, drawing water from the Upper Ganga Canal, it produces an average of 141 MGD.

Total Production from Water Treatment Plants: 803.00 MGD

2. **Recycling/Process Waste Water Plants:** Recycling plants at Wazirabad, Haiderpur, Bhagirathi, and Chandrawal collectively produce 31.5 MGD from recycled process waste.

   Total Production from Recycling Plants: 31.5 MGD

3. **Groundwater Sources:** Groundwater sources, including production from Ranney wells & Tube wells, contribute 877 MGD.

   Total Production from Groundwater Sources: 877 MGD

The water production in Delhi is diversified, drawing from various sources such as Yamuna water, Ganga water, recycling plants, and groundwater sources. Groundwater contributes significantly to the overall water supply, providing a substantial 877 MGD. The utilization of recycled process waste in certain plants indicates a commitment to sustainable water management practices (Yadav & Khandegar, 2019).

This analysis provides a comprehensive overview of the diverse sources and production capacities contributing to Delhi's water supply, highlighting the importance of managing multiple water sources to meet the city's demands.

As if it was not enough that Delhi's air is among the world's most polluted, a new study has now shown that the city's tap water is the most unsafe among 21 state capitals. The national capital is at the bottom of the list, ranking based on the water quality of tap water released by the Bureau of Indian Standards (BIS) (Delhi Jal Board, 2024).

The national capital, Delhi, could face a drinking water crisis in some areas as the Wazirabad, Chandrawal, and Okhla water treatment plants have been shut down due to the rising water level in the Yamuna River, as detailed in Table 9.3 (Business Today Desk, 2023).

Table 9.3 Daily water samples collected from different areas of Delhi

S. No.	Zonal lab	Total number of samples collected	Satisfactory	Total number of unsatisfactory	Address	Clarity	R/Cl_2
1	Wazirabad	77	76	1	H. No. 759 Chabi Ganj Kashmiri Gate	–	–
2	Haiderpur	37	36	1	H. No. 174, Pkt-5, Sector-2, Rohini	–	–
3	Bhagirathi / TYR	60	54	6	H. No. E-364, 365, 366, Nirman Vihar Vikash Marg; H. No.- B-186, 187, 188 Gali No. 7, Ashok Nagar, Shahdara	HAZY	NIL
4	Greater Kailash	42	41	1	H.No.-162 R/O Sachin Bidhuri, Alla Mohalla, Tehkhand Village	Turbid	N.D.
5	Okhla	45	45	Nil	N/A	–	–
6	Nangloi	130	129	1	B-434, B Block, JJ Colony, Camp No. 02, Nangloi	Sewage	Nil
7	Dwarka	49	45	4	Rz – G- 39/B, Jandelwan Chowk, Raj Nagar II; C – 127, Sector 03, Phase II, Dwarka; Rz – 2A, G. No. 17, Raj Nagar II; C – 2/80, Vijay Enclave	Sewage	Nil
8	Bawana	22	22	Nil	N/A	–	–
	Total	**462**	**448**	**14**	**N/A**	–	–

Source: Delhi Jal Board, Delhi, 2023

The data on water quality testing done by the Delhi Jal Board across zonal labs reveals that out of 462 samples collected, 448 were satisfactory, while 14 were found unsatisfactory, as shown in Table 9.3. Most zones reported minimal unsatisfactory cases, with Okhla and Bawana showing no issues. However, Bhagirathi/TYR had the highest number of unsatisfactory samples (6), with water appearing hazy and no residual chlorine detected. Dwarka (4) and Nangloi (1) also reported contamination, with samples indicating sewage presence and no residual chlorine. Greater Kailash reported one turbid sample with no detectable chlorine. These findings highlight the need for stricter monitoring in specific areas to ensure safe drinking water quality.

The CPCB, in collaboration with State Pollution Control Boards (SPCBs) and Pollution Control Committees (PCCs), has implemented a comprehensive National Water Quality Monitoring Programme (NWMP) aimed at assessing and managing water quality across India. This initiative has resulted in the establishment of a robust monitoring network spanning 4,294 locations nationwide, encompassing 28 States and 7 Union Territories (UTs) as shown in Table 9.4.

Table 9.4 Status of water quality monitoring network state-wise under NWMP

S. N.	State/Ut	River	Lake	Tank	Pond	Creek/ Sea/ Coastal	Canal	Drain	STP	Ground-water	Total
1	Andhra Pradesh	42	3	1	0	11	6	4	1	33	123
2	Arunachal Pradesh	0	0	0	0	0	0	0	0	0	29
3	Assam	100	6	1	27	0	0	0	0	64	198
4	Bihar	96	3	0	2	0	0	0	0	70	171
5	Chandigarh	0	1	0	0	0	0	3	0	0	11
6	Chhattisgarh	29	1	1	0	0	0	0	0	8	39
7	Daman & Diu, Dadra & Nagar Haveli	0	0	0	0	0	0	0	0	12	24

(Continued)

Table 9.4 (*Continued*)

S. N.	State/Ut	River	Lake	Tank	Pond	Creek/ Sea/ Coastal	Canal	Drain	STP	Ground-water	Total
8	Delhi	9	4	0	0	0	2	9	0	45	75
9	Goa	32	9	1	0	11	3	0	0	10	67
10	Gujarat	67	20	2	3	2	3	0	0	89	187
11	Haryana	22	3	3	0	0	14	1	0	29	73
12	Himachal Pradesh	143	5	0	0	0	0	23	0	49	220
13	Jammu & Kashmir and Ladakh	64	36	1	1	0	0	1	0	23	124
14	Jharkhand	65	4	4	0	0	0	0	0	3	76
15	Karnataka	109	95	5	0	0	0	0	0	3	287
16	Kerala	75	16	0	0	0	0	0	3	34	131
17	Lakshadweep	0	0	0	0	0	0	0	0	42	45
18	Madhya Pradesh	158	22	1	12	0	0	0	0	54	247
19	Maharashtra	162	0	0	0	0	34	0	0	50	256
20	Manipur	41	5	1	13	0	0	10	0	10	70
21	Meghalaya	64	7	1	2	0	0	0	0	13	84
22	Mizoram	46	1	0	2	0	0	0	0	26	76
23	Nagaland	19	2	0	0	0	0	0	0	10	31
24	Odisha	128	7	8	95	0	9	4	3	90	344
25	Puducherry	6	3	0	0	0	0	0	22	22	31
26	Punjab	59	3	3	0	0	0	0	0	46	129
27	Rajasthan	35	17	1	5	0	5	0	0	139	199
28	Sikkim	0	0	0	0	0	0	3	16	3	3
29	Tamil Nadu	86	1	1	1	34	5	5	0	22	177
30	Telangana	55	37	13	0	0	13	13	11	45	259
31	Tripura	8	10	10	0	0	0	7	7	57	120
32	Uttar Pradesh	10	3	1	1	0	1	0	0	40	160
33	Uttarakhand	3	1	0	0	0	2	4	3	19	69
34	West Bengal	59	376	138	106	189	0	0	0	68	4294

Source: CPCB Annual Report 2020–2021

Table 9.5 Water quality of River Yamuna ([March, 2020, pre-lockdown] and [April, 2020, lockdown])

Parameters	Primary water quality criteria for outdoor bathing	Palla-pre-lockdown	Palla-Lockdown	Nizamuddin Bridge-pre-lockdown	Nizamuddin Bridge-lockdown	Okhla Barrage u/s-pre-lockdown	Okhla Barrage u/s-lockdown
pH	6.5–8.5	8.7	7.8	7.3	7.2	7.2	7.1
Conductivity (µs/cm)	–	668	273 (−59.18%)	1369	460 (−66.40%)	861	488 (−43.32%)
DO (mg/l)	5	17.1	8.3 (−51.46%)	Not detectable	2.4	ND	1.2 (increase)
BOD (mg/l)	3	7.9	2 (−74.60%)	57	5.6 (−90.18%)	27	6.1 (−77.41%)
COD (mg/l)	–	28	6 (−78.57%)	90	16 (−82.22%)	95	18 (−81.05%)

The table provides a detailed overview of the distribution of monitoring sites across different states and a state-wise breakdown of the water quality monitoring network under the NWMP.

This network, strategically positioned to cover diverse geographic and ecological regions, serves as a vital tool for tracking water quality parameters and identifying areas requiring intervention to mitigate pollution. The data collected through this extensive network is invaluable for policymakers, researchers, and environmentalists in formulating effective strategies to safeguard water resources.

During the lockdown, water samples were collected from the Yamuna River in Delhi and from major drains contributing to pollution in the city, as shown in Table 9.5.

The analysis of these samples revealed the following findings:

- **Compliance with Water Quality Criteria:** The water sample collected at Palla met the primary water quality criteria for outdoor bathing. However, the other two locations, namely Nizamuddin Bridge and Okhla Barrage u/s, did not comply with the primary water quality criteria for bathing.
- **Trends in Water Quality Parameters:** A decreasing trend was observed regarding BOD and chemical oxygen demand (COD) at the monitored locations, except Palla. Conversely, DO showed an increasing trend.
- **Alterations in the Water Quality of Drains:** In April 2020, a declining pattern was observed in the water quality of two drains, specifically the Najafgarh and Shahdara drains, as indicated by reductions in suspended solids, BOD, and COD.

The changes in water quality of the Yamuna River can be attributed to several factors:

- **Dilution Effect:** The release of fresh water from the Wazirabad Barrage contributed to the dilution of drain water, thereby improving the overall water quality.
- **Self-Purification:** The availability of dilution aided in the self-purification process downstream of the Yamuna River.

- **Reduction in Industrial Effluent Discharge:** Due to lockdown measures, there was no discharge of industrial effluents (approximately 35.9 MLD) from both upstream and downstream sources in Delhi, further improving water quality.
- **Improved Solar Light Penetration:** With reduced human activity and industrial pollution, there was better penetration of solar light, leading to improved physical visibility and potentially aiding in water quality improvement.
- **Reduction in Human Activities:** The closure of industries and restrictions on human activities such as the disposal of religious materials, solid waste, bathing, and clothes washing also contributed to the improved water quality during the lockdown period.

These findings highlight the significant impact that human activities, industrial discharges, and dilution effects have on the water quality of the Yamuna River. The temporary improvements observed during the lockdown period underscore the importance of effective water management practices and pollution control measures to ensure urban water bodies' long-term health and sustainability. Decentralized water treatment (DWT) systems are designed to process the water from individual sources. In urban areas like Delhi, a blend of centralized, decentralized, and on-site water management systems may be employed to collectively address the drinking water needs of the entire city or town. Utilizing post-treatment data from WTPs in Delhi, it is evident that improvements have been made in water quality. However, a comprehensive approach that includes the integration of decentralized wastewater management can further enhance the city's water supply and positively impact public health. The analysis provides a data-driven basis for considering decentralized systems as a complementary solution to address water quality challenges in Delhi, thereby contributing to the overall well-being of its residents.

Delhi's water sources are contaminated with several pollutants that exceed permissible limits, posing significant public health risks. Key contaminants include:

- **Fluoride**: Elevated fluoride levels have been detected in Delhi's groundwater, with concentrations surpassing the BIS limit of 1.5 mg/l. Excessive fluoride intake can lead to dental and skeletal fluorosis (Ahmad, 2025).
- **Nitrate**: Nitrate contamination, primarily from agricultural runoff and improper waste disposal, affects approximately 20% of groundwater samples nationwide, exceeding the BIS limit of 45 mg/l. While specific data for Delhi is limited, similar urban areas have reported nitrate levels surpassing safe thresholds, which can cause health issues like methemoglobinemia, especially in infants.
- **Chloride**: High chloride concentrations, indicative of salinity, have been observed in groundwater samples, particularly in regions like Haryana. Although direct data for Delhi is scarce, the proximity suggests potential similar challenges. Excessive chloride levels can affect water taste and corrode plumbing systems.
- **Iron**: Iron contamination is prevalent in northern and central India, with 13.2% of groundwater samples exceeding the BIS limit of 1.0 mg/l. States like Uttar Pradesh and Bihar report significant exceedances. While specific figures for Delhi are not detailed, the regional trend indicates potential concerns. High iron content can impart a metallic taste and stain laundry and fixtures.
- **Arsenic**: Arsenic contamination has been identified in various parts of India, posing severe health risks such as cancer and skin lesions. While the provided sources do not specify arsenic levels in Delhi, the presence of arsenic in neighboring regions suggests a need for vigilance.
- **Total Coliforms**: The CPCB specifies that for water classified under "Drinking water source after conventional treatment and disinfection" (Class C), total coliform organism count should be 5000 MPN/100 ml or less. Elevated coliform counts indicate fecal contamination, raising concerns about waterborne diseases.
- **BOD**: For Class C water, the CPCB sets a BOD limit of 3 mg/l or less. Higher BOD levels suggest organic pollution, which can deplete oxygen in water bodies, harming aquatic life.

These contaminants often exceed regulatory standards, underscoring the need for enhanced water treatment processes, pollution control measures, and regular monitoring to safeguard public health in Delhi.

9.4 Discussion

Delhi has implemented various water policy interventions aimed at improving water quality and management. The effectiveness of these measures has been mixed, with notable successes and ongoing challenges:

1. **Free Water Policy**: In 2013, the Delhi government introduced a policy providing 20,000 liters of free water per month to households with metered connections. This initiative incentivized the installation of water meters, leading to an increase in metered households. However, it did not significantly reduce non-revenue water (NRW), which includes water lost due to leaks and theft. Additionally, unmetered households, often in lower-income areas, did not benefit from this policy, highlighting issues of equity in water distribution (Sharma & Harvey, 2023).
2. **Water Conservation Measures**: To address water scarcity, the Delhi government has imposed fines for water wastage, such as overflowing tanks and excessive use. This policy aimed to promote responsible water usage among residents. While it raised awareness, the overall impact on water conservation has been limited, as enforcement remains inconsistent (Addo, Thoms, & Parsons, 2019; Golladay et al., 2021).
3. **Wastewater Treatment and Reuse**: Policies have been introduced to encourage the treatment and reuse of wastewater for non-potable purposes. The Master Plan for Delhi emphasizes 100% treatment and maximum reuse of wastewater in new developments. However, implementation has been slow, and existing infrastructure struggles to meet these goals, resulting in continued discharge of untreated or partially treated wastewater into the Yamuna River (Goyal & Kumar, 2020).

4. **Collaborative Planning Initiatives**: Efforts to integrate water policies into urban development plans through collaborative planning have been proposed. These initiatives aim to involve various stakeholders in the planning process to create more effective and sustainable water management strategies. While the framework exists, practical application has faced challenges due to bureaucratic hurdles and a lack of coordination among agencies (Kumar, 2022; Kumar & Goyal, 2025).
5. **Groundwater Regulation**: To prevent overexploitation of groundwater, authorities have implemented measures to limit the installation of new tube wells. Despite these interventions, illegal extraction persists, leading to continued depletion and contamination of groundwater resources (Roy et al., 2020).
6. **Infrastructure Development**: The Delhi Jal Board has undertaken projects to augment water supply and improve distribution networks. While these efforts have enhanced access to piped water in some areas, challenges such as aging infrastructure, leakage, and unequal distribution remain prevalent.

Delhi's water policy interventions have led to some improvements in water access and awareness, but significant challenges persist in achieving comprehensive water quality enhancement. Issues such as policy enforcement, infrastructural limitations, and socio-economic disparities continue to hinder the effectiveness of these interventions.

Delhi faces significant challenges in water management due to rapid urbanization, population growth, and limited water resources. To address these issues, the city has implemented various strategies, including rainwater harvesting mandates and wastewater recycling initiatives. However, these efforts have seen mixed success due to factors such as enforcement challenges and infrastructural limitations. By examining water management practices from other major global cities, valuable insights can be gained to enhance Delhi's approach (Parveen & Ahmad, 2024).

Table 9.6 provides a comparative analysis of water management strategies employed by Delhi and other global cities.

Table 9.6 Comparative analysis of water management strategies employed by Delhi and other global cities

City	Water management strategy	Details	Outcome/Impact
Delhi	**Rainwater harvesting mandate**	Since 2016, Delhi has mandated the installation of rainwater harvesting systems in all public and private properties measuring 100 square meters or above. The Delhi Jal Board has constructed rainwater harvesting structures in 594 of its buildings.	Implementation has faced challenges, including a lack of awareness, maintenance issues, and inadequate enforcement, leading to suboptimal utilization of harvested rainwater.
Delhi	**Wastewater recycling and reuse**	Efforts are underway to enhance sewage treatment capacity and promote the reuse of treated wastewater for non-potable purposes such as irrigation, horticulture, and industrial cooling.	Approximately 16% of treated sewage is supplied for non-potable uses. However, gaps remain between sewage generation and treatment capacity, necessitating further infrastructure development and policy support.
Singapore	**NEWater initiative**	Singapore has developed the NEWater program, which treats and reclaims wastewater to produce high-quality potable water. This involves microfiltration, reverse osmosis, and ultraviolet disinfection.	NEWater meets up to 40% of Singapore's water demand, reducing reliance on imported water and enhancing water security.

(*Continued*)

Table 9.6 (*Continued*)

City	Water management strategy	Details	Outcome/Impact
Tokyo	**Leakage control program**	Tokyo has implemented an extensive leakage detection and control program, utilizing advanced technologies and regular maintenance to minimize water loss in its distribution system.	The city has achieved one of the lowest water leakage rates globally, at around 3%, thereby conserving significant amounts of water and improving system efficiency.
Copenhagen	**Integrated stormwater management**	Copenhagen employs green infrastructure solutions, such as permeable surfaces, green roofs, and urban wetlands, to manage stormwater. This approach reduces runoff, mitigates flood risks, and enhances groundwater recharge.	These measures have improved the city's resilience to heavy rainfall events and contributed to overall urban livability.
Stockholm	**Advanced wastewater treatment**	Stockholm has implemented advanced wastewater treatment technologies and strict regulations on industrial discharges to protect and restore water bodies, including lakes, rivers, and the Baltic Sea.	These efforts have led to improved water quality, reduced nutrient runoff, and healthier aquatic ecosystems.
Austin	**Wastewater treatment plant expansion**	Austin is investing over $1 billion to upgrade the Walnut Creek Wastewater Treatment Plant, increasing its capacity by 25 million gallons per day and incorporating advanced treatment technologies.	The expansion aims to meet the needs of a growing population, improve water quality in the Colorado River, and enhance resilience against drought conditions.

By learning from these global examples, Delhi can refine its water management strategies to address current challenges effectively. Implementing comprehensive policies, investing in advanced technologies, and promoting community engagement are essential steps toward achieving sustainable water management in the city.

Urban water quality management is crucial in safeguarding public health in rapidly growing urban areas. Access to clean and safe water is essential for human well-being, as it directly impacts drinking water supplies, recreational activities, and the overall environment of cities. Therefore, effective management strategies are necessary to address the challenges posed by high population density, extensive infrastructure, and various sources of pollution in urban environments (Sharma et al., 2017). One of the key goals of urban water quality management is the protection, preservation, and enhancement of water resources. This involves monitoring and assessing the quality of water sources, such as rivers, lakes, and groundwater, to identify potential contaminants and ensure compliance with water quality standards. Regular testing and analysis of water samples help identify pollutants and assess their potential risks to public health.

The implementation of appropriate treatment processes is another crucial aspect of urban water quality management. Water treatment facilities play a vital role in removing contaminants and pathogens from water supplies, making it safe for consumption. Processes such as filtration, disinfection, and chemical treatment are commonly employed to ensure that water meets the required quality standards and minimizes the risk of waterborne diseases (Lenka & Patra, 2017). Regulatory measures are essential to prevent pollution and enforce water quality standards in urban areas. Policies and regulations governing wastewater discharge, industrial activities, and waste management practices help mitigate pollution sources and reduce the impact on water bodies. Compliance monitoring, enforcement mechanisms, and penalties for non-compliance are necessary to ensure adherence to these regulations (Priya, 1993). Education and awareness programs also play a crucial role in promoting responsible water use and reducing contamination at the source. Public outreach campaigns, community engagement initiatives, and educational programs help raise awareness about the importance of water quality, proper waste disposal, and the potential health risks associated with contaminated water. By empowering individuals and communities with knowledge, they can make informed choices and take actions to protect water resources and their health.

Waterborne diseases are a significant concern in urban environments due to the high population density and potential contamination sources. Contaminated water can transmit various diseases, including gastrointestinal infections, cholera, typhoid fever, and hepatitis A. Vulnerable populations, such as children, the elderly, and those with compromised immune systems, are particularly at risk. Therefore, urban water quality management focuses on implementing robust water treatment systems, disinfection protocols, and strict water quality standards to minimize the risk of waterborne diseases and improve public health outcomes (Dagar & Singh, 2021). An integrated approach to water management is crucial for achieving sustainable urban development and ensuring good public health. Collaboration among urban planners, policymakers, water authorities, and public health agencies is necessary to develop comprehensive, holistic strategies that address water quality concerns. Considering the entire water cycle, including source protection, wastewater treatment, stormwater management, and water reuse, helps optimize resource efficiency, minimize pollution, and safeguard public health (Ghosh et al., 2019). Urban water quality management is critical to ensuring good public health in urban areas. Urban communities can access clean and safe water by prioritizing protecting, preserving, and enhancing water resources, implementing effective treatment processes, enforcing regulations, and promoting awareness. This, in turn, reduces the risks of waterborne diseases, improves public health outcomes, and contributes to the overall well-being and sustainability of urban populations. Continued research, innovation, and collaboration are essential for further advancements in urban water quality management practices and their positive impact on public health.

9.4.1 Challenges in Policy Implementation

Key challenges in implementing water management policies in Delhi:

1. **Pollution from Untreated Sewage**
    - A significant portion of Delhi's sewage remains untreated due to inadequate sewage treatment infrastructure.
    - Overloaded and inefficient sewage treatment plants (STPs) result in the direct discharge of wastewater into the Yamuna River.
2. **Industrial Effluent Discharge**
    - Many small and unregulated industries discharge untreated effluents containing heavy metals and toxic chemicals into water bodies.
    - Weak enforcement of pollution control norms exacerbates water contamination.
3. **Groundwater Depletion and Contamination**
    - Over-extraction of groundwater, coupled with contamination from leachates, nitrates, and heavy metals, reduces the availability of clean drinking water.
    - Illegal borewells and poor groundwater recharge practices worsen the situation.
4. **Stormwater Runoff and Urban Drainage Issues**
    - Unregulated stormwater runoff carries pollutants from roads, construction sites, and solid waste dumps into water sources.
    - Encroachment and clogging of drainage systems lead to urban flooding and further water quality deterioration.
5. **Policy Implementation and Governance Gaps**
    - Lack of coordination among multiple agencies, such as the Delhi Jal Board, the Delhi Pollution Control Committee (DPCC), and municipal bodies, delays effective policy execution.
    - Weak enforcement of environmental regulations results in non-compliance by industries and residents.

6. **Public Awareness and Community Participation**
   - Low awareness among residents about water conservation and pollution control leads to excessive wastage and improper disposal of waste.
   - Limited community-driven initiatives hinder the successful implementation of water management strategies.
7. **Climate Change and Water Scarcity**
   - Irregular monsoons, rising temperatures, and extreme weather events affect Delhi's water availability and increase pressure on existing resources.
   - Sustainable water conservation measures, such as rainwater harvesting, are not widely adopted.

Addressing these challenges requires an integrated approach, including stricter regulations, improved infrastructure, community involvement, and climate-resilient water management strategies.

9.5 Conclusions

The 2024 reports from the DPCC and the CPCB reveal persistent challenges in managing urban water quality in Delhi, with significant implications for public health. Monitoring data from the DPCC indicates that the River Yamuna continues to suffer from high levels of pollution. For instance, the analysis report dated April 18, 2024, highlights elevated concentrations of pollutants, such as total suspended solids, COD, and BOD, all exceeding permissible limits. These findings suggest ongoing contamination from untreated sewage, industrial discharges, and urban runoff.

The CPCB's "Groundwater Quality in Problem Areas – A Status Report (Part-V)" underscores concerns regarding groundwater contamination in Delhi. The report identifies elevated levels of contaminants, including nitrates and heavy metals, in several areas, posing risks to public health and indicating the need for improved groundwater management strategies. The DPCC's analysis of STPs for September 2024 reveals that out of 38 STPs, 16 met the prescribed standards, while 22 failed to comply with them. This non-compliance contributes to the discharge of inadequately treated wastewater into water bodies, further degrading water quality.

The 2024 pollution control board reports highlight that despite ongoing efforts, Delhi's urban water quality remains compromised due to factors such as untreated sewage, industrial effluents, and ineffective stormwater management. Addressing these challenges requires a comprehensive approach, including enhancing wastewater treatment infrastructure, enforcing pollution control regulations, and implementing sustainable urban planning practices. Improving stormwater management through green infrastructure and low-impact development can mitigate pollutant loads entering water bodies. Additionally, regular monitoring and public awareness campaigns are essential to protect water resources and public health in Delhi.

9.6 Recommendations

Recommendations for improving urban water quality management for good public health:

- **Strengthen Water Quality Monitoring:** Enhance the frequency and coverage of water quality monitoring programs in urban areas to improve water quality. This includes regular sampling and analysis of water sources, ensuring compliance with established water quality standards. The use of advanced monitoring technologies and data-sharing platforms can facilitate real-time monitoring and early detection of contamination events.
- **Upgrade Water Treatment Infrastructure:** Invest in modernizing and expanding water treatment facilities to accommodate the growing population and increasing pollution challenges. Incorporate advanced treatment technologies that effectively remove contaminants and pathogens from water supplies. Regular maintenance and periodic audits of treatment plants should be conducted to ensure optimal performance.

- **Implement Source Water Protection:** Focus on source water protection by implementing measures to prevent pollution and degradation of water sources. This involves enforcing strict regulations on industrial discharges, agricultural runoff, and other potential pollution sources near water bodies. Encourage land-use planning that preserves and protects water catchment areas.
- **Strengthen Regulatory Frameworks:** Develop and enforce stringent regulatory frameworks to govern water quality management in urban areas. Set clear guidelines and standards for water quality parameters, including permissible pollutant levels, and regularly update them based on scientific research and emerging contaminants. Implement robust compliance monitoring and enforcement mechanisms to hold polluters accountable.
- **Promote Integrated Water Resource Management:** Adopt an integrated approach to water resource management that considers the entire water cycle. This includes stormwater management, wastewater treatment, water reuse, and green infrastructure implementation. Encourage collaboration among water management agencies, urban planners, public health departments, and other stakeholders to develop comprehensive strategies that optimize water resource utilization and protect public health.
- **Enhance Public Education and Awareness:** Conduct awareness campaigns and educational programs targeting urban residents to promote responsible water use and pollution prevention. Increase public understanding of the importance of clean water for public health and individuals' role in conserving water resources and reducing contamination risks. Encourage proper waste disposal practices and discourage behaviors that contribute to water pollution.
- **Strengthen Data Sharing and Research Collaboration:** Encourage data sharing and collaboration among researchers, water management agencies, and public health institutions.

Foster interdisciplinary research projects to better understand the relationship between water quality and public health outcomes in urban areas. Use research findings to inform evidence-based decision-making and policy formulation.

- **Invest in Green Infrastructure:** Integrate green infrastructure solutions, such as constructed wetlands, permeable pavements, and green roofs, into urban water management plans. These nature-based solutions can help mitigate stormwater runoff, improve water quality, and enhance urban aesthetics while providing additional benefits such as urban cooling and biodiversity conservation.
- **Foster Public-Private Partnerships:** Promote collaboration between the public and private sectors to leverage expertise, resources, and innovative technologies for effective water quality management. Public-private partnerships can improve infrastructure management, technological advancements, and knowledge exchange, ultimately benefiting public health and water quality outcomes.
- **Regular Review and Adaptation:** Continuously evaluate the effectiveness of water quality management strategies, policies, and programs. Regularly review and update approaches based on emerging challenges, scientific advancements, and changing urban landscapes. Foster a culture of adaptive management to ensure that water quality management practices remain responsive and resilient in evolving urban environments.

By implementing these recommendations, urban areas can improve their water quality management practices, protect public health, and ensure the sustainable use of water resources for present and future generations.

Declarations

- There is no funding for this research.
- The authors have no conflict of interest in the publication of this chapter.

References

Acharya, S., Sharma, S. K., & Khandegar, V. (2018). Assessment of groundwater quality by water quality indices for irrigation and drinking in South West Delhi, India. *Data in Brief, 18*, 2019–2028. https://doi.org/10.1016/j.dib.2018.04.120.

Addo, I. B., Thoms, M. C., & Parsons, M. (2019). The influence of water-conservation messages on reducing household water use. *Applied Water Science*, 9(5), 126. https://doi.org/10.1007/s13201-019-1002-0.

Ahiablame, L. M., Engel, B. A., & Chaubey, I. (2012). Effectiveness of low impact development practices: Literature review and suggestions for future research. *Water, Air, & Soil Pollution*, *223*(7), 4253–4273. https://doi.org/10.1007/s11270-012-1189-2.

Ahmad, F. (2025, January 15). India's groundwater quality report underscores systemic inertia and fragmented efforts undermining water security. *Down To Earth*. https://www.downtoearth.org.in/water/indias-groundwater-quality-report-underscores-systemic-inertia-and-fragmented-efforts-undermining-water-security.

Bidhuri, S., & Khan, M. M. A. (2020). Assessment of ground water quality of central and southeast districts of NCT of Delhi. *Journal of the Geological Society of India*, *95*(1), 95–103. https://doi.org/10.1007/s12594-020-1390-7.

Business Today Desk. (2023, July 13). Delhi flood situation: 25% of the water supply in Delhi will go down, says CM Kejriwal [News]. Business Today. https://www.businesstoday.in/latest/trends/story/delhi-flood-situation-25-of-the-water-supply-in-delhi-will-go-down-says-cm-kejriwal-389537-2023-07-13.

Central Pollution & Control Board. (2008). *Guidelines for Water Quality Management*. Central Pollution Control Board.

Dagar, S., & Singh, S. K. (2021). Seasonal variation of water quality index of an urban water body Bhalswa Lake, Delhi (India). In R. M. Singari, K. Mathiyazhagan, & H. Kumar (Eds.), *Advances in Manufacturing and Industrial Engineering* (pp. 179–190). Springer Nature Singapore. https://doi.org/10.1007/978-981-15-8542-5_16.

Dehalwar, K., & Sharma, S. N. (2023). *Fundamentals of Research Writing and Uses of Research Methodologies*. https://doi.org/10.5281/ZENODO.10117851.

Delhi Jal Board. (2024). *Daily Drinking Water Quality.* https://delhijalboard.delhi.gov.in/daily-drinking-water-quality.

Dietz, M. E. (2007). Low impact development practices: A review of current research and recommendations for future directions. *Water, Air, and Soil Pollution, 186*(1–4), 351–363. https://doi.org/10.1007/s11270-007-9484-z.

Fletcher, T. D., Andrieu, H., & Hamel, P. (2013). Understanding, management and modelling of urban hydrology and its consequences for receiving waters: A state of the art. *Advances in Water Resources, 51*, 261–279. https://doi.org/10.1016/j.advwatres.2012.09.001.

Ghosh, R., Kansal, A., & Venkatesh, G. (2019). Urban water security assessment using an integrated metabolism approach—Case study of the National Capital Territory of Delhi in India. *Resources, 8*(2), 62. https://doi.org/10.3390/resources8020062.

Golladay, S. W., Craig, L. S., DePalma-Dow, A. D., Emanuel, B. N., & Rogers, S. G. (2021). Building resilience into water management through public engagement. *Freshwater Science*, 40(1), 238–244. https://doi.org/10.1086/712514.

Goyal, K., & Kumar, A. (2020). A modelling approach to assess wastewater reuse potential for Delhi city. *Water Supply*, 20(5), 1716–1725. https://doi.org/10.2166/ws.2020.080.

Hatt, B. E., Deletic, A., & Fletcher, T. D. (2006). Integrated treatment and recycling of stormwater: A review of Australian practice. *Journal of Environmental Management, 79*(1), 102–113. https://doi.org/10.1016/j.jenvman.2005.06.003.

Jamwal, P., Mittal, A. K., & Mouchel, J.-M. (2008). Effects of urbanisation on the quality of the urban runoff for Delhi watershed. *Urban Water Journal, 5*(3), 247–257. https://doi.org/10.1080/15730620701780348.

Kumar, A. (2022). Water governance in the national capital territory of Delhi, India. In A. Kumar & D. S. Meshram, *Future of Cities* (1st ed., pp. 94–111). Routledge India. https://doi.org/10.4324/9781003296218-6.

Kumar, S., & Goyal, M. K. (2025). Water policy review: Ensuring sustainable water management for India. *Journal of Environmental Management*, 388, 125823. https://doi.org/10.1016/j.jenvman.2025.125823.

Lenka, A. K., & Patra, G. B. (2017). Water and sanitation and public health issues in Delhi. In S. S. Acharya, S. Sen, M. Punia, & S. Reddy (Eds.), *Marginalization in Globalizing Delhi: Issues of Land, Livelihoods and*

Health (pp. 403–417). Springer India. https://doi.org/10.1007/978-81-322-3583-5_22.

Parveen, A., & Ahmad, S. N. (2024). Urban water system of the National Capital Territory (NCT) of Delhi: A comprehensive study. *Water Supply, 24*(11), 3639–3651. https://doi.org/10.2166/ws.2024.233.

Priya, R. (1993). Town planning, public health and urban poor: Some explorations from Delhi. *Economic and Political Weekly, 28*, 824–834.

Patel, R. S., Taneja, S., Singh, J., & Sharma, S. N. (2024). Modelling of surface run-off using SWMM and GIS for efficient stormwater management. *Current Science, 126*(4), 243–249.

Roy, A. H., Wenger, S. J., Fletcher, T. D., Walsh, C. J., Ladson, A. R., Shuster, W. D., Thurston, H. W., & Brown, R. R. (2008). Impediments and solutions to sustainable, watershed-scale urban stormwater management: Lessons from Australia and the United States. *EnvironmentalManagement,42*(2),344–359.https://doi.org/10.1007/s00267-008-9119-1.

Roy, D. (2016). Revival of Hauz Khas Lake in Delhi: Approaches to urban water resource management in India. *Journal of Management and Sustainability*, *6*(4), 73. https://doi.org/10.5539/jms.v6n4p73.

Roy, S. S., Rahman, A., Ahmed, S., Shahfahad, & Ahmad, I. A. (2020). Alarming groundwater depletion in the Delhi Metropolitan Region: A long-term assessment. *Environmental Monitoring and Assessment*, 192(10), 620. https://doi.org/10.1007/s10661-020-08585-8.

Sharma, S., Jha, P. K., Ranjan, M. R., Singh, U. K., & Jindal, T. (2017). Water quality monitoring of Yamuna River by using GIS based water quality index in Delhi, India. *International Journal of Current Microbiology and Applied Sciences*, *6*(2), 1249–1263. https://doi.org/10.20546/ijcmas.2017.602.141.

Sharma, A., & Harvey, M. (2023). Economies of water in Delhi: A neo-Polanyian analysis. *Water International*, 48(1), 98–119. https://doi.org/10.1080/02508060.2022.2122323.

Shuster, W. D., Bonta, J., Thurston, H., Warnemuende, E., & Smith, D. R. (2005). Impacts of impervious surface on watershed hydrology: A review. *Urban Water Journal*, *2*(4), 263–275. https://doi.org/10.1080/ 15730620500386529.

Somnath Pal, C. B. (2023, January 23). Decentralised waste water treatment systems to improve water security. Mongabay-India. https://india.mongabay.com/2023/01/commentary-decentralised-waste-water-treatment-systems-to-improve-water-security/.

Trowsdale, S. A., & Simcock, R. (2011). Urban stormwater treatment using bioretention. *Journal of Hydrology, 397*(3–4), 167–174. https://doi.org/10.1016/j.jhydrol.2010.11.023.

Verma, N., Singh, G., & Ahsan, N. (2022). Development of water quality management strategies for an urban river reach: A case study of the river Yamuna, Delhi, India. *Arabian Journal of Geosciences, 15*(24), 1767. https://doi.org/10.1007/s12517-022-11030-4.

Xiang, X., Li, Q., Khan, S., & Khalaf, O. I. (2021). Urban water resource management for sustainable environment planning using artificial intelligence techniques. *Environmental Impact Assessment Review, 86*, 106515. https://doi.org/10.1016/j.eiar.2020.106515.

Yadav, A., & Khandegar, V. (2019). Dataset on assessment of River Yamuna, Delhi, India using indexing approach. *Data in Brief, 22*, 1–10. https://doi.org/10.1016/j.dib.2018.11.130.

Index

For Product Safety Concerns and Information please contact our EU representative GPSR@taylorandfrancis.com Taylor & Francis Verlag GmbH, Kaufingerstraße 24, 80331 München, Germany